冨樫義博

I'm just barely getting by.

Yoshihiro Togashi

Yoshihiro Togashi's manga career began in 1986 at the age of 20, when he won the coveted Osamu Tezuka Award for new manga artists. He debuted in the Japanese **Weekly Shonen Jump** magazine in 1989 with the romantic comedy **Tende Shôwaru Cupid**. From 1990 to 1994 he wrote and drew the hit manga **YuYu Hakusho**, which was followed by the dark comedy science-fiction series **Level E**, and finally this adventure series, **Hunter x Hunter**, available from VIZ Media's SHONEN JUMP Advanced imprint. In 1999 he married the manga artist Naoko Takeuchi.

HUNTER X HUNTER Volume 21
SHONEN JUMP ADVANCED Manga Edition

STORY AND ART BY
YOSHIHIRO TOGASHI

English Adaptation & Translation/Lillian Olsen
Touch-up Art & Lettering/Mark Griffin
Design/Matt Hinrichs
Editor/Yuki Murashige

Printed in the U.S.A.

Published by VIZ Media, LLC
P.O. Box 77010
San Francisco, CA 94107

10 9 8 7 6 5 4 3 2
First printing, July 2008
Second printing, May 2016

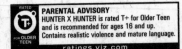

SHONEN [redacted]

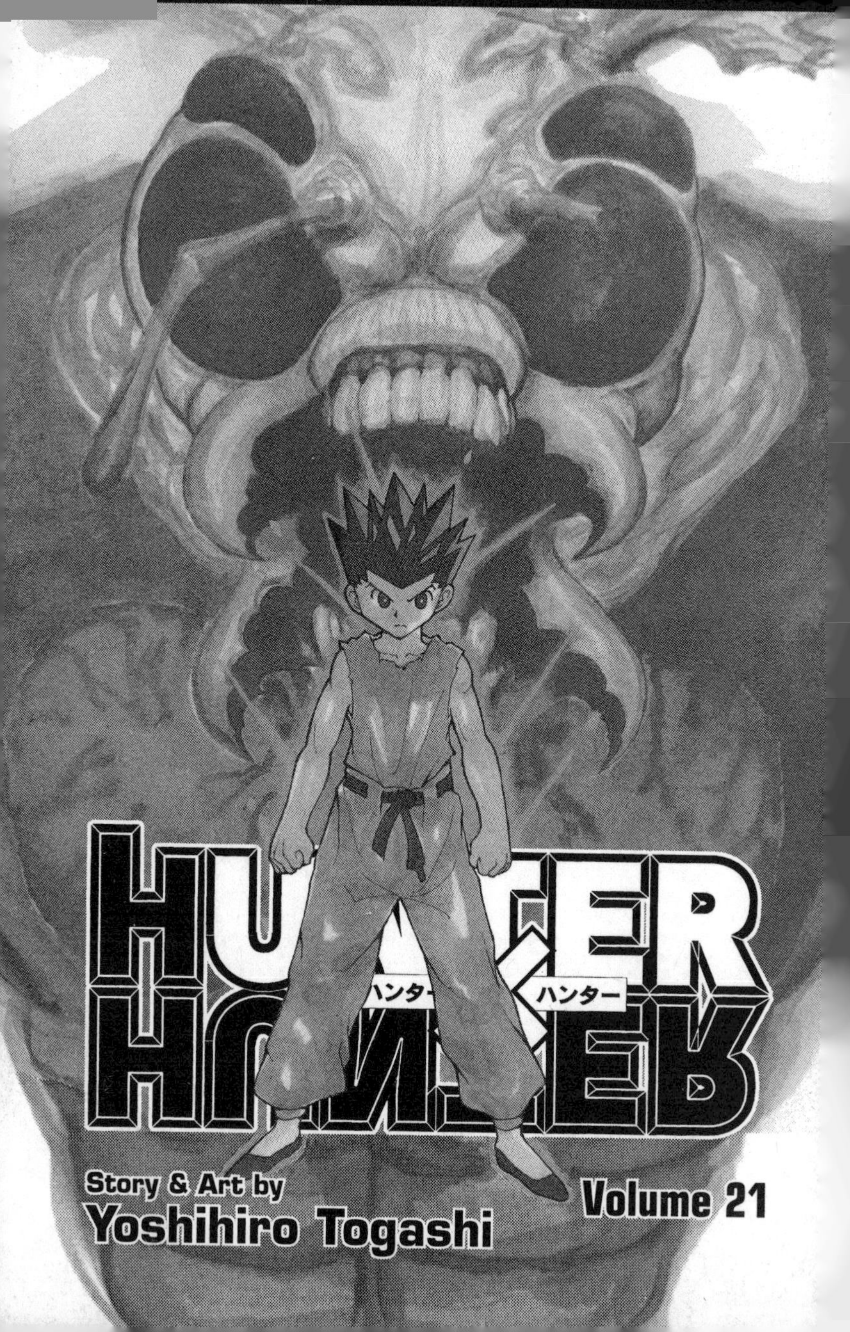
HUNTER×HUNTER
ハンター×ハンター
Story & Art by
Yoshihiro Togashi
Volume 21

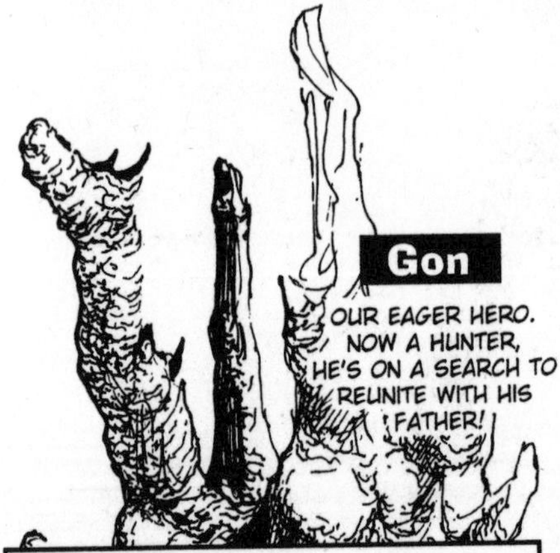

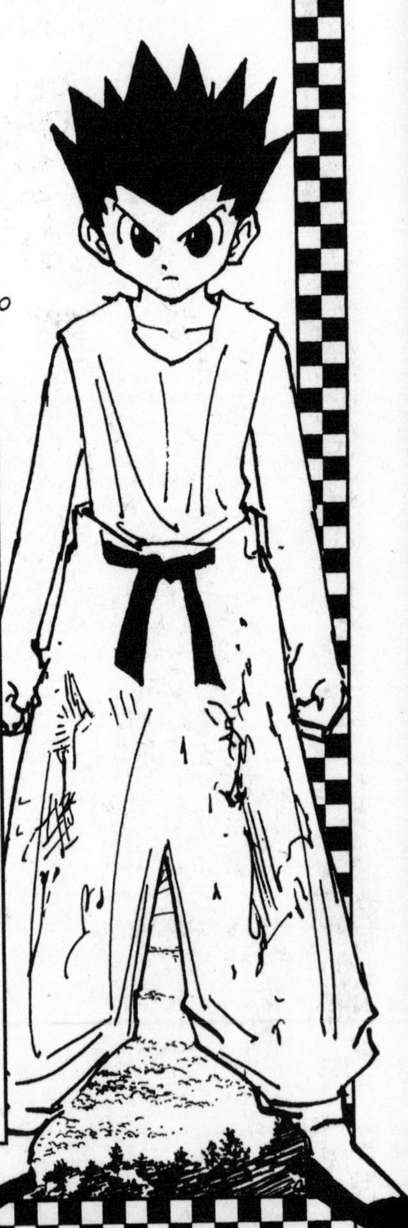

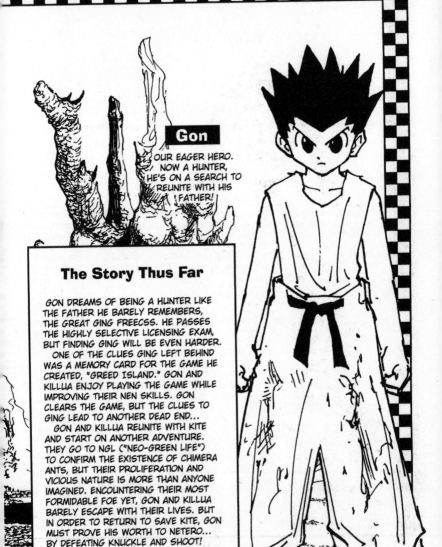

Gon

OUR EAGER HERO. NOW A HUNTER, HE'S ON A SEARCH TO REUNITE WITH HIS FATHER!

The Story Thus Far

GON DREAMS OF BEING A HUNTER LIKE THE FATHER HE BARELY REMEMBERS, THE GREAT GING FREECSS. HE PASSES THE HIGHLY SELECTIVE LICENSING EXAM, BUT FINDING GING WILL BE EVEN HARDER.

ONE OF THE CLUES GING LEFT BEHIND WAS A MEMORY CARD FOR THE GAME HE CREATED, "GREED ISLAND." GON AND KILLUA ENJOY PLAYING THE GAME WHILE IMPROVING THEIR NEN SKILLS. GON CLEARS THE GAME, BUT THE CLUES TO GING LEAD TO ANOTHER DEAD END...

GON AND KILLUA REUNITE WITH KITE AND START ON ANOTHER ADVENTURE. THEY GO TO NGL ("NEO-GREEN LIFE") TO CONFIRM THE EXISTENCE OF CHIMERA ANTS, BUT THEIR PROLIFERATION AND VICIOUS NATURE IS MORE THAN ANYONE IMAGINED. ENCOUNTERING THEIR MOST FORMIDABLE FOE YET, GON AND KILLUA BARELY ESCAPE WITH THEIR LIVES. BUT IN ORDER TO RETURN TO SAVE KITE, GON MUST PROVE HIS WORTH TO NETERO... BY DEFEATING KNUCKLE AND SHOOT!

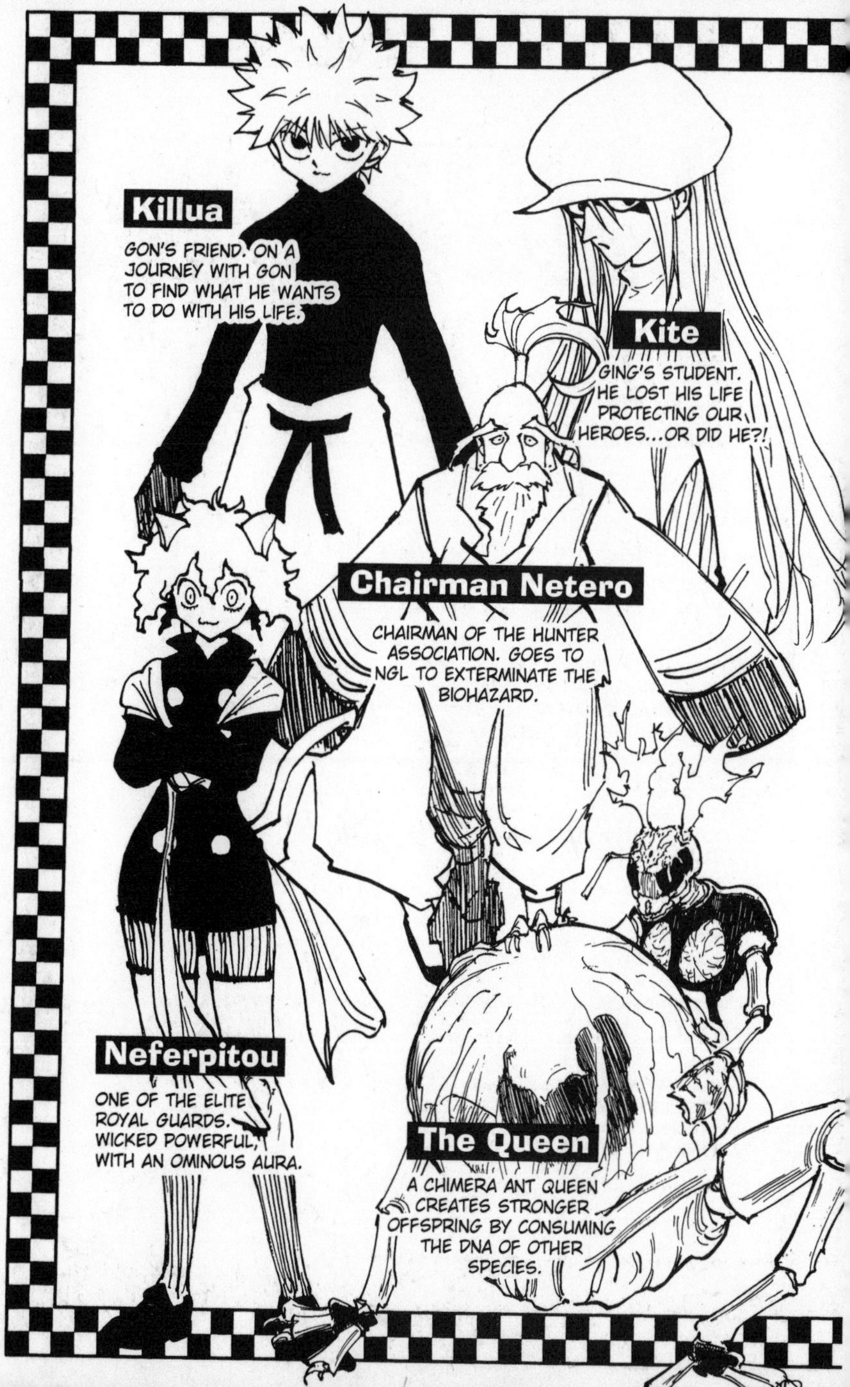

Killua
GON'S FRIEND. ON A JOURNEY WITH GON TO FIND WHAT HE WANTS TO DO WITH HIS LIFE.
Kite
GING'S STUDENT. HE LOST HIS LIFE PROTECTING OUR HEROES...OR DID HE?!
Chairman Netero
CHAIRMAN OF THE HUNTER ASSOCIATION. GOES TO NGL TO EXTERMINATE THE BIOHAZARD.
Neferpitou
ONE OF THE ELITE ROYAL GUARDS. WICKED POWERFUL, WITH AN OMINOUS AURA.
The Queen
A CHIMERA ANT QUEEN CREATES STRONGER OFFSPRING BY CONSUMING THE DNA OF OTHER SPECIES.

HUNTER × HUNTER

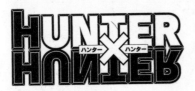

Volume 21

CONTENTS

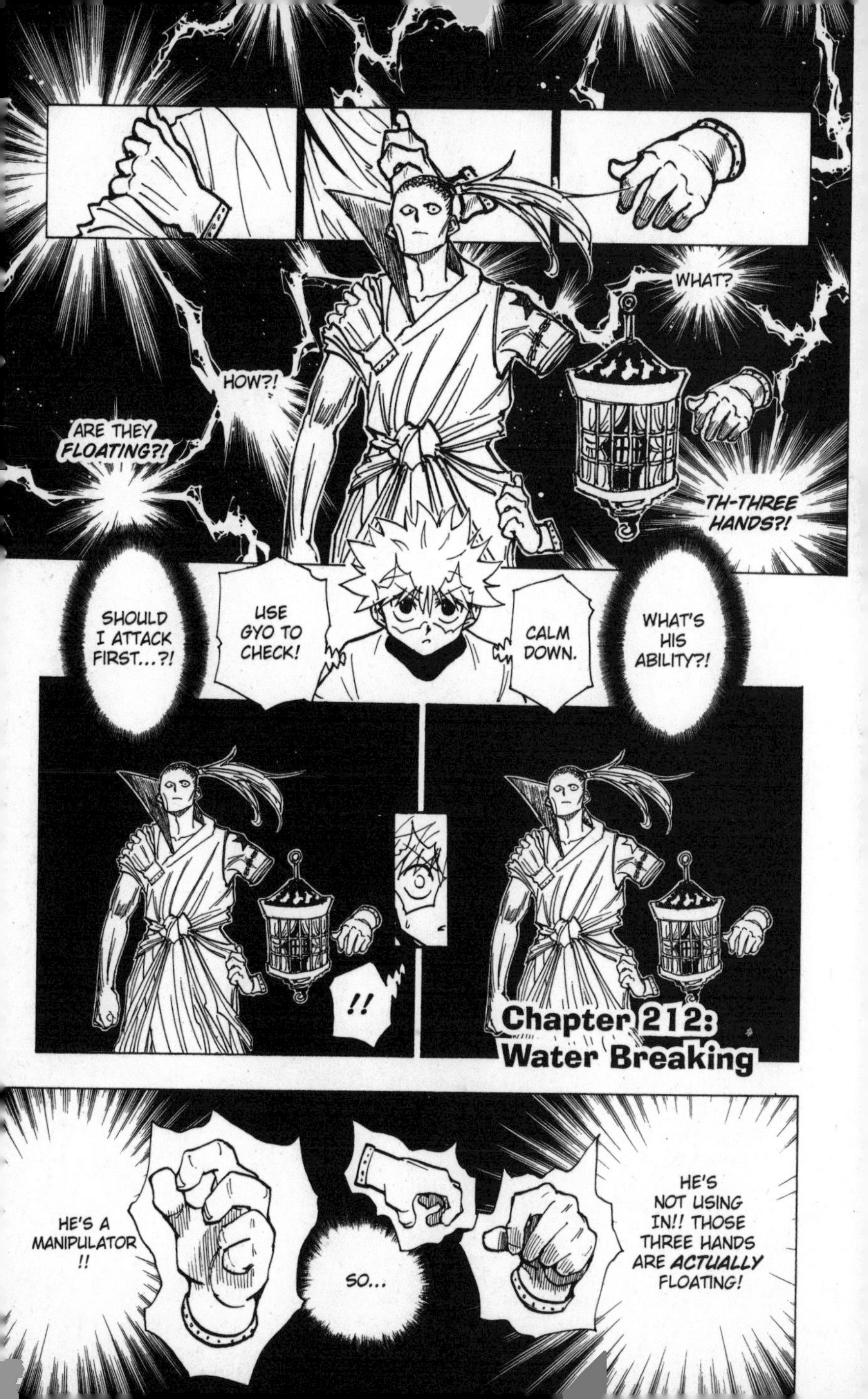
WHAT?
TH-THREE HANDS?!
HOW?!
ARE THEY FLOATING?!
WHAT'S HIS ABILITY?!
CALM DOWN.
USE GYO TO CHECK!
SHOULD I ATTACK FIRST...?!
Chapter 212: Water Breaking
!!
HE'S NOT USING IN!! THOSE THREE HANDS ARE ACTUALLY FLOATING!
SO...
HE'S A MANIPULATOR !!

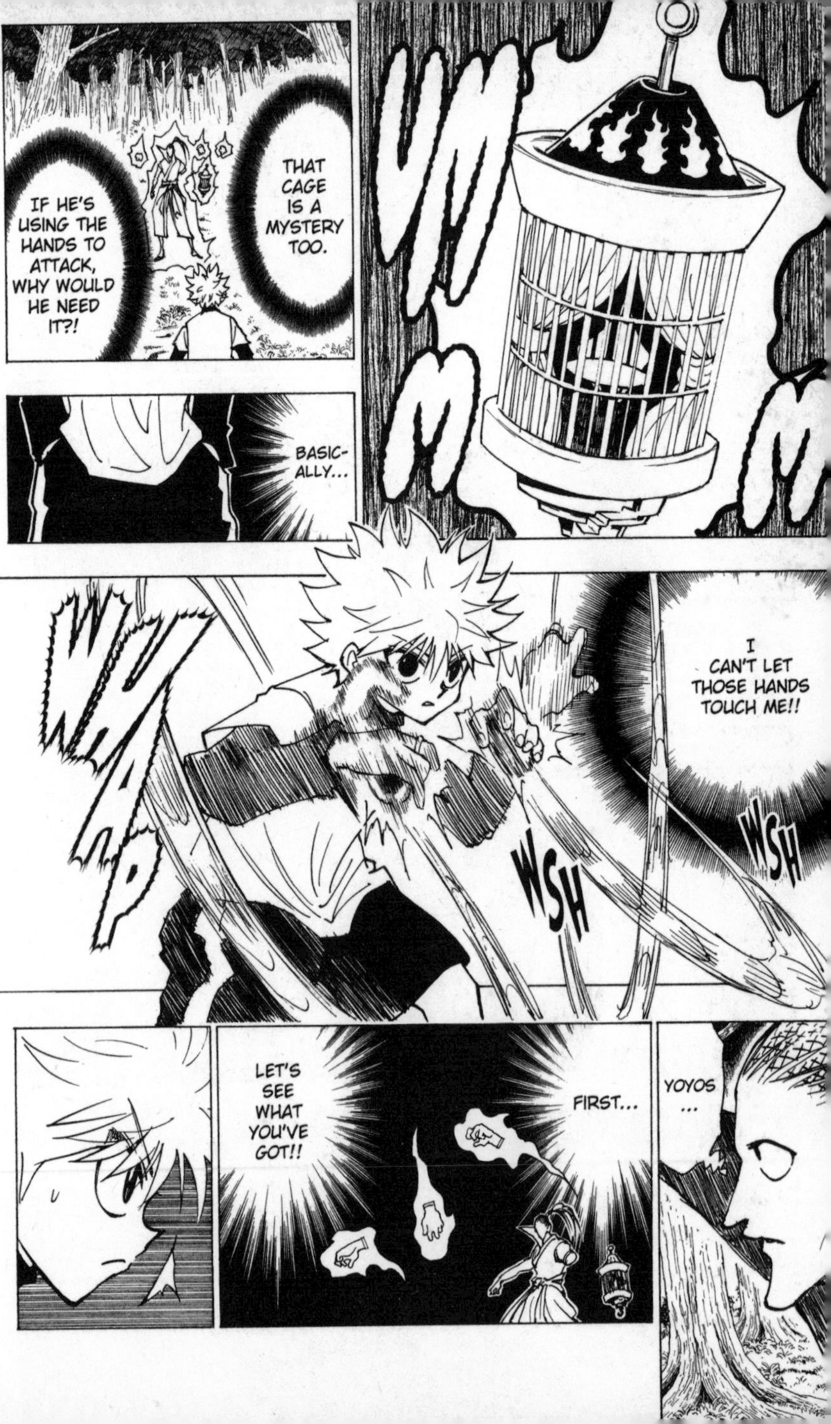
THAT CAGE IS A MYSTERY TOO.
IF HE'S USING THE HANDS TO ATTACK, WHY WOULD HE NEED IT?!
BASIC-ALLY...
I CAN'T LET THOSE HANDS TOUCH ME!!
WSH
WSH
YOYOS ...
FIRST...
LET'S SEE WHAT YOU'VE GOT!!

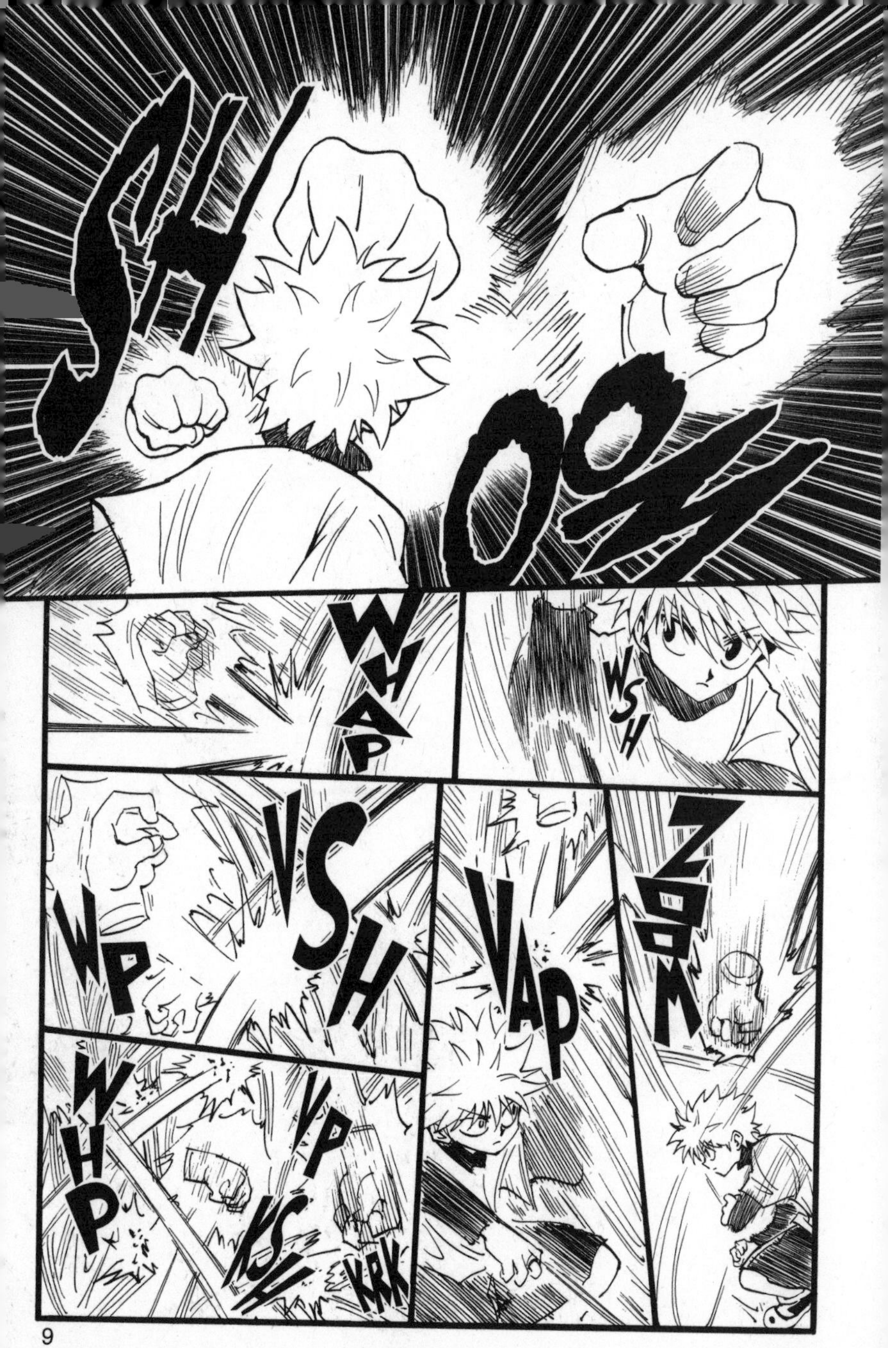
SHOOM
WSH
WHAP
ZOOM
VAP
VSH
WP
VP
KSH
KRK
WHP

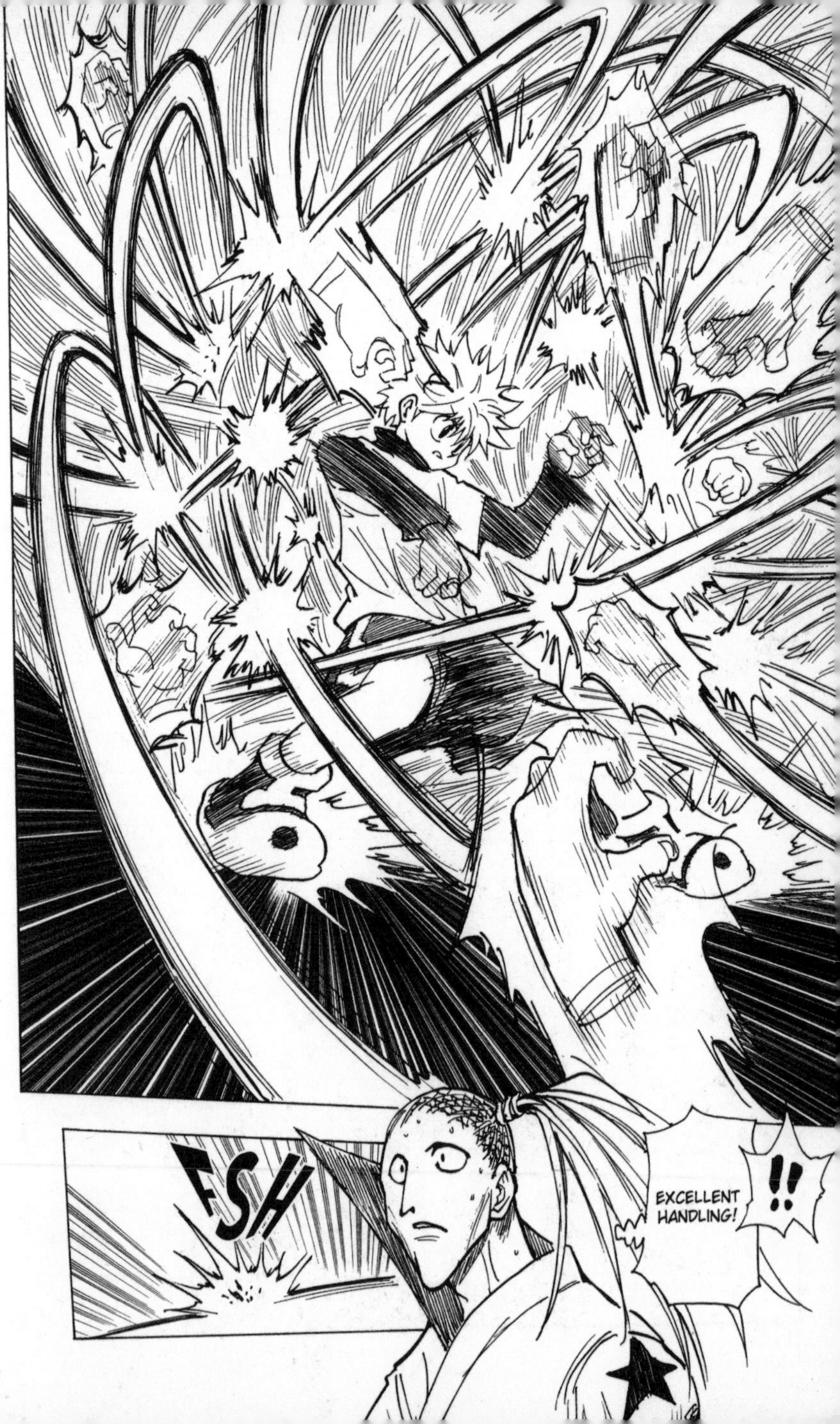
EXCELLENT HANDLING!
!!
FSH

READ THIS WAY

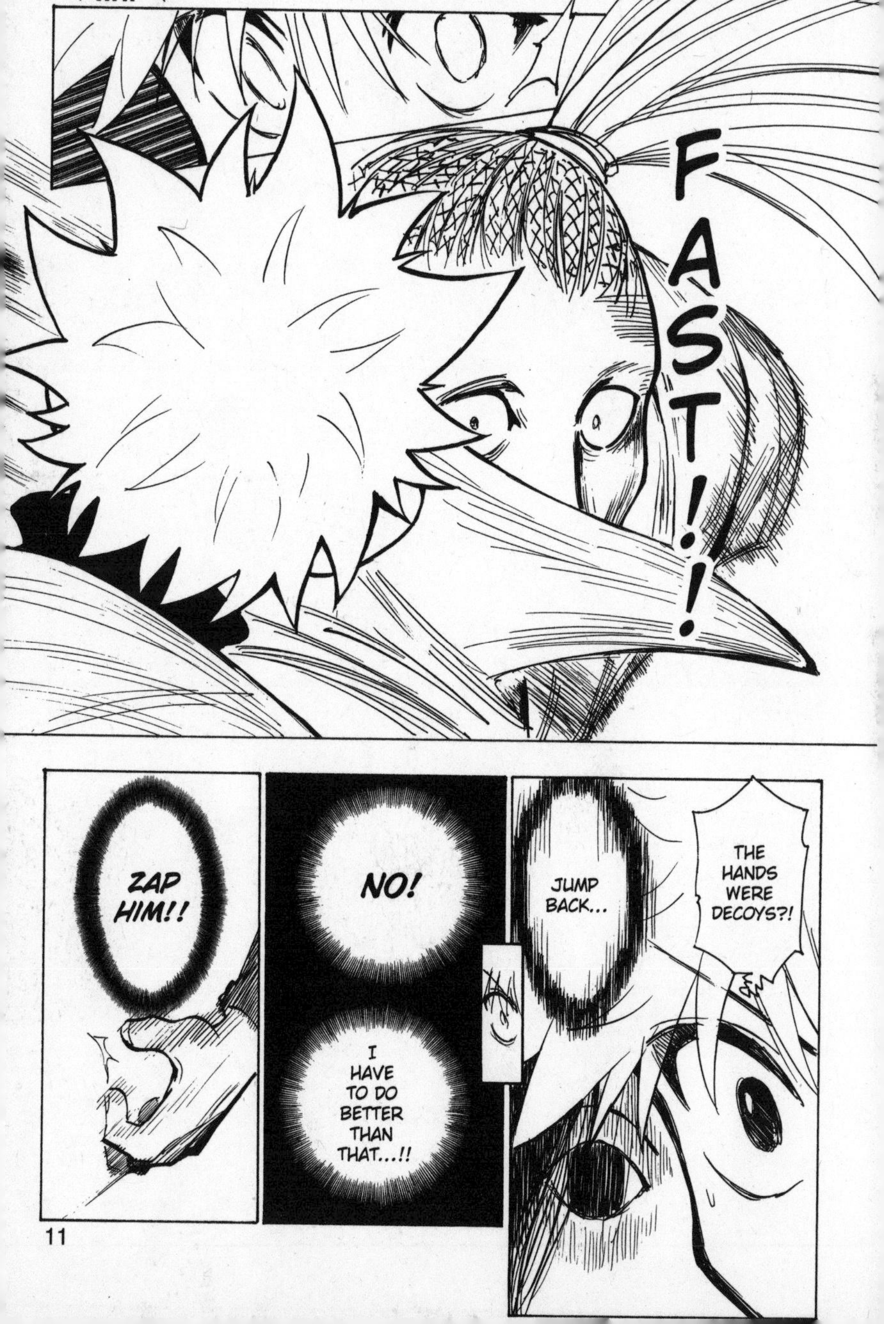
FAST!!!
THE HANDS WERE DECOYS?!
JUMP BACK...
NO!
I HAVE TO DO BETTER THAN THAT...!!
ZAP HIM!!

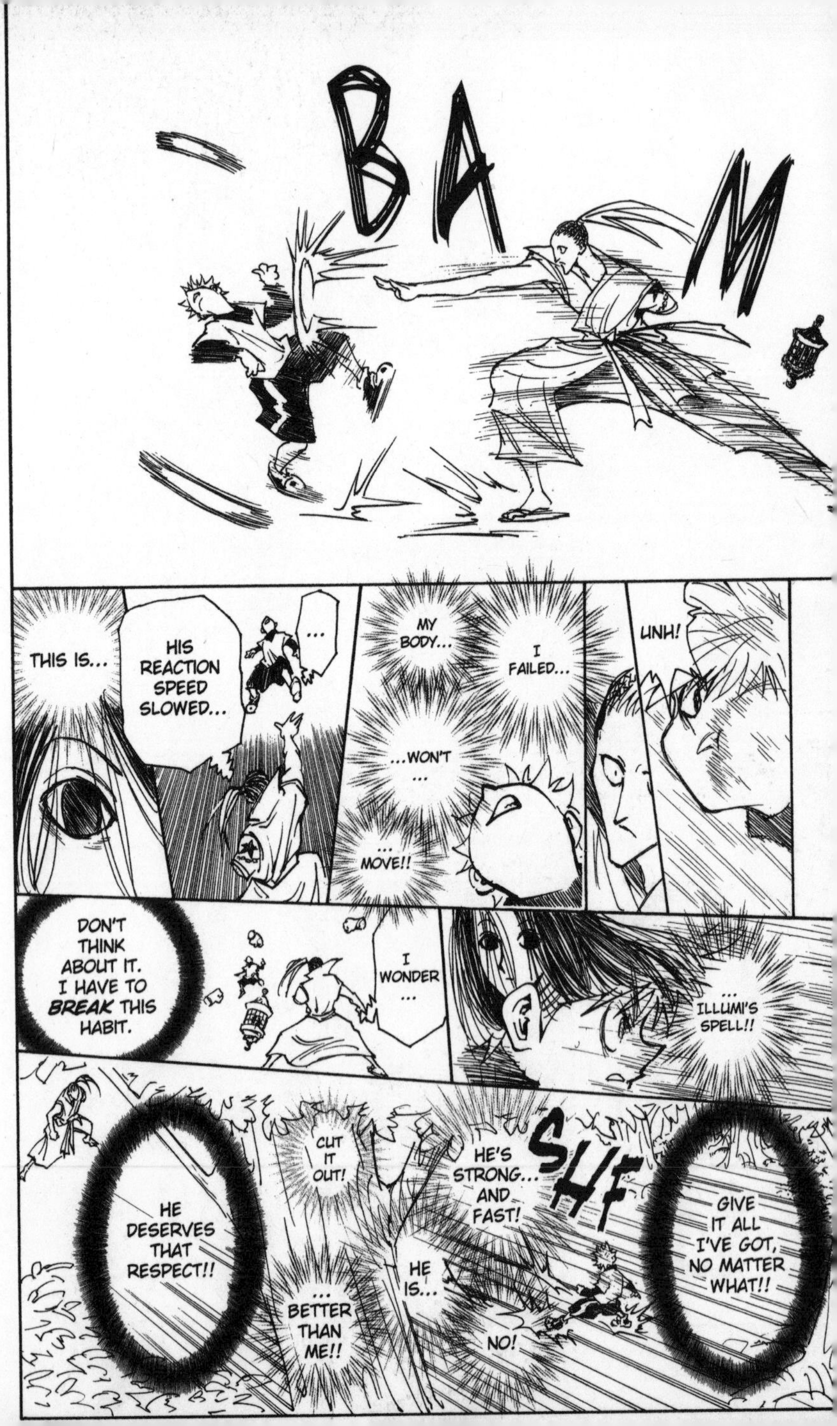
BAM
UNH!
I FAILED...
MY BODY...
...WON'T ...
... MOVE!!
...
HIS REACTION SPEED SLOWED...
THIS IS...
... ILLUMI'S SPELL!!
I WONDER ...
DON'T THINK ABOUT IT. I HAVE TO ***BREAK*** THIS HABIT.
GIVE IT ALL I'VE GOT, NO MATTER WHAT!!
SHF
HE'S STRONG... AND FAST!
NO!
HE IS...
CUT IT OUT!
... BETTER THAN ME!!
HE DESERVES THAT RESPECT!!

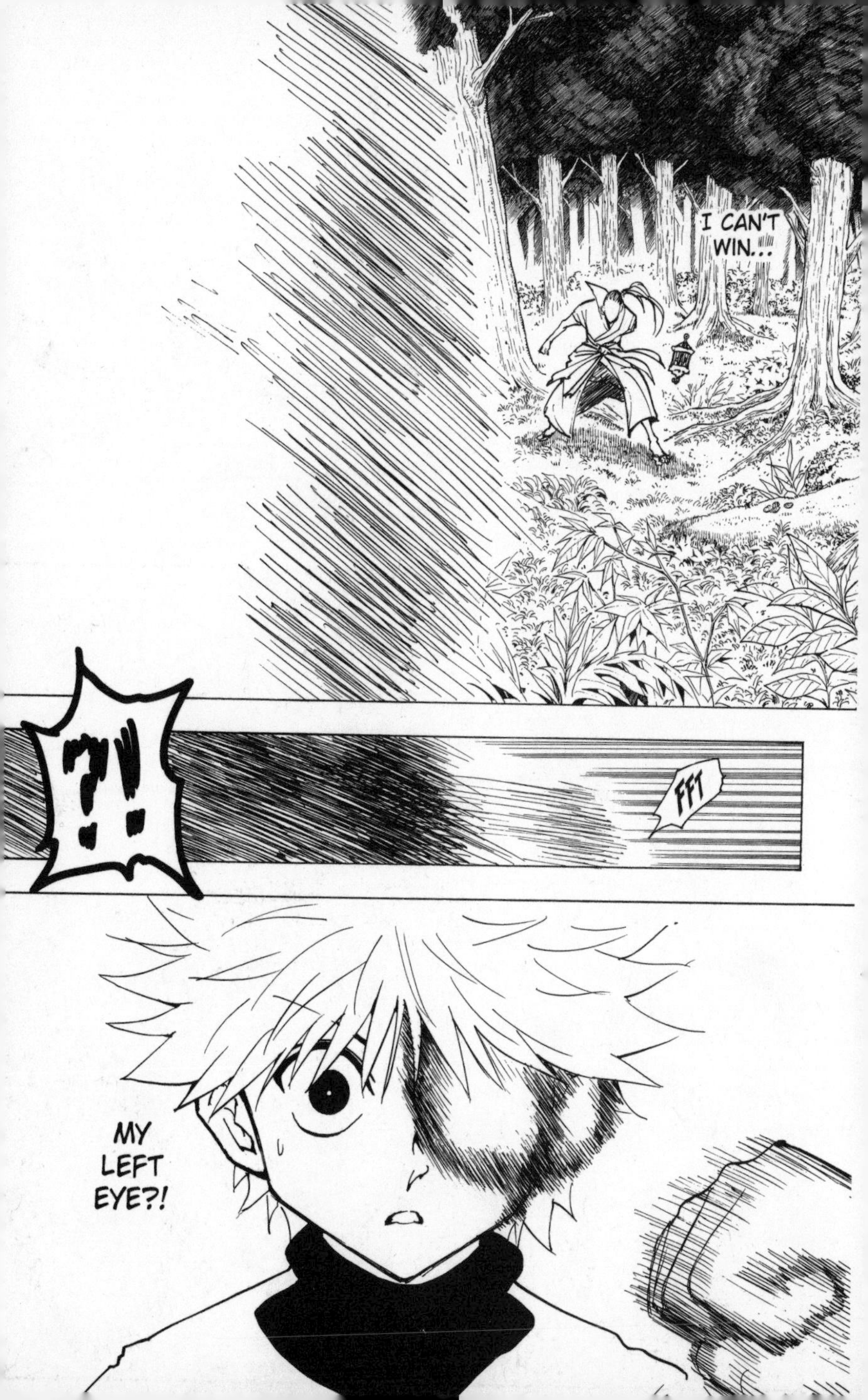
I CAN'T WIN...
?!
FFT
MY LEFT EYE?!

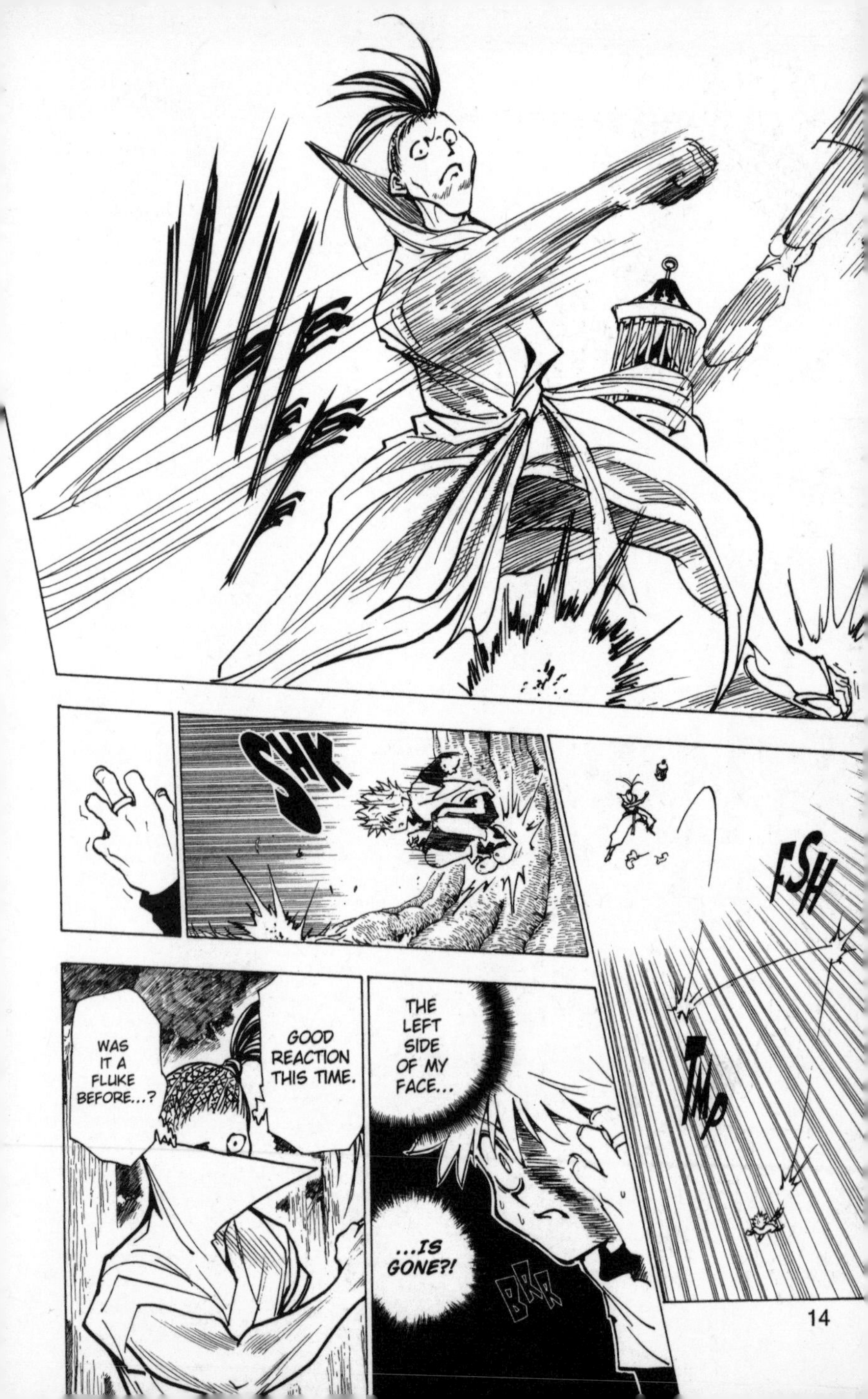
WHFFF
FSH
TMP
SHK
THE LEFT SIDE OF MY FACE...
...IS GONE?!
BRR
GOOD REACTION THIS TIME.
WAS IT A FLUKE BEFORE...?

READ THIS WAY

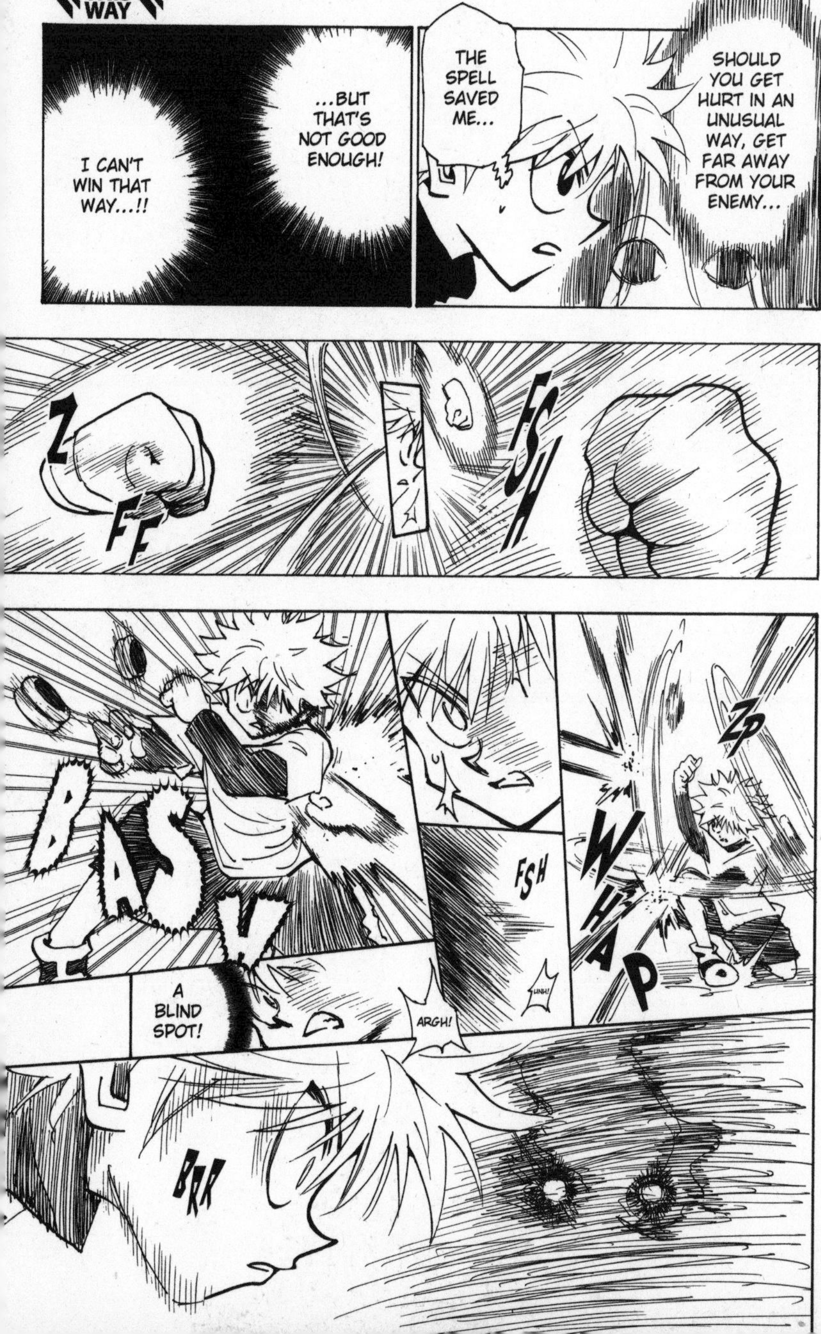
SHOULD YOU GET HURT IN AN UNUSUAL WAY, GET FAR AWAY FROM YOUR ENEMY...
THE SPELL SAVED ME...
...BUT THAT'S NOT GOOD ENOUGH!
I CAN'T WIN THAT WAY...!!
FSH
ZFF
ZP
WHAP
FSH
UNH!
BASH
A BLIND SPOT!
ARGH!
BRR

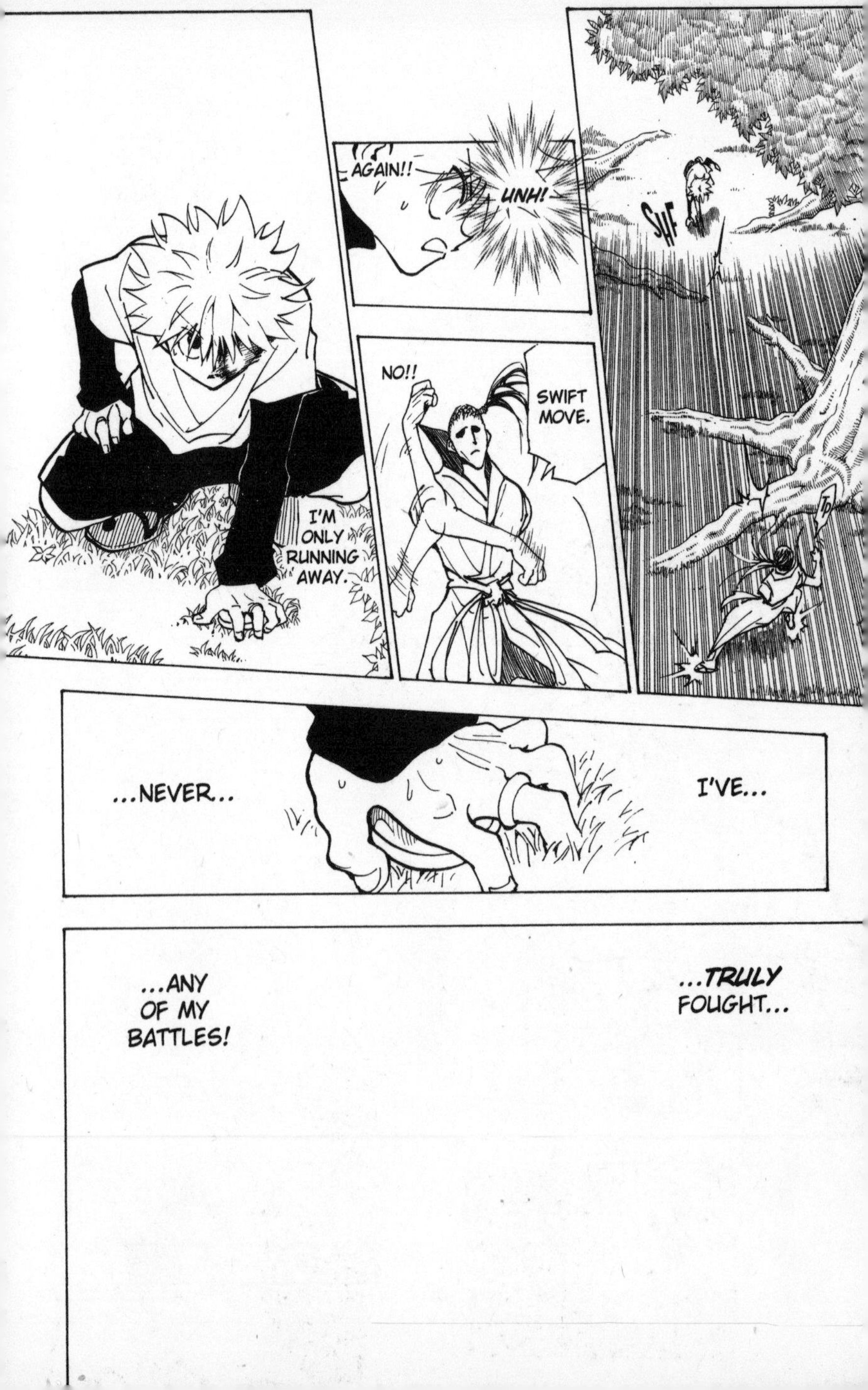
SHF
UNH!
AGAIN!!
SWIFT MOVE.
NO!!
I'M ONLY RUNNING AWAY.
I'VE...
...NEVER...
...TRULY FOUGHT...
...ANY OF MY BATTLES!

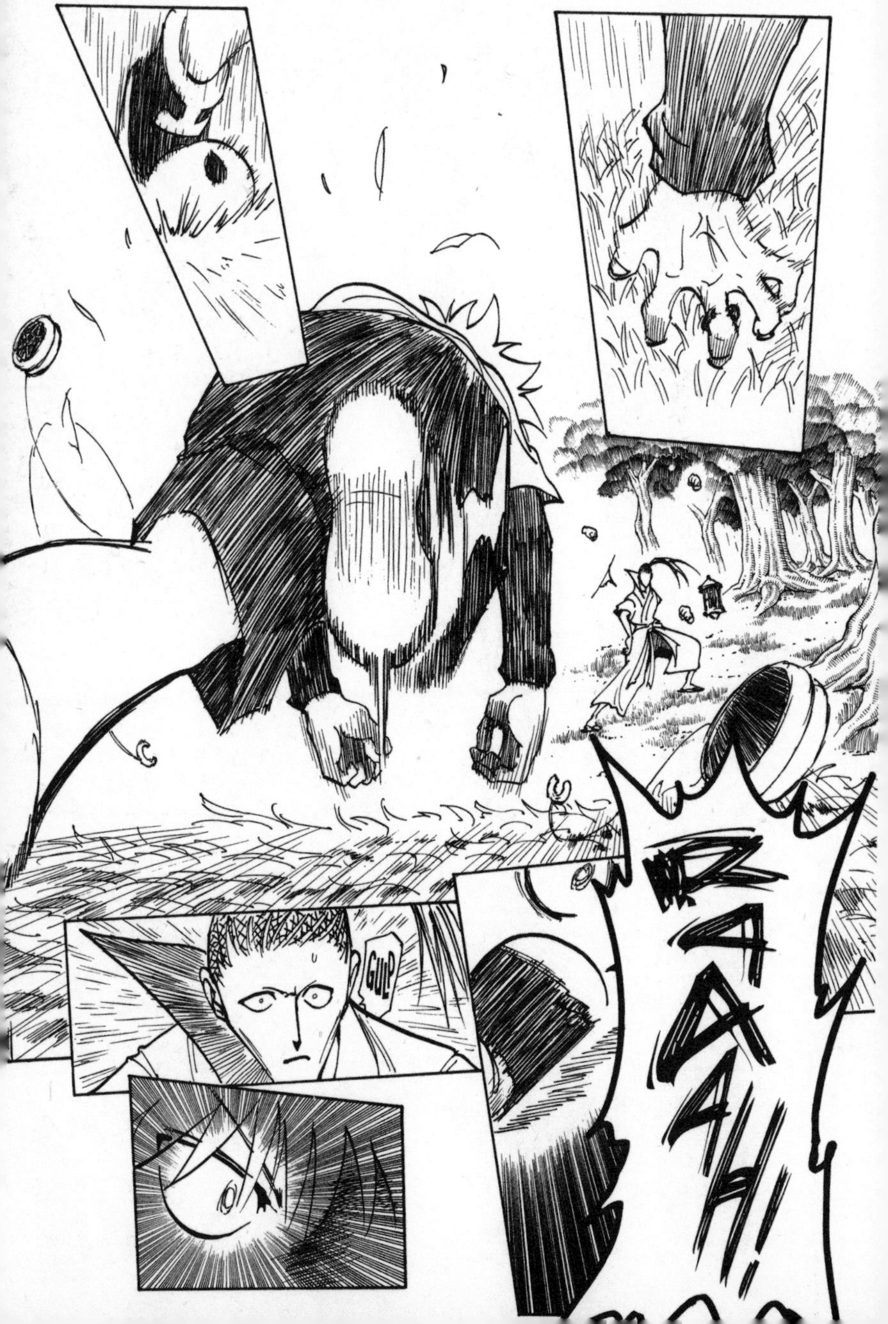
GULP
WRAAAAH!!

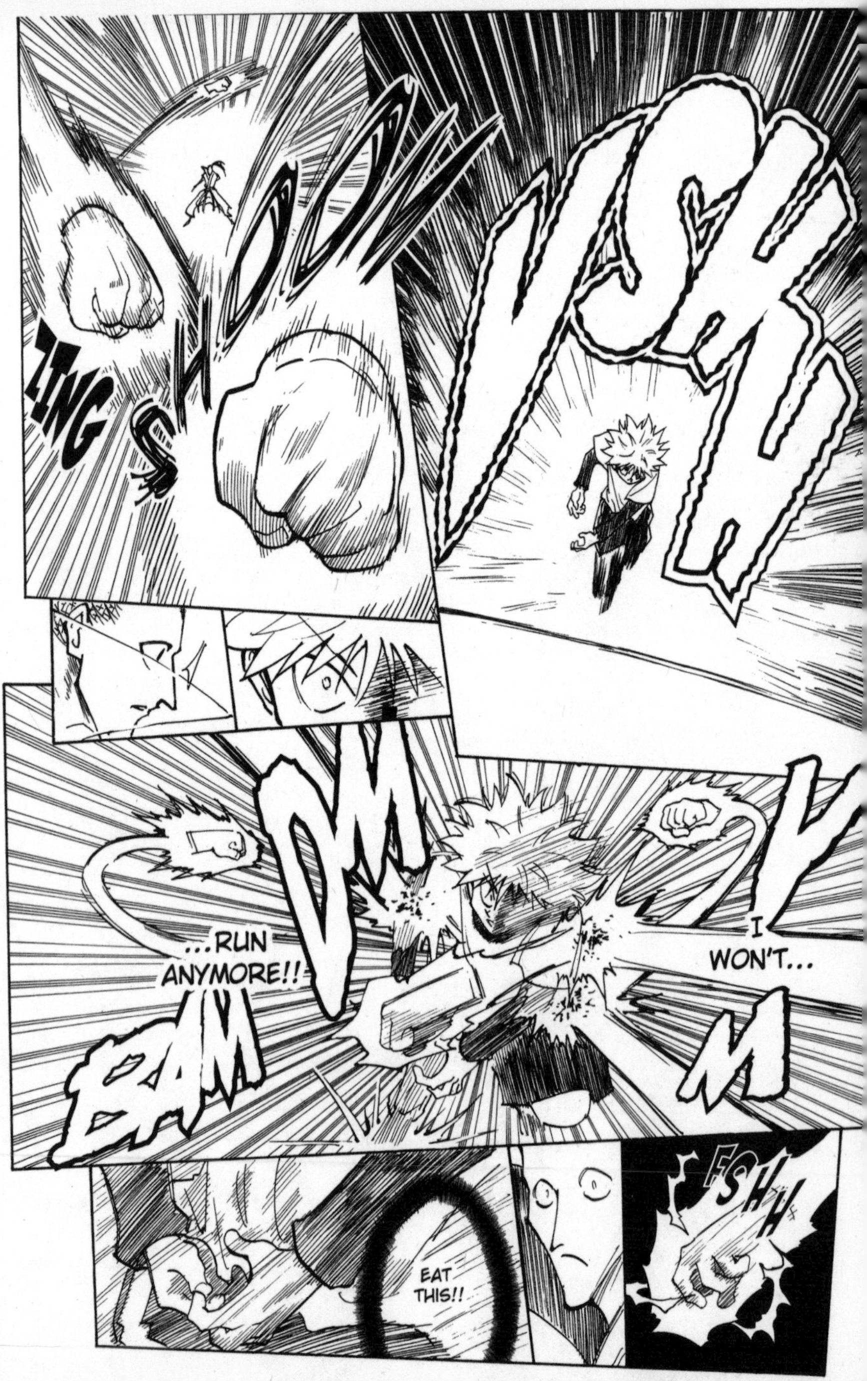
ZING
I WON'T...
...RUN ANYMORE!!
BAM
FSHH
EAT THIS!!

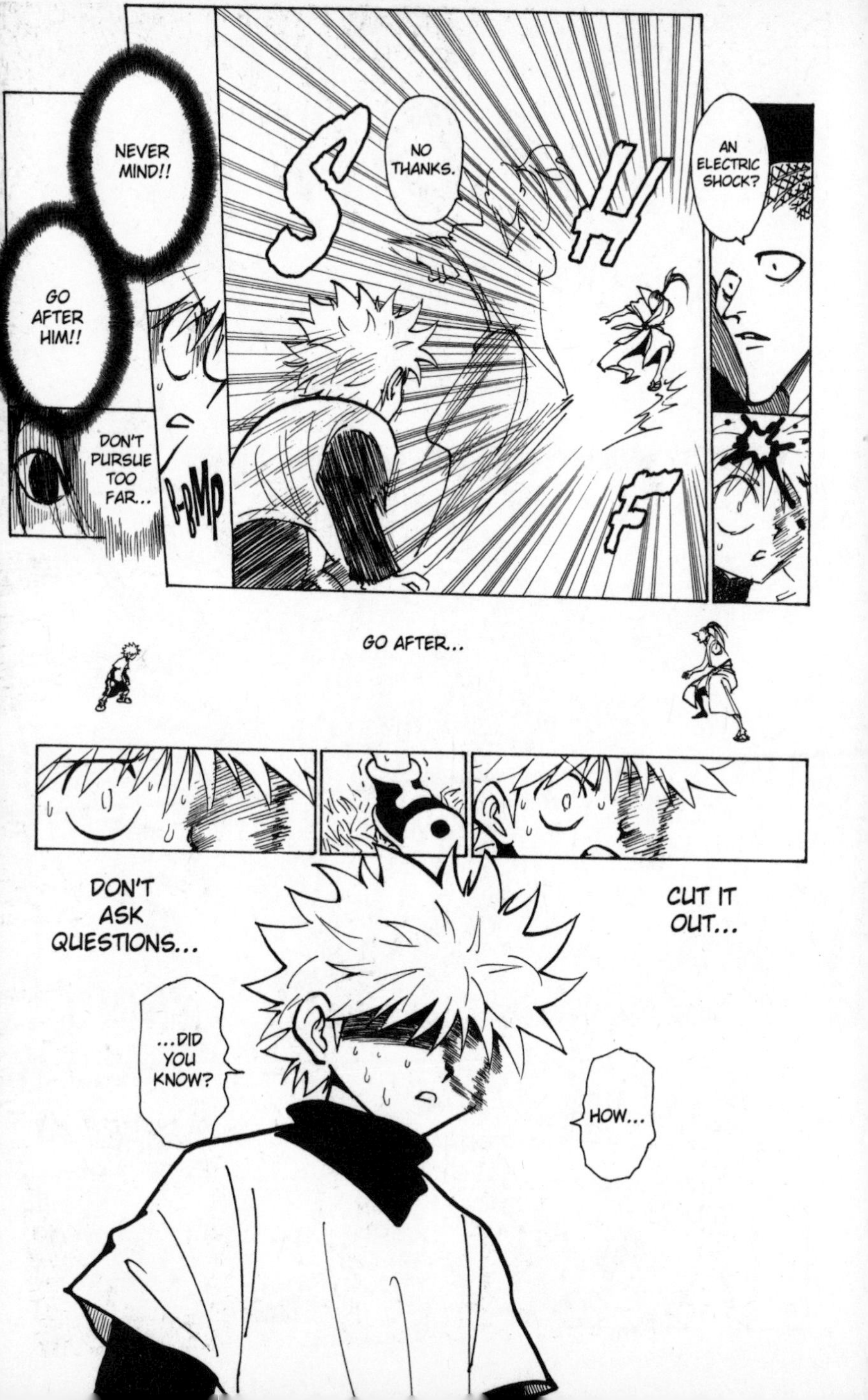
AN ELECTRIC SHOCK?
NO THANKS.
B-BMP
NEVER MIND!!
GO AFTER HIM!!
DON'T PURSUE TOO FAR...
GO AFTER...
CUT IT OUT...
DON'T ASK QUESTIONS...
HOW...
...DID YOU KNOW?

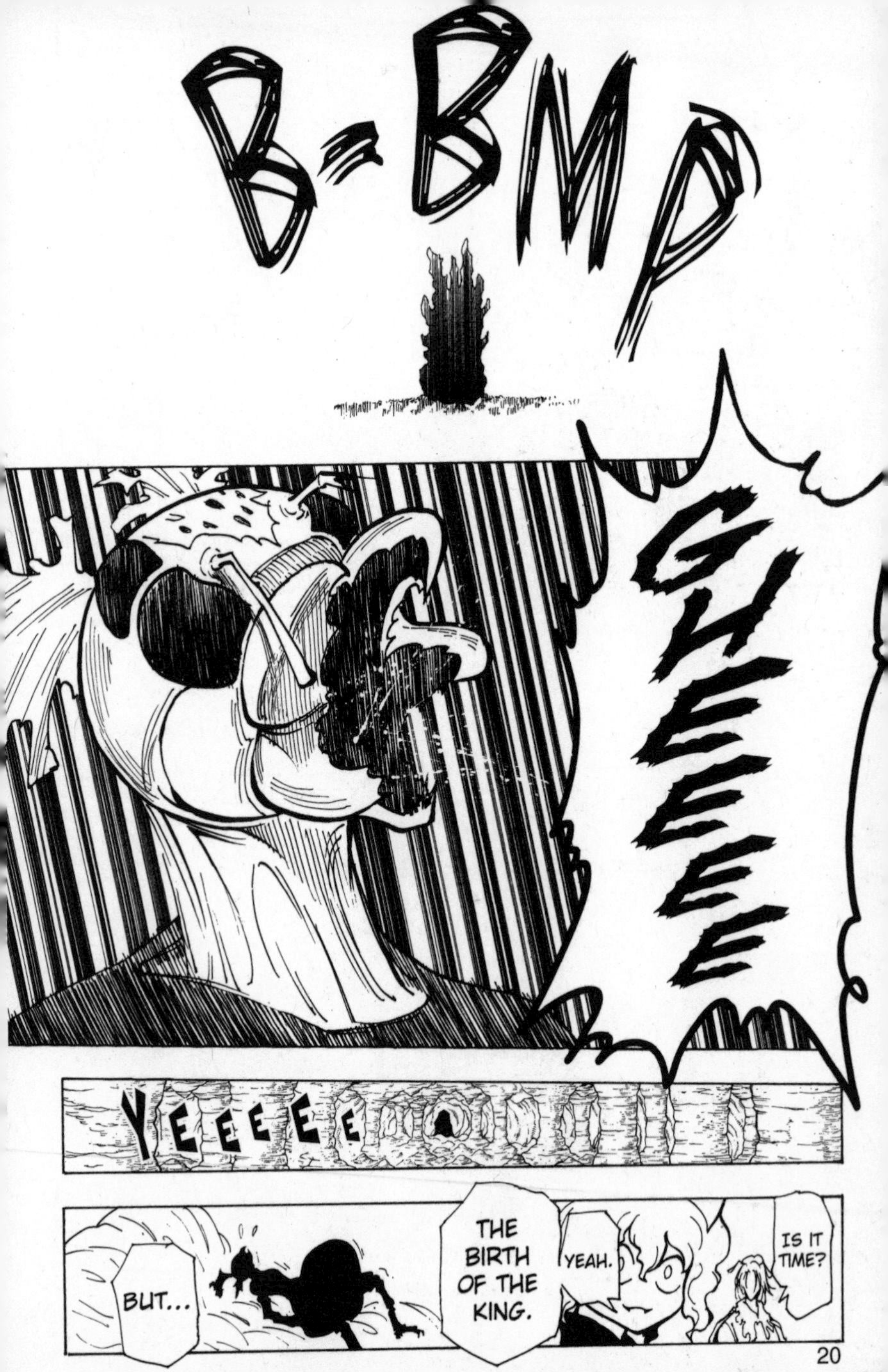
B-BMP
GHEEEEE
YEEEEE
IS IT TIME?
YEAH.
THE BIRTH OF THE KING.
BUT...

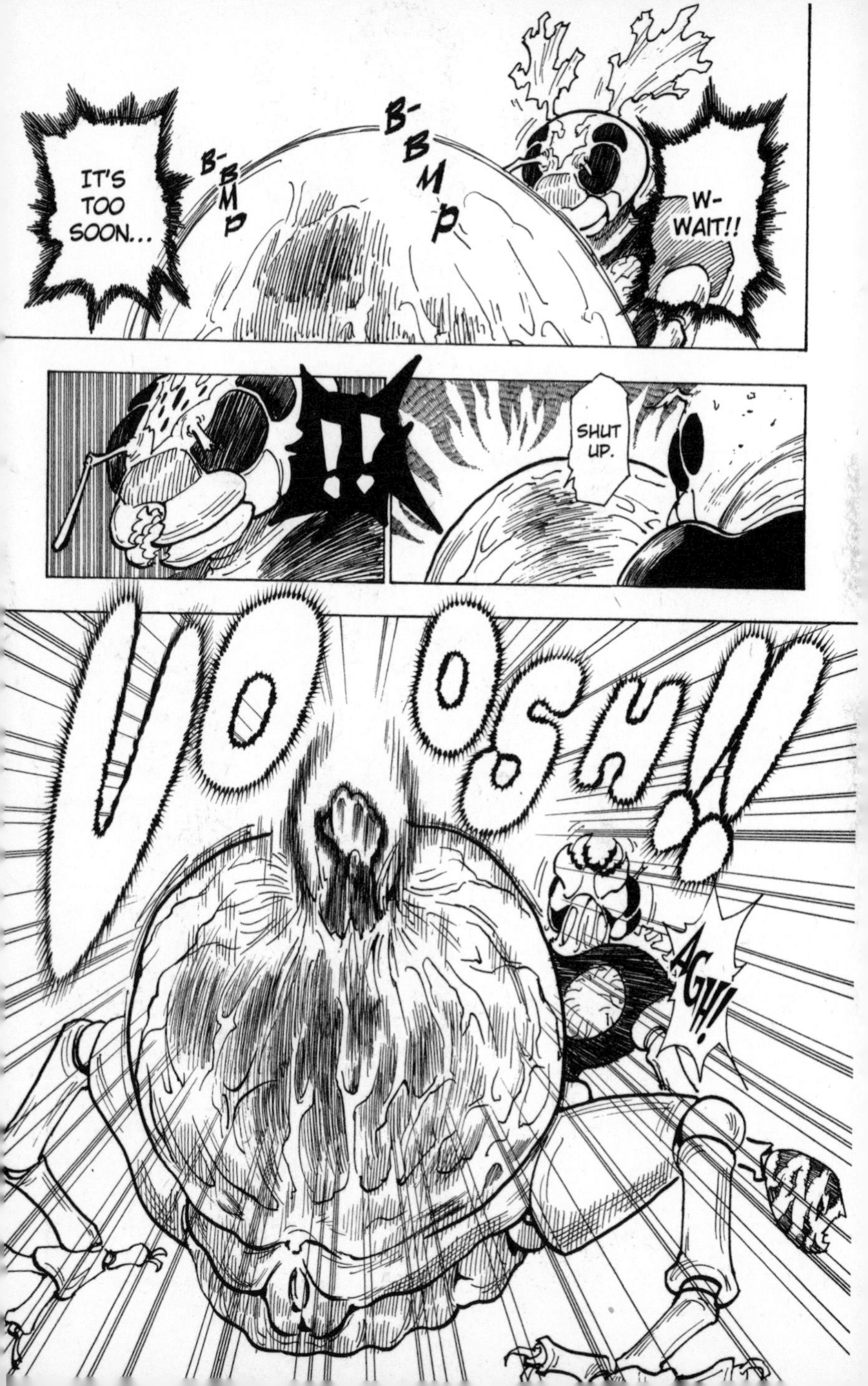
W-WAIT!!
B-BMP
B-BMP
IT'S TOO SOON...
SHUT UP.
!!
VOOSH!!
AGH!!

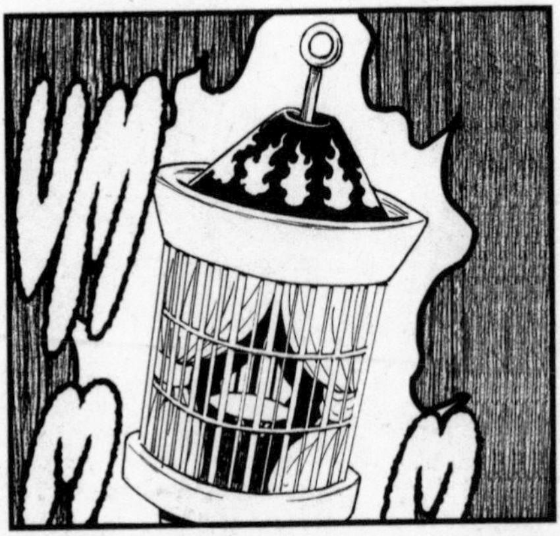
UMM

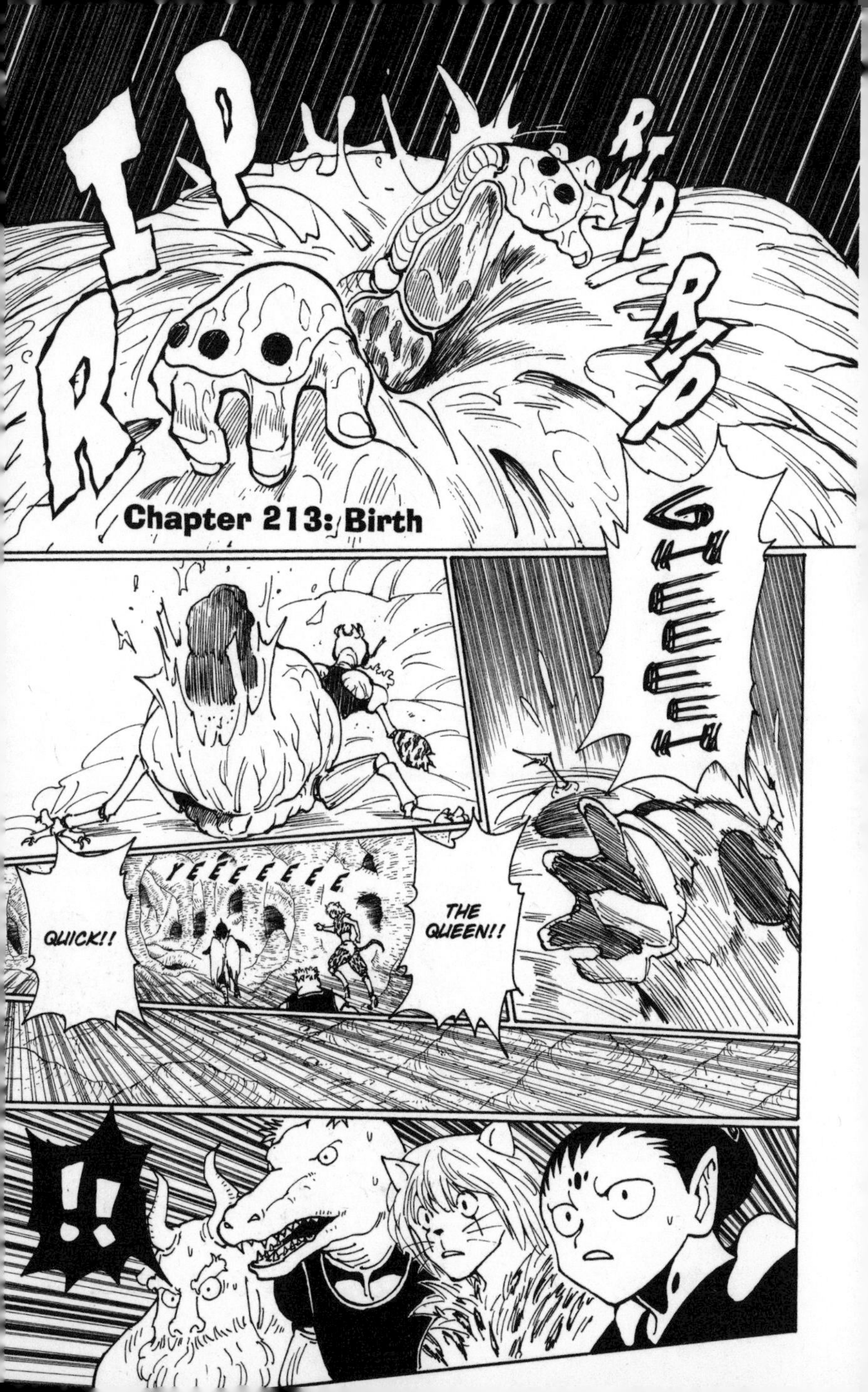
RIP
RIP
RIP
Chapter 213: Birth
GHEEEEH
THE QUEEN!!
YEEEEEEE
QUICK!!
!!

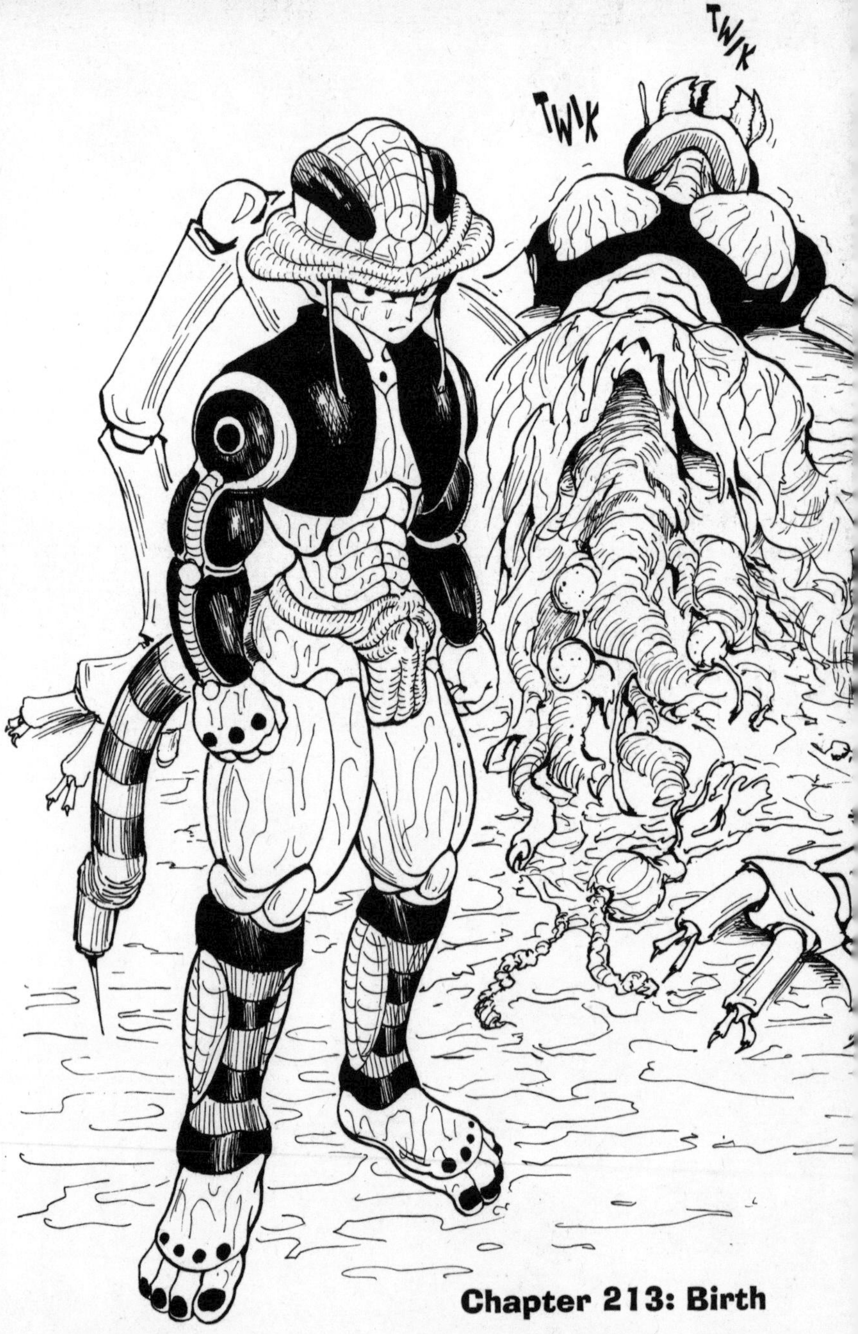
TWIK
TWIK

Chapter 213: Birth

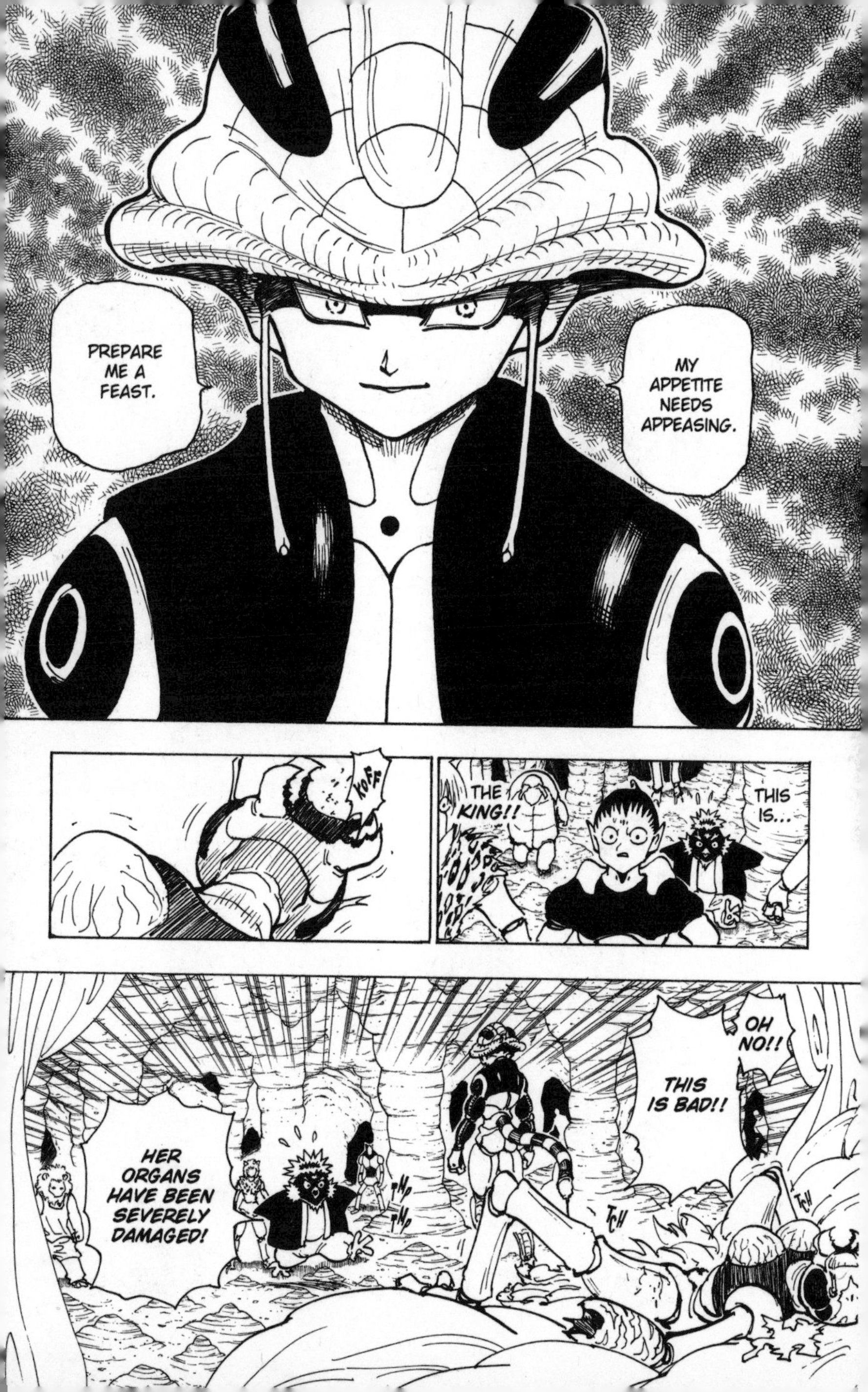
MY APPETITE NEEDS APPEASING.
PREPARE ME A FEAST.
THIS IS...
THE KING!!
KOFF
OH NO!!
THIS IS BAD!!
TCH
TCH
HER ORGANS HAVE BEEN SEVERELY DAMAGED!
TMP
TMP

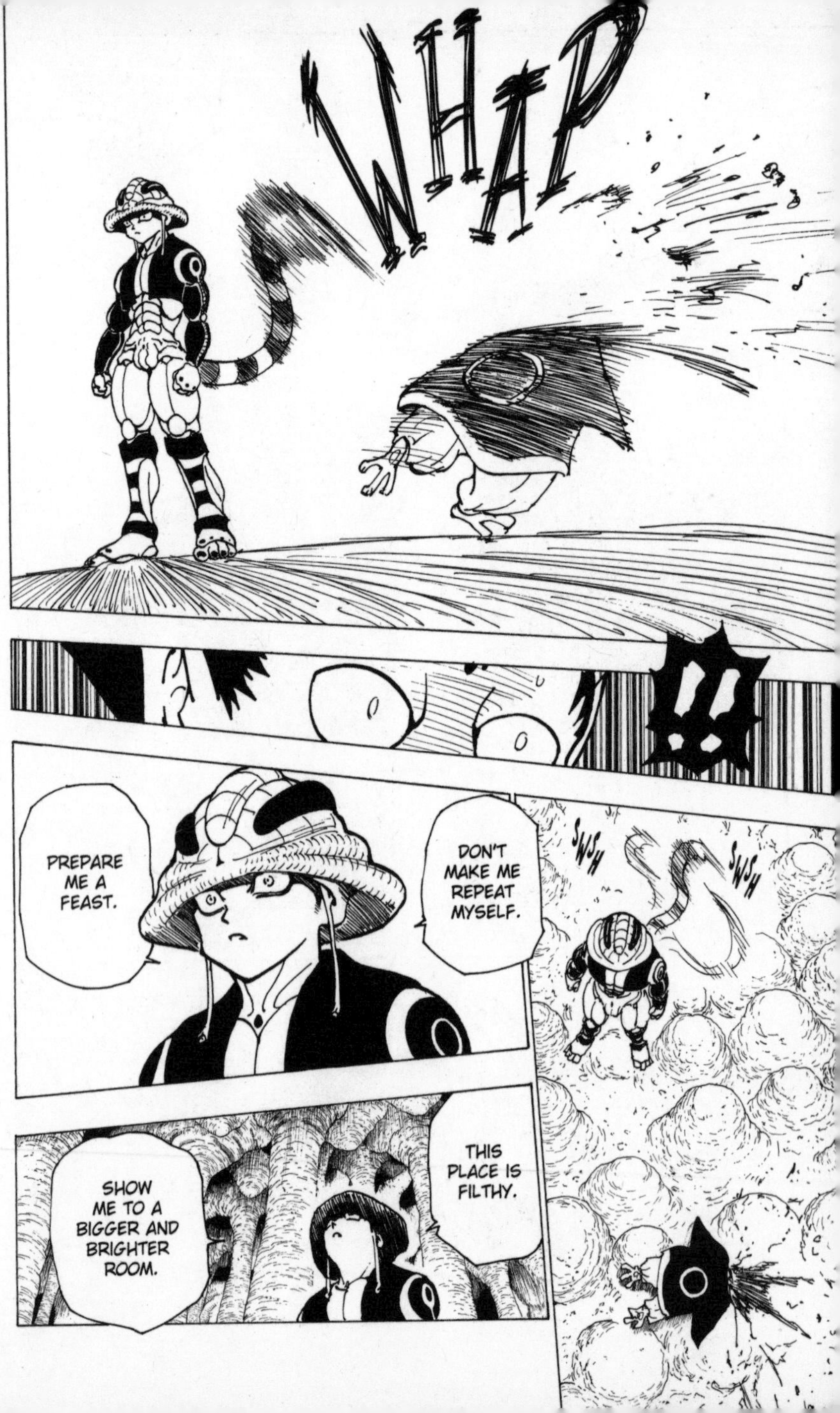
WHAP
SWSH
SWSH
DON'T MAKE ME REPEAT MYSELF.
PREPARE ME A FEAST.
THIS PLACE IS FILTHY.
SHOW ME TO A BIGGER AND BRIGHTER ROOM.

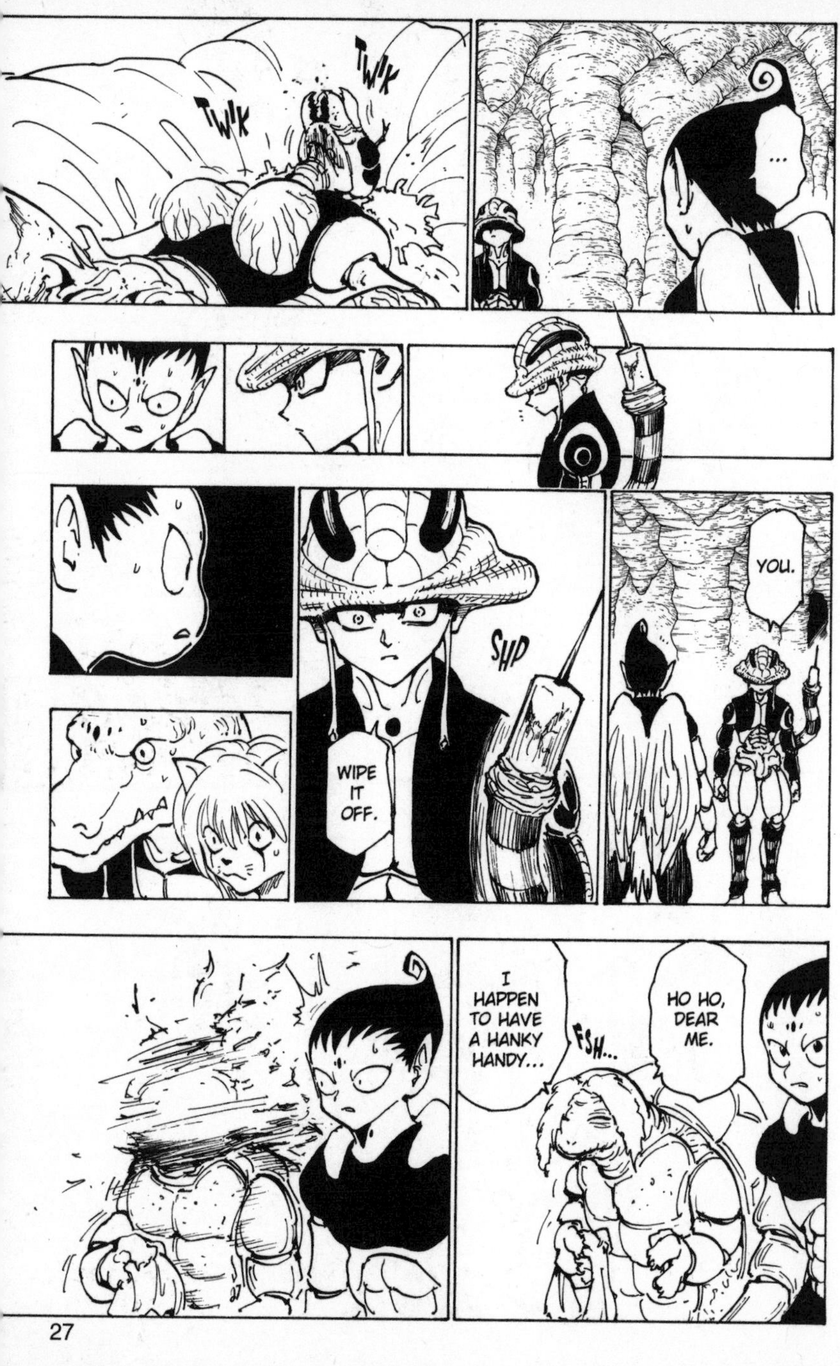
...
TWIK
TWIK
YOU.
SHP
WIPE IT OFF.
HO HO, DEAR ME.
I HAPPEN TO HAVE A HANKY HANDY...
FSH...

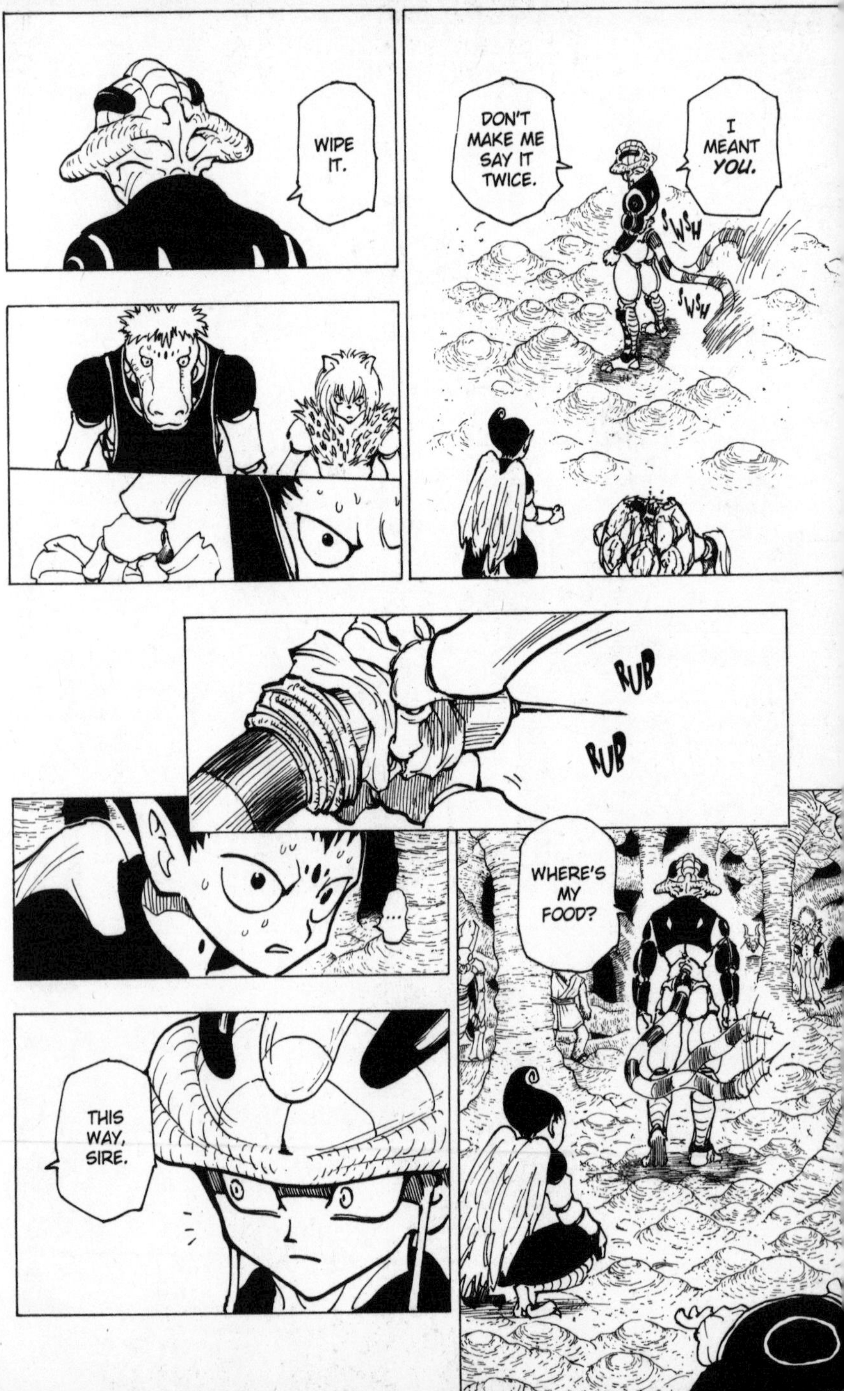
I MEANT *YOU.*
DON'T MAKE ME SAY IT TWICE.
SWSH
SWSH
WIPE IT.
RUB
RUB
WHERE'S MY FOOD?
...
THIS WAY, SIRE.

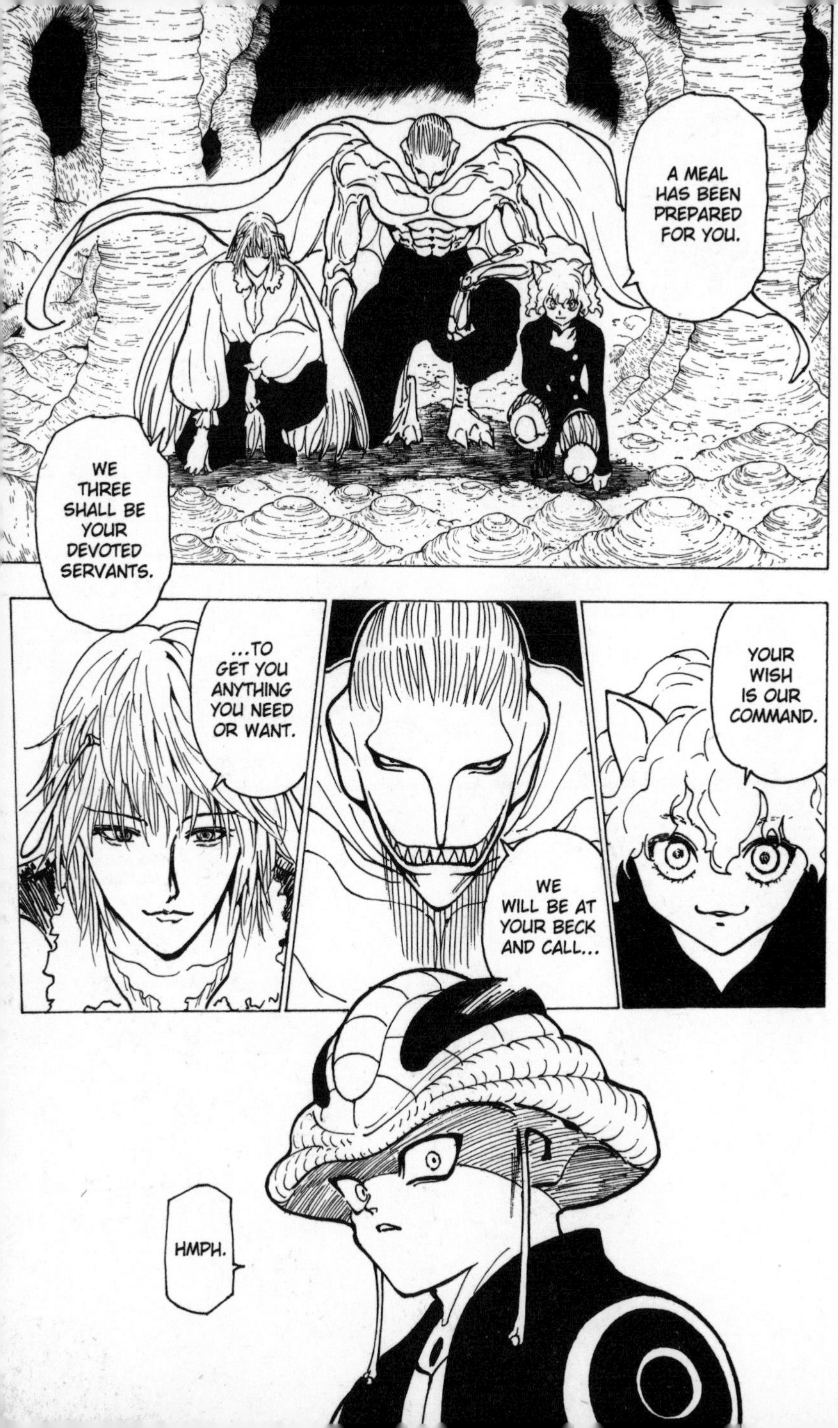
A MEAL HAS BEEN PREPARED FOR YOU.
WE THREE SHALL BE YOUR DEVOTED SERVANTS.
YOUR WISH IS OUR COMMAND.
WE WILL BE AT YOUR BECK AND CALL...
...TO GET YOU ANYTHING YOU NEED OR WANT.
HMPH.

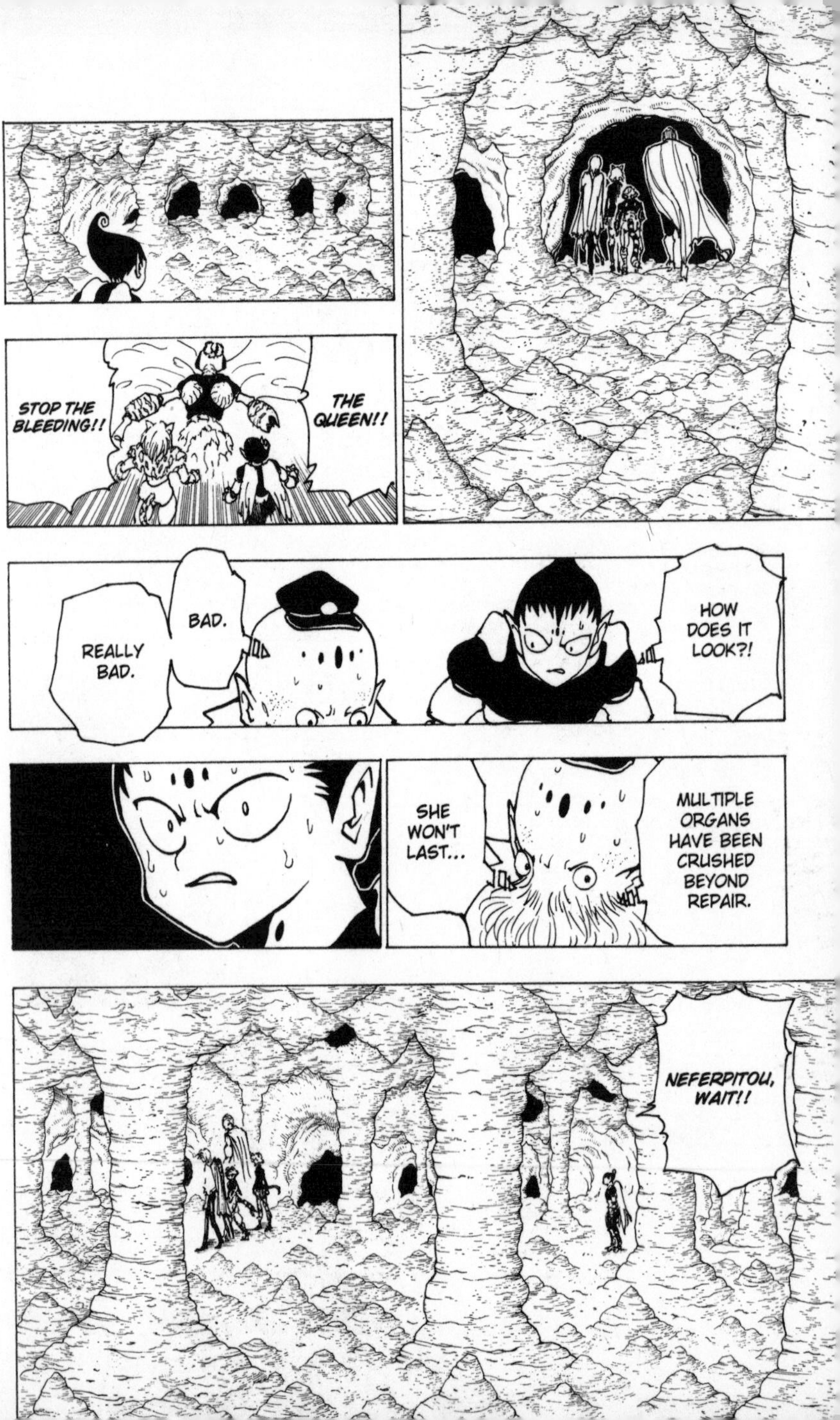
THE QUEEN!!
STOP THE BLEEDING!!
HOW DOES IT LOOK?!
BAD.
REALLY BAD.
MULTIPLE ORGANS HAVE BEEN CRUSHED BEYOND REPAIR.
SHE WON'T LAST...
NEFERPITOU, WAIT!!

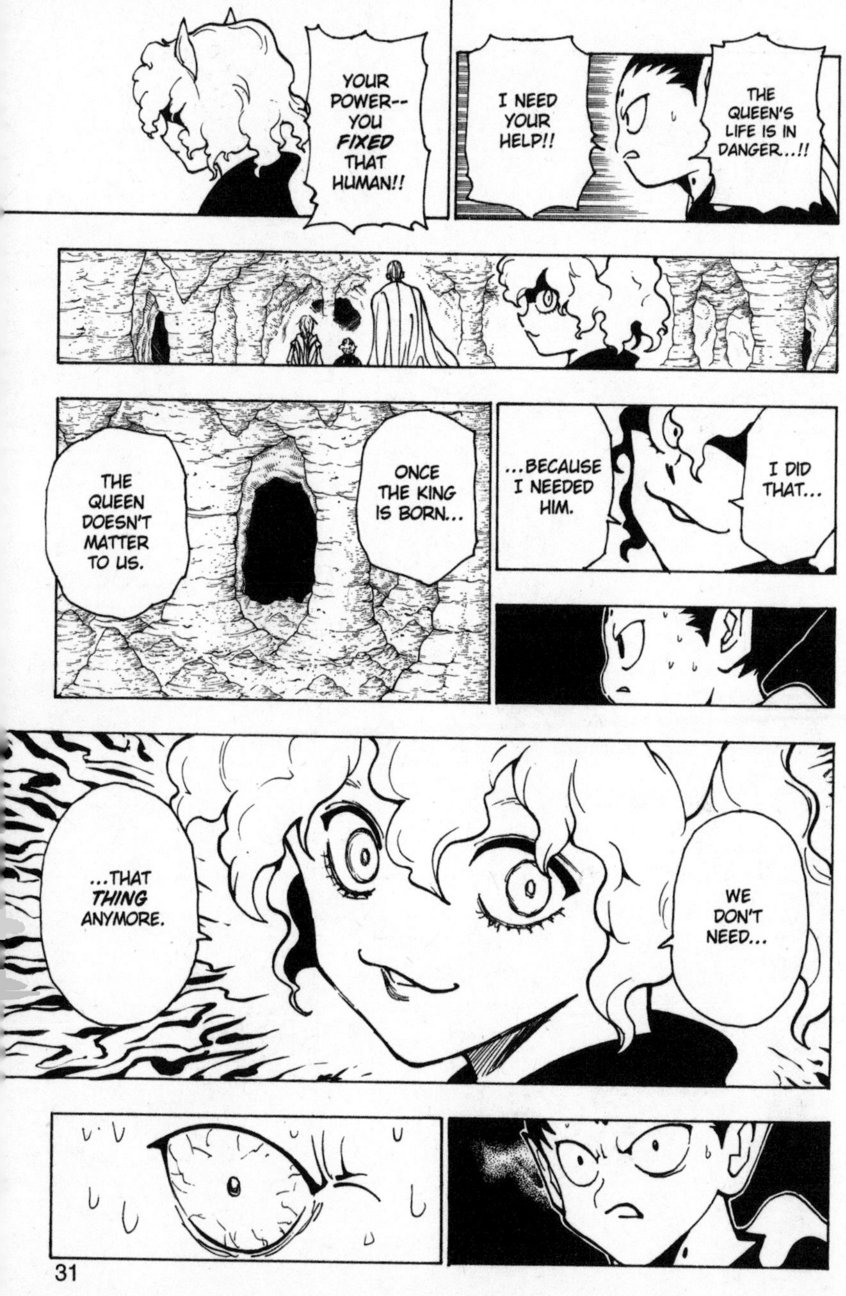
THE QUEEN'S LIFE IS IN DANGER...!!
I NEED YOUR HELP!!
YOUR POWER-- YOU *FIXED* THAT HUMAN!!
I DID THAT...
...BECAUSE I NEEDED HIM.
ONCE THE KING IS BORN...
THE QUEEN DOESN'T MATTER TO US.
WE DON'T NEED...
...THAT *THING* ANYMORE.

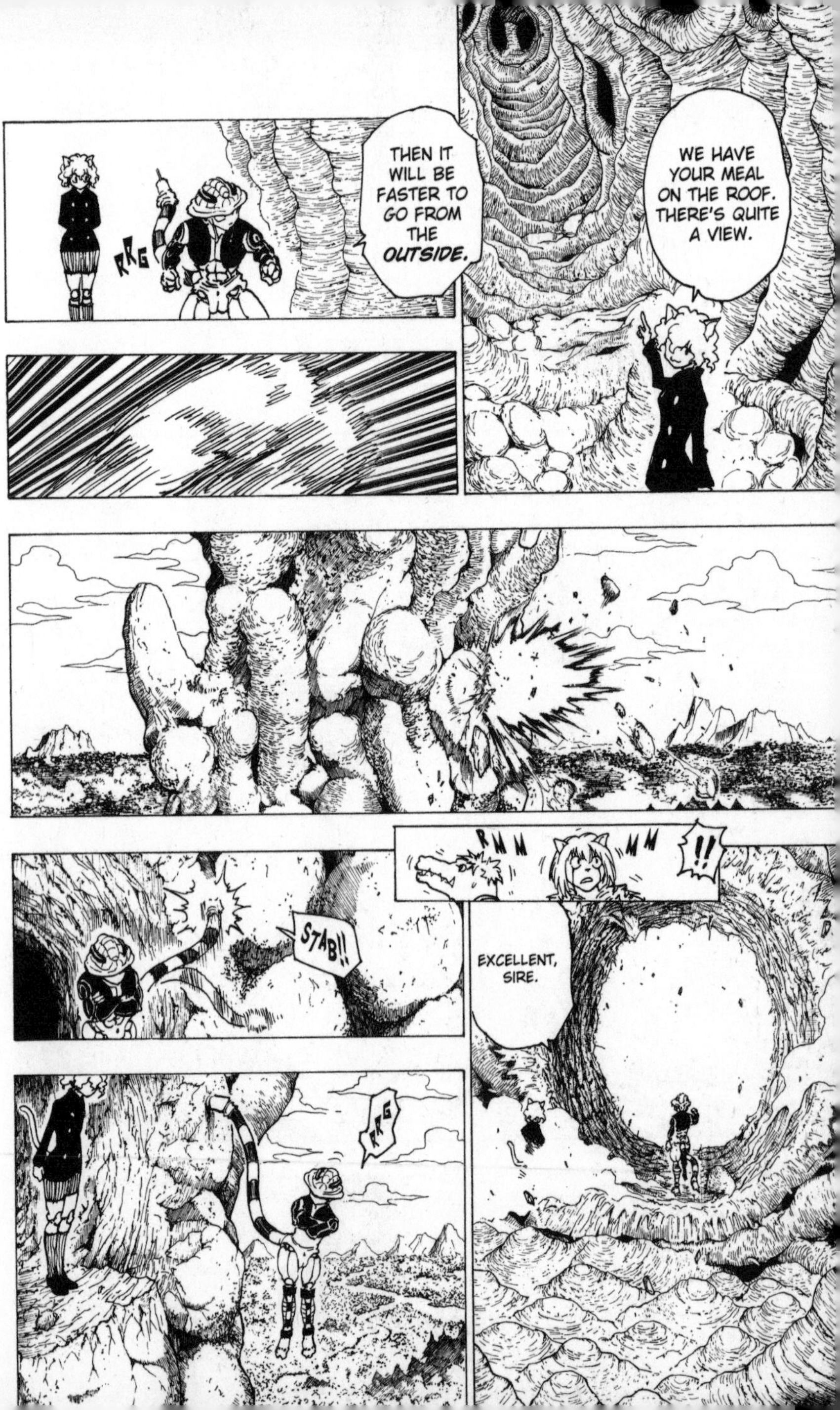
WE HAVE YOUR MEAL ON THE ROOF. THERE'S QUITE A VIEW.
THEN IT WILL BE FASTER TO GO FROM THE *OUTSIDE.*
RRG
!!
MM
RMM
EXCELLENT, SIRE.
STAB!!
RRG

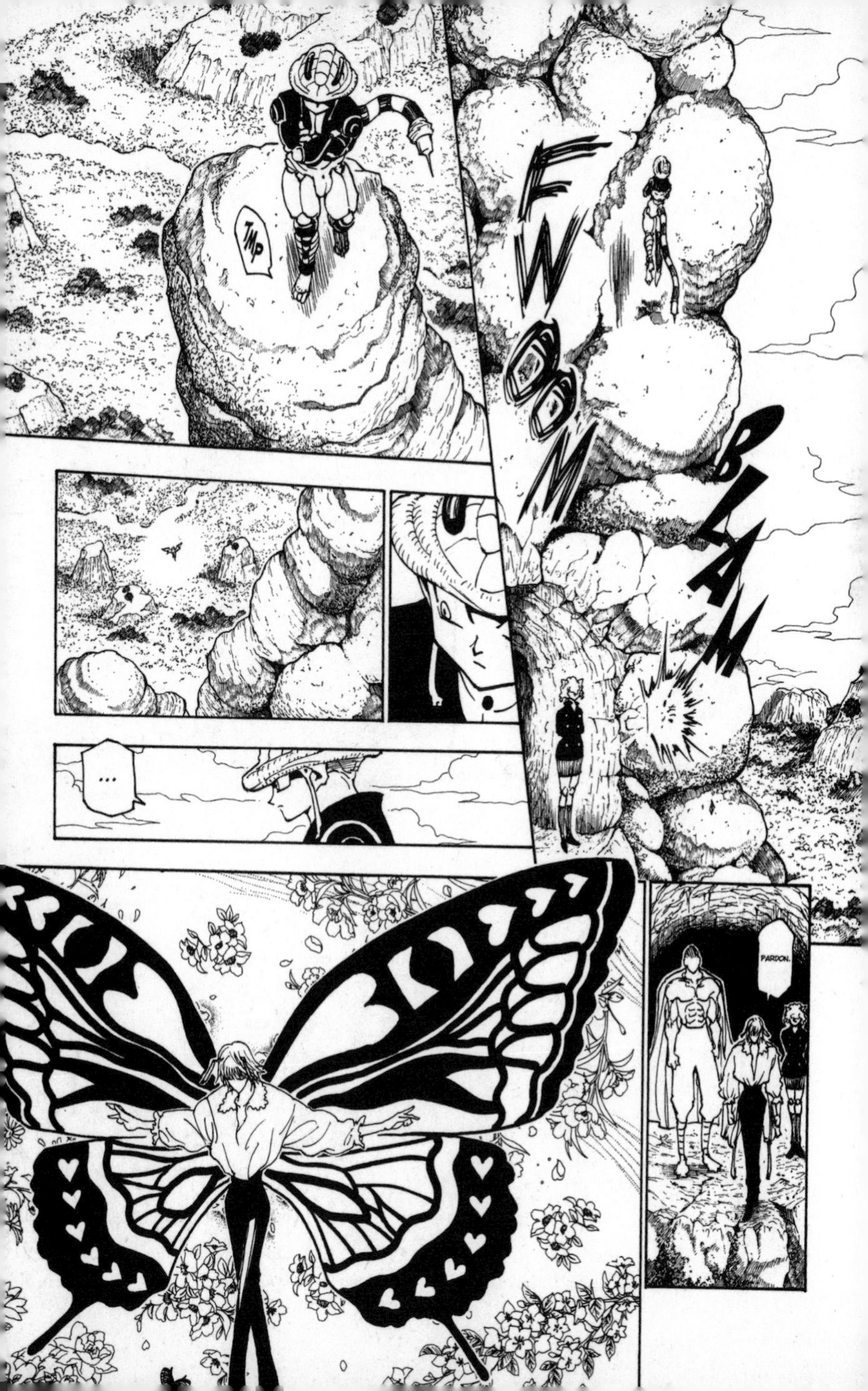
FWOOM
BLAM
TMP
...
PARDON.

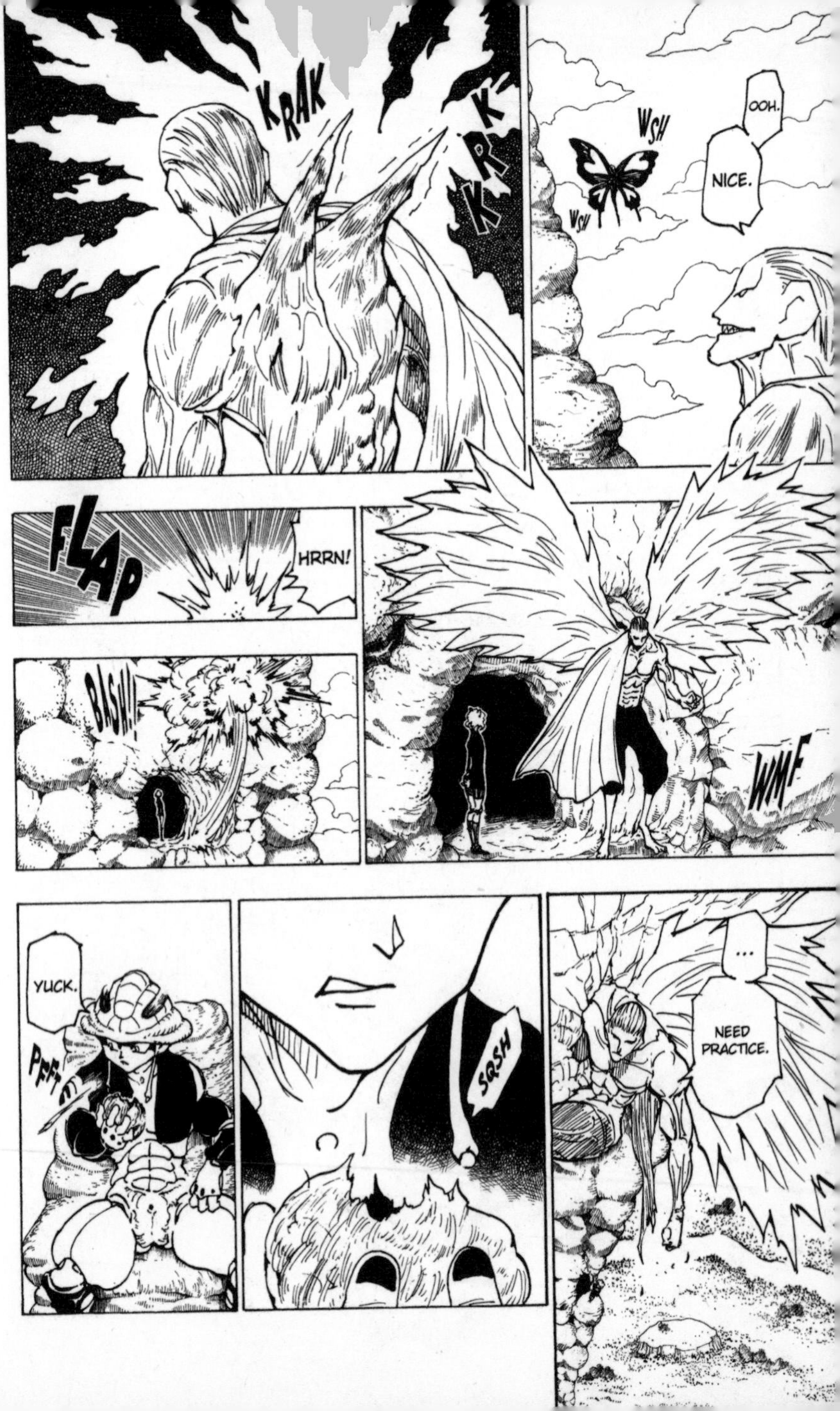

WSH
WSH
OOH.
NICE.
KRAK
KRK
WMF
HRRN!
FLAP
BASH!!
...
NEED PRACTICE.
SQSH
YUCK.
PFFT

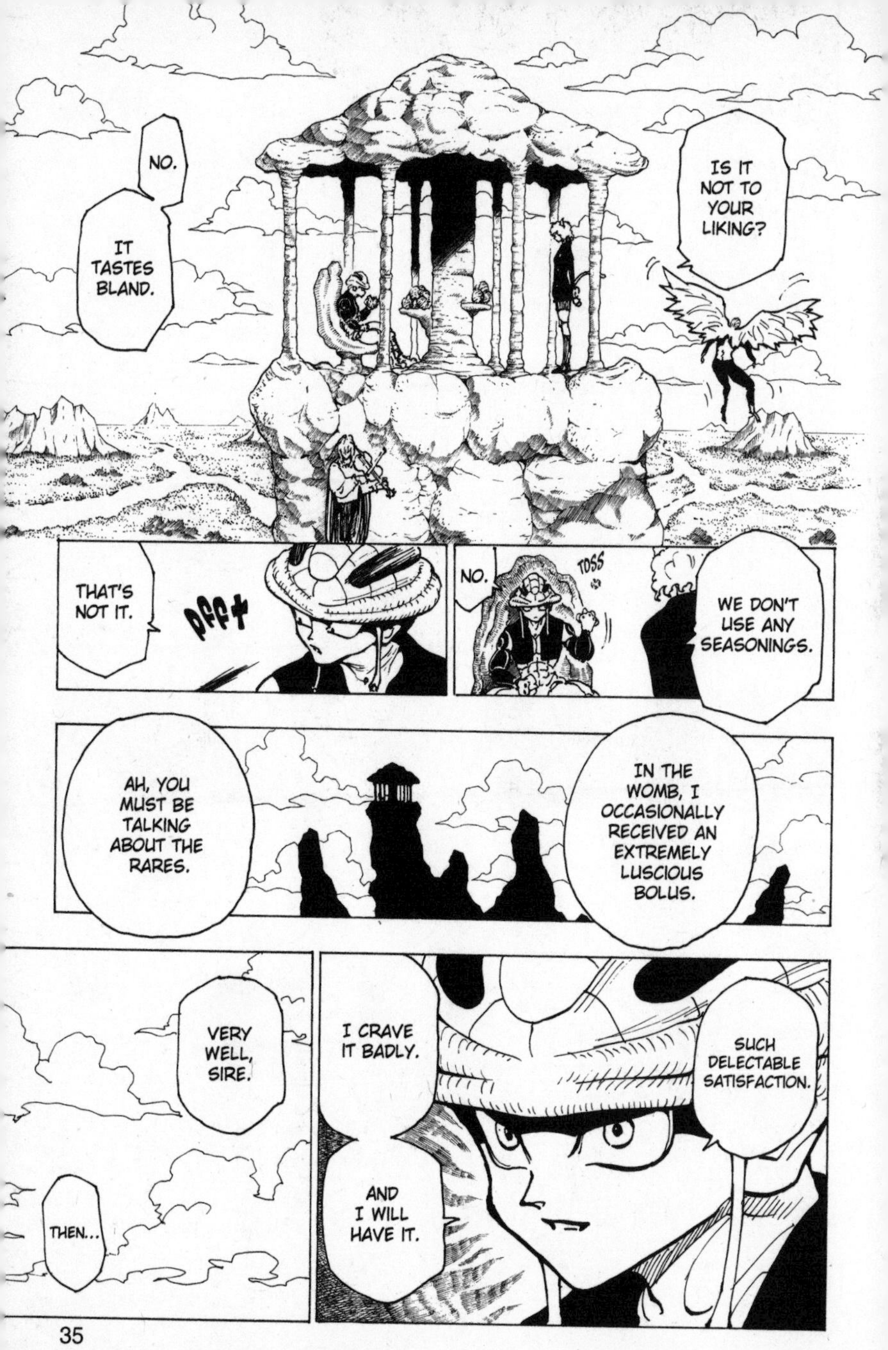
IS IT NOT TO YOUR LIKING?
NO.
IT TASTES BLAND.
WE DON'T USE ANY SEASONINGS.
TOSS
NO.
THAT'S NOT IT.
PFFT
IN THE WOMB, I OCCASIONALLY RECEIVED AN EXTREMELY LUSCIOUS BOLUS.
AH, YOU MUST BE TALKING ABOUT THE RARES.
SUCH DELECTABLE SATISFACTION.
I CRAVE IT BADLY.
AND I WILL HAVE IT.
VERY WELL, SIRE.
THEN...

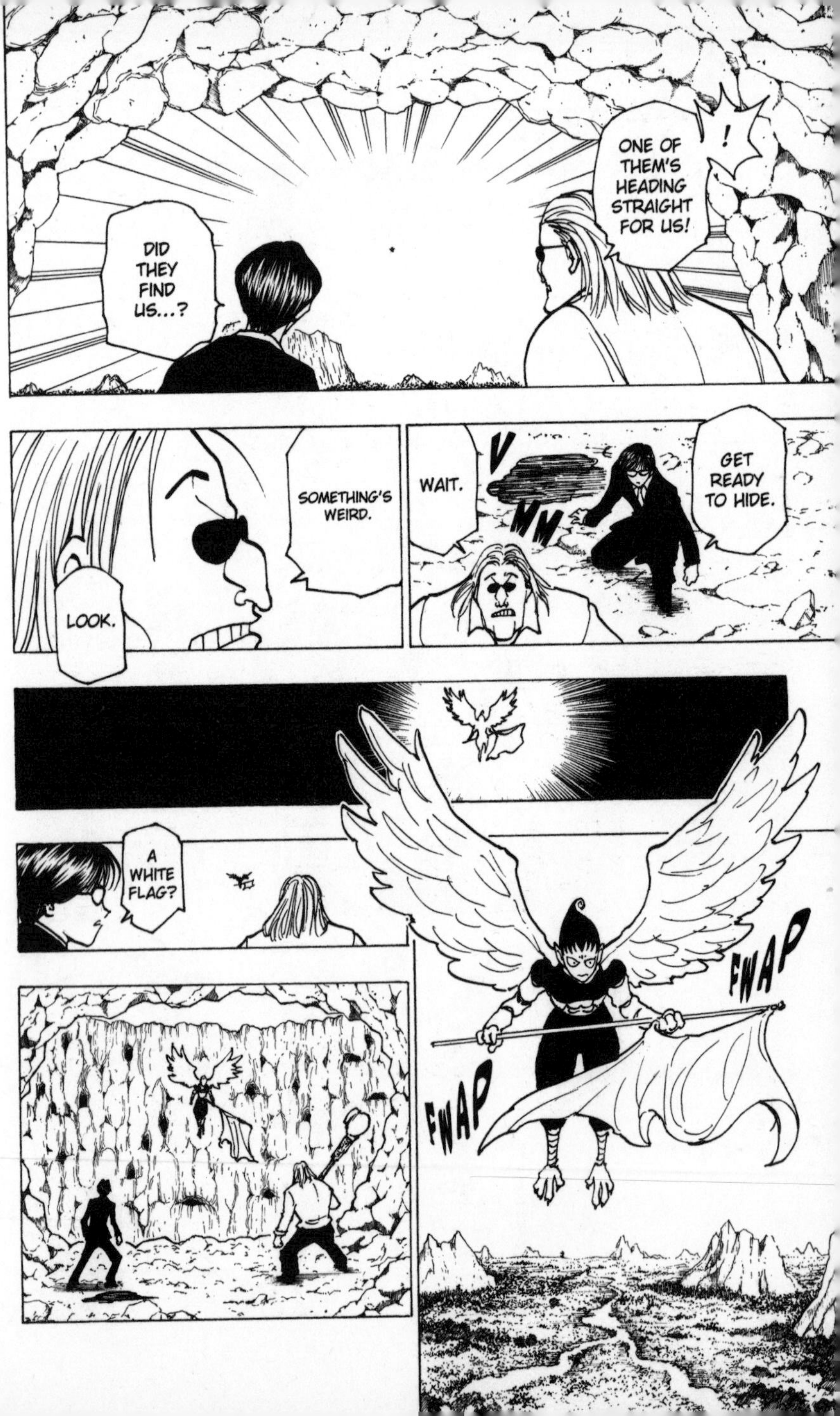
!
ONE OF THEM'S HEADING STRAIGHT FOR US!
DID THEY FIND US...?
GET READY TO HIDE.
VMM
WAIT.
SOMETHING'S WEIRD.
LOOK.
FWAP
FWAP
A WHITE FLAG?

READ THIS WAY

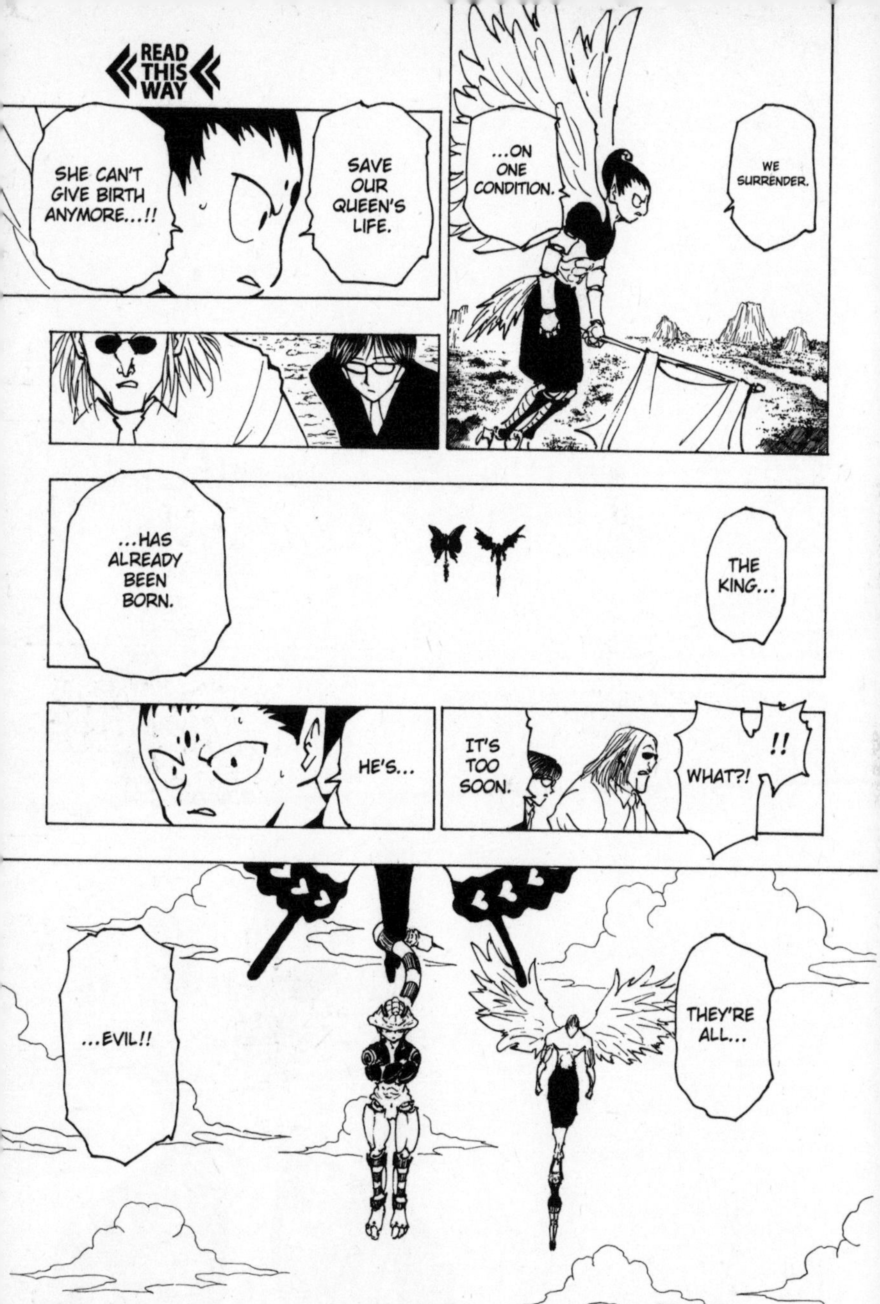
WE SURRENDER.
...ON ONE CONDITION.
SAVE OUR QUEEN'S LIFE.
SHE CAN'T GIVE BIRTH ANYMORE...!!
THE KING...
...HAS ALREADY BEEN BORN.
!! WHAT?!
IT'S TOO SOON.
HE'S...
THEY'RE ALL...
...EVIL!!

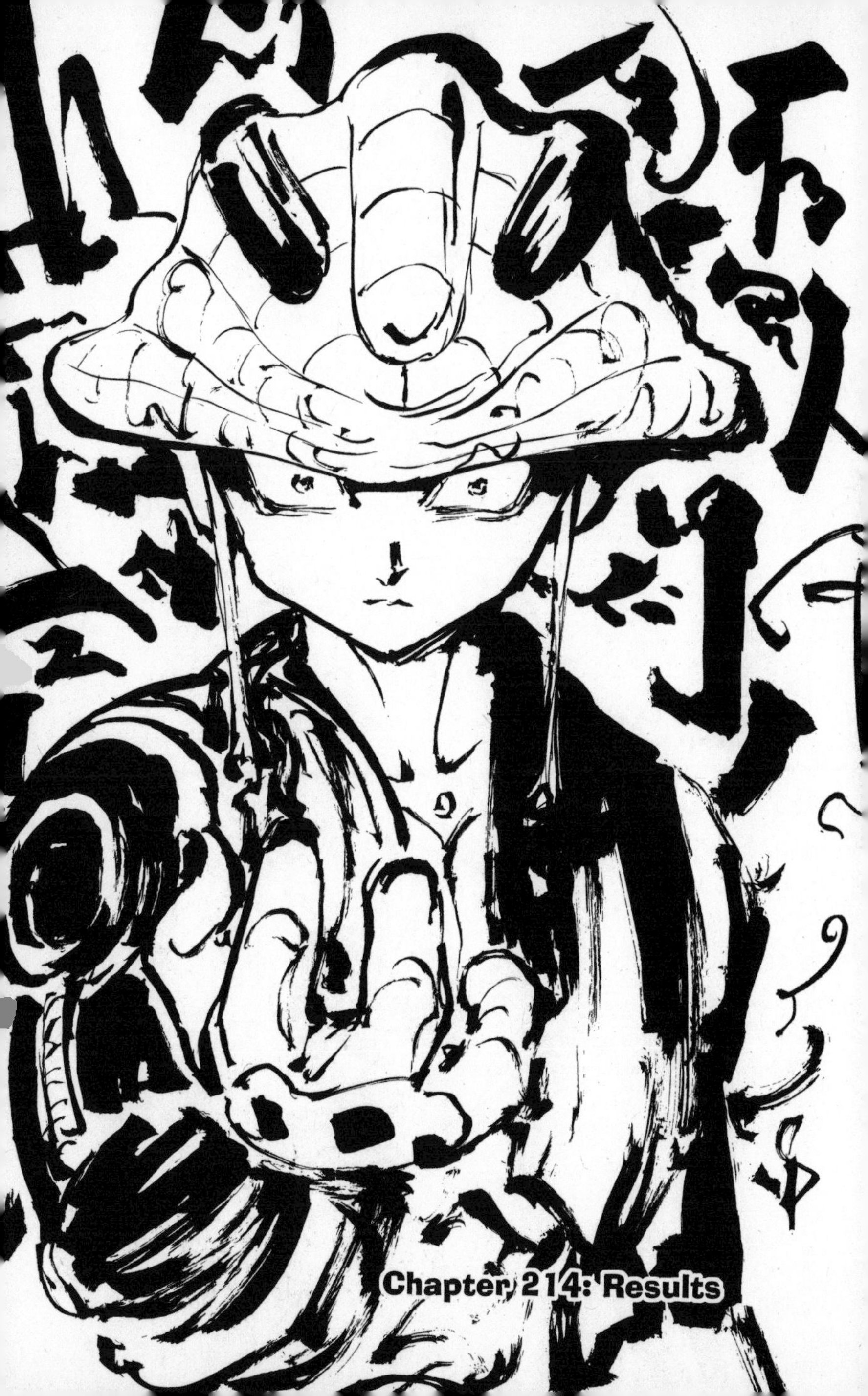

Chapter 214: Results

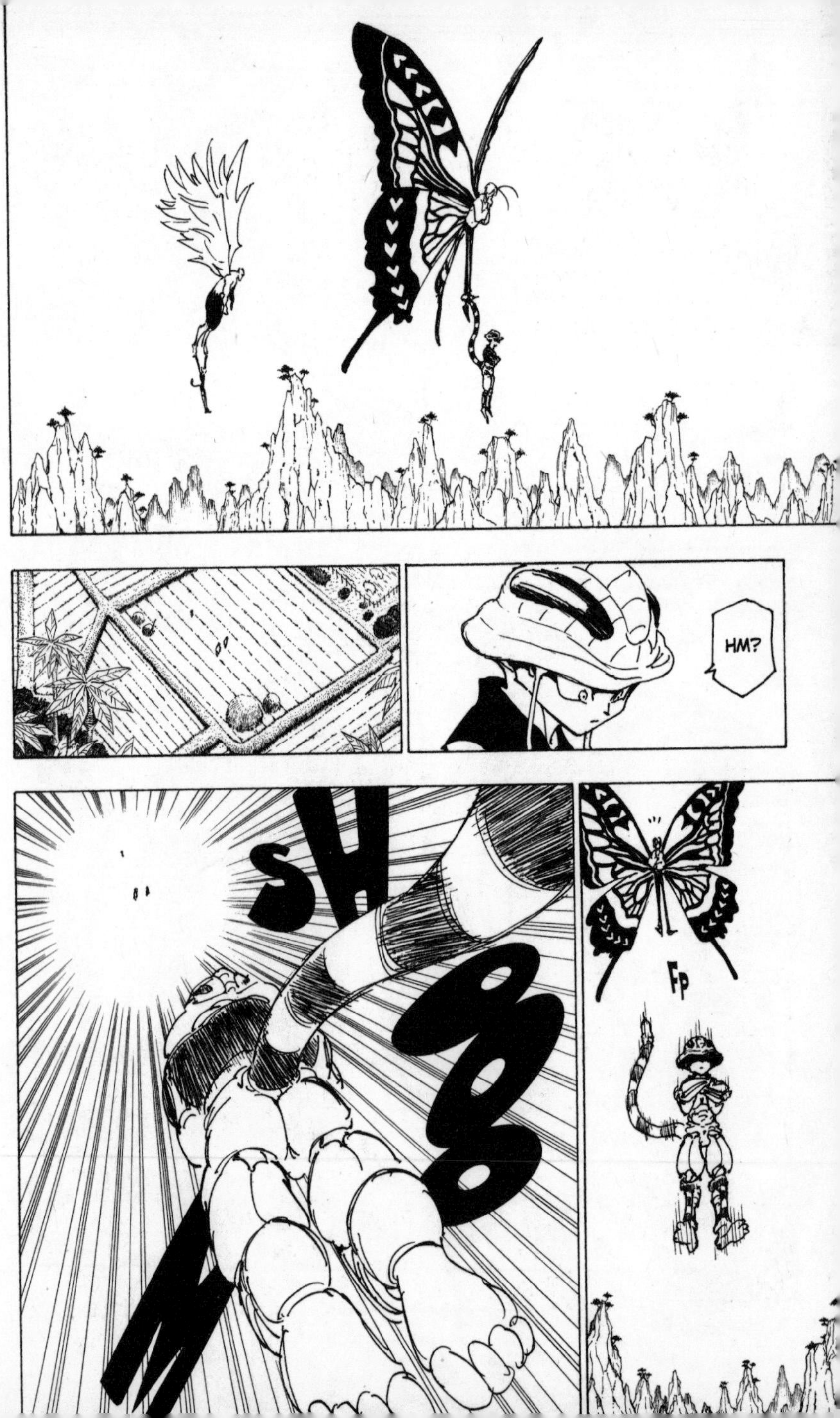
HM?
Fp
SHOOOM

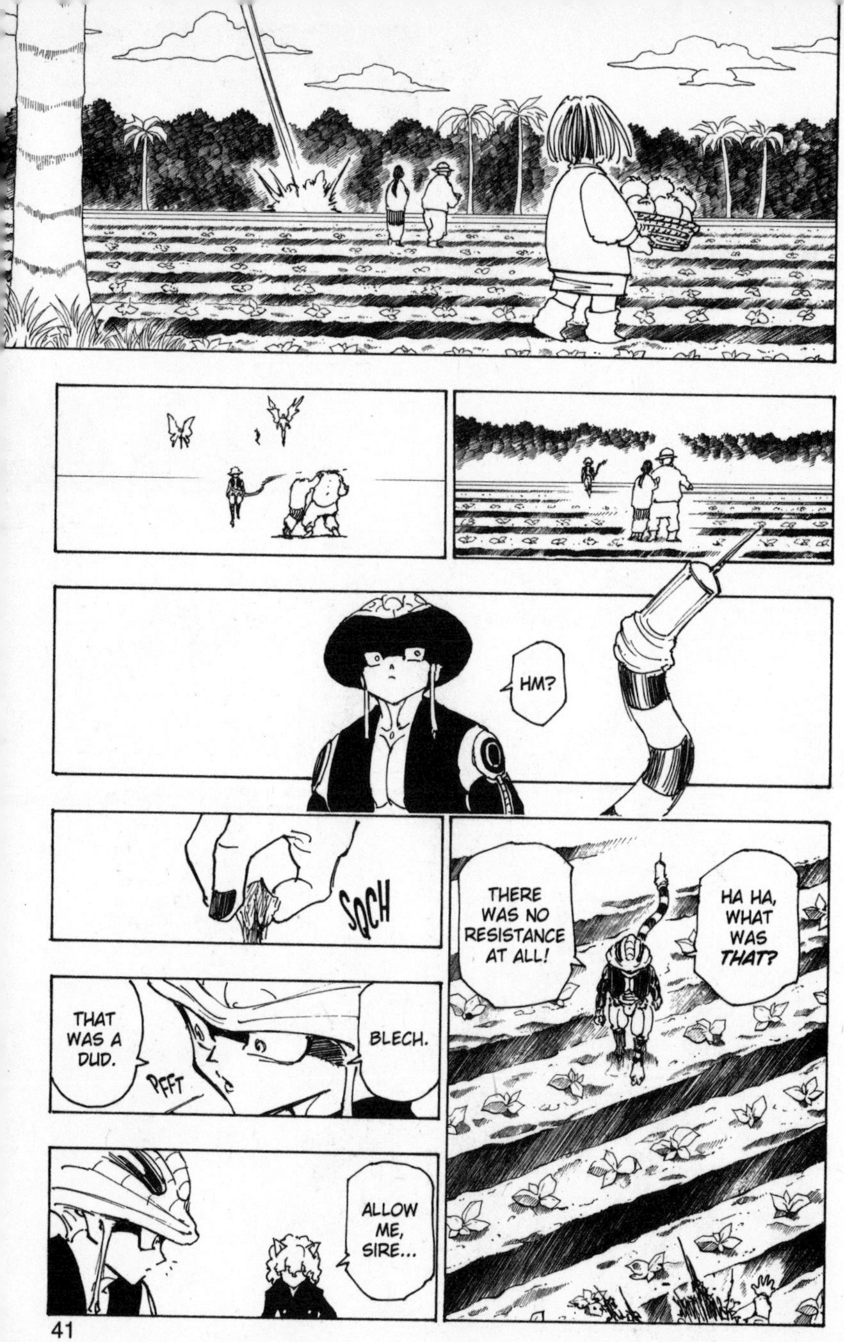
HM?
HA HA, WHAT WAS *THAT?*
THERE WAS NO RESISTANCE AT ALL!
SQCH
BLECH.
THAT WAS A DUD.
PFFT
ALLOW ME, SIRE...

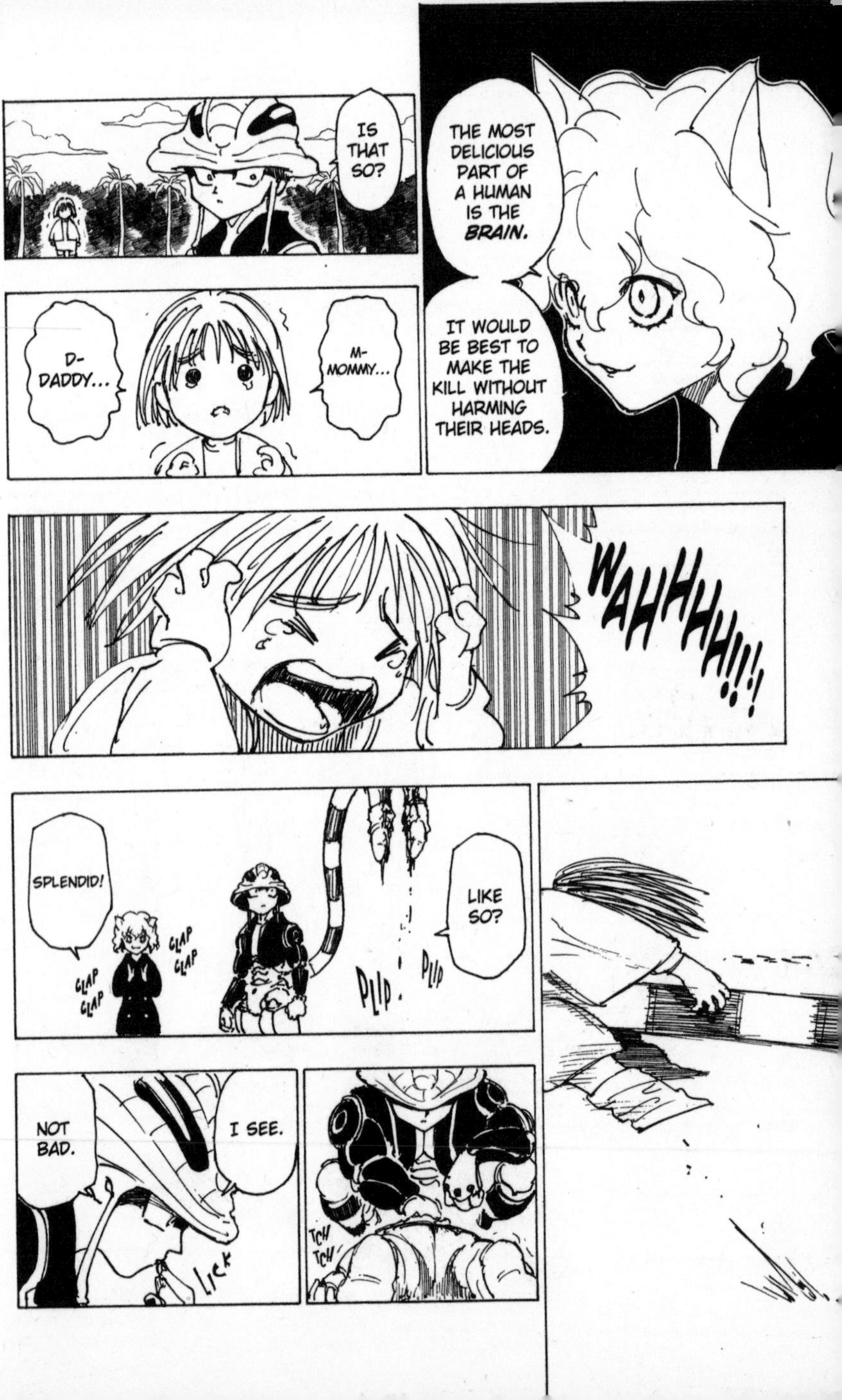
THE MOST DELICIOUS PART OF A HUMAN IS THE ***BRAIN.***
IT WOULD BE BEST TO MAKE THE KILL WITHOUT HARMING THEIR HEADS.
IS THAT SO?
M-MOMMY...
D-DADDY...
WAHHHH!!!!
LIKE SO?
PLIP
PLIP
CLAP CLAP
CLAP CLAP
SPLENDID!
TCH TCH
I SEE.
NOT BAD.
LICK

READ THIS WAY

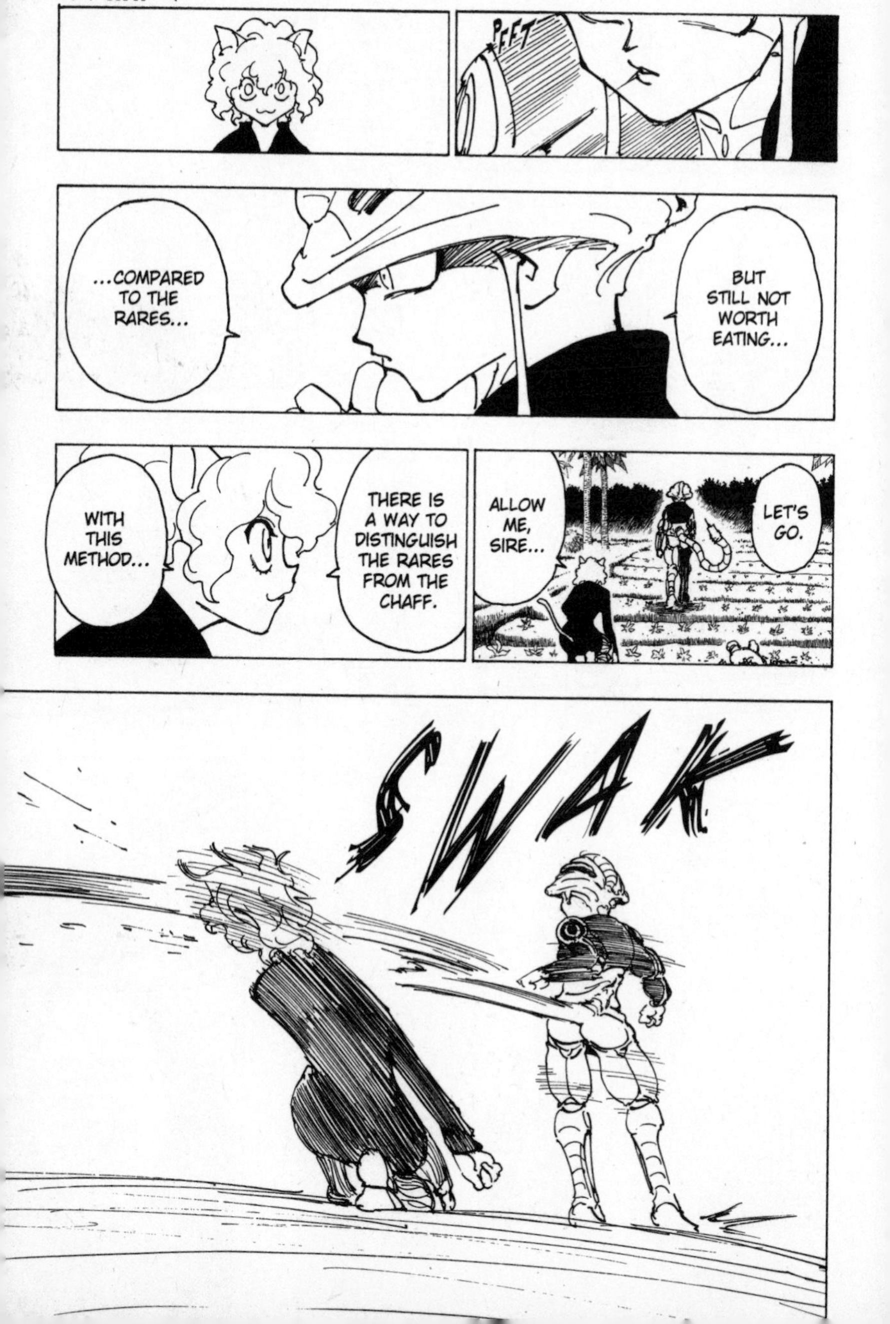
PFFT
BUT STILL NOT WORTH EATING...
...COMPARED TO THE RARES...
LET'S GO.
ALLOW ME, SIRE...
THERE IS A WAY TO DISTINGUISH THE RARES FROM THE CHAFF.
WITH THIS METHOD...
SWAK

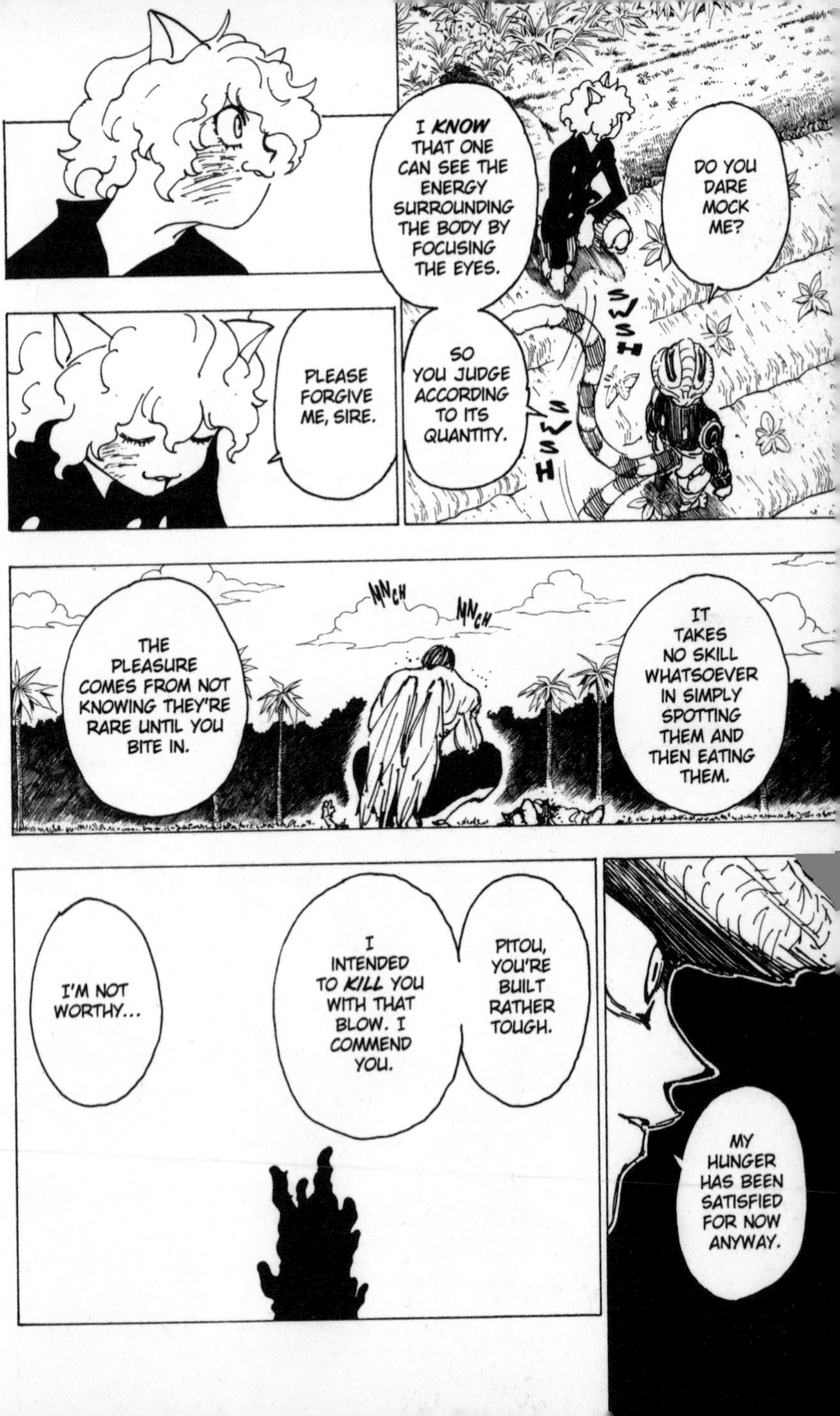
DO YOU DARE MOCK ME?
I KNOW THAT ONE CAN SEE THE ENERGY SURROUNDING THE BODY BY FOCUSING THE EYES.
SWSH
SWSH
SO YOU JUDGE ACCORDING TO ITS QUANTITY.
PLEASE FORGIVE ME, SIRE.
IT TAKES NO SKILL WHATSOEVER IN SIMPLY SPOTTING THEM AND THEN EATING THEM.
MNCH
MNCH
THE PLEASURE COMES FROM NOT KNOWING THEY'RE RARE UNTIL YOU BITE IN.
MY HUNGER HAS BEEN SATISFIED FOR NOW ANYWAY.
PITOU, YOU'RE BUILT RATHER TOUGH.
I INTENDED TO KILL YOU WITH THAT BLOW. I COMMEND YOU.
I'M NOT WORTHY...

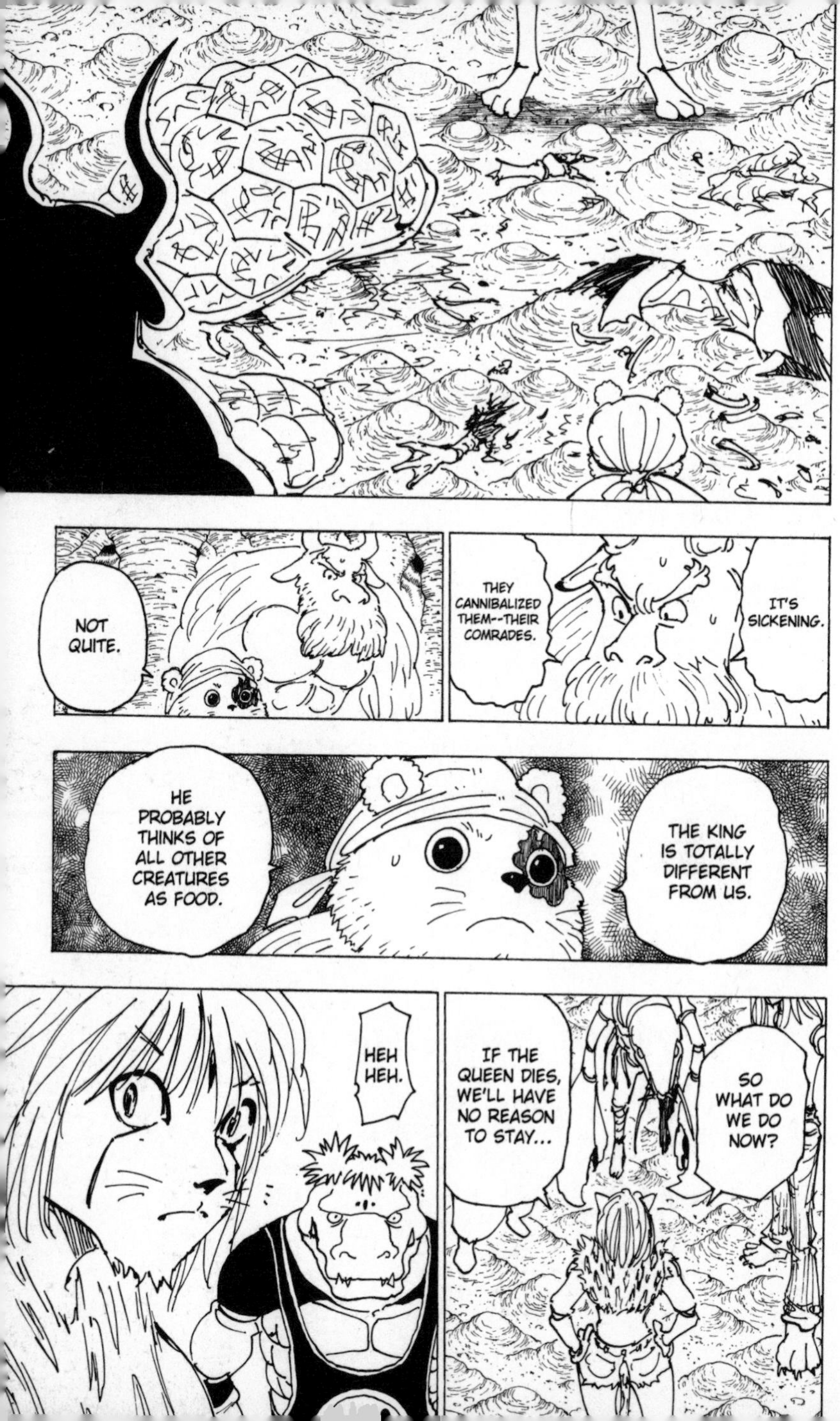
IT'S SICKENING.
THEY CANNIBALIZED THEM--THEIR COMRADES.
NOT QUITE.
THE KING IS TOTALLY DIFFERENT FROM US.
HE PROBABLY THINKS OF ALL OTHER CREATURES AS FOOD.
SO WHAT DO WE DO NOW?
IF THE QUEEN DIES, WE'LL HAVE NO REASON TO STAY...
HEH HEH.
...

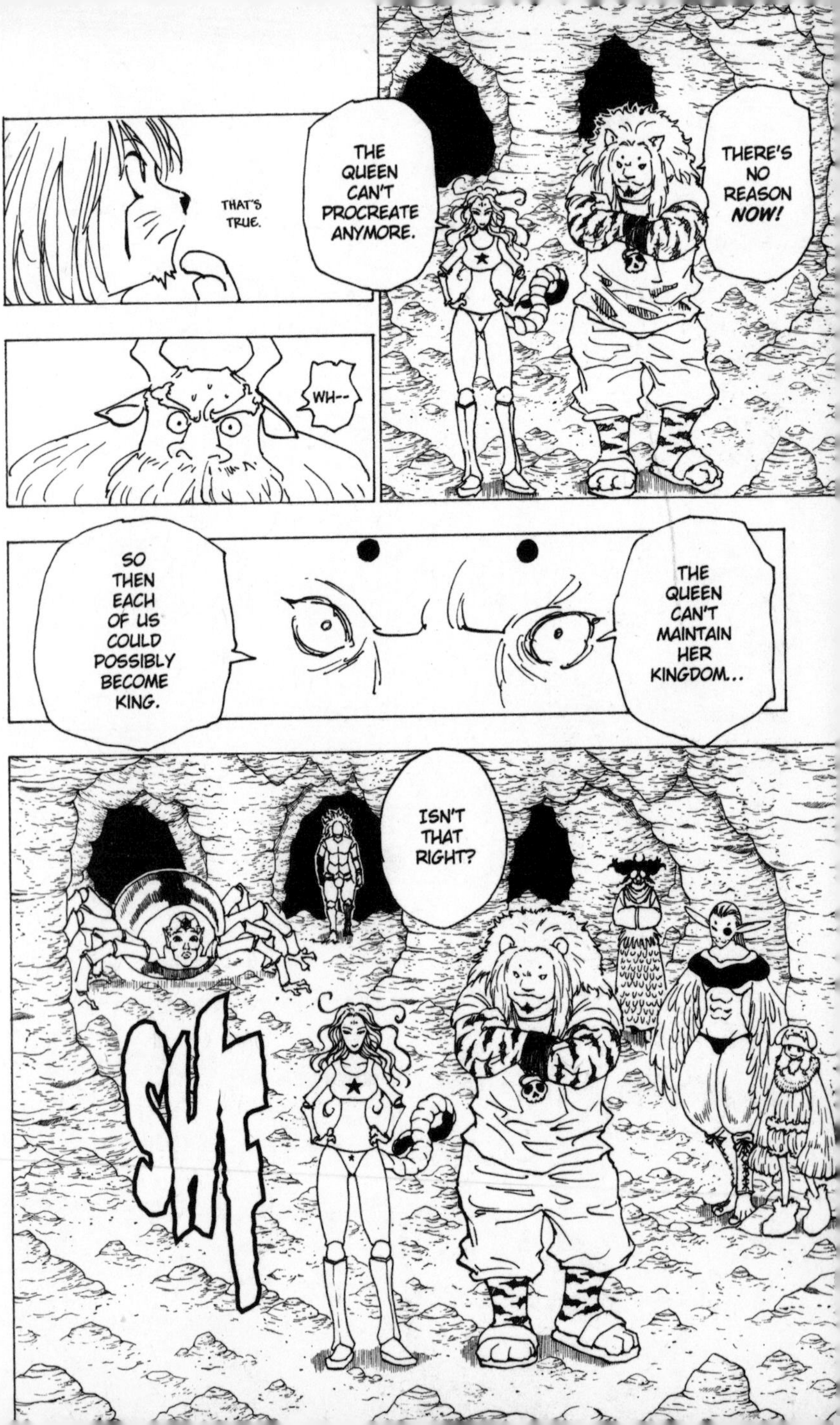
THERE'S NO REASON NOW!
THE QUEEN CAN'T PROCREATE ANYMORE.
THAT'S TRUE.
WH--
THE QUEEN CAN'T MAINTAIN HER KINGDOM...
SO THEN EACH OF US COULD POSSIBLY BECOME KING.
ISN'T THAT RIGHT?

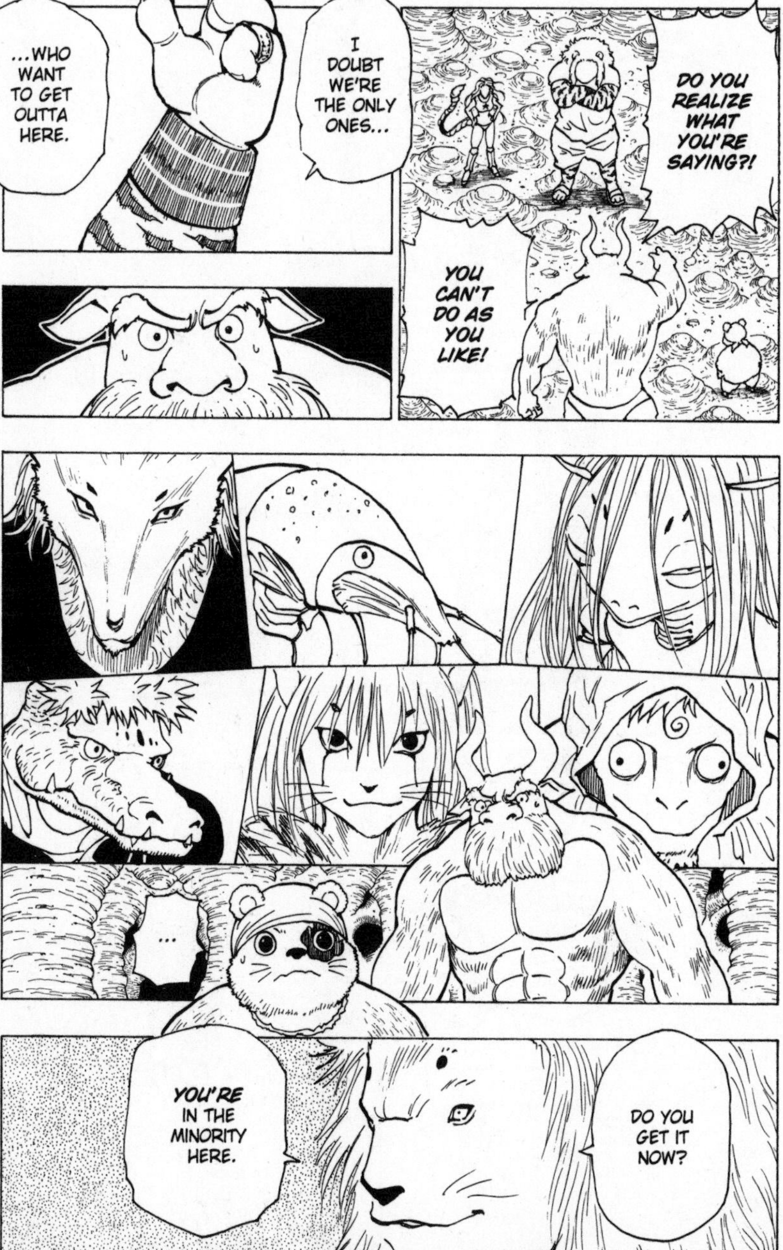
DO YOU REALIZE WHAT YOU'RE SAYING?!
YOU CAN'T DO AS YOU LIKE!
I DOUBT WE'RE THE ONLY ONES...
...WHO WANT TO GET OUTTA HERE.
...
DO YOU GET IT NOW?
YOU'RE IN THE MINORITY HERE.

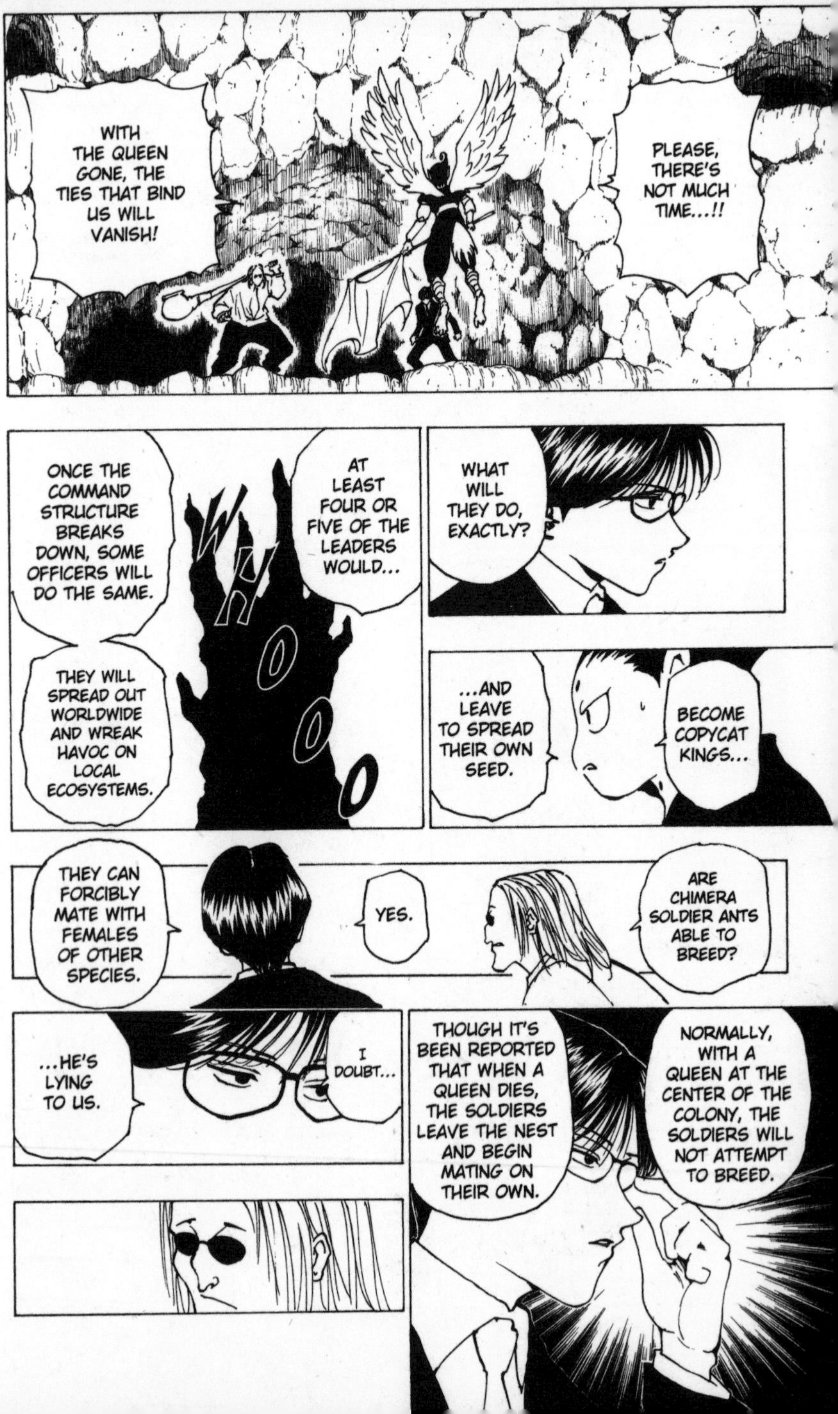
PLEASE, THERE'S NOT MUCH TIME...!!
WITH THE QUEEN GONE, THE TIES THAT BIND US WILL VANISH!
WHAT WILL THEY DO, EXACTLY?
BECOME COPYCAT KINGS...
...AND LEAVE TO SPREAD THEIR OWN SEED.
AT LEAST FOUR OR FIVE OF THE LEADERS WOULD...
ONCE THE COMMAND STRUCTURE BREAKS DOWN, SOME OFFICERS WILL DO THE SAME.
WHOOOO
THEY WILL SPREAD OUT WORLDWIDE AND WREAK HAVOC ON LOCAL ECOSYSTEMS.
ARE CHIMERA SOLDIER ANTS ABLE TO BREED?
YES.
THEY CAN FORCIBLY MATE WITH FEMALES OF OTHER SPECIES.
NORMALLY, WITH A QUEEN AT THE CENTER OF THE COLONY, THE SOLDIERS WILL NOT ATTEMPT TO BREED.
THOUGH IT'S BEEN REPORTED THAT WHEN A QUEEN DIES, THE SOLDIERS LEAVE THE NEST AND BEGIN MATING ON THEIR OWN.
I DOUBT...
...HE'S LYING TO US.

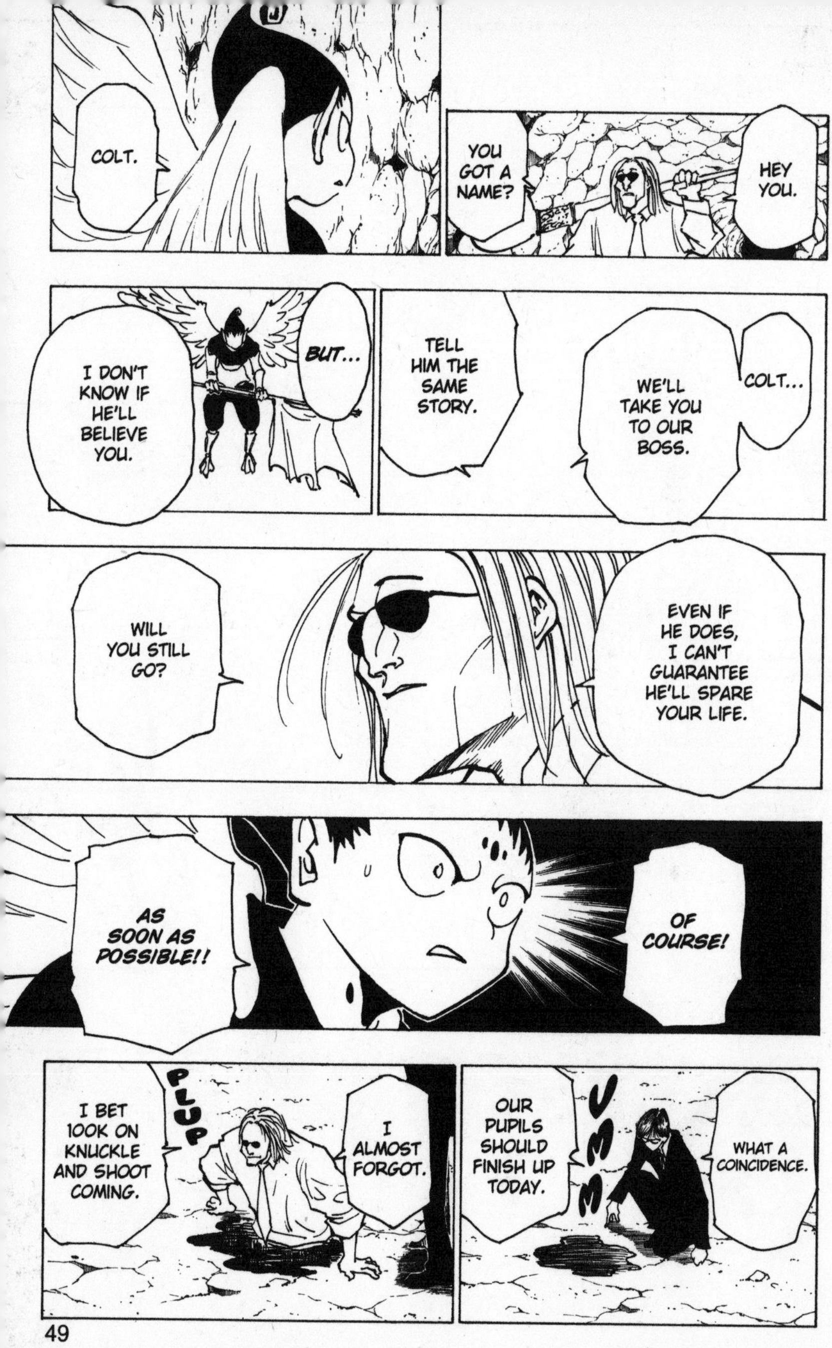
HEY YOU.
YOU GOT A NAME?
COLT.
COLT...
WE'LL TAKE YOU TO OUR BOSS.
TELL HIM THE SAME STORY.
BUT...
I DON'T KNOW IF HE'LL BELIEVE YOU.
EVEN IF HE DOES, I CAN'T GUARANTEE HE'LL SPARE YOUR LIFE.
WILL YOU STILL GO?
OF COURSE!
AS SOON AS POSSIBLE!!
WHAT A COINCIDENCE.
UMMM
OUR PUPILS SHOULD FINISH UP TODAY.
I ALMOST FORGOT.
PLUP
I BET 100K ON KNUCKLE AND SHOOT COMING.

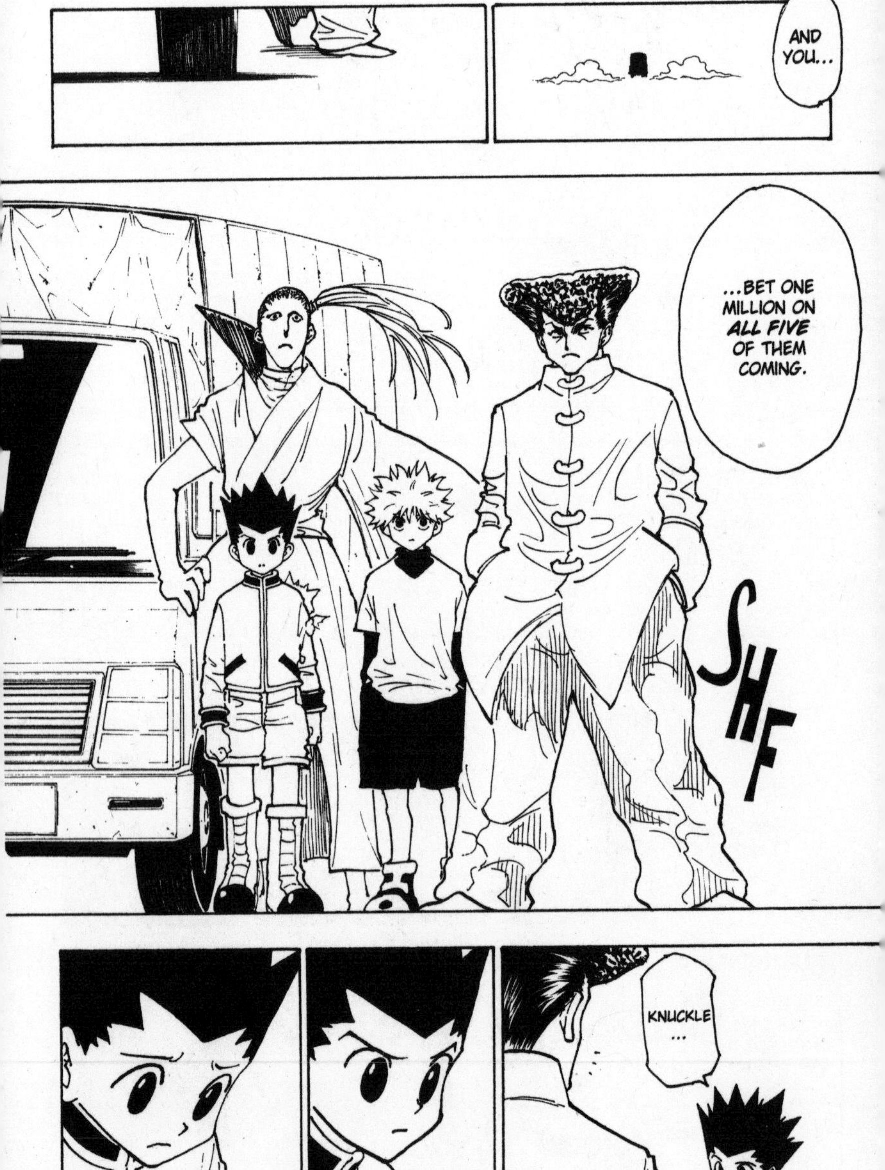
AND YOU...
...BET ONE MILLION ON ALL FIVE OF THEM COMING.
SHF
KNUCKLE ...

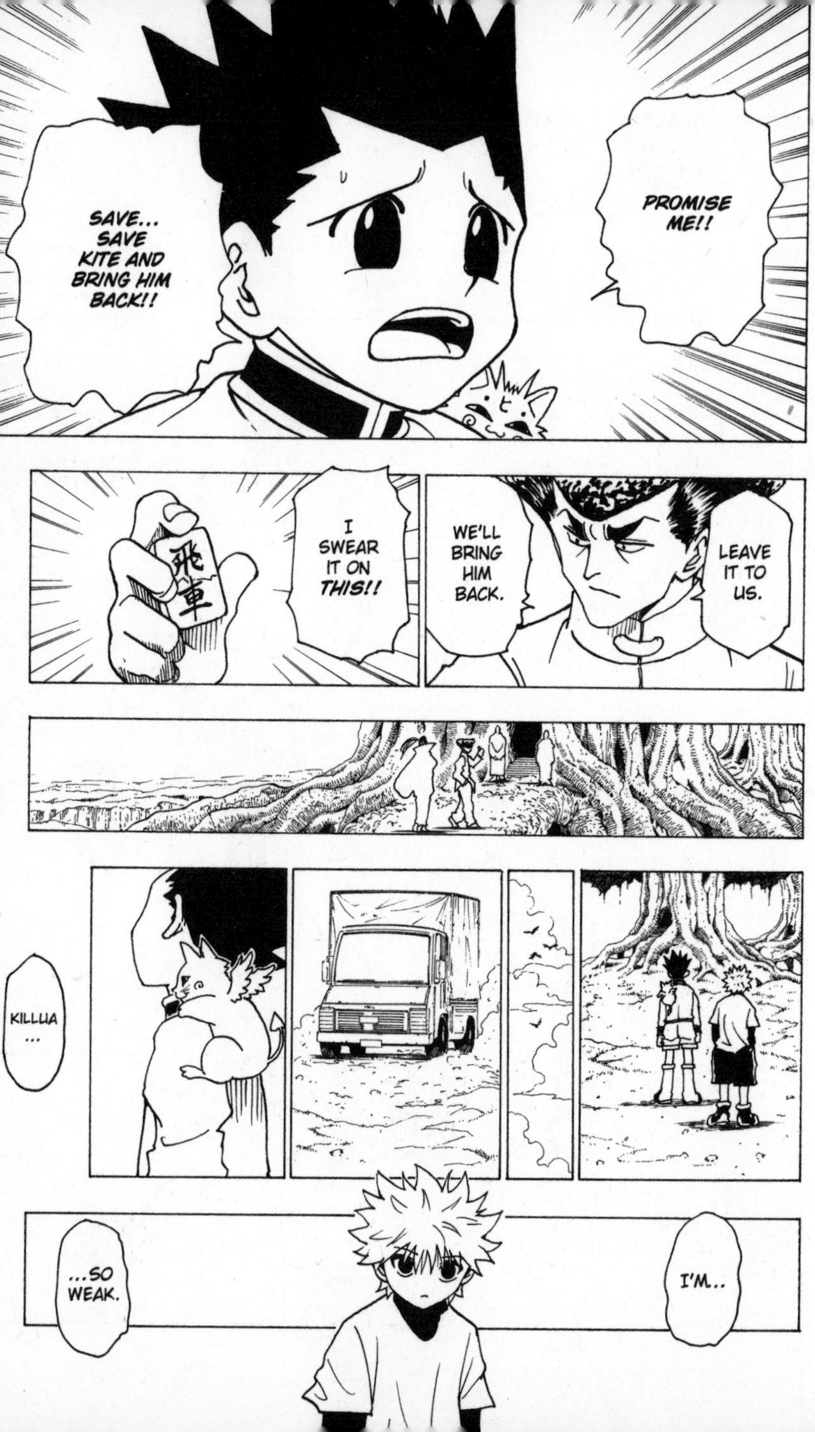
PROMISE ME!!
SAVE... SAVE KITE AND BRING HIM BACK!!
LEAVE IT TO US.
WE'LL BRING HIM BACK.
I SWEAR IT ON THIS!!
KILLUA...
I'M...
...SO WEAK.

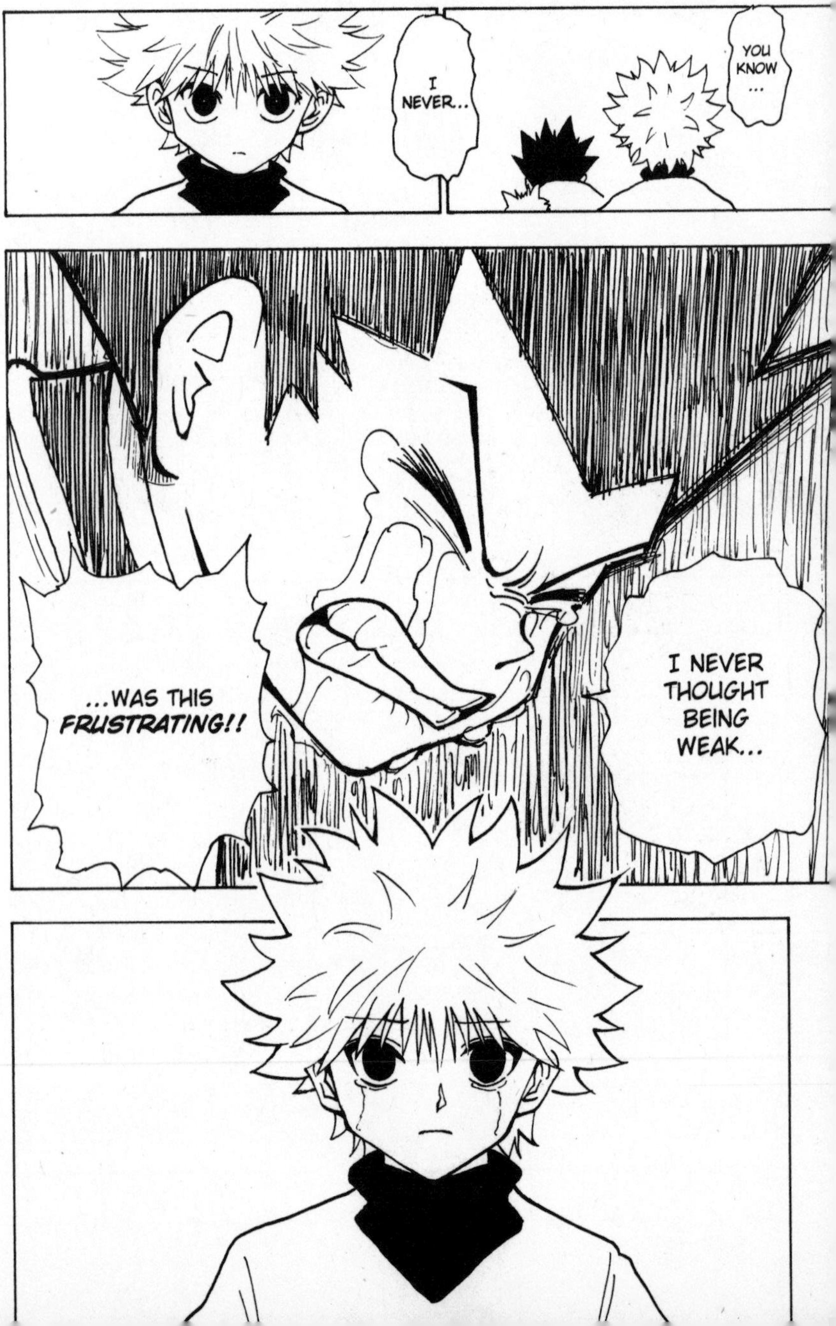
YOU KNOW ...
I NEVER...
I NEVER THOUGHT BEING WEAK...
...WAS THIS FRUSTRATING!!

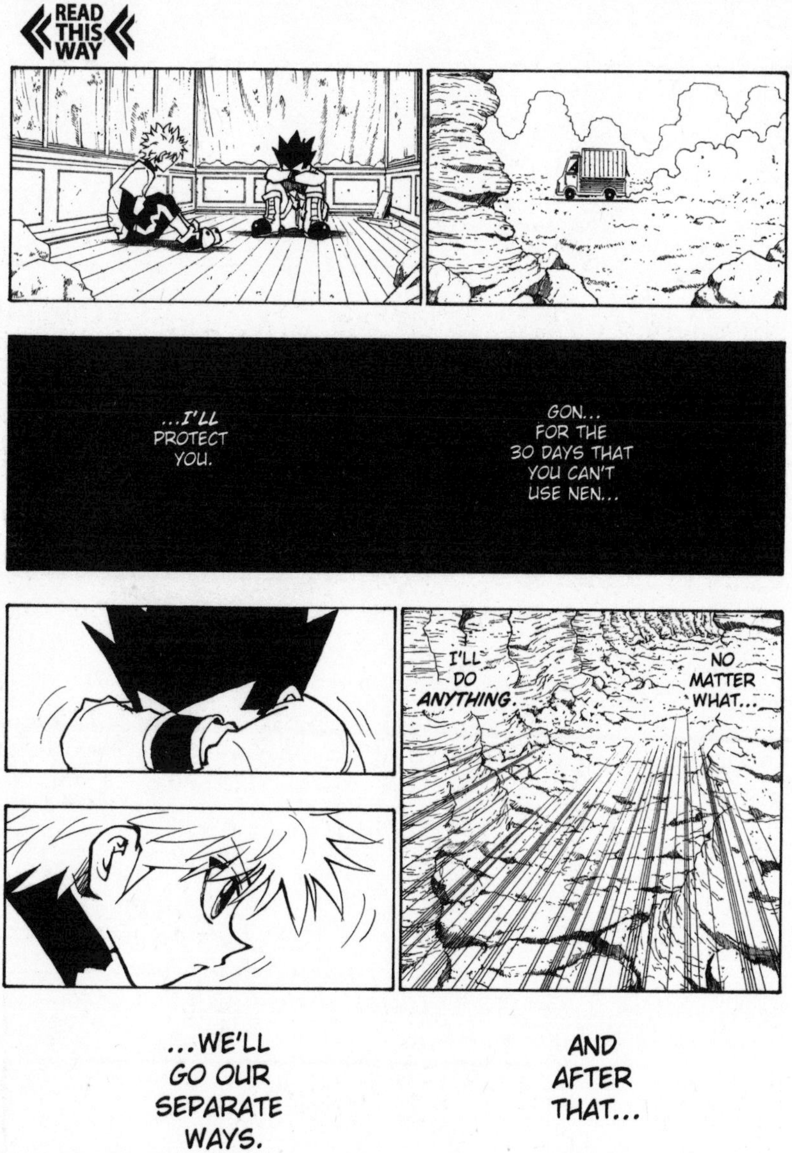
READ THIS WAY
GON... FOR THE 30 DAYS THAT YOU CAN'T USE NEN...
...I'LL PROTECT YOU.
NO MATTER WHAT...
I'LL DO ANYTHING.
AND AFTER THAT...
...WE'LL GO OUR SEPARATE WAYS.

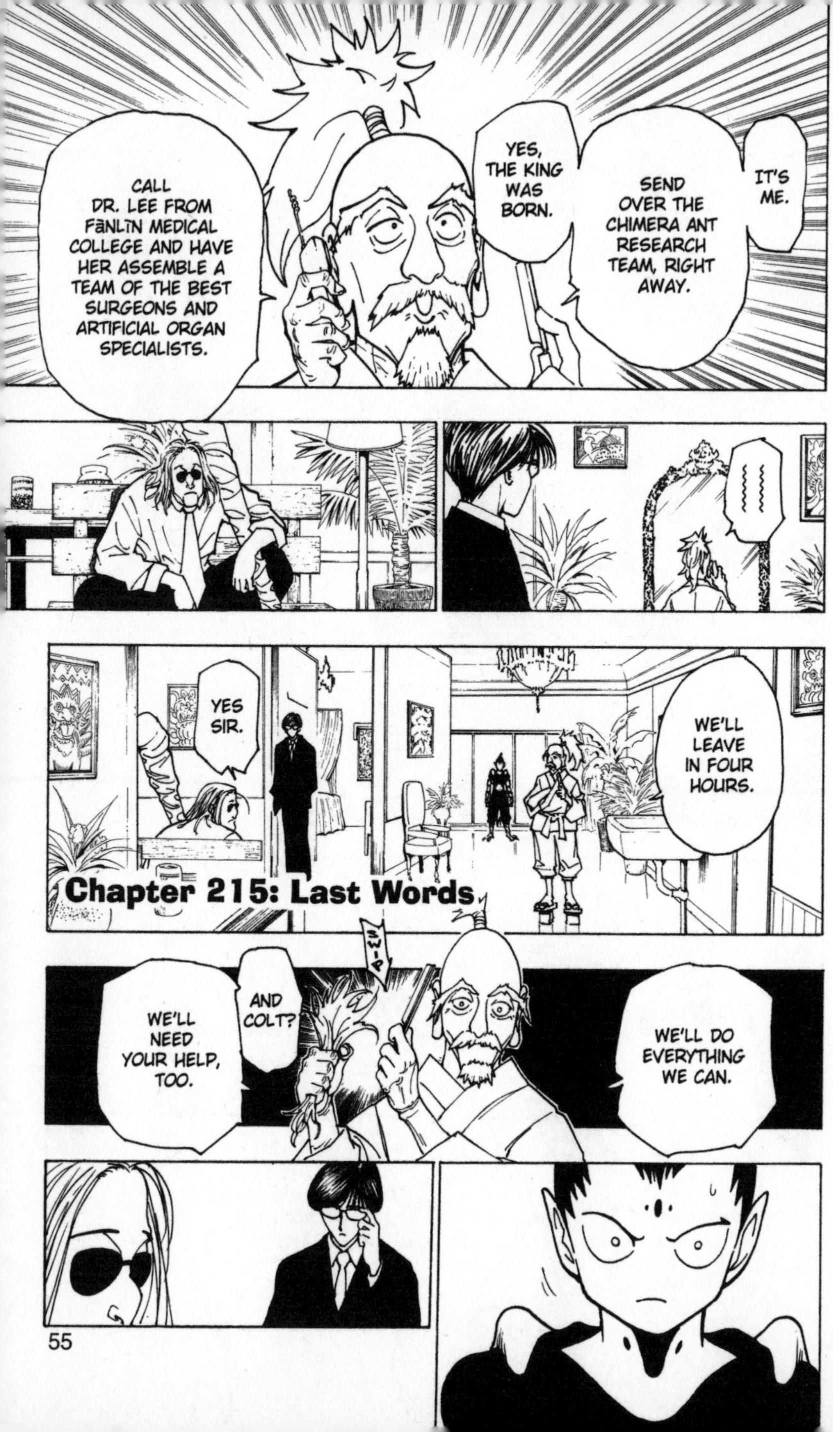
IT'S ME.
SEND OVER THE CHIMERA ANT RESEARCH TEAM, RIGHT AWAY.
YES, THE KING WAS BORN.
CALL DR. LEE FROM Fānlīn MEDICAL COLLEGE AND HAVE HER ASSEMBLE A TEAM OF THE BEST SURGEONS AND ARTIFICIAL ORGAN SPECIALISTS.
WE'LL LEAVE IN FOUR HOURS.
YES SIR.
Chapter 215: Last Words
WE'LL DO EVERYTHING WE CAN.
SWIP
AND COLT?
WE'LL NEED YOUR HELP, TOO.

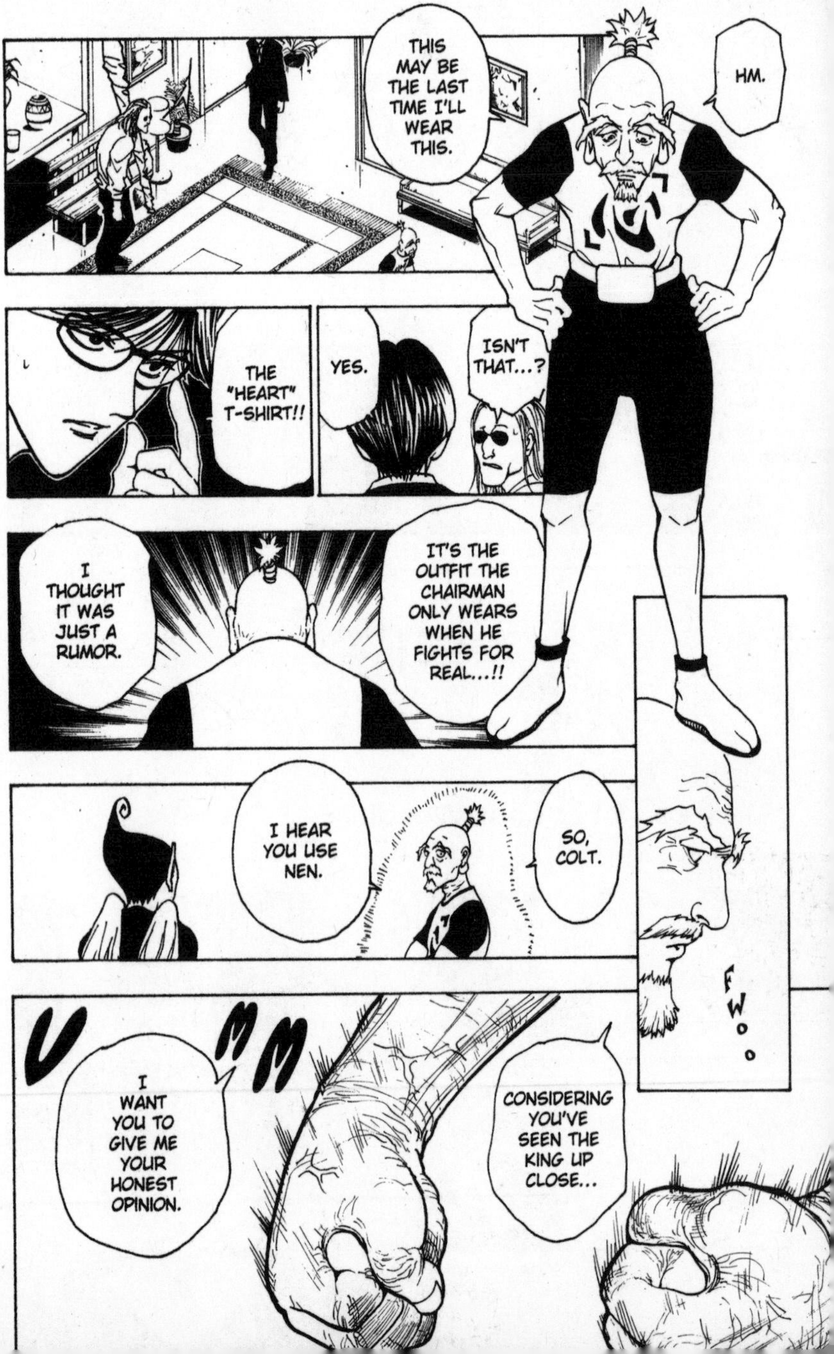
HM.
THIS MAY BE THE LAST TIME I'LL WEAR THIS.
ISN'T THAT...?
YES.
THE "HEART" T-SHIRT!!
IT'S THE OUTFIT THE CHAIRMAN ONLY WEARS WHEN HE FIGHTS FOR REAL...!!
I THOUGHT IT WAS JUST A RUMOR.
FWOO
SO, COLT.
I HEAR YOU USE NEN.
CONSIDERING YOU'VE SEEN THE KING UP CLOSE...
I WANT YOU TO GIVE ME YOUR HONEST OPINION.
UMM

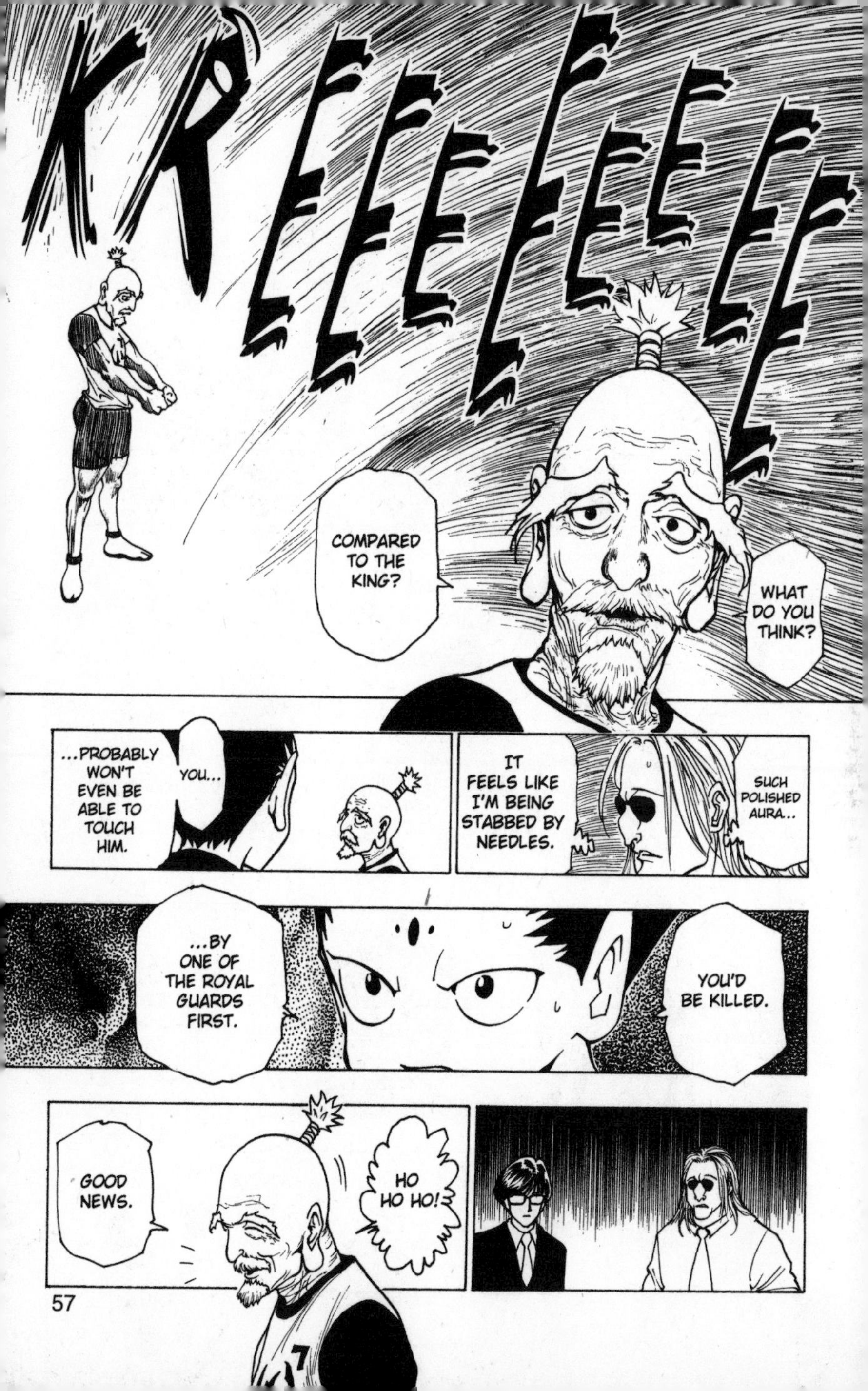
KREEEEEEEEE
WHAT DO YOU THINK?
COMPARED TO THE KING?
SUCH POLISHED AURA...
IT FEELS LIKE I'M BEING STABBED BY NEEDLES.
YOU...
...PROBABLY WON'T EVEN BE ABLE TO TOUCH HIM.
YOU'D BE KILLED.
...BY ONE OF THE ROYAL GUARDS FIRST.
HO HO HO!
GOOD NEWS.

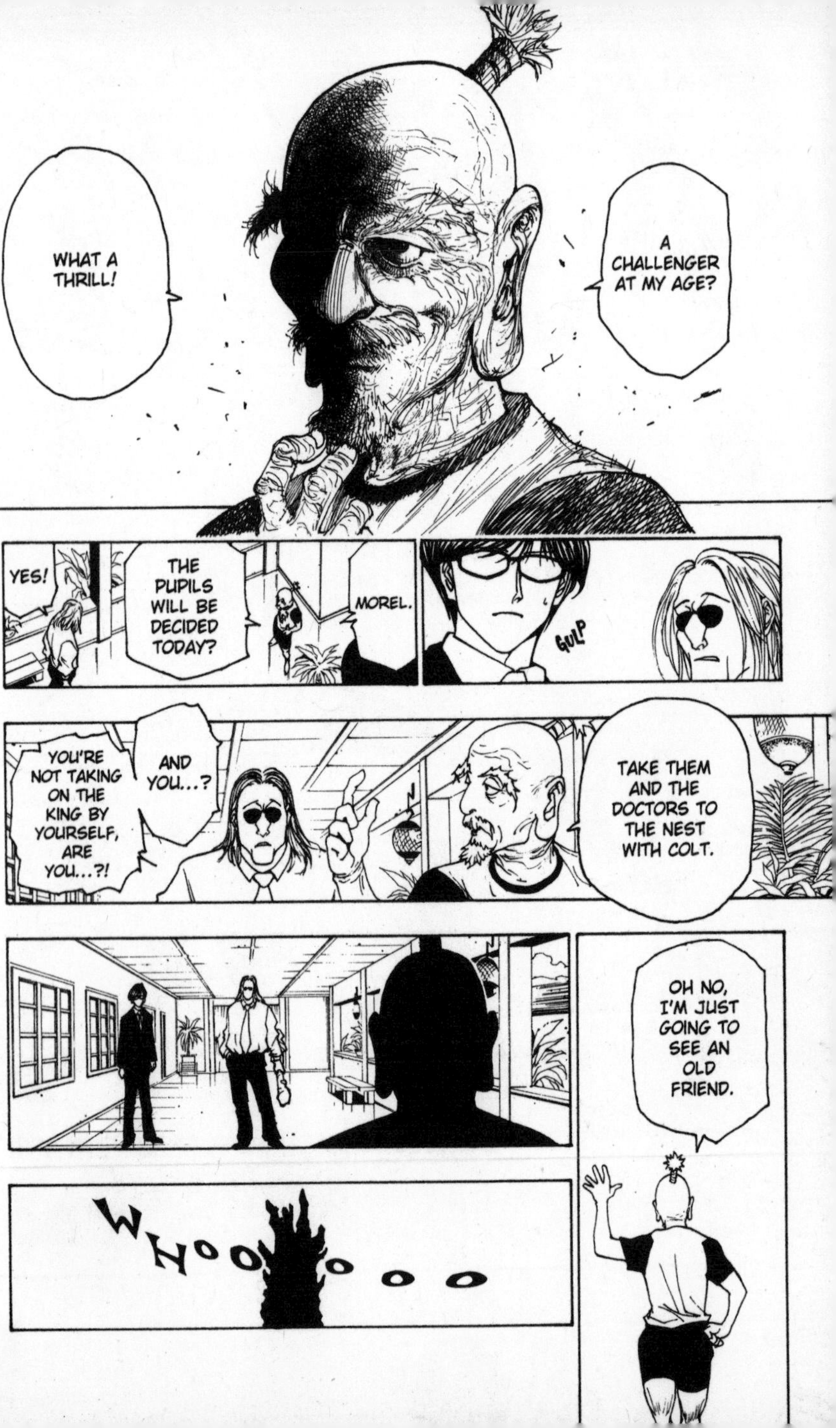
A CHALLENGER AT MY AGE?
WHAT A THRILL!
GULP
MOREL.
THE PUPILS WILL BE DECIDED TODAY?
YES!
TAKE THEM AND THE DOCTORS TO THE NEST WITH COLT.
AND YOU...?
YOU'RE NOT TAKING ON THE KING BY YOURSELF, ARE YOU...?!
OH NO, I'M JUST GOING TO SEE AN OLD FRIEND.
WHOOOOOO

READ THIS WAY

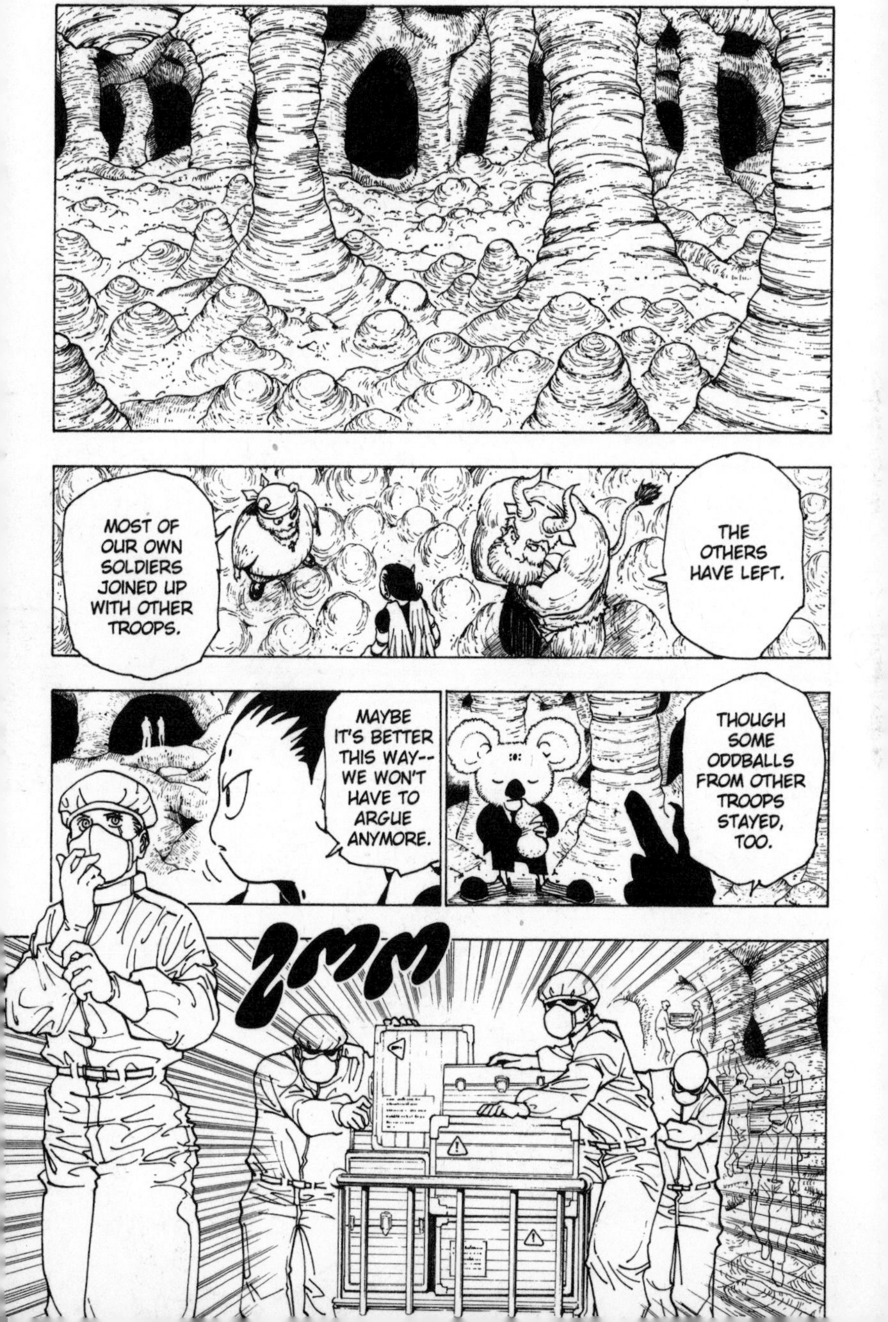

THE OTHERS HAVE LEFT.
MOST OF OUR OWN SOLDIERS JOINED UP WITH OTHER TROOPS.
THOUGH SOME ODDBALLS FROM OTHER TROOPS STAYED, TOO.
MAYBE IT'S BETTER THIS WAY--WE WON'T HAVE TO ARGUE ANYMORE.

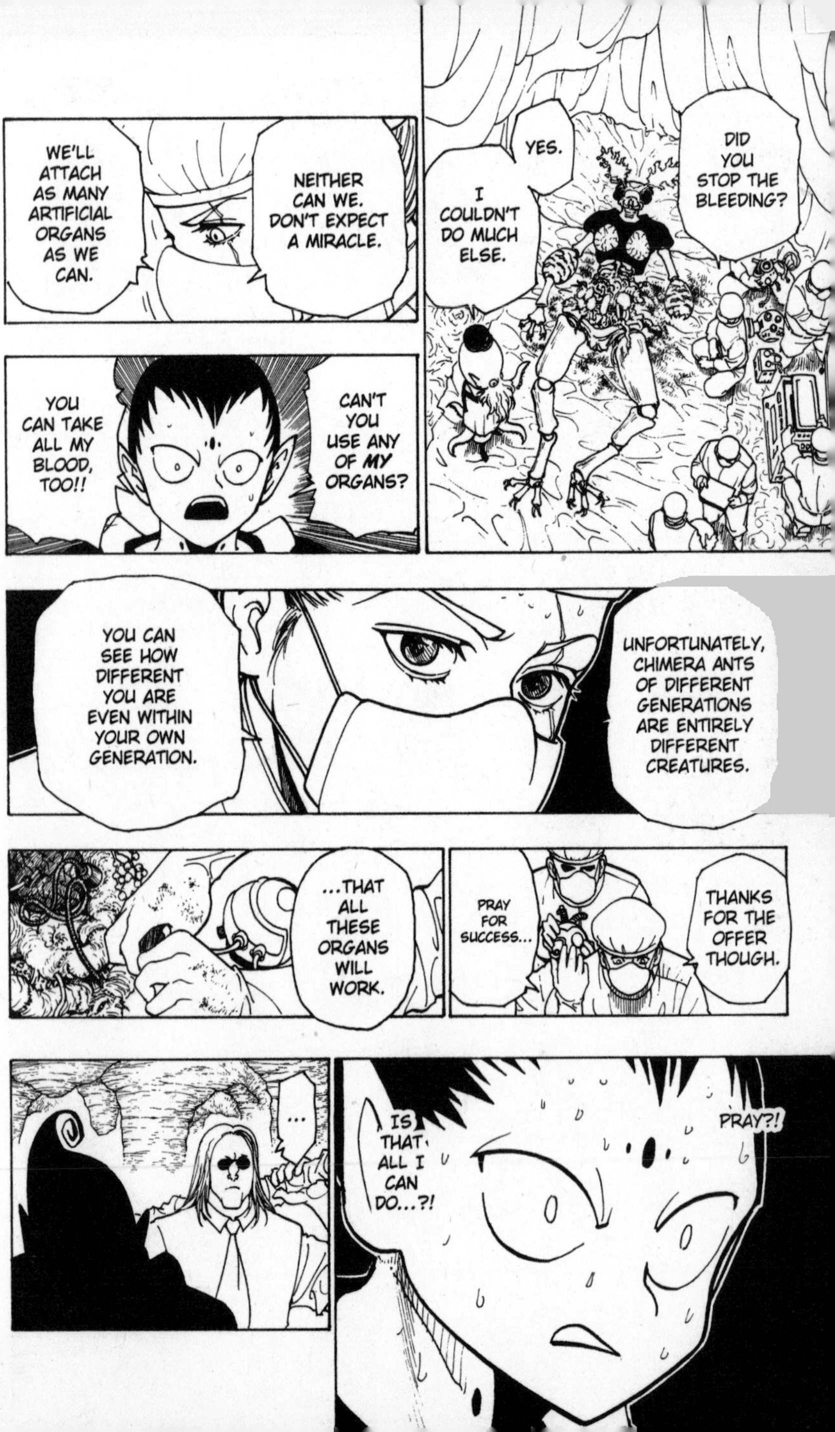
DID YOU STOP THE BLEEDING?
YES.
I COULDN'T DO MUCH ELSE.
NEITHER CAN WE. DON'T EXPECT A MIRACLE.
WE'LL ATTACH AS MANY ARTIFICIAL ORGANS AS WE CAN.
CAN'T YOU USE ANY OF *MY* ORGANS?
YOU CAN TAKE ALL MY BLOOD, TOO!!
UNFORTUNATELY, CHIMERA ANTS OF DIFFERENT GENERATIONS ARE ENTIRELY DIFFERENT CREATURES.
YOU CAN SEE HOW DIFFERENT YOU ARE EVEN WITHIN YOUR OWN GENERATION.
THANKS FOR THE OFFER THOUGH.
PRAY FOR SUCCESS...
...THAT ALL THESE ORGANS WILL WORK.
PRAY?!
IS THAT ALL I CAN DO...?!
...

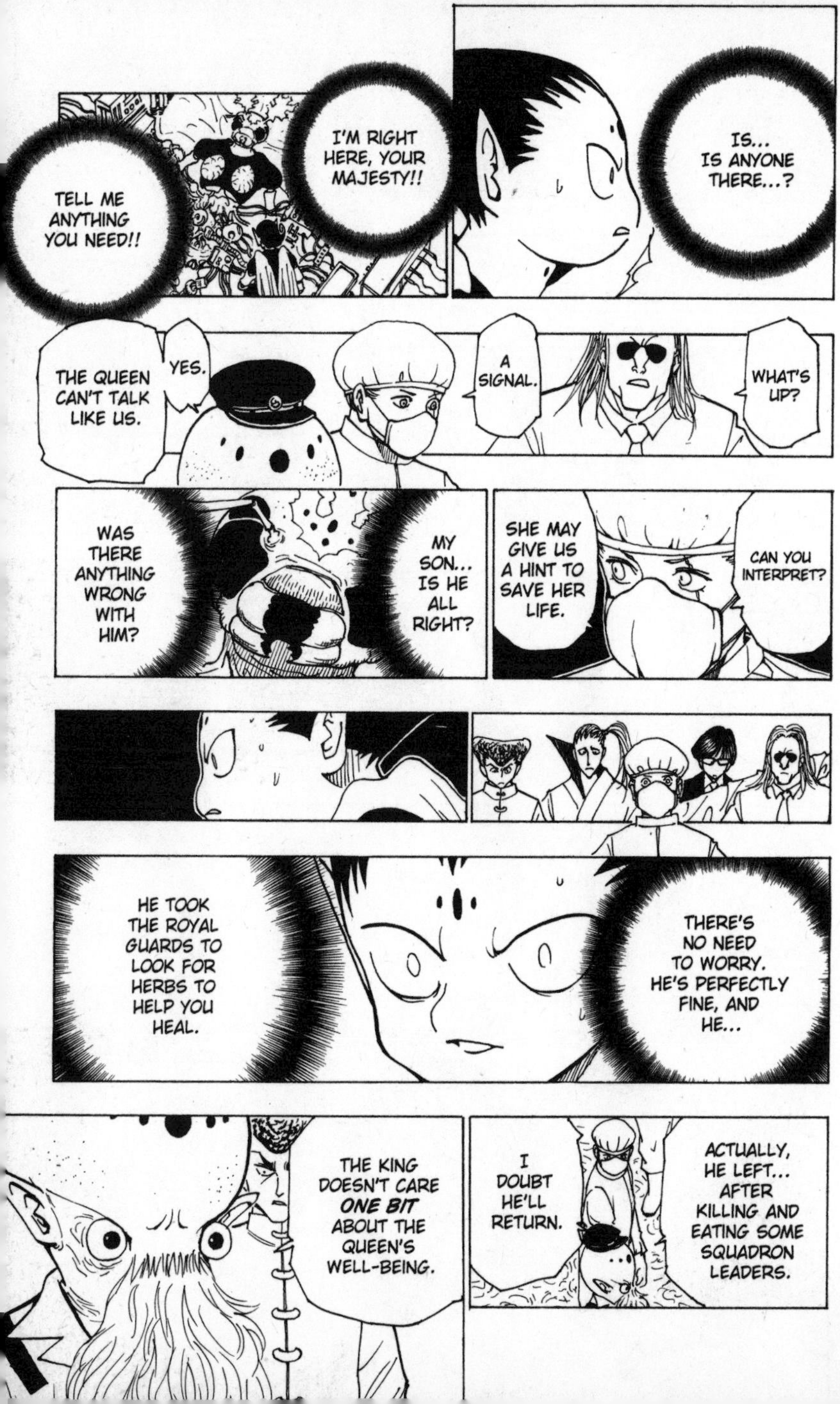
IS... IS ANYONE THERE...?
I'M RIGHT HERE, YOUR MAJESTY!!
TELL ME ANYTHING YOU NEED!!
WHAT'S UP?
A SIGNAL.
YES.
THE QUEEN CAN'T TALK LIKE US.
CAN YOU INTERPRET?
SHE MAY GIVE US A HINT TO SAVE HER LIFE.
MY SON... IS HE ALL RIGHT?
WAS THERE ANYTHING WRONG WITH HIM?
THERE'S NO NEED TO WORRY. HE'S PERFECTLY FINE, AND HE...
HE TOOK THE ROYAL GUARDS TO LOOK FOR HERBS TO HELP YOU HEAL.
ACTUALLY, HE LEFT... AFTER KILLING AND EATING SOME SQUADRON LEADERS.
I DOUBT HE'LL RETURN.
THE KING DOESN'T CARE ONE BIT ABOUT THE QUEEN'S WELL-BEING.

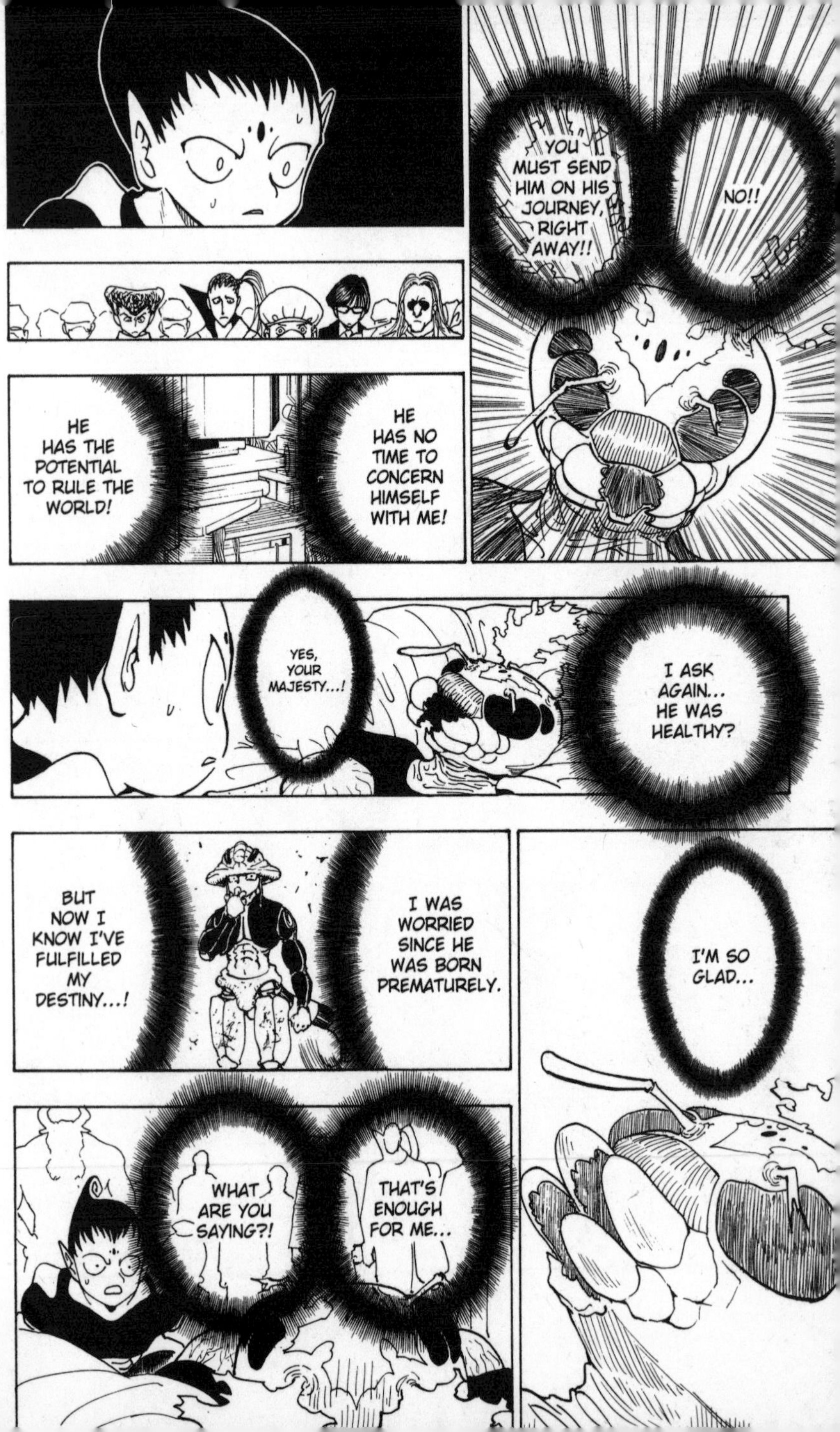
NO!!
YOU MUST SEND HIM ON HIS JOURNEY, RIGHT AWAY!!
HE HAS NO TIME TO CONCERN HIMSELF WITH ME!
HE HAS THE POTENTIAL TO RULE THE WORLD!
I ASK AGAIN... HE WAS HEALTHY?
YES, YOUR MAJESTY...!
I'M SO GLAD...
I WAS WORRIED SINCE HE WAS BORN PREMATURELY.
BUT NOW I KNOW I'VE FULFILLED MY DESTINY...!
THAT'S ENOUGH FOR ME...
WHAT ARE YOU SAYING?!

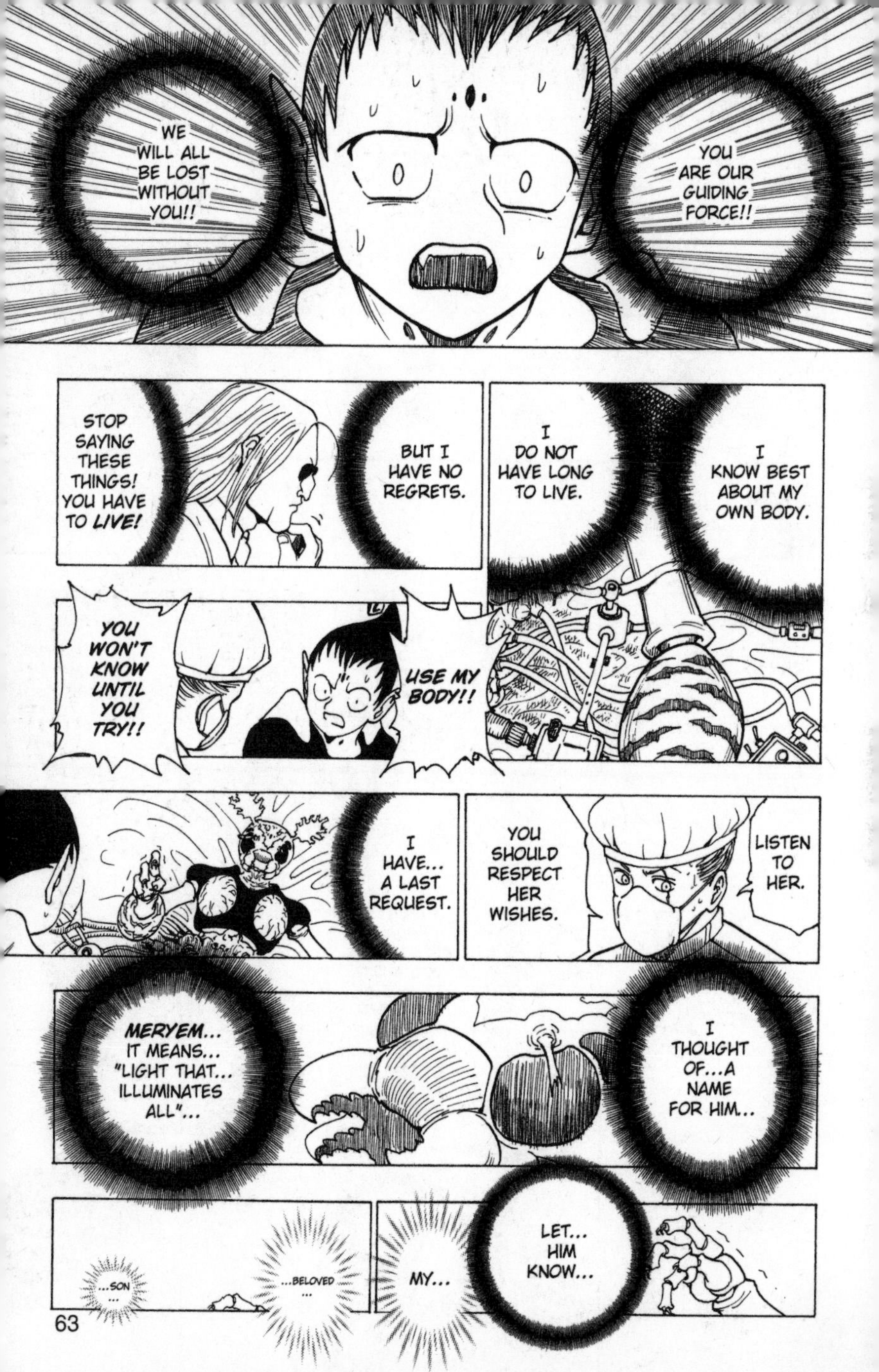
YOU ARE OUR GUIDING FORCE!!
WE WILL ALL BE LOST WITHOUT YOU!!
I KNOW BEST ABOUT MY OWN BODY.
I DO NOT HAVE LONG TO LIVE.
BUT I HAVE NO REGRETS.
STOP SAYING THESE THINGS! YOU HAVE TO LIVE!
USE MY BODY!!
YOU WON'T KNOW UNTIL YOU TRY!!
LISTEN TO HER.
YOU SHOULD RESPECT HER WISHES.
I HAVE... A LAST REQUEST.
I THOUGHT OF...A NAME FOR HIM...
MERYEM... IT MEANS... "LIGHT THAT... ILLUMINATES ALL"...
LET... HIM KNOW...
MY...
...BELOVED ...
...SON ...

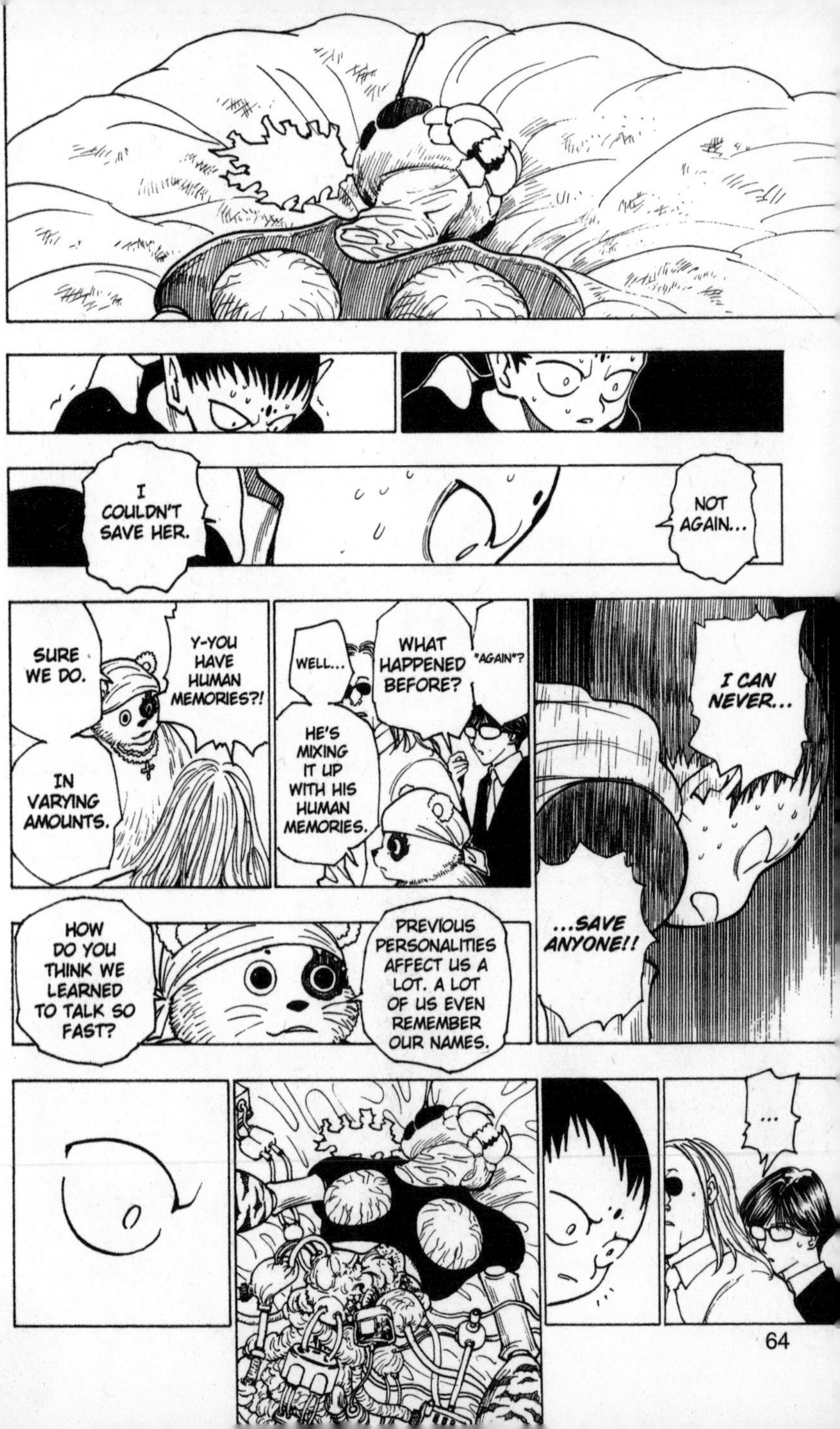
NOT AGAIN...
I COULDN'T SAVE HER.
I CAN NEVER...
...SAVE ANYONE!!
"AGAIN"?
WHAT HAPPENED BEFORE?
WELL...
HE'S MIXING IT UP WITH HIS HUMAN MEMORIES.
Y-YOU HAVE HUMAN MEMORIES?!
SURE WE DO.
IN VARYING AMOUNTS.
PREVIOUS PERSONALITIES AFFECT US A LOT. A LOT OF US EVEN REMEMBER OUR NAMES.
HOW DO YOU THINK WE LEARNED TO TALK SO FAST?
...

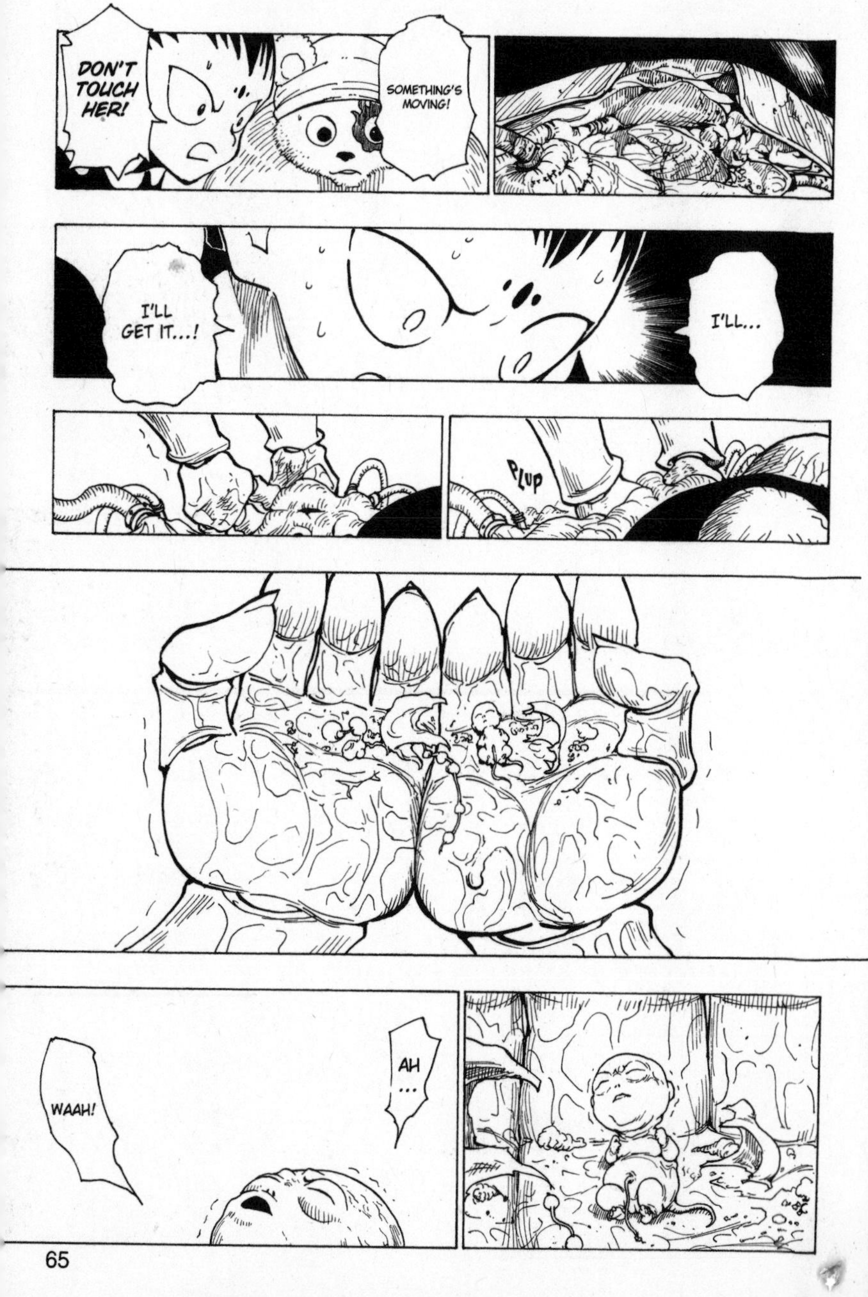
SOMETHING'S MOVING!
DON'T TOUCH HER!
I'LL...
I'LL GET IT...!
PLUP
AH ...
WAAH!

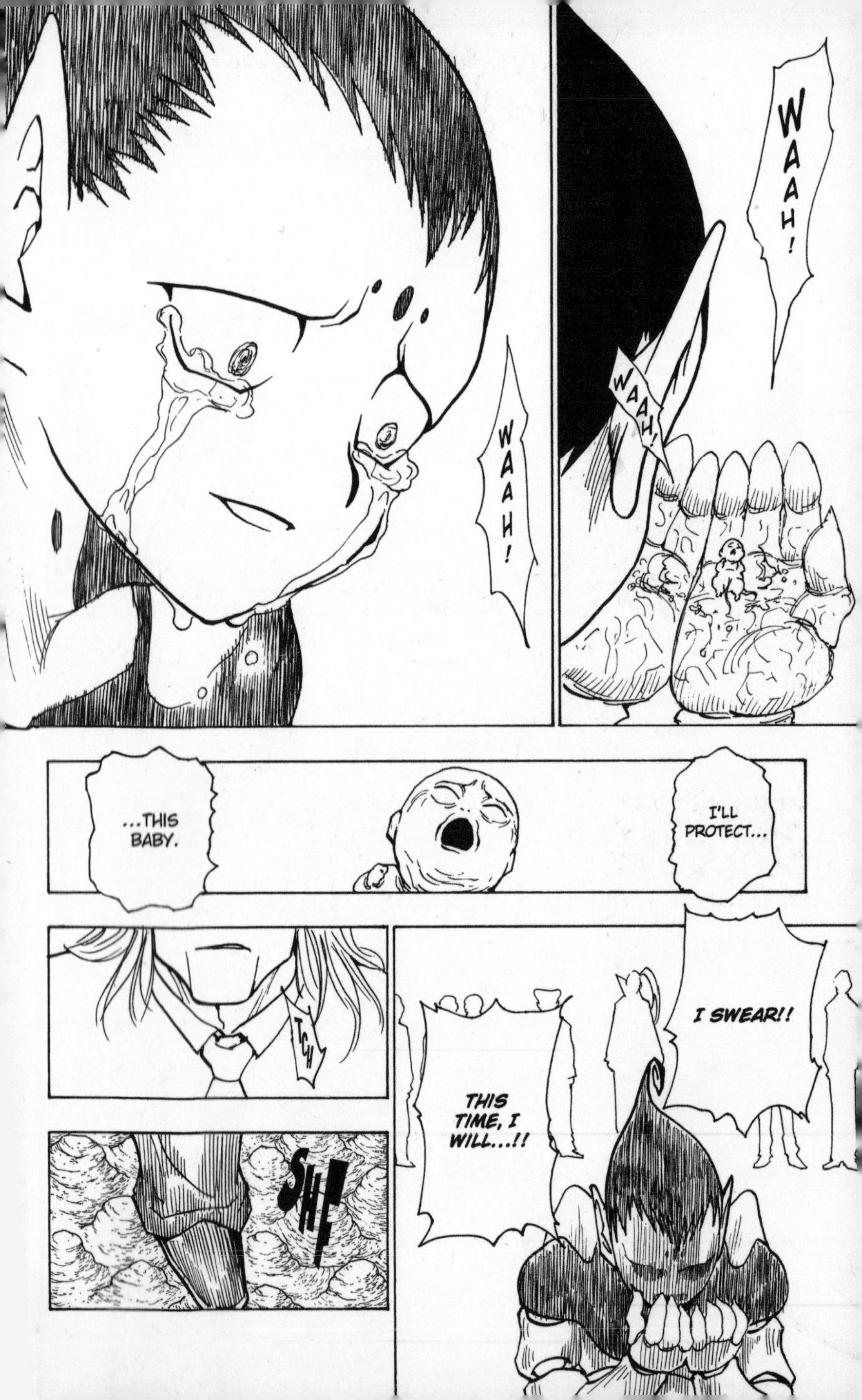
WAAAH!
WAAH!
WAAH!
I'LL PROTECT...
...THIS BABY.
I SWEAR!!
THIS TIME, I WILL...!!
TCH
SHF

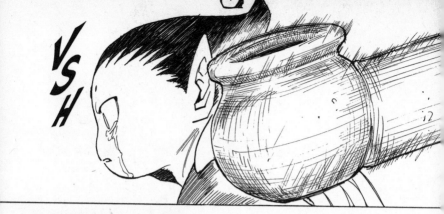

...THAT YOU AND THAT BABY WILL NEVER EAT A HUMAN?

CAN YOU SWEAR...

MOREL?

COLT.

...IF YOU CAN...

BUT...

...GO SOMEWHERE I'LL NEVER FIND YOU.

IF YOU CAN'T...

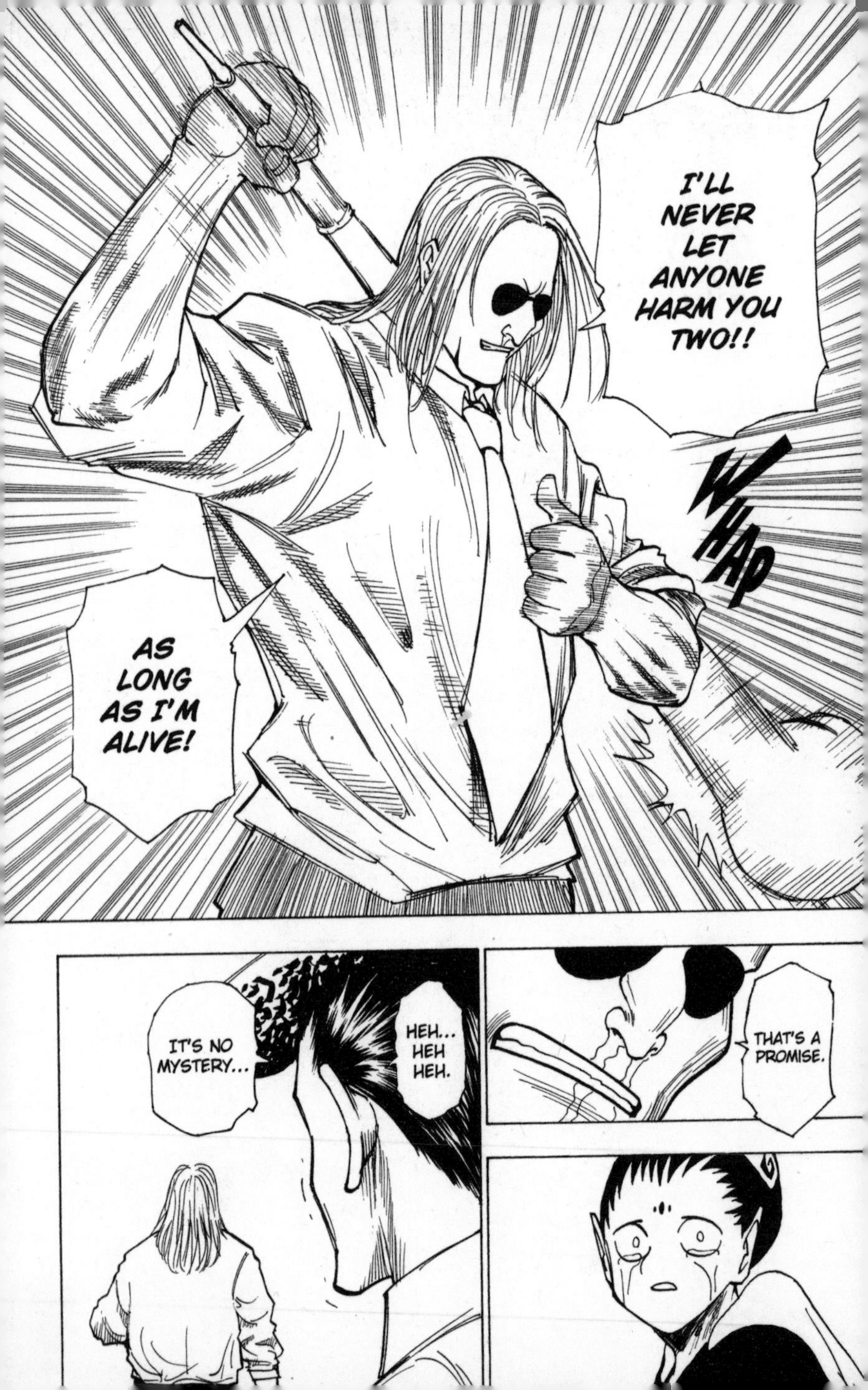
I'LL NEVER LET ANYONE HARM YOU TWO!!
WHAP
AS LONG AS I'M ALIVE!
THAT'S A PROMISE.
HEH... HEH HEH.
IT'S NO MYSTERY...

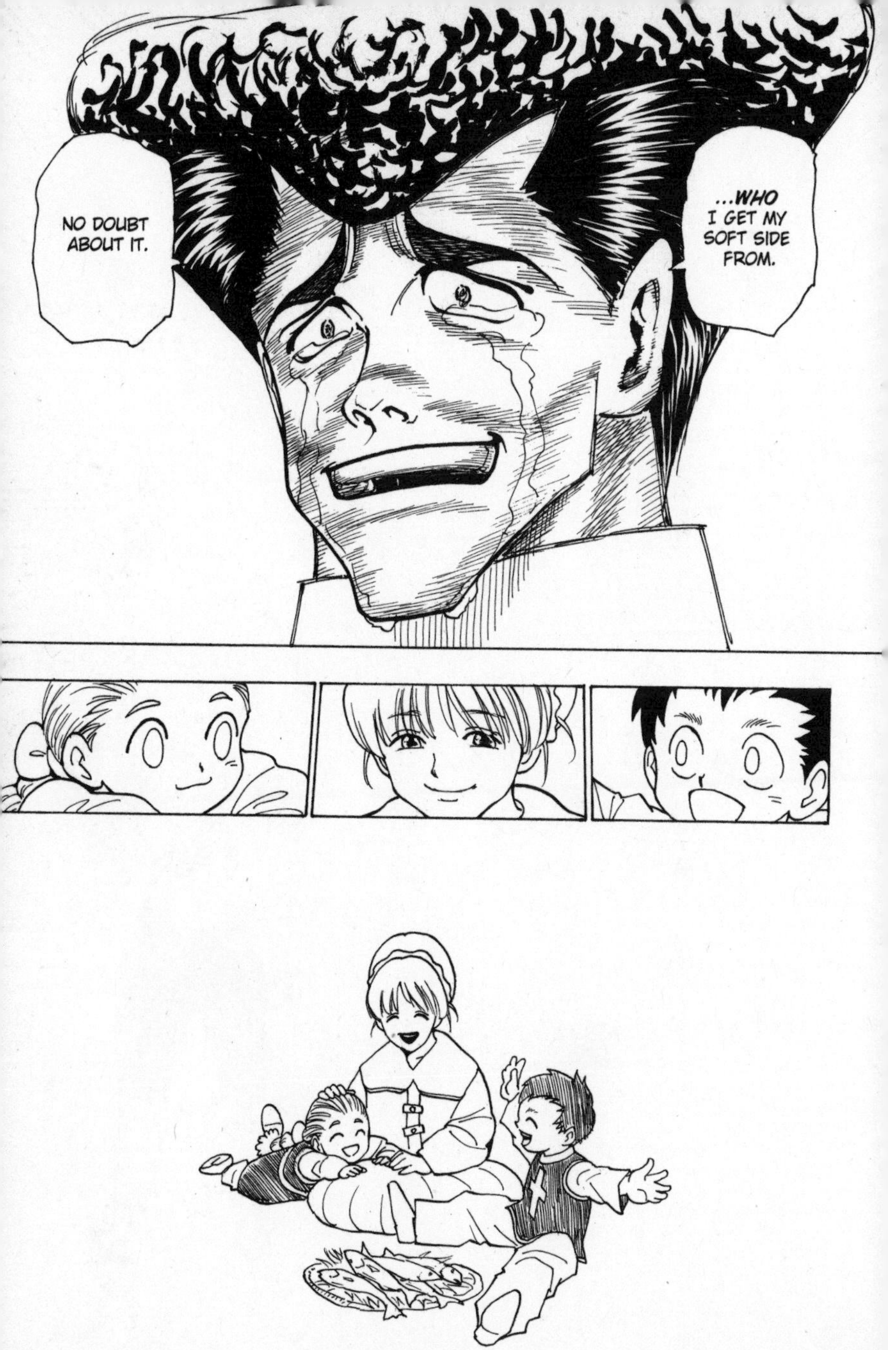
...WHO I GET MY SOFT SIDE FROM.
NO DOUBT ABOUT IT.

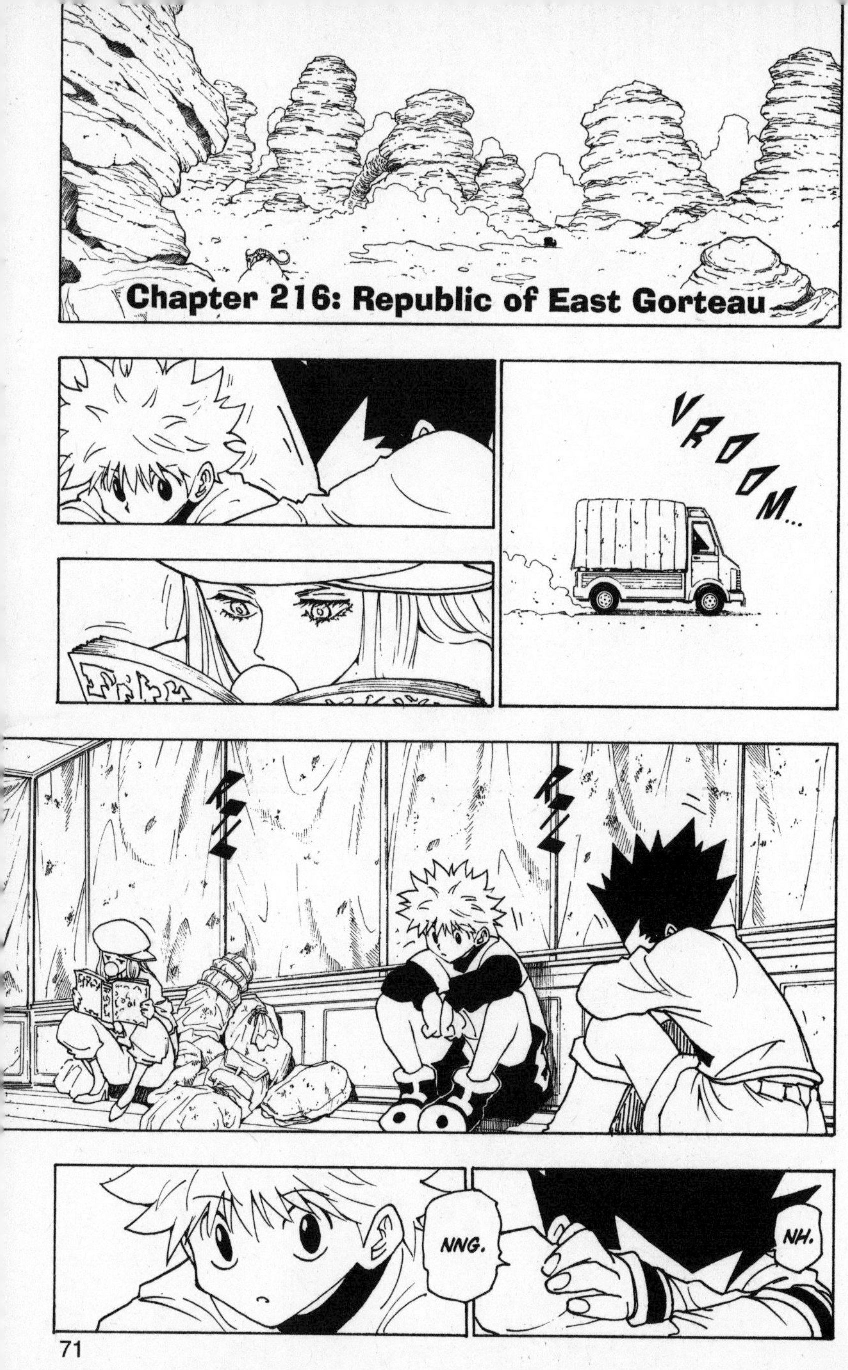
Chapter 216: Republic of East Gorteau
VROOM...
NH.
NNG.

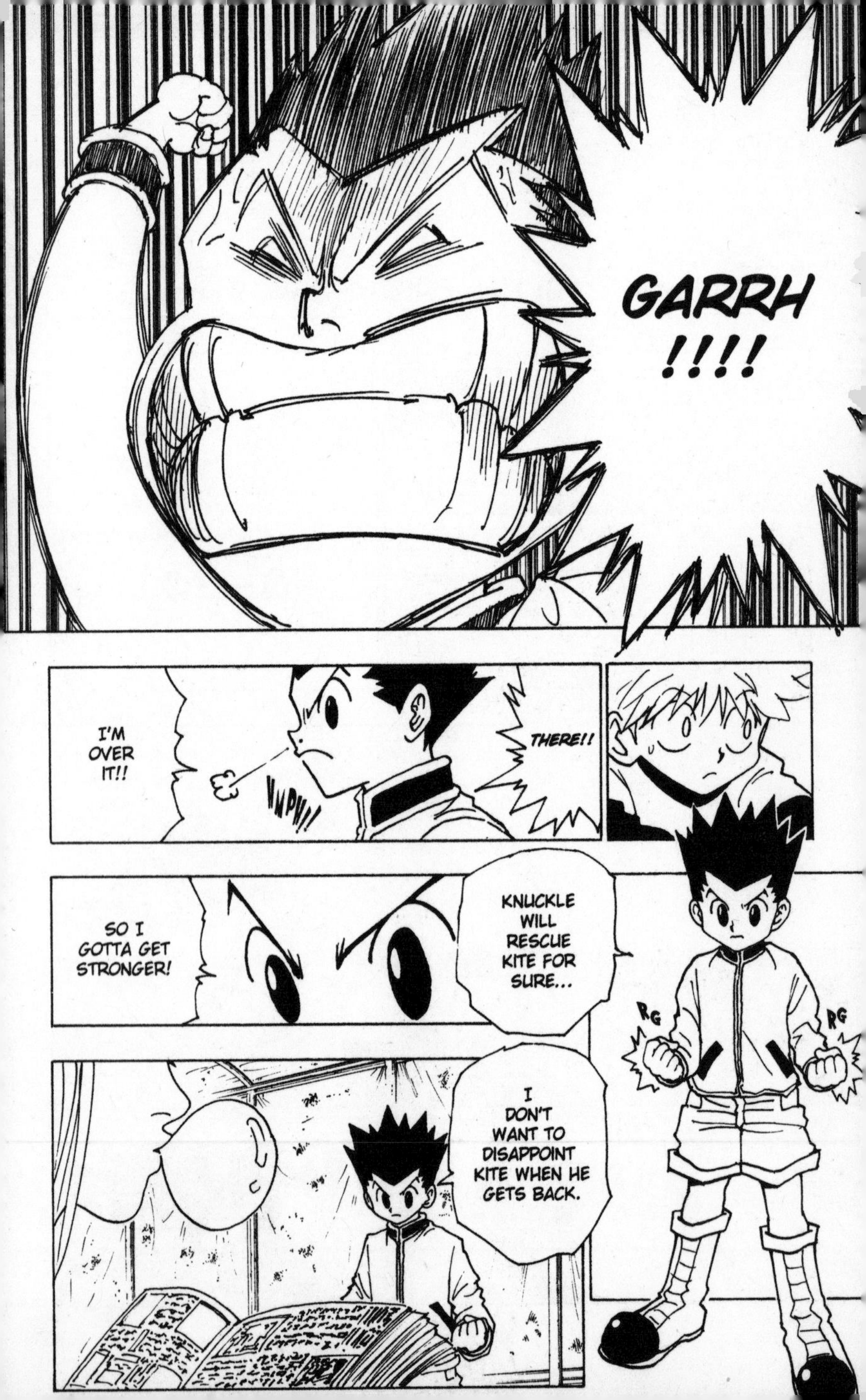
GARRH !!!!
THERE!!
HMPH!!
I'M OVER IT!!
RG
RG
KNUCKLE WILL RESCUE KITE FOR SURE...
SO I GOTTA GET STRONGER!
I DON'T WANT TO DISAPPOINT KITE WHEN HE GETS BACK.

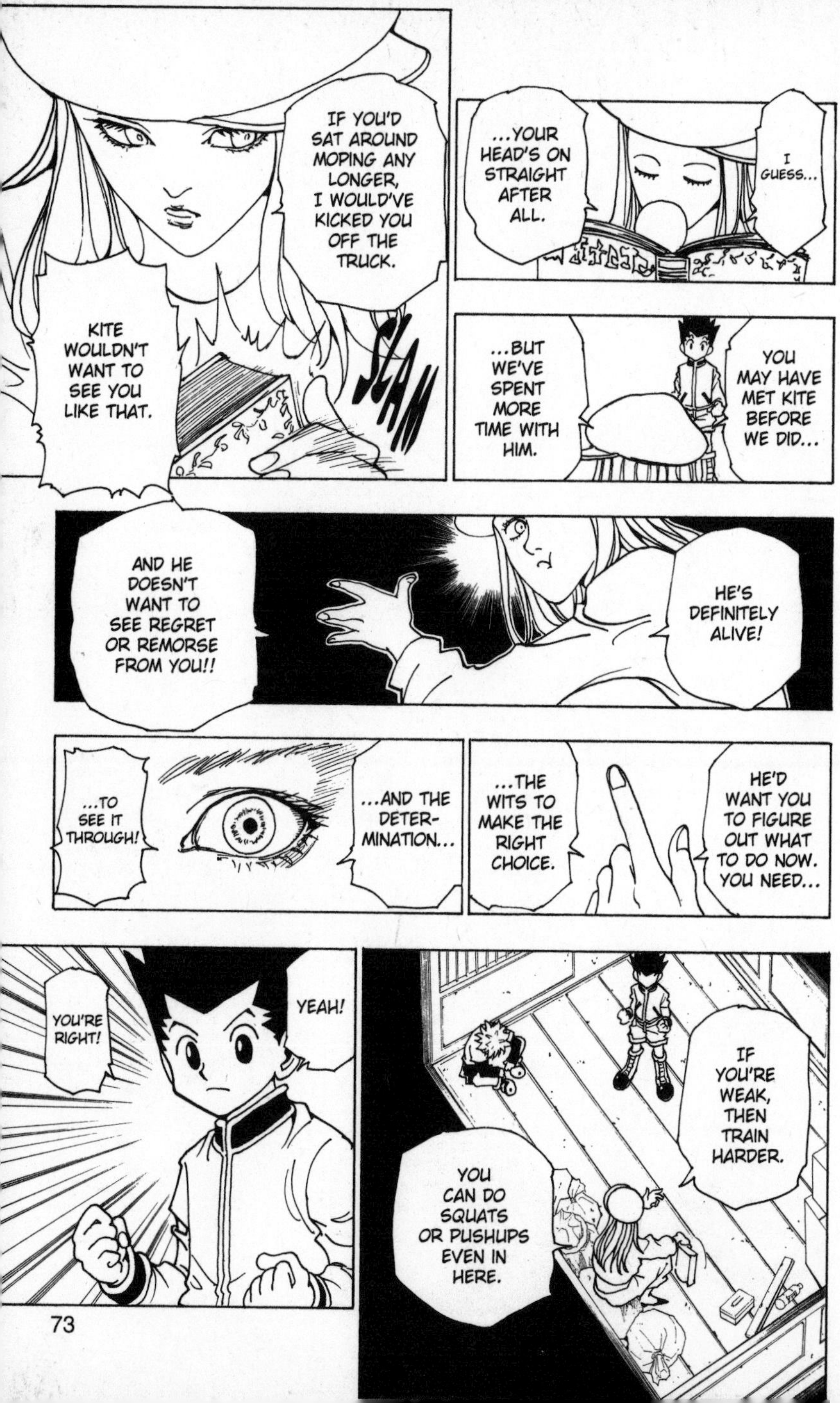
I GUESS...
...YOUR HEAD'S ON STRAIGHT AFTER ALL.
YOU MAY HAVE MET KITE BEFORE WE DID...
...BUT WE'VE SPENT MORE TIME WITH HIM.
IF YOU'D SAT AROUND MOPING ANY LONGER, I WOULD'VE KICKED YOU OFF THE TRUCK.
SLAM
KITE WOULDN'T WANT TO SEE YOU LIKE THAT.
HE'S DEFINITELY ALIVE!
AND HE DOESN'T WANT TO SEE REGRET OR REMORSE FROM YOU!!
HE'D WANT YOU TO FIGURE OUT WHAT TO DO NOW. YOU NEED...
...THE WITS TO MAKE THE RIGHT CHOICE.
...AND THE DETER-MINATION...
...TO SEE IT THROUGH!
IF YOU'RE WEAK, THEN TRAIN HARDER.
YOU CAN DO SQUATS OR PUSHUPS EVEN IN HERE.
YEAH!
YOU'RE RIGHT!

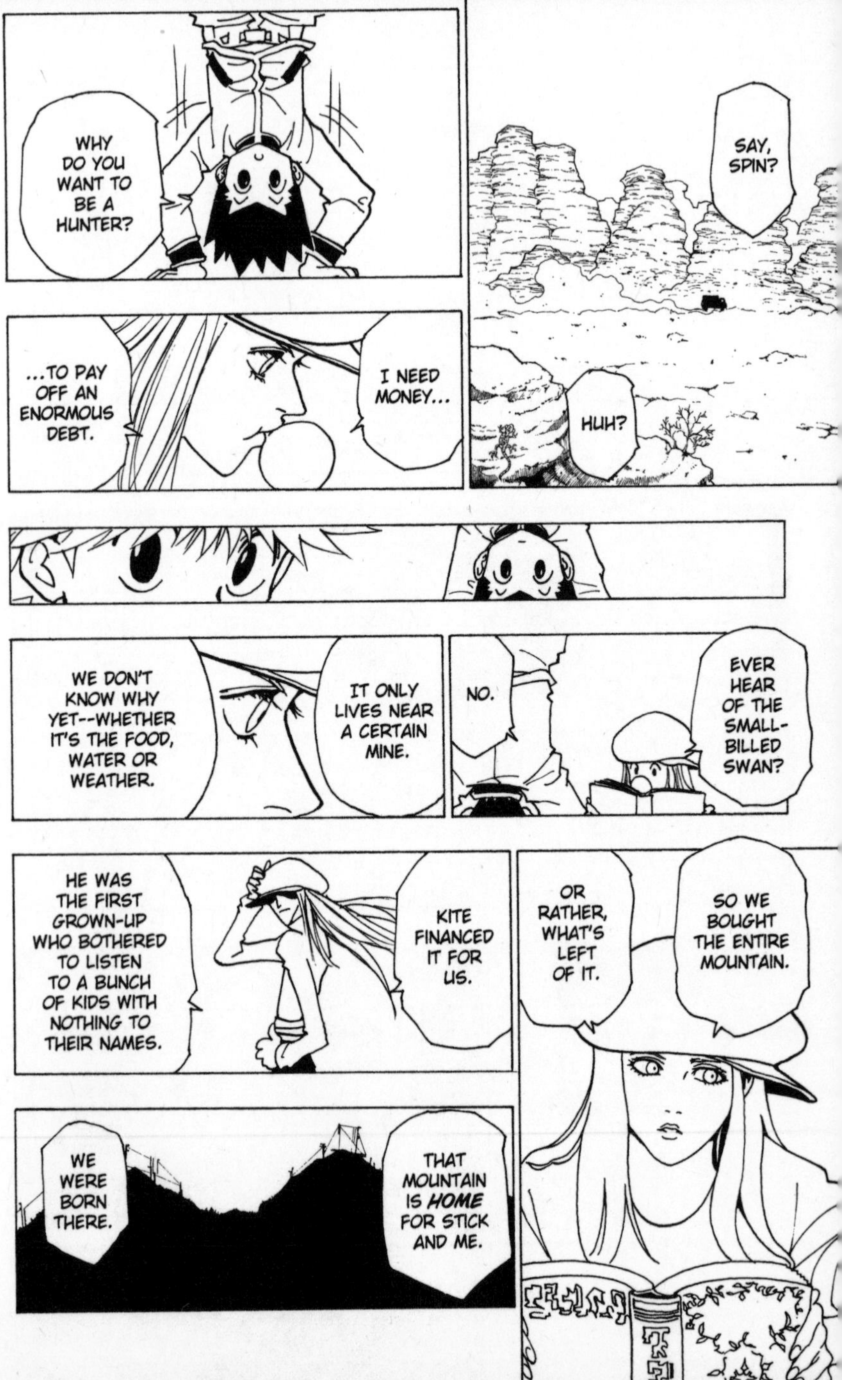
SAY, SPIN?
HUH?
WHY DO YOU WANT TO BE A HUNTER?
I NEED MONEY...
...TO PAY OFF AN ENORMOUS DEBT.
EVER HEAR OF THE SMALL-BILLED SWAN?
NO.
IT ONLY LIVES NEAR A CERTAIN MINE.
WE DON'T KNOW WHY YET--WHETHER IT'S THE FOOD, WATER OR WEATHER.
SO WE BOUGHT THE ENTIRE MOUNTAIN.
OR RATHER, WHAT'S LEFT OF IT.
KITE FINANCED IT FOR US.
HE WAS THE FIRST GROWN-UP WHO BOTHERED TO LISTEN TO A BUNCH OF KIDS WITH NOTHING TO THEIR NAMES.
THAT MOUNTAIN IS *HOME* FOR STICK AND ME.
WE WERE BORN THERE.

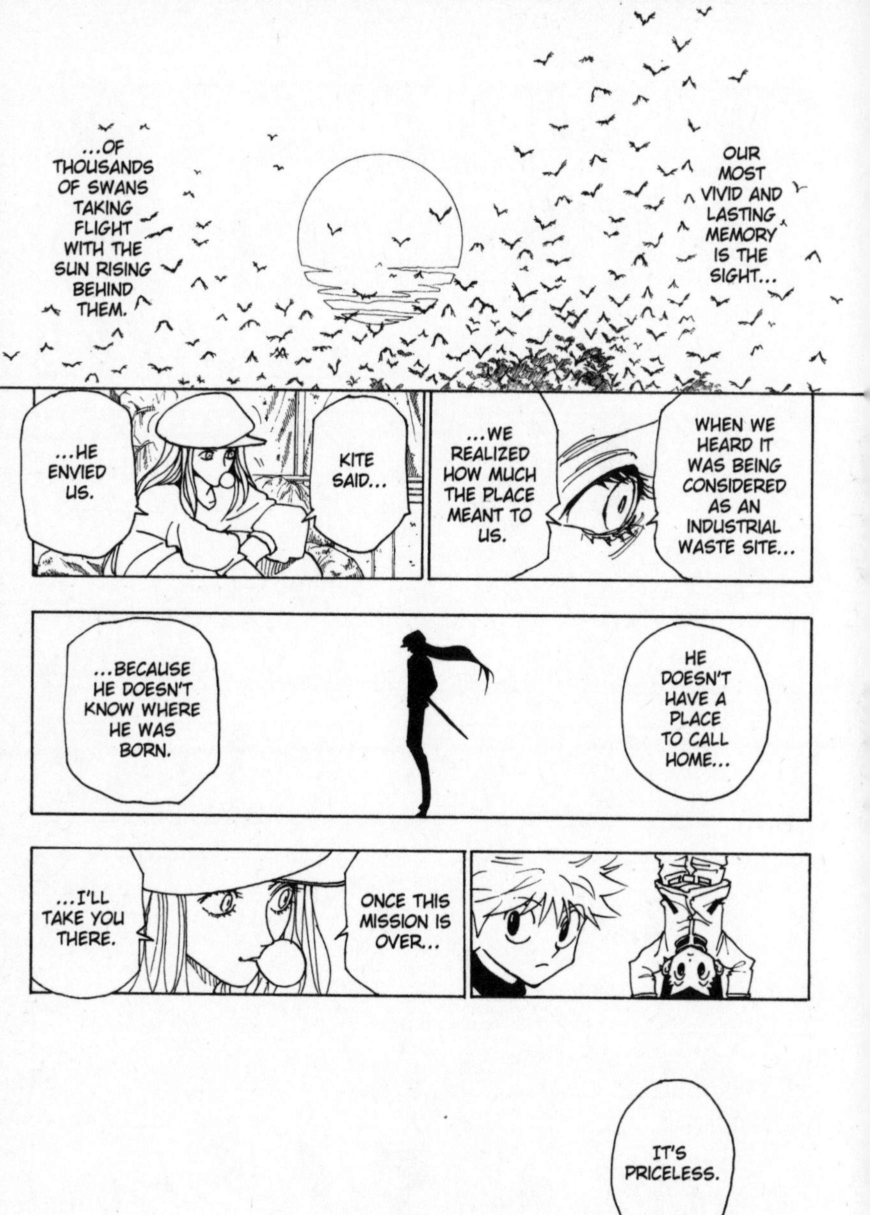
OUR MOST VIVID AND LASTING MEMORY IS THE SIGHT...
...OF THOUSANDS OF SWANS TAKING FLIGHT WITH THE SUN RISING BEHIND THEM.
WHEN WE HEARD IT WAS BEING CONSIDERED AS AN INDUSTRIAL WASTE SITE...
...WE REALIZED HOW MUCH THE PLACE MEANT TO US.
KITE SAID...
...HE ENVIED US.
HE DOESN'T HAVE A PLACE TO CALL HOME...
...BECAUSE HE DOESN'T KNOW WHERE HE WAS BORN.
ONCE THIS MISSION IS OVER...
...I'LL TAKE YOU THERE.
IT'S PRICELESS.

WHOOSH
?
ROLL
PSSHH
ARNNG
FSSHHH

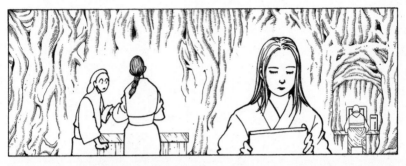

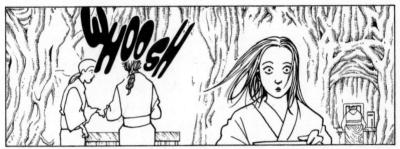

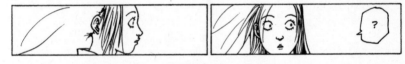

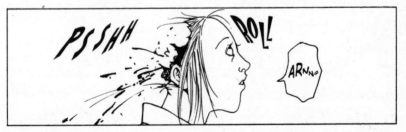

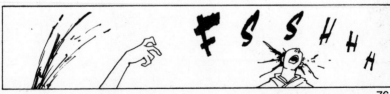

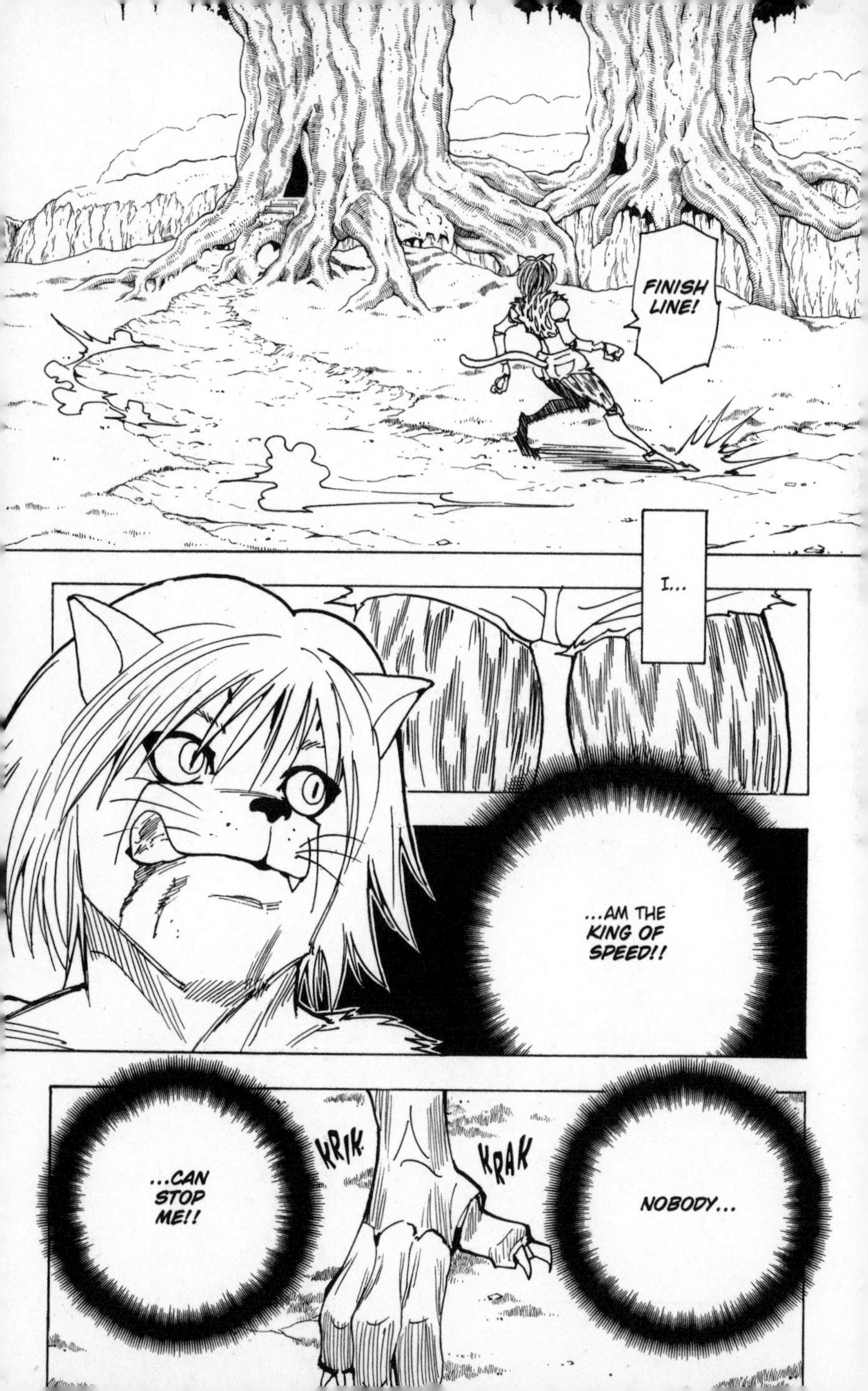
FINISH LINE!
I...
...AM THE KING OF SPEED!!
NOBODY...
KRAK
KRIK
...CAN STOP ME!!

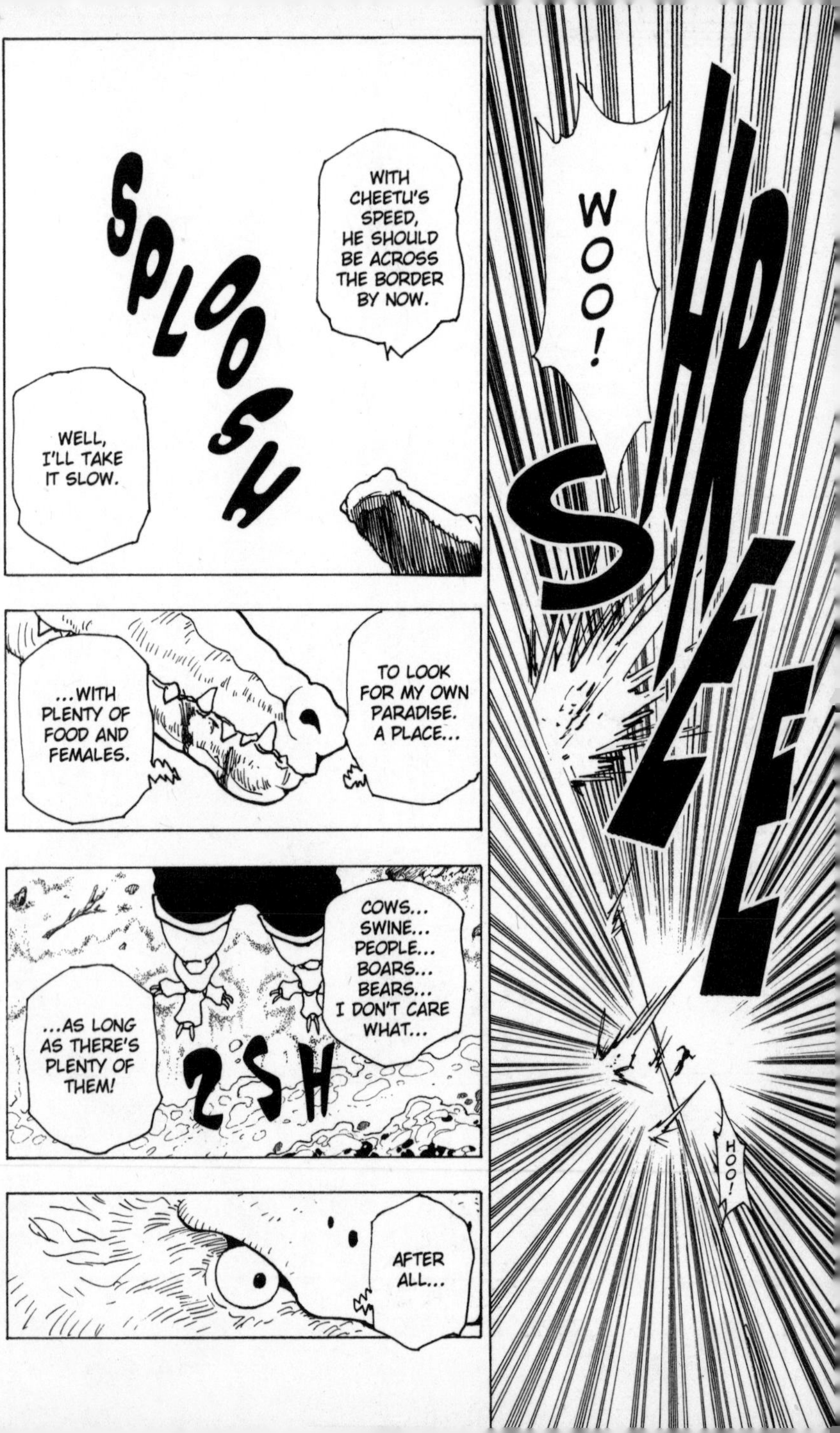
WOO!
HOO!
WITH CHEETU'S SPEED, HE SHOULD BE ACROSS THE BORDER BY NOW.
SPLOOSH
WELL, I'LL TAKE IT SLOW.
TO LOOK FOR MY OWN PARADISE. A PLACE...
...WITH PLENTY OF FOOD AND FEMALES.
COWS... SWINE... PEOPLE... BOARS... BEARS... I DON'T CARE WHAT...
ZSH
...AS LONG AS THERE'S PLENTY OF THEM!
AFTER ALL...

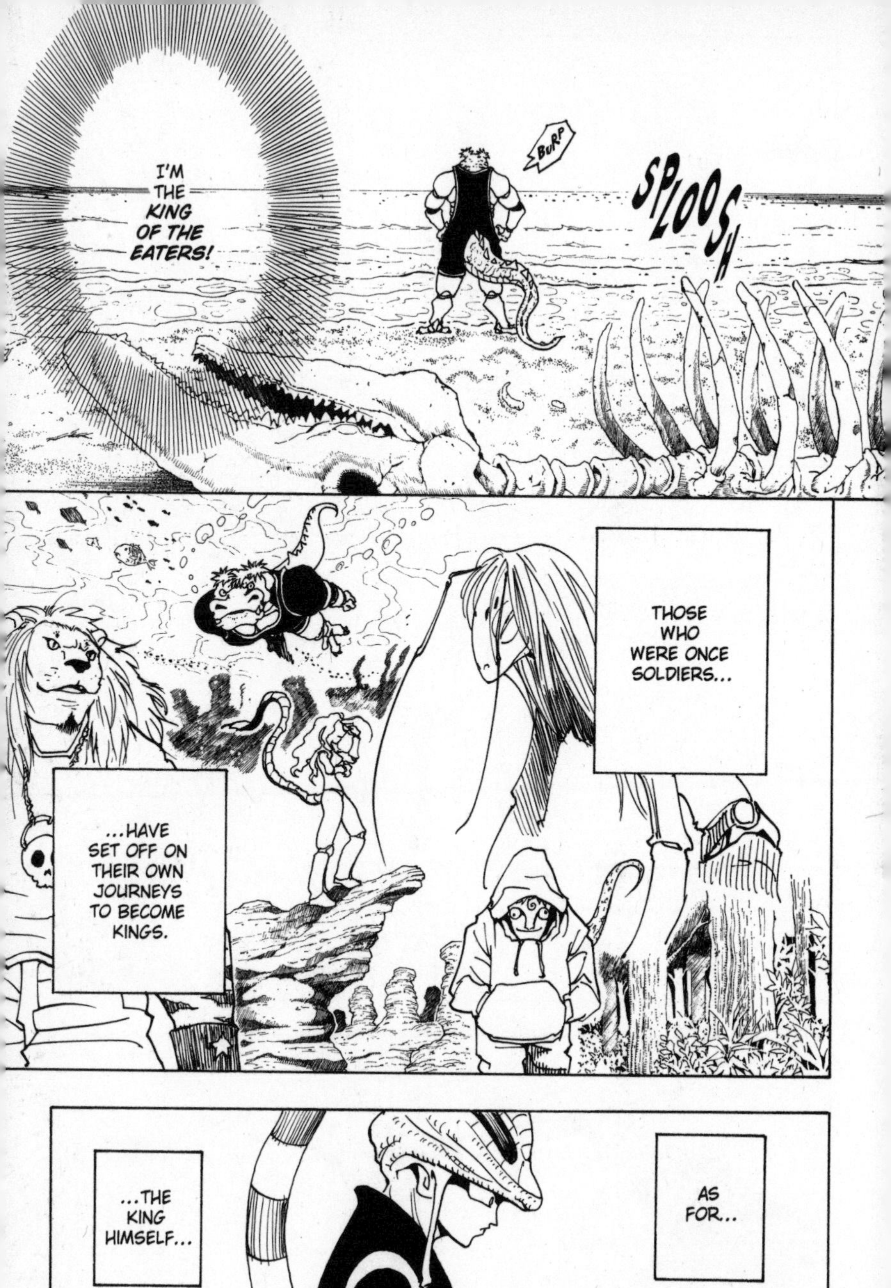
SPLOOSH
BURP
I'M THE KING OF THE EATERS!
THOSE WHO WERE ONCE SOLDIERS...
...HAVE SET OFF ON THEIR OWN JOURNEYS TO BECOME KINGS.
AS FOR...
...THE KING HIMSELF...

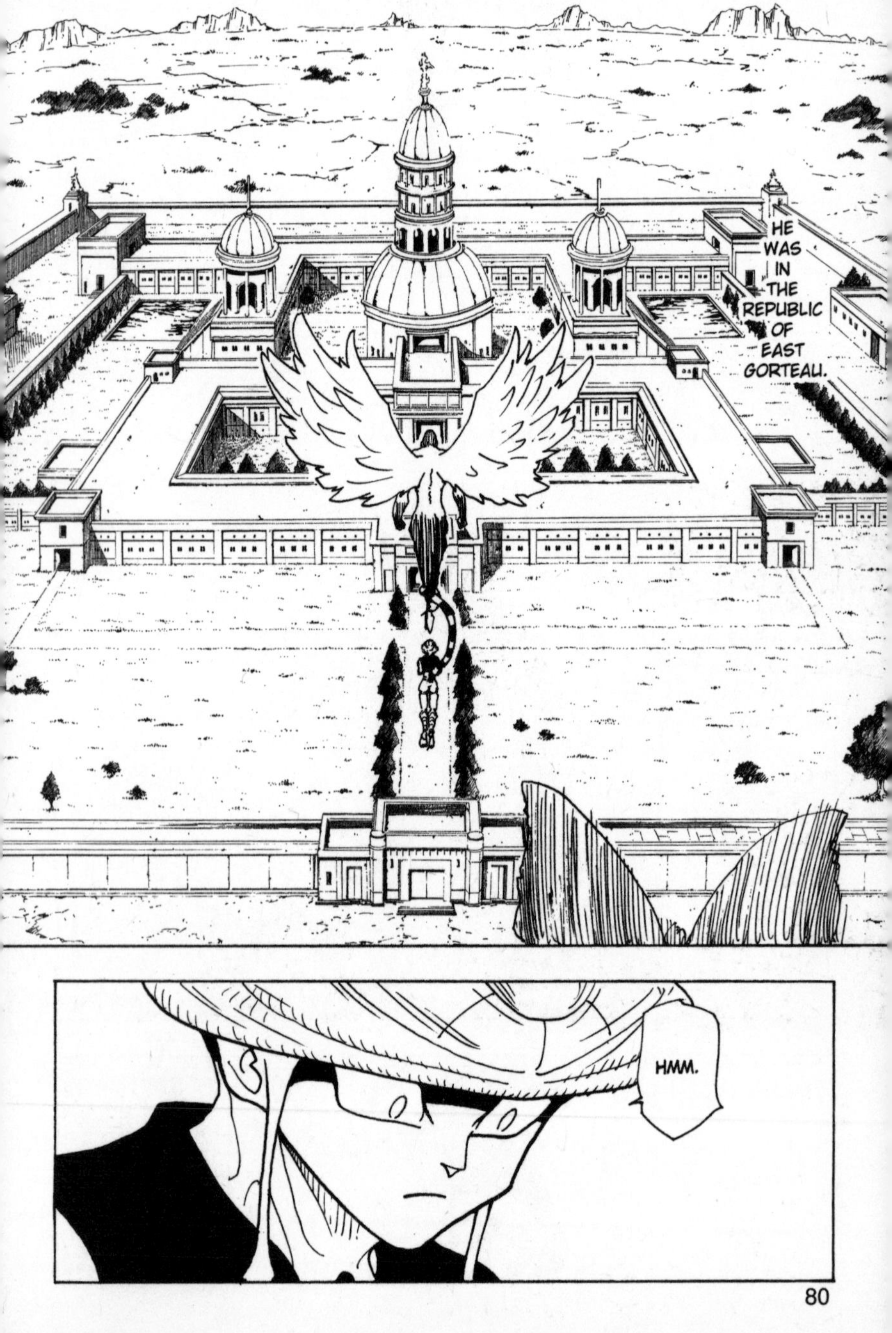
HE WAS IN THE REPUBLIC OF EAST GORTEAU.
HMM.

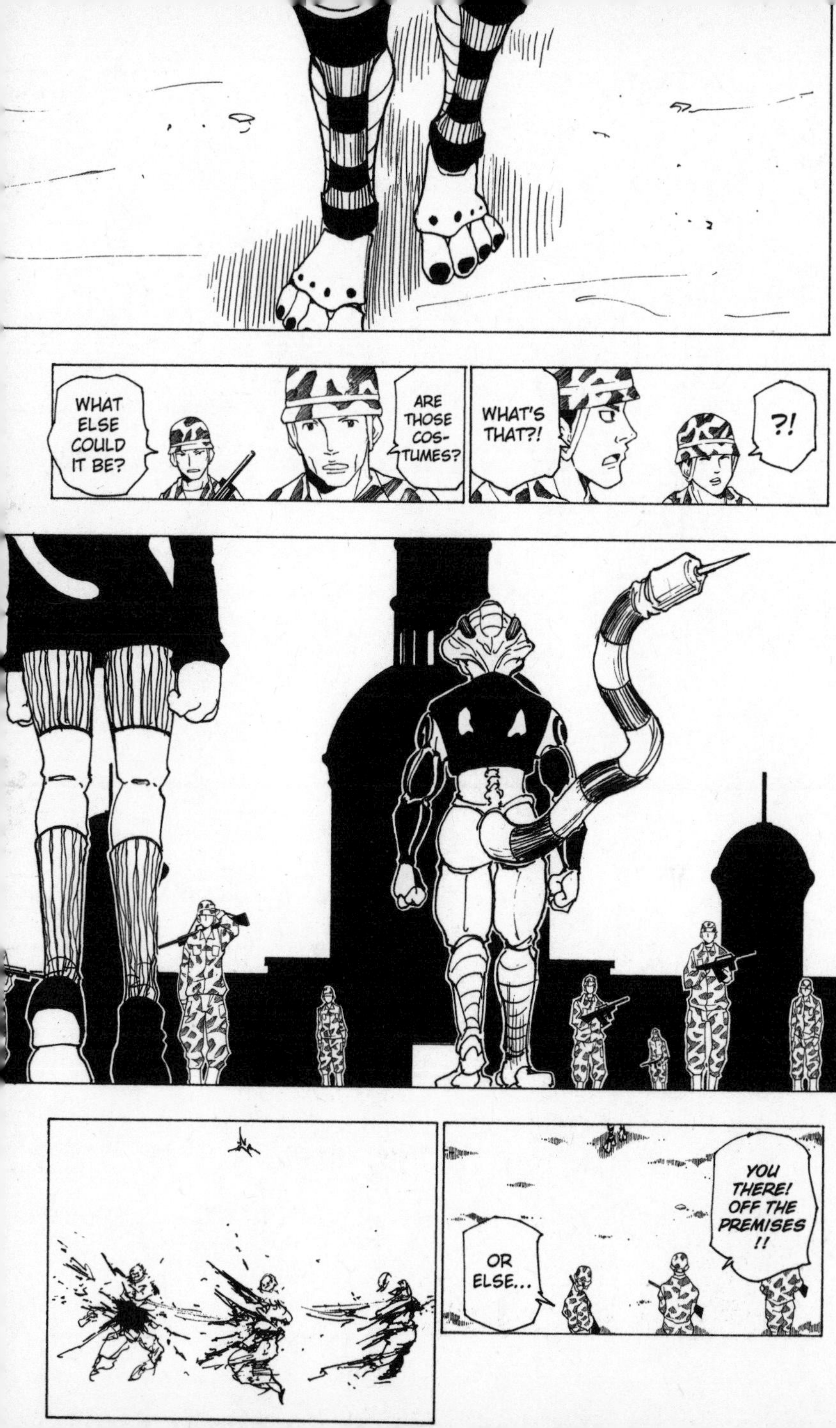
?!
WHAT'S THAT?!
ARE THOSE COS-TUMES?
WHAT ELSE COULD IT BE?
YOU THERE! OFF THE PREMISES!!
OR ELSE...

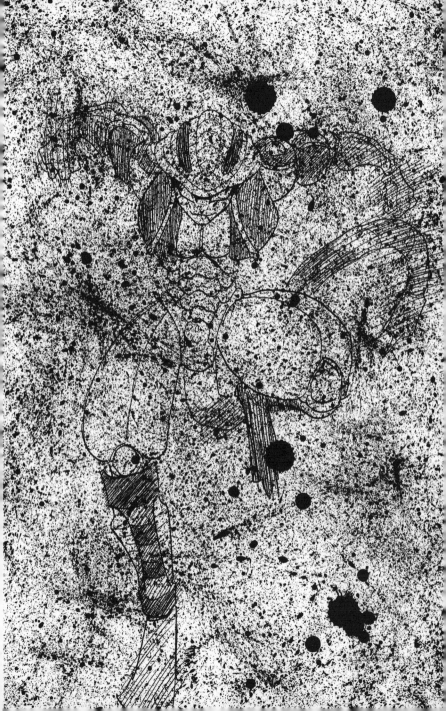

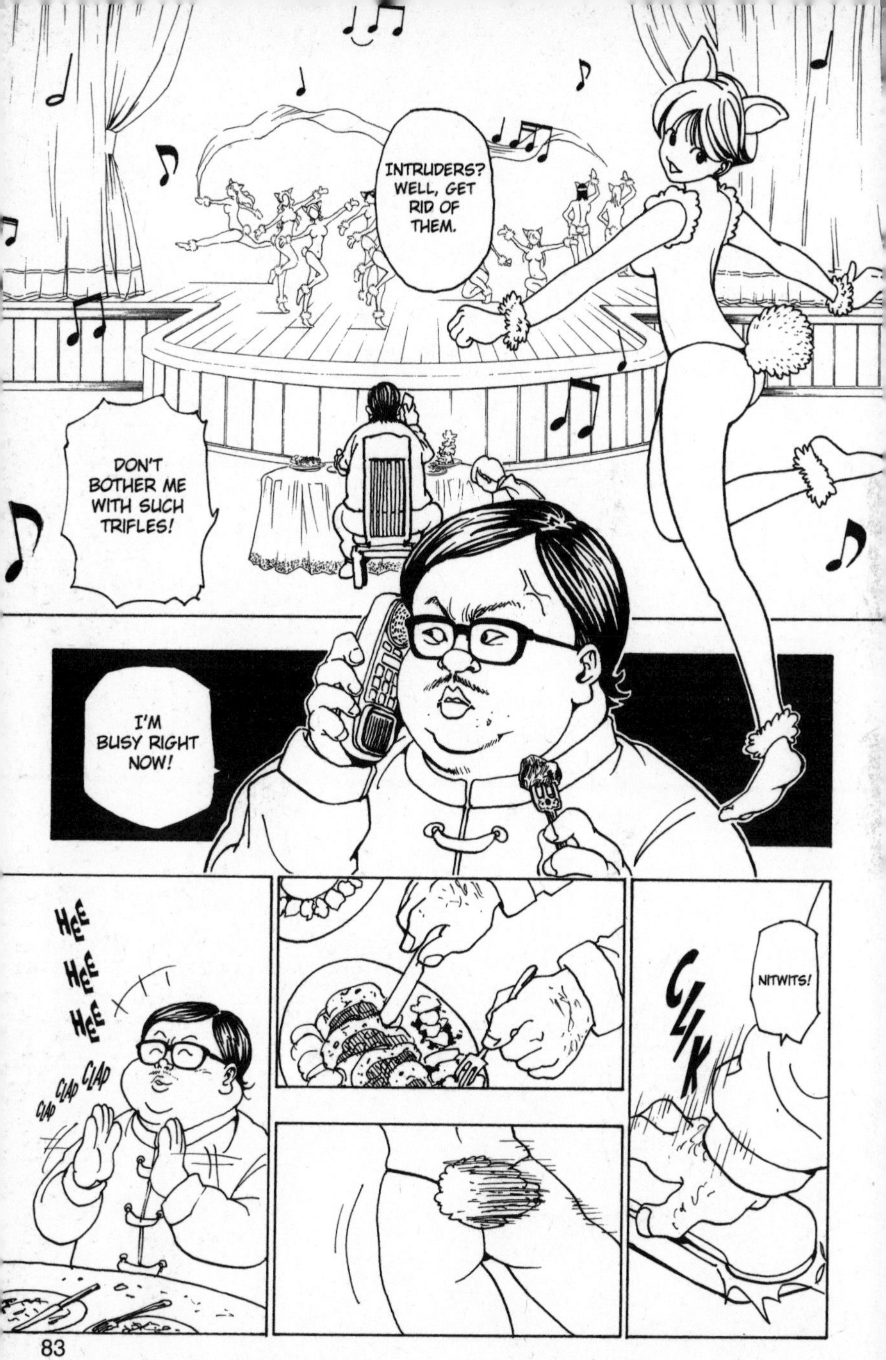
INTRUDERS? WELL, GET RID OF THEM.
DON'T BOTHER ME WITH SUCH TRIFLES!
I'M BUSY RIGHT NOW!
NITWITS!
CLIK
HEE HEE HEE
CLAP CLAP CLAP

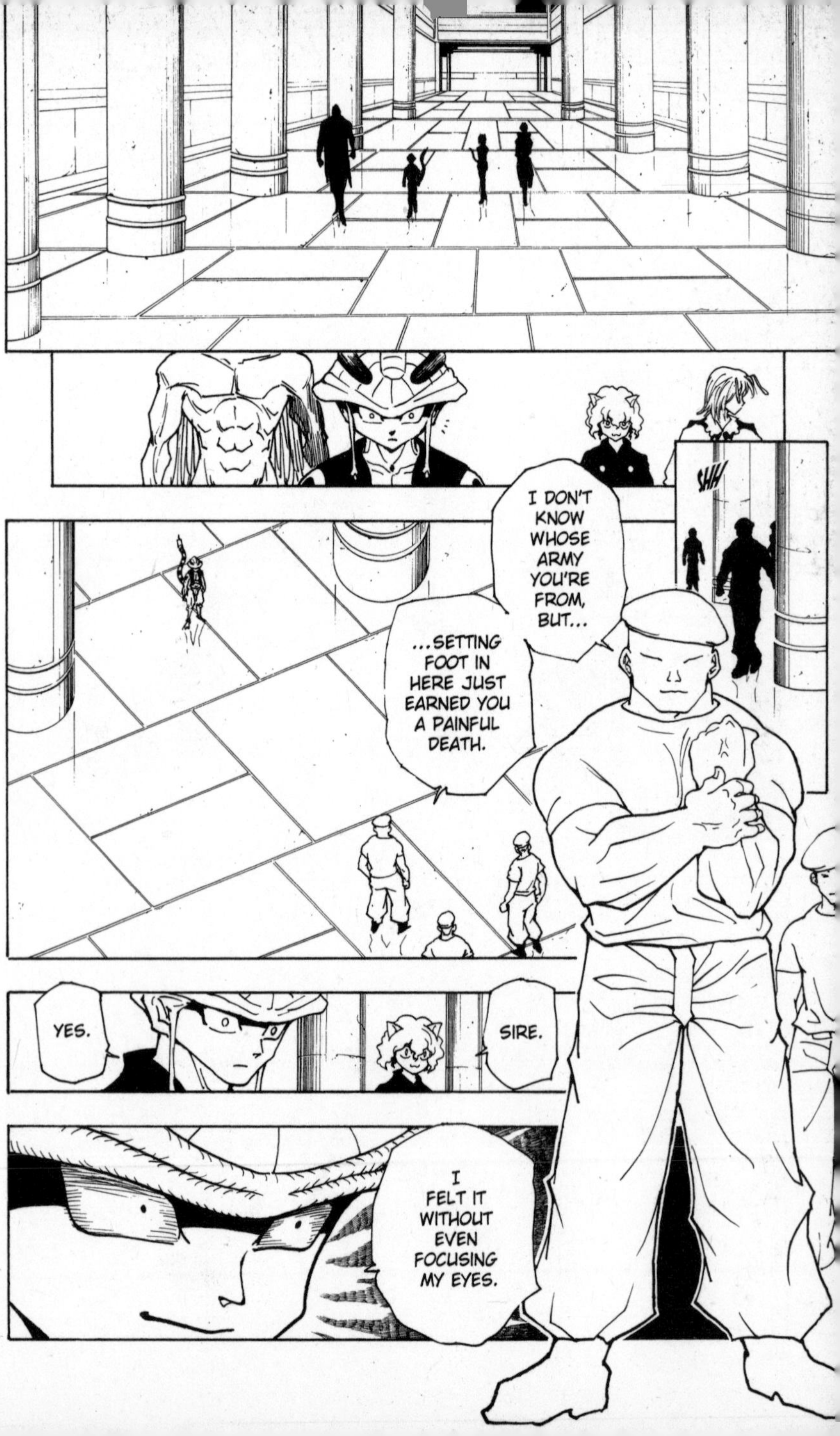
SHH
I DON'T KNOW WHOSE ARMY YOU'RE FROM, BUT...
...SETTING FOOT IN HERE JUST EARNED YOU A PAINFUL DEATH.
SIRE.
YES.
I FELT IT WITHOUT EVEN FOCUSING MY EYES.

IT'S A RARE.

LOOKS TASTY...

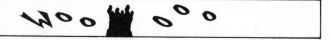

WOO OOO

OH...

MAN...

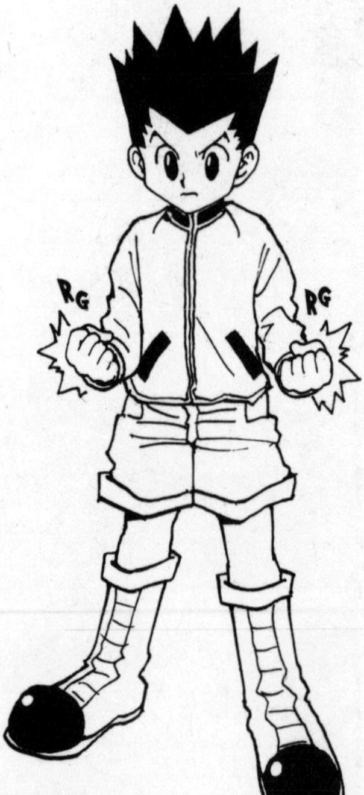
RG
RG

Chapter 217: Meat Orchard

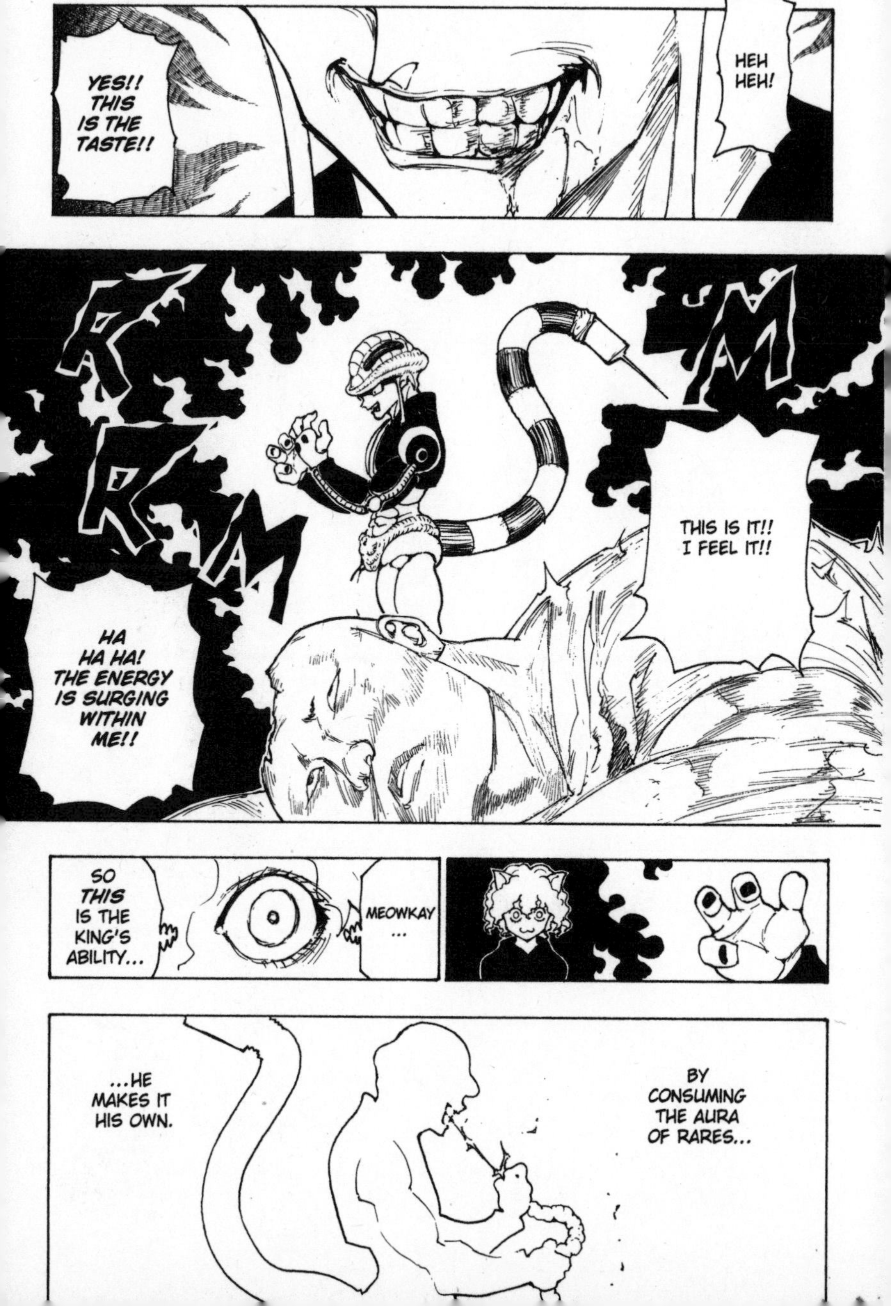

HEH HEH!
YES!! THIS IS THE TASTE!!
THIS IS IT!! I FEEL IT!!
HA HA HA! THE ENERGY IS SURGING WITHIN ME!!
MEOWKAY...
SO THIS IS THE KING'S ABILITY...
BY CONSUMING THE AURA OF RARES...
...HE MAKES IT HIS OWN.

Chapter 217: Meat Orchard

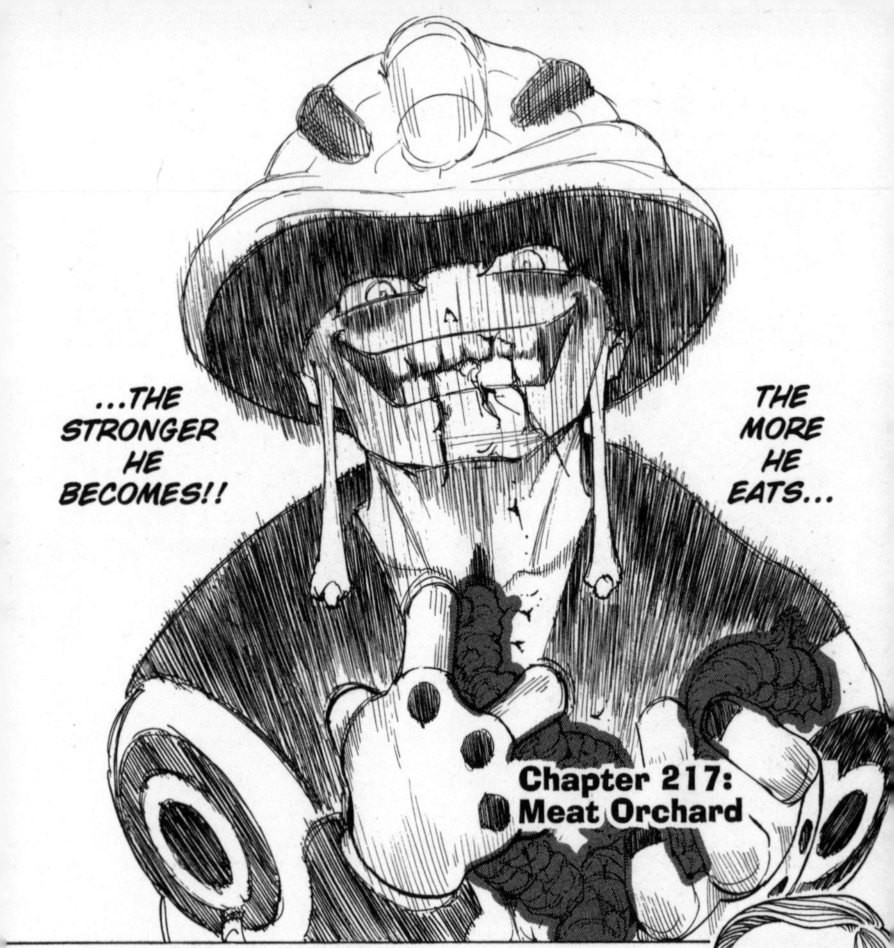
THE MORE HE EATS...
...THE STRONGER HE BECOMES!!

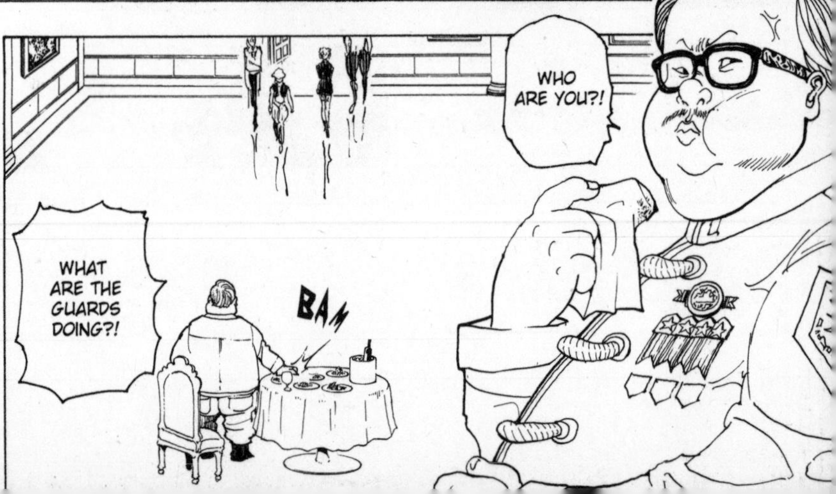
WHO ARE YOU?!
BAM
WHAT ARE THE GUARDS DOING?!

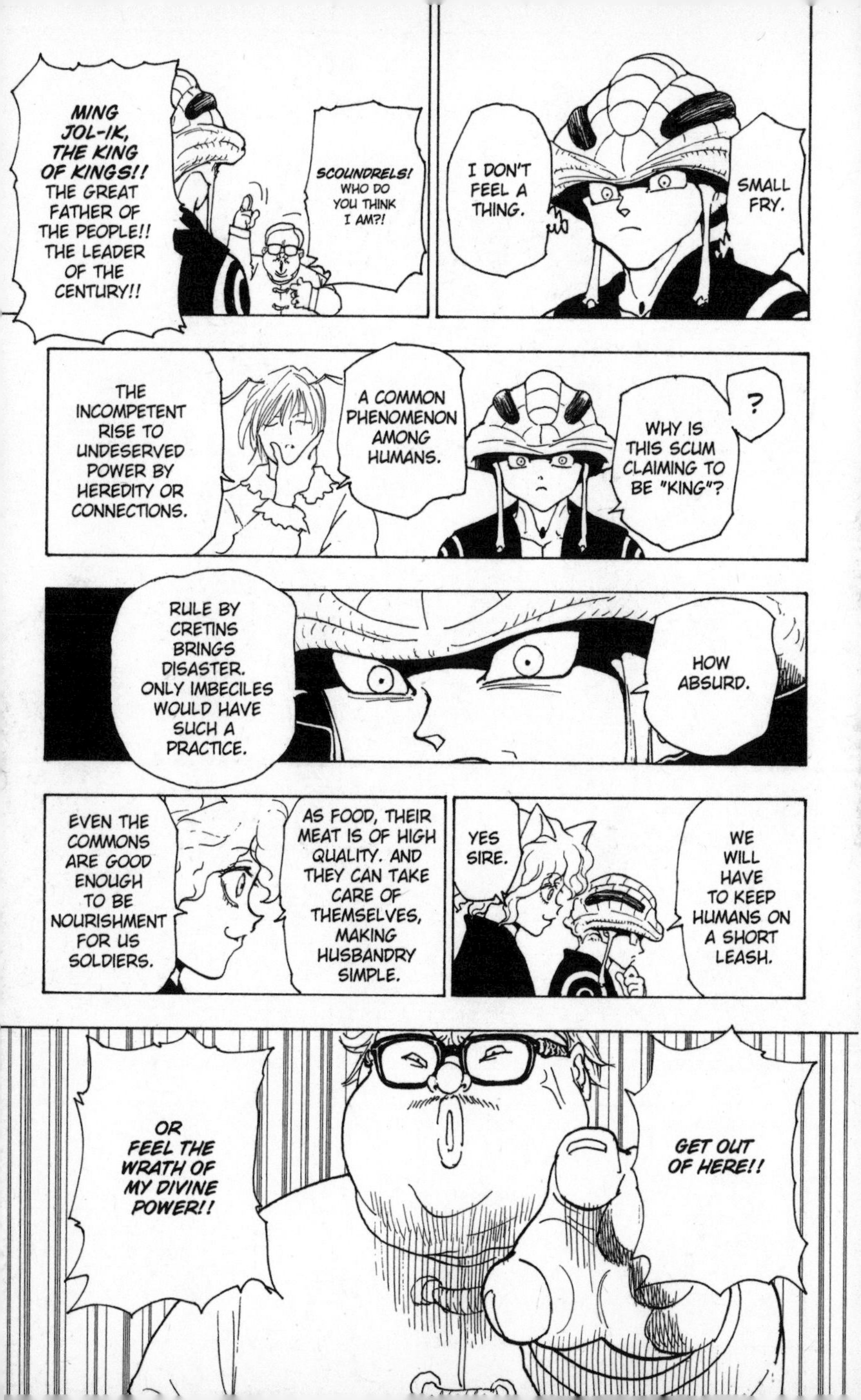
SMALL FRY.
I DON'T FEEL A THING.
SCOUNDRELS! WHO DO YOU THINK I AM?!
MING JOL-IK, THE KING OF KINGS!! THE GREAT FATHER OF THE PEOPLE!! THE LEADER OF THE CENTURY!!
?
WHY IS THIS SCUM CLAIMING TO BE "KING"?
A COMMON PHENOMENON AMONG HUMANS.
THE INCOMPETENT RISE TO UNDESERVED POWER BY HEREDITY OR CONNECTIONS.
HOW ABSURD.
RULE BY CRETINS BRINGS DISASTER. ONLY IMBECILES WOULD HAVE SUCH A PRACTICE.
WE WILL HAVE TO KEEP HUMANS ON A SHORT LEASH.
YES SIRE.
AS FOOD, THEIR MEAT IS OF HIGH QUALITY. AND THEY CAN TAKE CARE OF THEMSELVES, MAKING HUSBANDRY SIMPLE.
EVEN THE COMMONS ARE GOOD ENOUGH TO BE NOURISHMENT FOR US SOLDIERS.
GET OUT OF HERE!!
OR FEEL THE WRATH OF MY DIVINE POWER!!

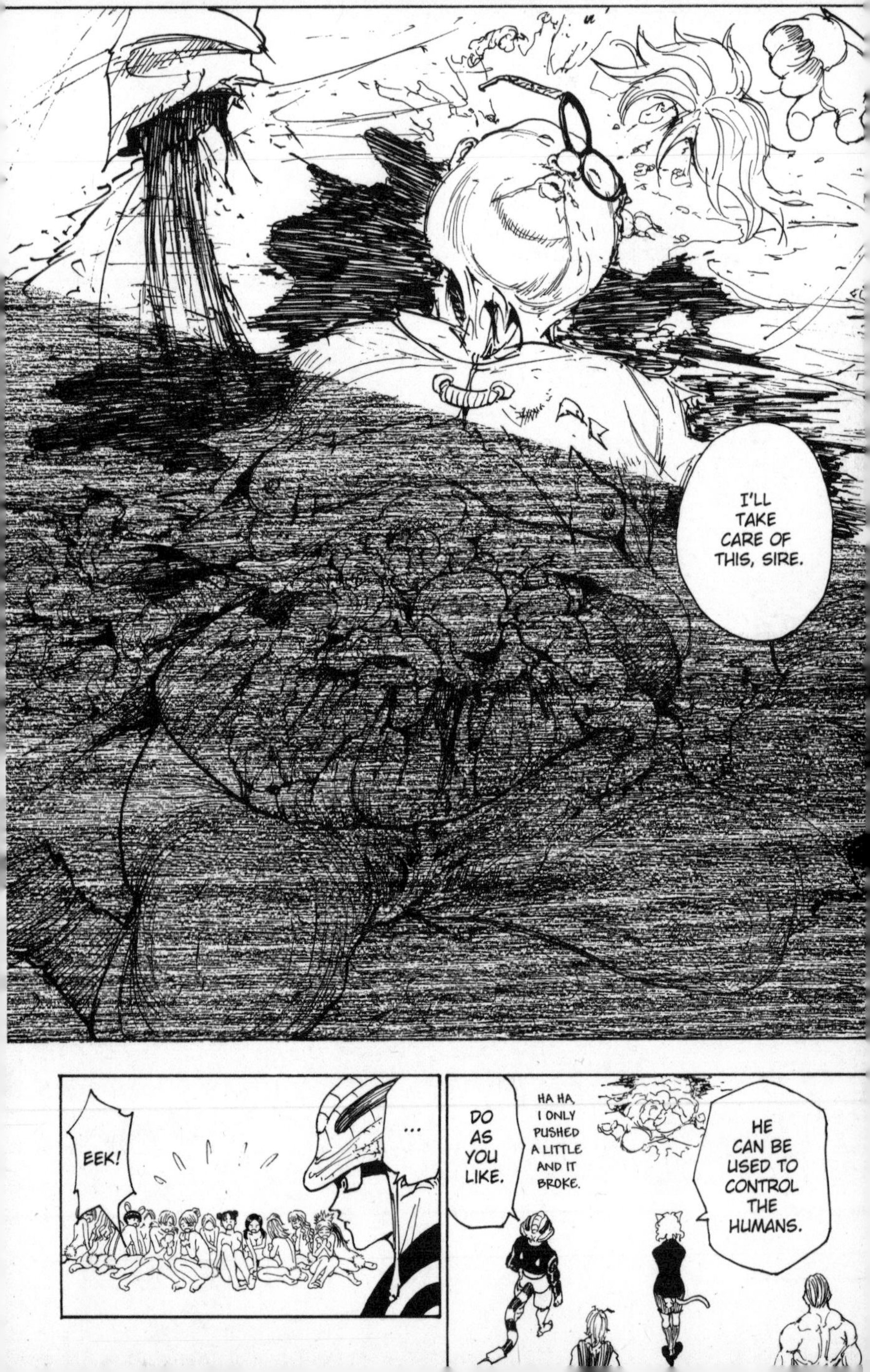
I'LL TAKE CARE OF THIS, SIRE.
HE CAN BE USED TO CONTROL THE HUMANS.
HA HA, I ONLY PUSHED A LITTLE AND IT BROKE.
DO AS YOU LIKE.
...
EEK!

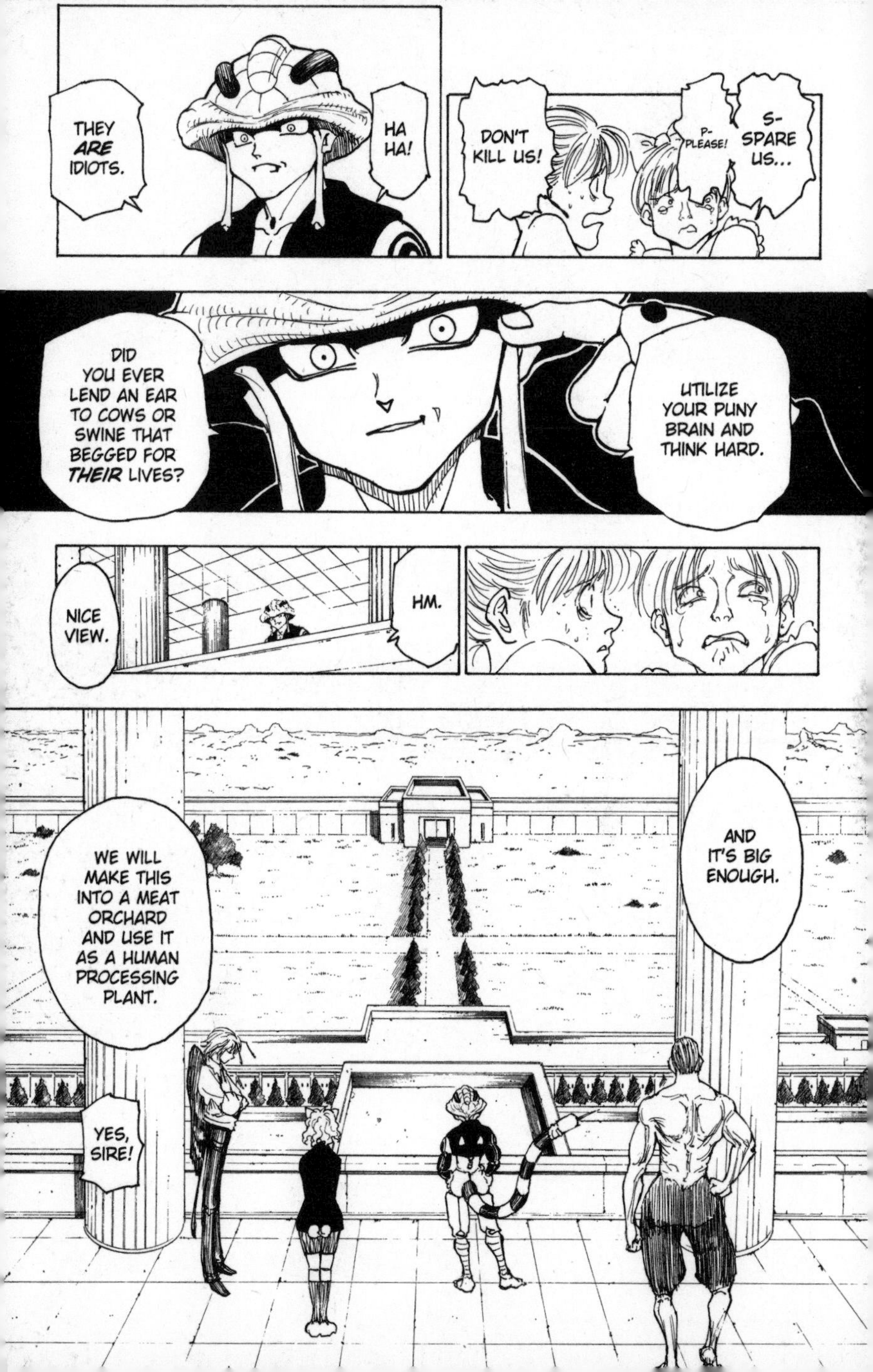
S-SPARE US...
P-PLEASE!
DON'T KILL US!
HA HA!
THEY *ARE* IDIOTS.
DID YOU EVER LEND AN EAR TO COWS OR SWINE THAT BEGGED FOR *THEIR* LIVES?
UTILIZE YOUR PUNY BRAIN AND THINK HARD.
HM.
NICE VIEW.
AND IT'S BIG ENOUGH.
WE WILL MAKE THIS INTO A MEAT ORCHARD AND USE IT AS A HUMAN PROCESSING PLANT.
YES, SIRE!

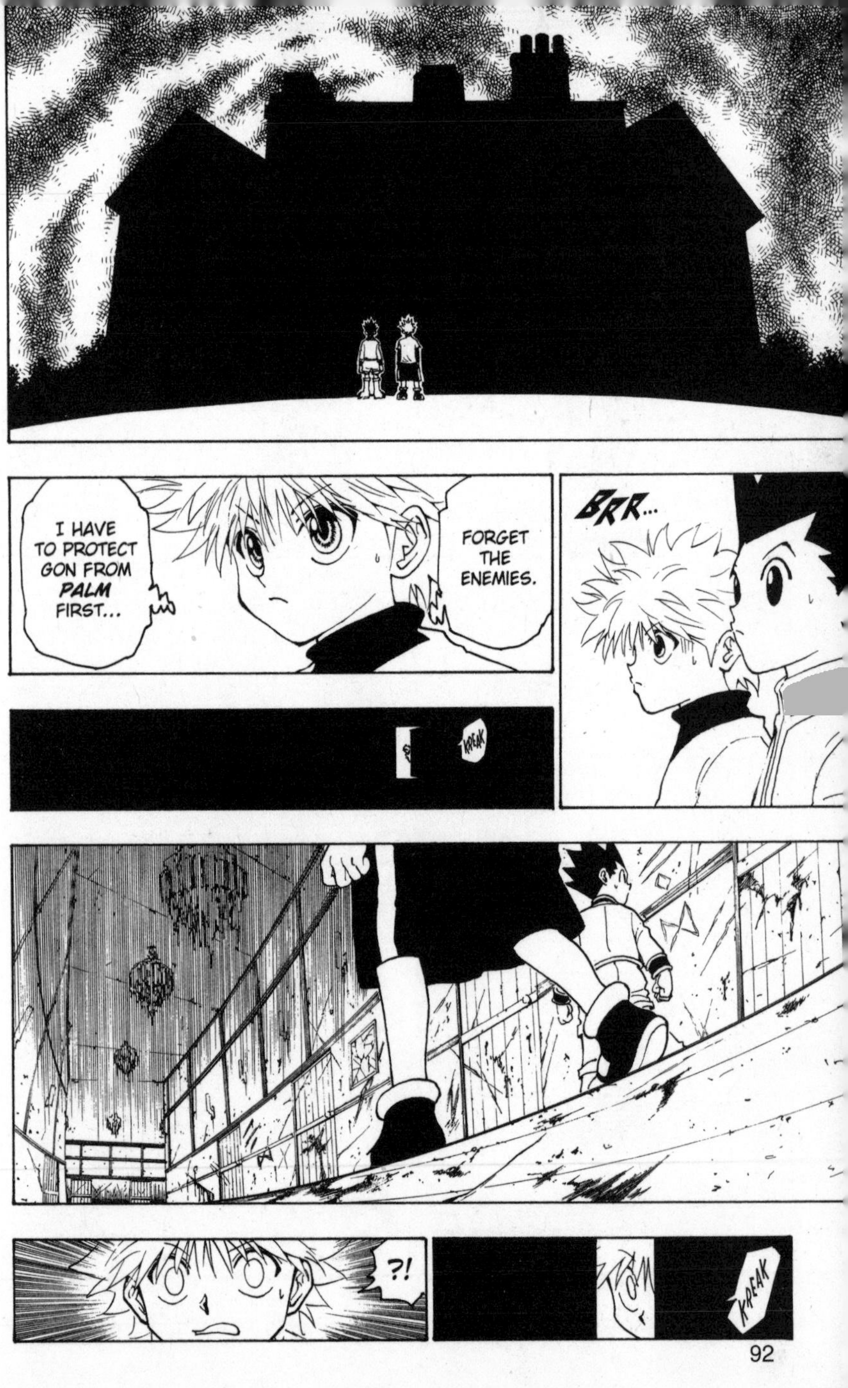
BRR...
FORGET THE ENEMIES.
I HAVE TO PROTECT GON FROM *PALM* FIRST...
KREAK
KREAK
?!

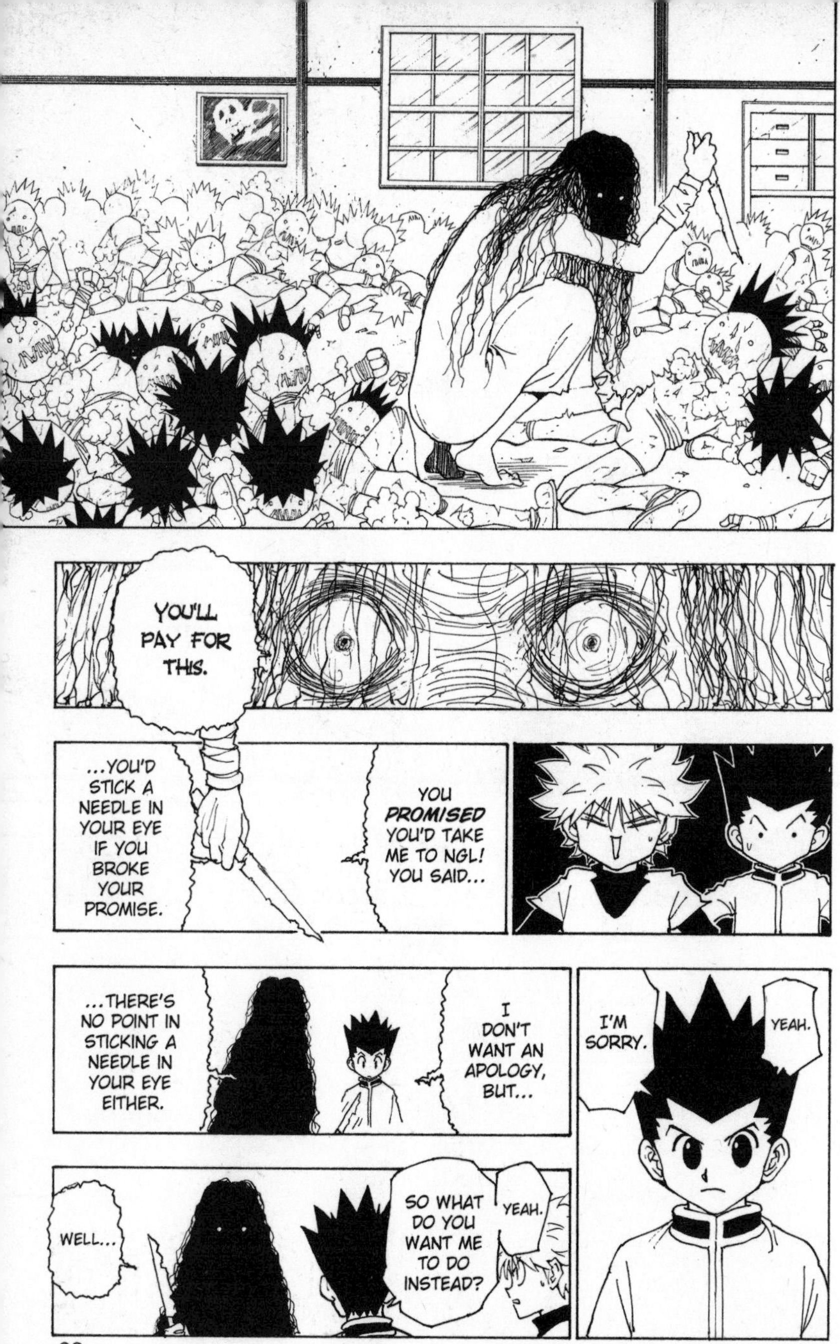
YOU'LL PAY FOR THIS.
YOU *PROMISED* YOU'D TAKE ME TO NGL! YOU SAID...
...YOU'D STICK A NEEDLE IN YOUR EYE IF YOU BROKE YOUR PROMISE.
YEAH.
I'M SORRY.
I DON'T WANT AN APOLOGY, BUT...
...THERE'S NO POINT IN STICKING A NEEDLE IN YOUR EYE EITHER.
YEAH.
SO WHAT DO YOU WANT ME TO DO INSTEAD?
WELL...

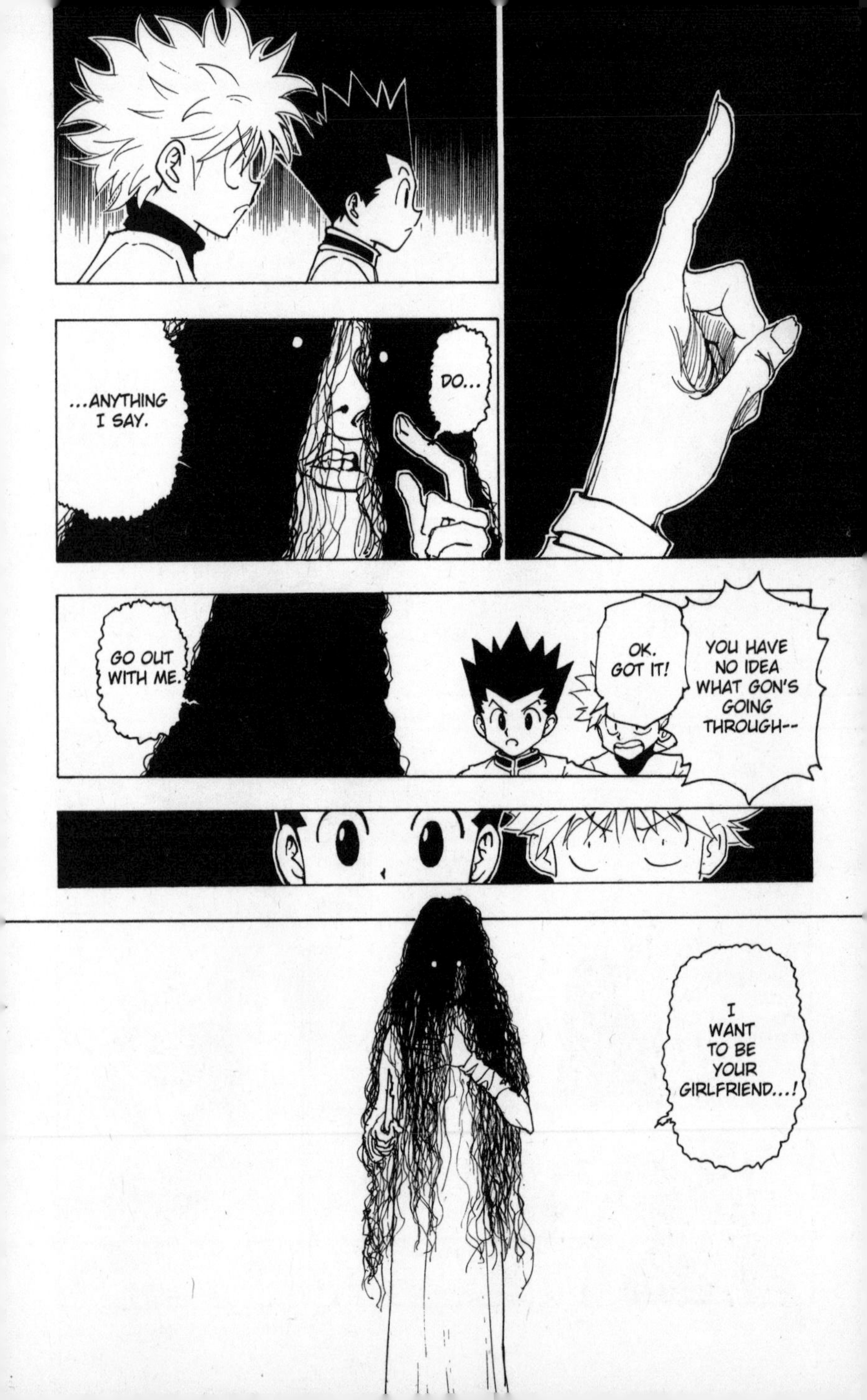
DO...
...ANYTHING I SAY.
YOU HAVE NO IDEA WHAT GON'S GOING THROUGH--
OK. GOT IT!
GO OUT WITH ME.
I WANT TO BE YOUR GIRLFRIEND...!

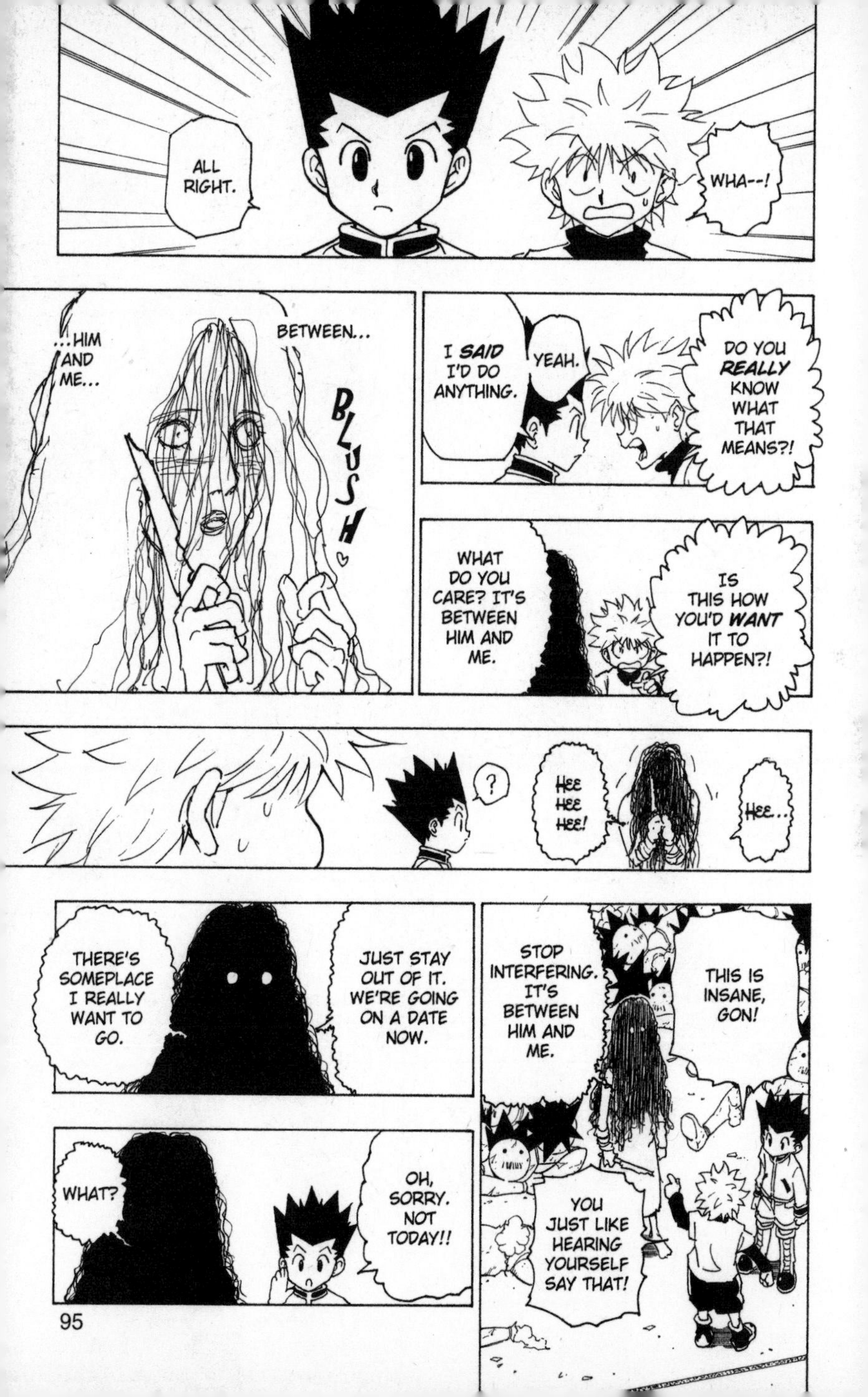
WHA--!
ALL RIGHT.
DO YOU REALLY KNOW WHAT THAT MEANS?!
YEAH.
I SAID I'D DO ANYTHING.
IS THIS HOW YOU'D WANT IT TO HAPPEN?!
WHAT DO YOU CARE? IT'S BETWEEN HIM AND ME.
BETWEEN...
...HIM AND ME...
BLUSH
HEE...
HEE HEE HEE!
?
THIS IS INSANE, GON!
STOP INTERFERING. IT'S BETWEEN HIM AND ME.
YOU JUST LIKE HEARING YOURSELF SAY THAT!
JUST STAY OUT OF IT. WE'RE GOING ON A DATE NOW.
THERE'S SOMEPLACE I REALLY WANT TO GO.
OH, SORRY. NOT TODAY!!
WHAT?

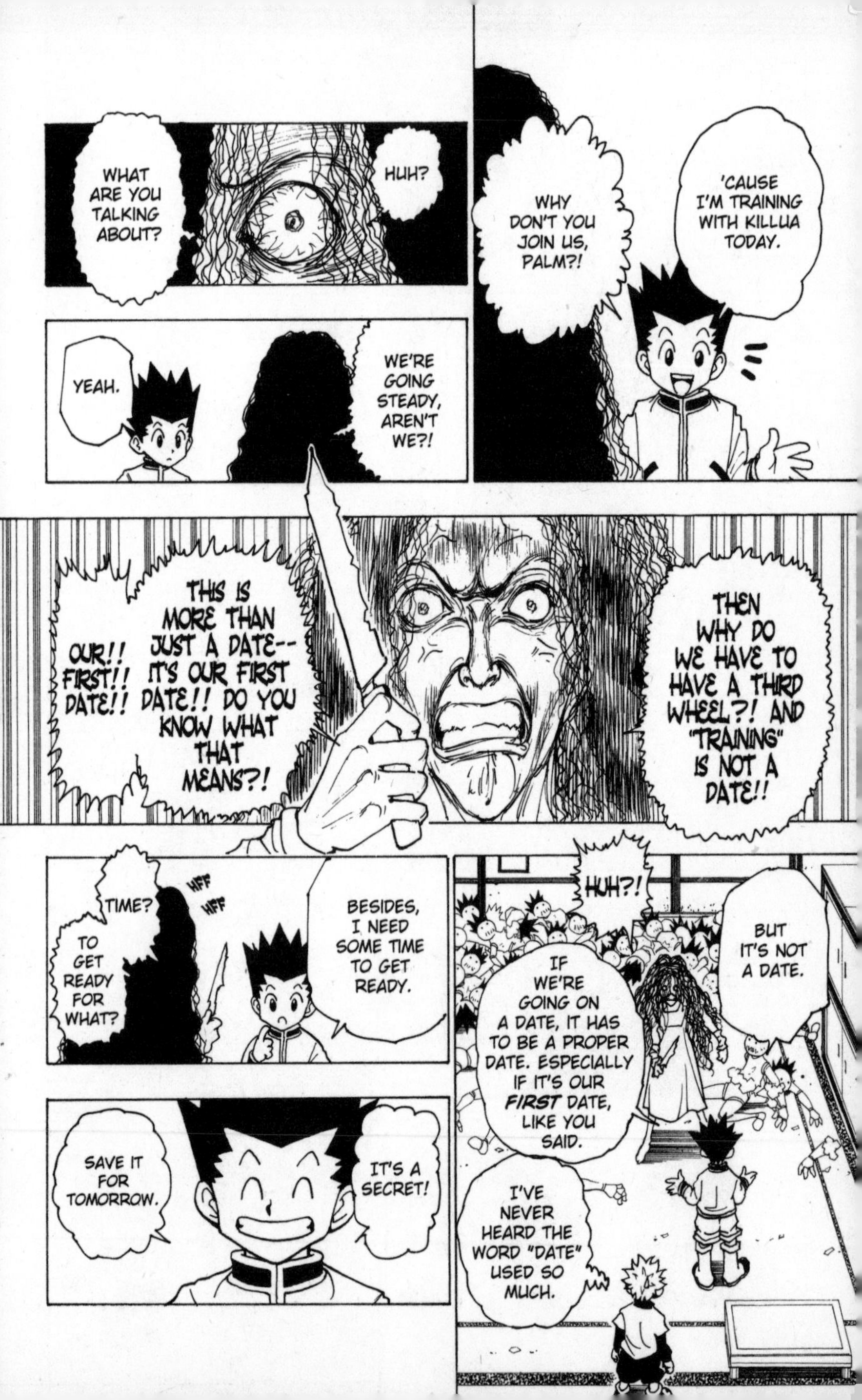

'CAUSE I'M TRAINING WITH KILLUA TODAY.
WHY DON'T YOU JOIN US, PALM?!
HUH?
WHAT ARE YOU TALKING ABOUT?
WE'RE GOING STEADY, AREN'T WE?!
YEAH.
THEN WHY DO WE HAVE TO HAVE A THIRD WHEEL?! AND "TRAINING" IS NOT A DATE!!
THIS IS MORE THAN JUST A DATE-- IT'S OUR FIRST DATE!! DO YOU KNOW WHAT THAT MEANS?!
OUR!! FIRST!! DATE!!
BUT IT'S NOT A DATE.
HUH?!
IF WE'RE GOING ON A DATE, IT HAS TO BE A PROPER DATE. ESPECIALLY IF IT'S OUR FIRST DATE, LIKE YOU SAID.
I'VE NEVER HEARD THE WORD "DATE" USED SO MUCH.
BESIDES, I NEED SOME TIME TO GET READY.
HFF HFF
TIME?
TO GET READY FOR WHAT?
IT'S A SECRET!
SAVE IT FOR TOMORROW.

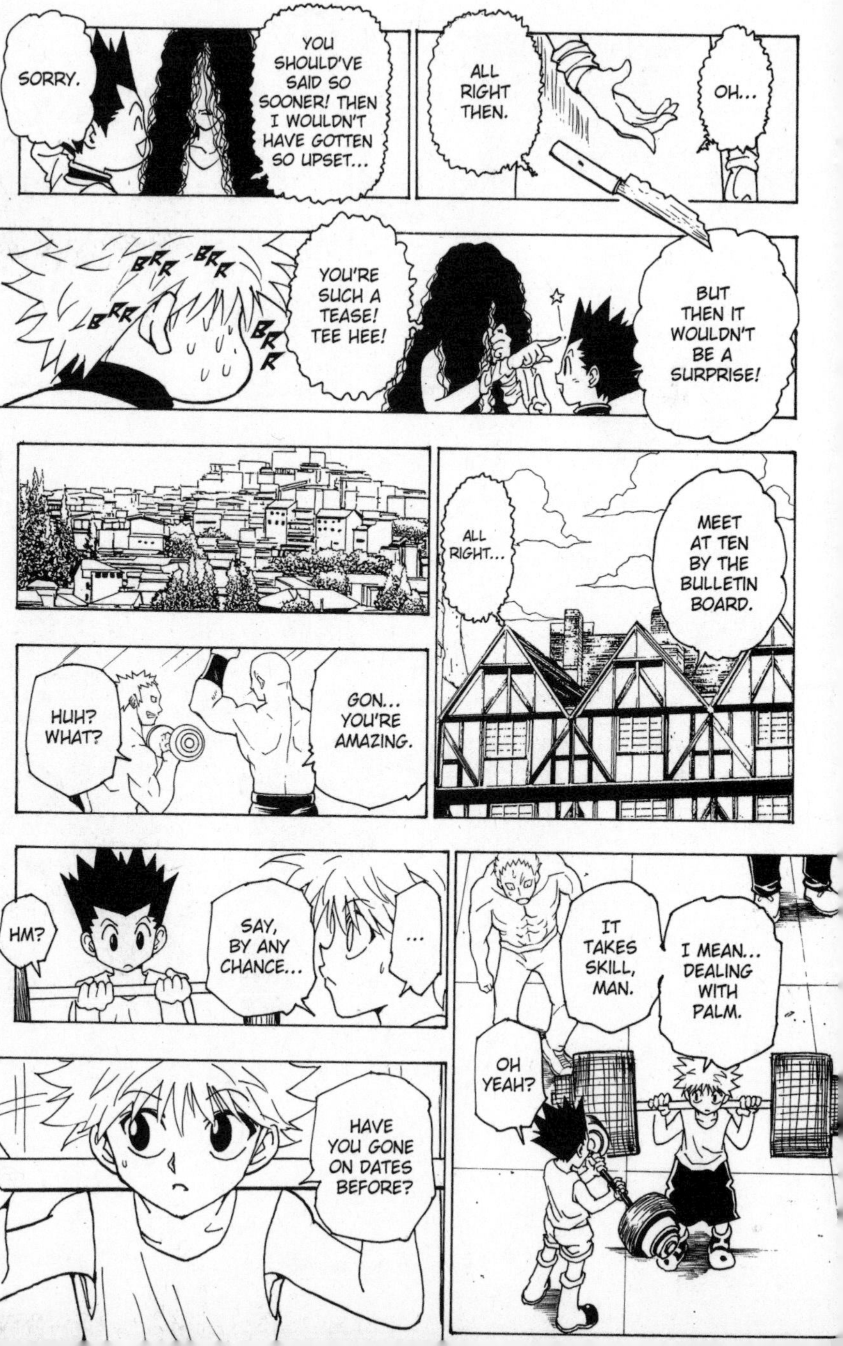
OH...
ALL RIGHT THEN.
YOU SHOULD'VE SAID SO SOONER! THEN I WOULDN'T HAVE GOTTEN SO UPSET...
SORRY.
BUT THEN IT WOULDN'T BE A SURPRISE!
YOU'RE SUCH A TEASE! TEE HEE!
BRR BRR BRR BRR
MEET AT TEN BY THE BULLETIN BOARD.
ALL RIGHT...
GON... YOU'RE AMAZING.
HUH? WHAT?
I MEAN... DEALING WITH PALM.
IT TAKES SKILL, MAN.
OH YEAH?
...
SAY, BY ANY CHANCE...
HM?
HAVE YOU GONE ON DATES BEFORE?

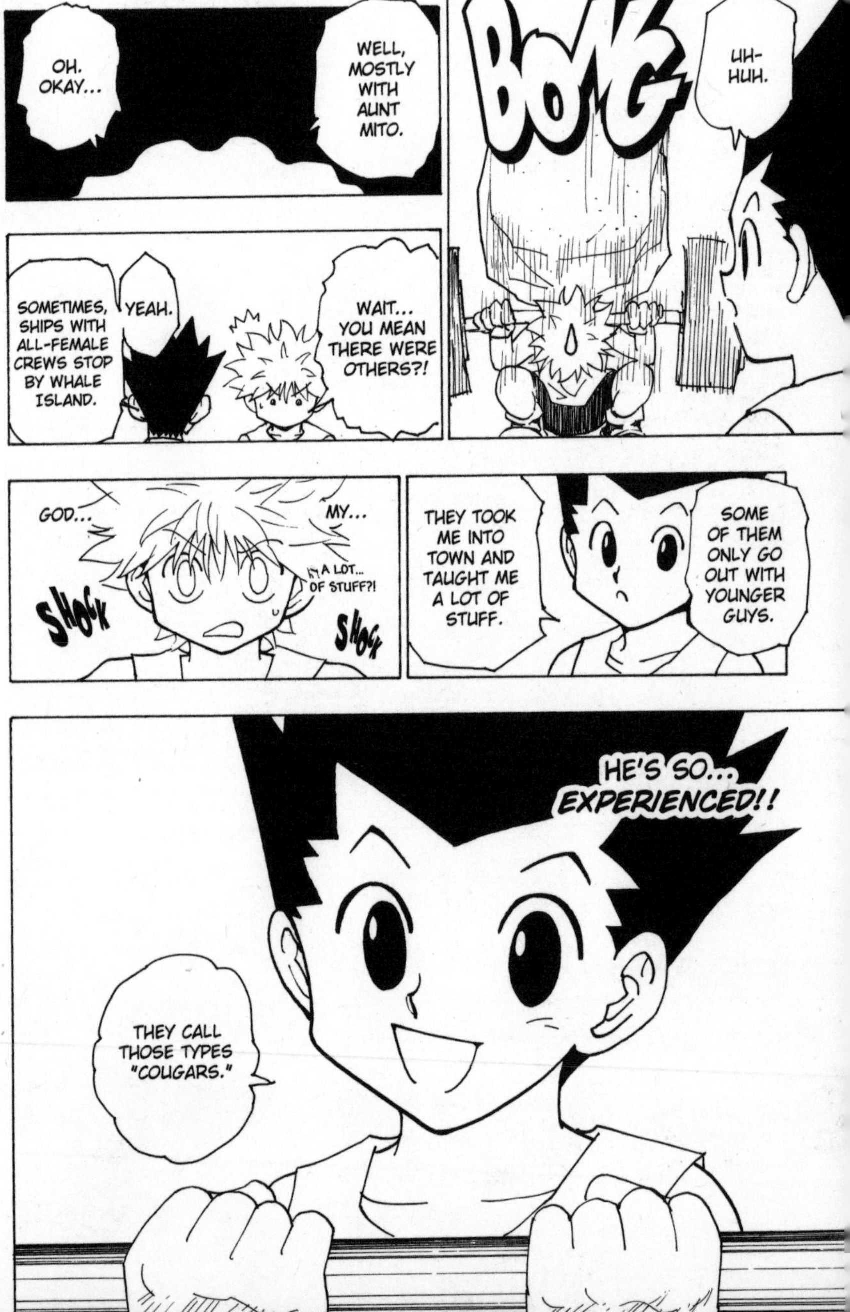
UH-HUH.
BONG
WELL, MOSTLY WITH AUNT MITO.
OH. OKAY...
WAIT... YOU MEAN THERE WERE OTHERS?!
YEAH.
SOMETIMES, SHIPS WITH ALL-FEMALE CREWS STOP BY WHALE ISLAND.
SOME OF THEM ONLY GO OUT WITH YOUNGER GUYS.
THEY TOOK ME INTO TOWN AND TAUGHT ME A LOT OF STUFF.
MY...
SHOCK
A LOT... OF STUFF?!
GOD...
SHOCK
HE'S SO... EXPERIENCED!!
THEY CALL THOSE TYPES "COUGARS."

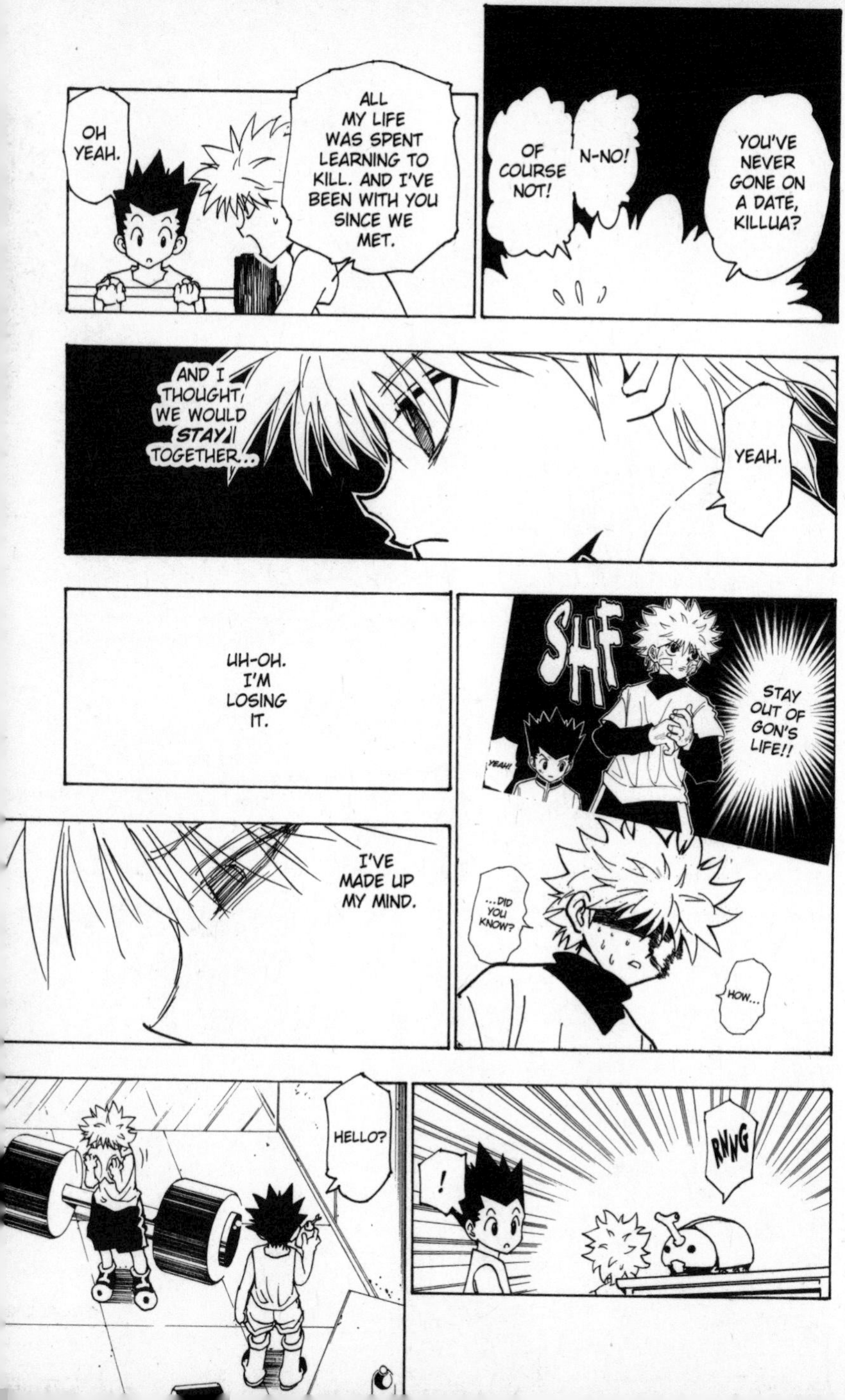
YOU'VE NEVER GONE ON A DATE, KILLUA?
N-NO!
OF COURSE NOT!
ALL MY LIFE WAS SPENT LEARNING TO KILL. AND I'VE BEEN WITH YOU SINCE WE MET.
OH YEAH.
YEAH.
AND I THOUGHT WE WOULD STAY TOGETHER...
SHF
STAY OUT OF GON'S LIFE!!
YEAH!
HOW...
...DID YOU KNOW?
UH-OH. I'M LOSING IT.
I'VE MADE UP MY MIND.
RNNG
!
HELLO?

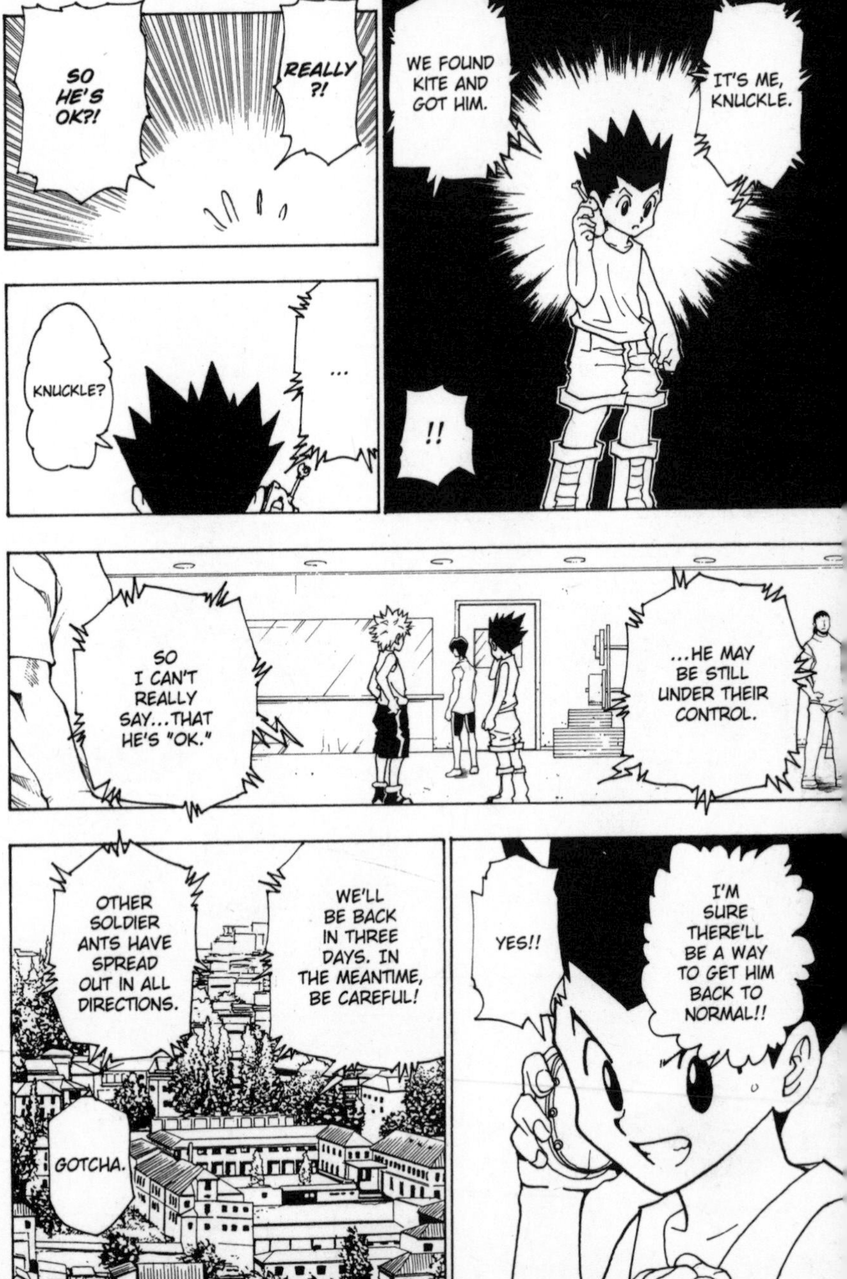
IT'S ME, KNUCKLE.
WE FOUND KITE AND GOT HIM.
!!
REALLY?!
SO HE'S OK?!
...
KNUCKLE?
...HE MAY BE STILL UNDER THEIR CONTROL.
SO I CAN'T REALLY SAY...THAT HE'S "OK."
I'M SURE THERE'LL BE A WAY TO GET HIM BACK TO NORMAL!!
YES!!
WE'LL BE BACK IN THREE DAYS. IN THE MEANTIME, BE CAREFUL!
OTHER SOLDIER ANTS HAVE SPREAD OUT IN ALL DIRECTIONS.
GOTCHA.

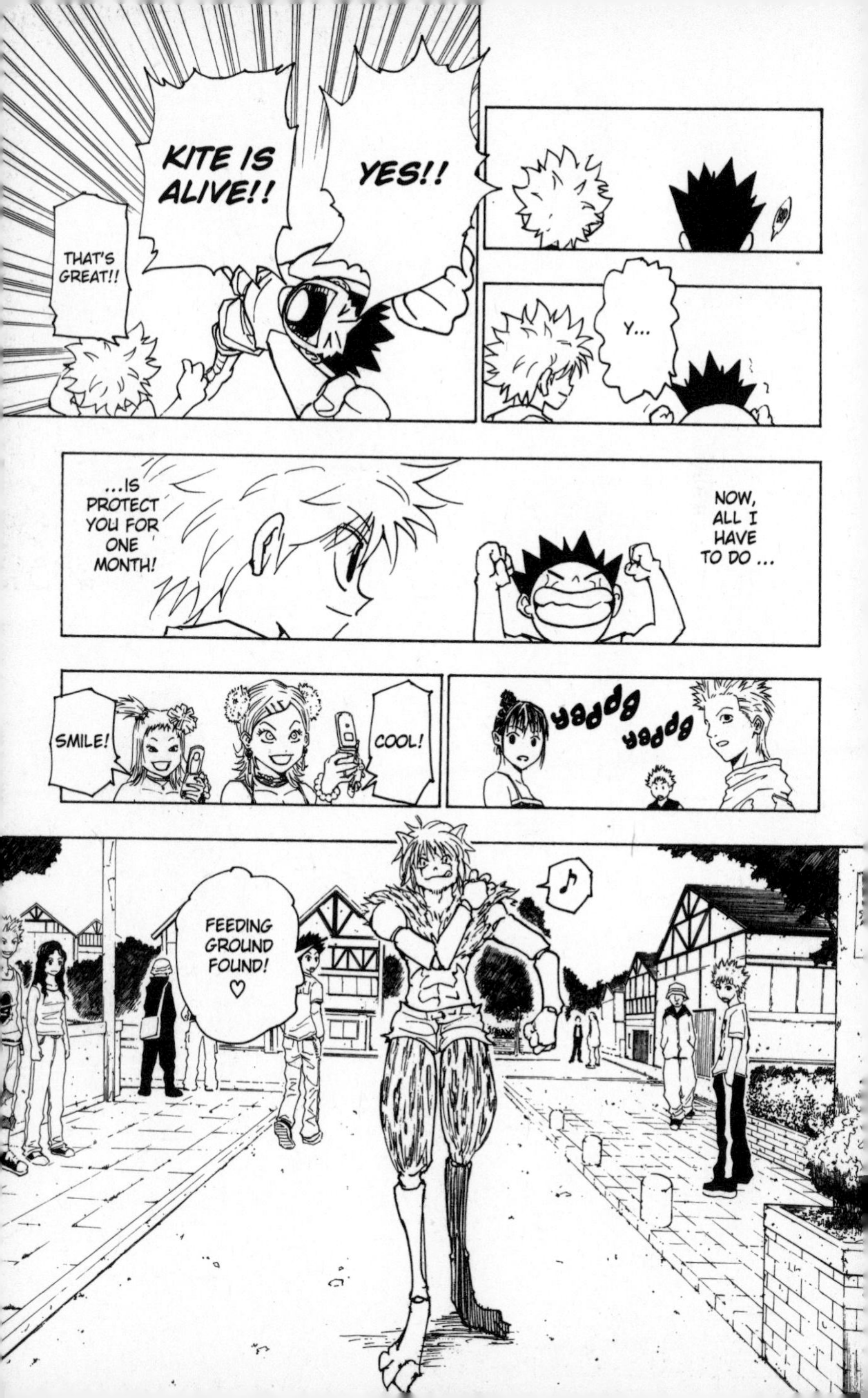
Y...
YES!!
KITE IS ALIVE!!
THAT'S GREAT!!
NOW, ALL I HAVE TO DO ...
...IS PROTECT YOU FOR ONE MONTH!
COOL!
SMILE!
♪
FEEDING GROUND FOUND! ♡

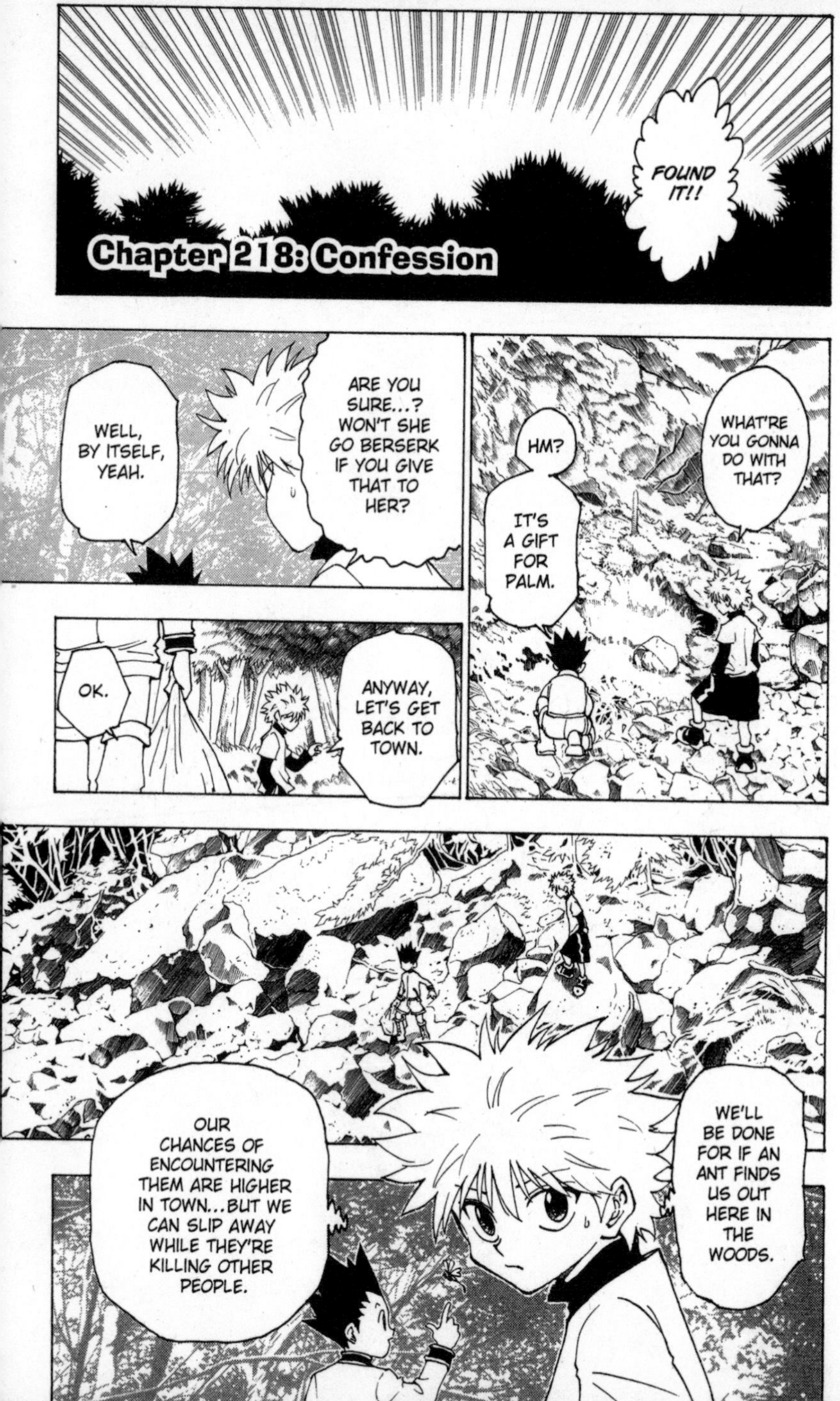
FOUND IT!!
Chapter 218: Confession
WHAT'RE YOU GONNA DO WITH THAT?
HM?
IT'S A GIFT FOR PALM.
ARE YOU SURE...? WON'T SHE GO BERSERK IF YOU GIVE THAT TO HER?
WELL, BY ITSELF, YEAH.
ANYWAY, LET'S GET BACK TO TOWN.
OK.
WE'LL BE DONE FOR IF AN ANT FINDS US OUT HERE IN THE WOODS.
OUR CHANCES OF ENCOUNTERING THEM ARE HIGHER IN TOWN...BUT WE CAN SLIP AWAY WHILE THEY'RE KILLING OTHER PEOPLE.

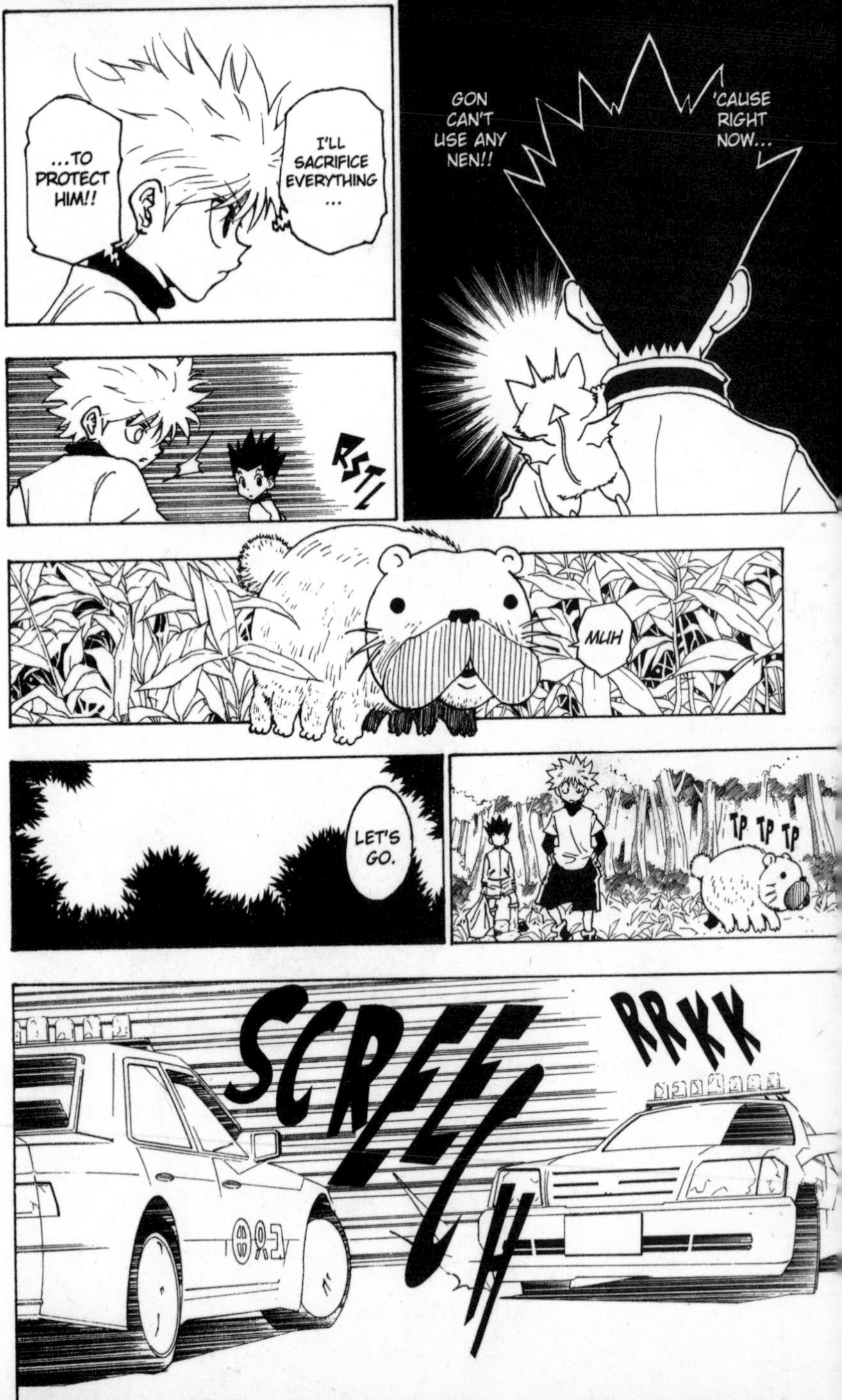
'CAUSE RIGHT NOW...
GON CAN'T USE ANY NEN!!
I'LL SACRIFICE EVERYTHING ...
...TO PROTECT HIM!!
RSTL
MUH
TP TP TP
LET'S GO.
RRKK
SCREECH

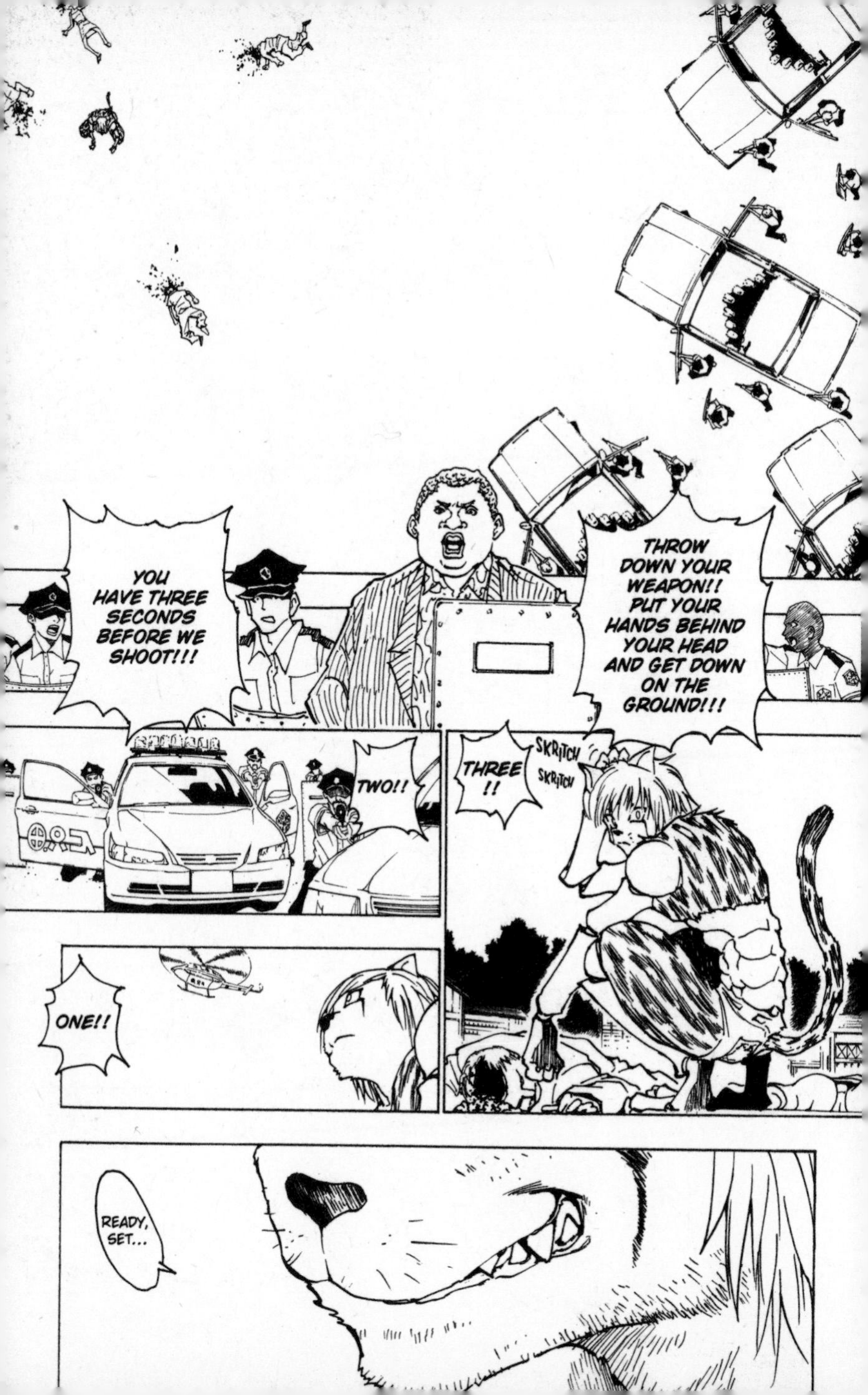
THROW DOWN YOUR WEAPON!! PUT YOUR HANDS BEHIND YOUR HEAD AND GET DOWN ON THE GROUND!!!
YOU HAVE THREE SECONDS BEFORE WE SHOOT!!!
SKRITCH
SKRITCH
THREE!!
TWO!!
ONE!!
READY, SET...

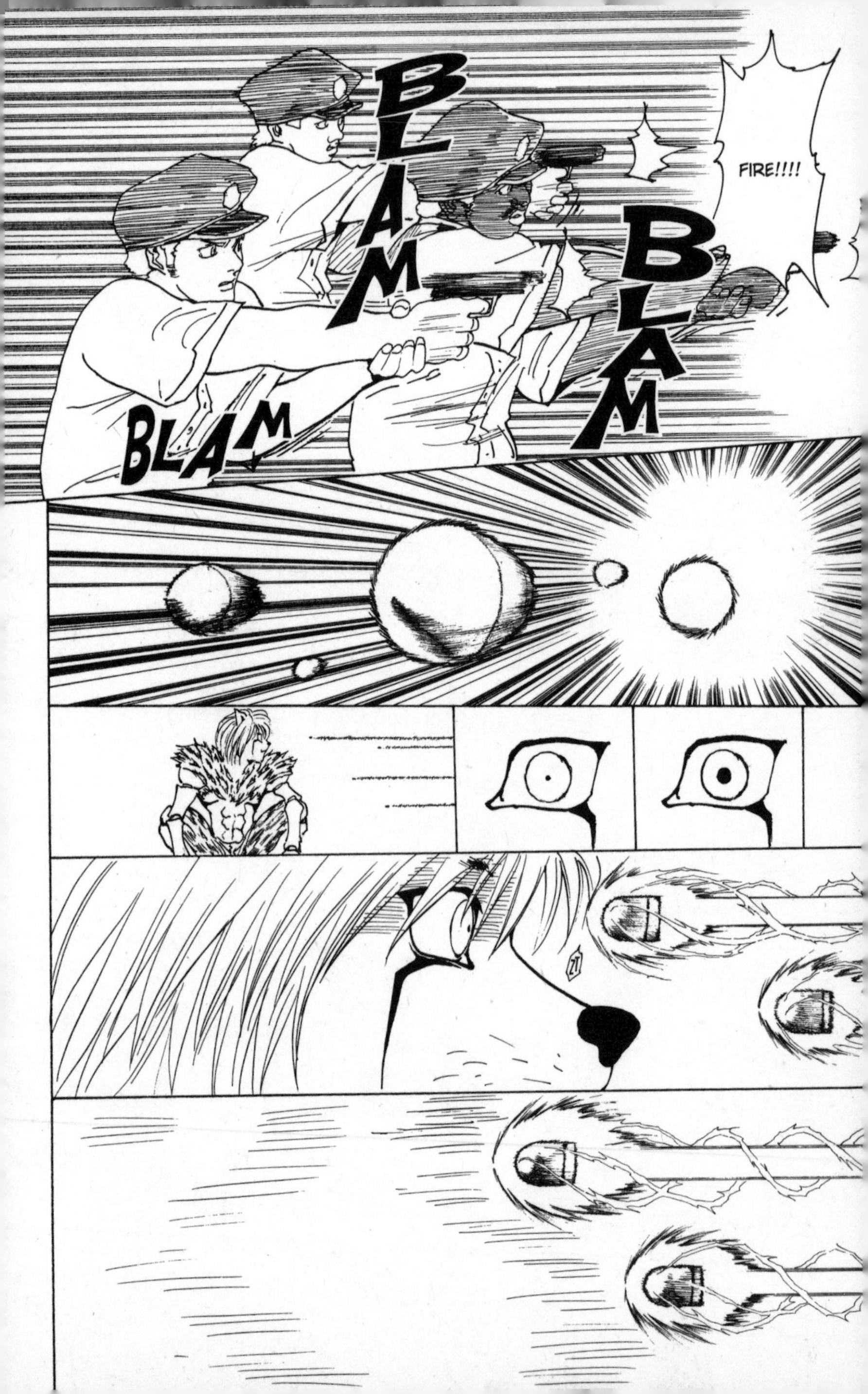
FIRE!!!!
BLAM
BLAM
BLAM

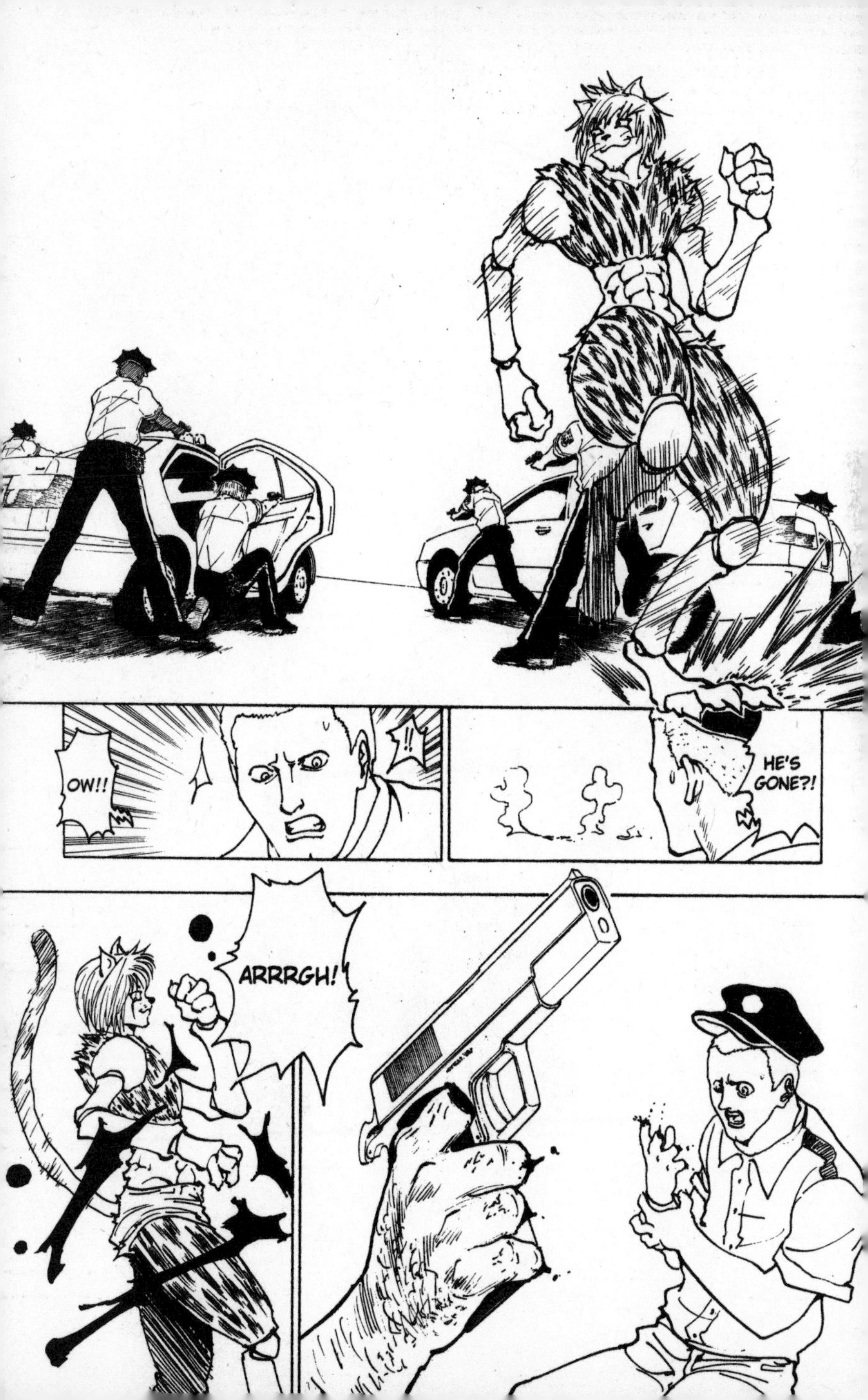
HE'S GONE?!
!!
OW!!
ARRRGH!

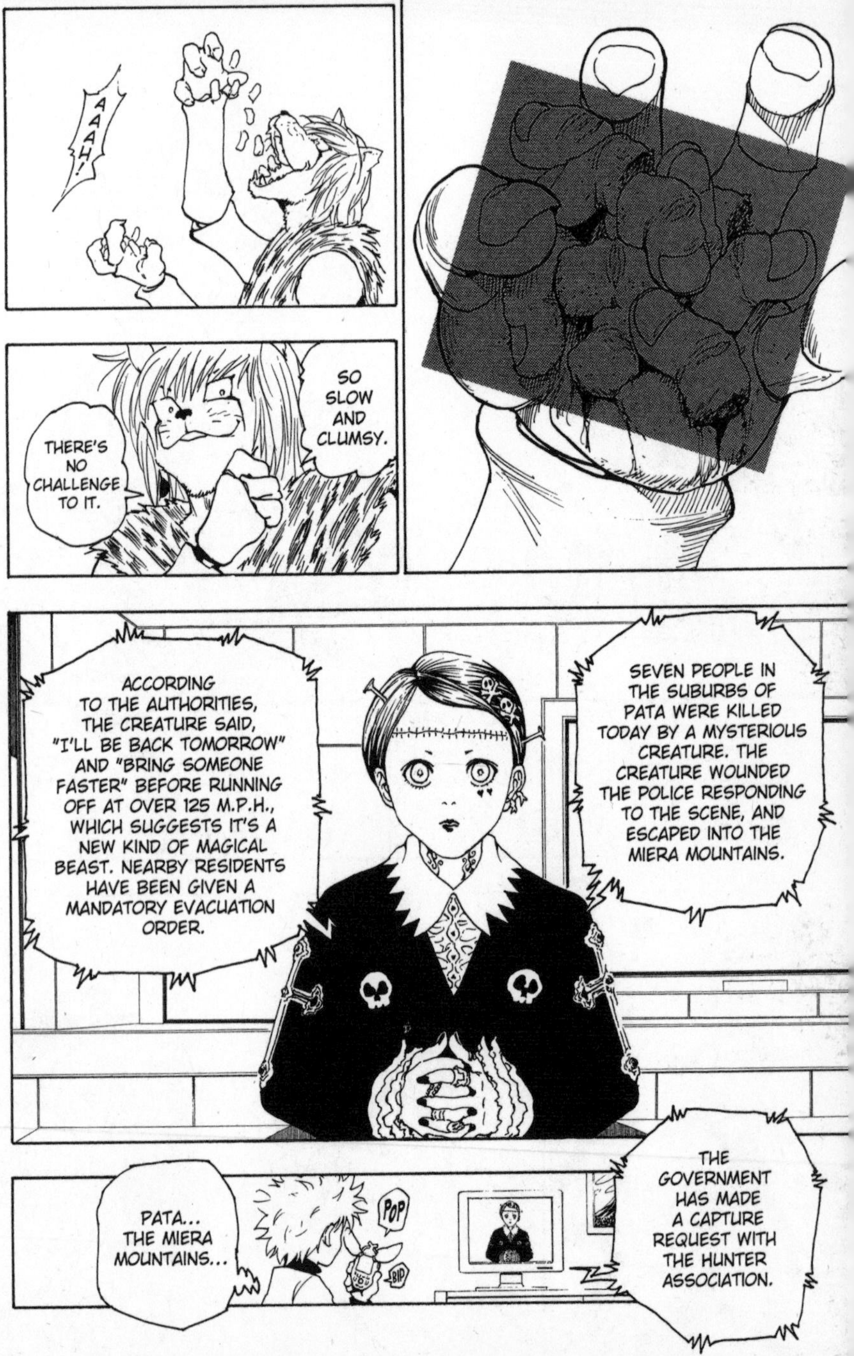
AAAH!
SO SLOW AND CLUMSY.
THERE'S NO CHALLENGE TO IT.
SEVEN PEOPLE IN THE SUBURBS OF PATA WERE KILLED TODAY BY A MYSTERIOUS CREATURE. THE CREATURE WOUNDED THE POLICE RESPONDING TO THE SCENE, AND ESCAPED INTO THE MIERA MOUNTAINS.
ACCORDING TO THE AUTHORITIES, THE CREATURE SAID, "I'LL BE BACK TOMORROW" AND "BRING SOMEONE FASTER" BEFORE RUNNING OFF AT OVER 125 M.P.H., WHICH SUGGESTS IT'S A NEW KIND OF MAGICAL BEAST. NEARBY RESIDENTS HAVE BEEN GIVEN A MANDATORY EVACUATION ORDER.
THE GOVERNMENT HAS MADE A CAPTURE REQUEST WITH THE HUNTER ASSOCIATION.
POP
BIP
PATA... THE MIERA MOUNTAINS...

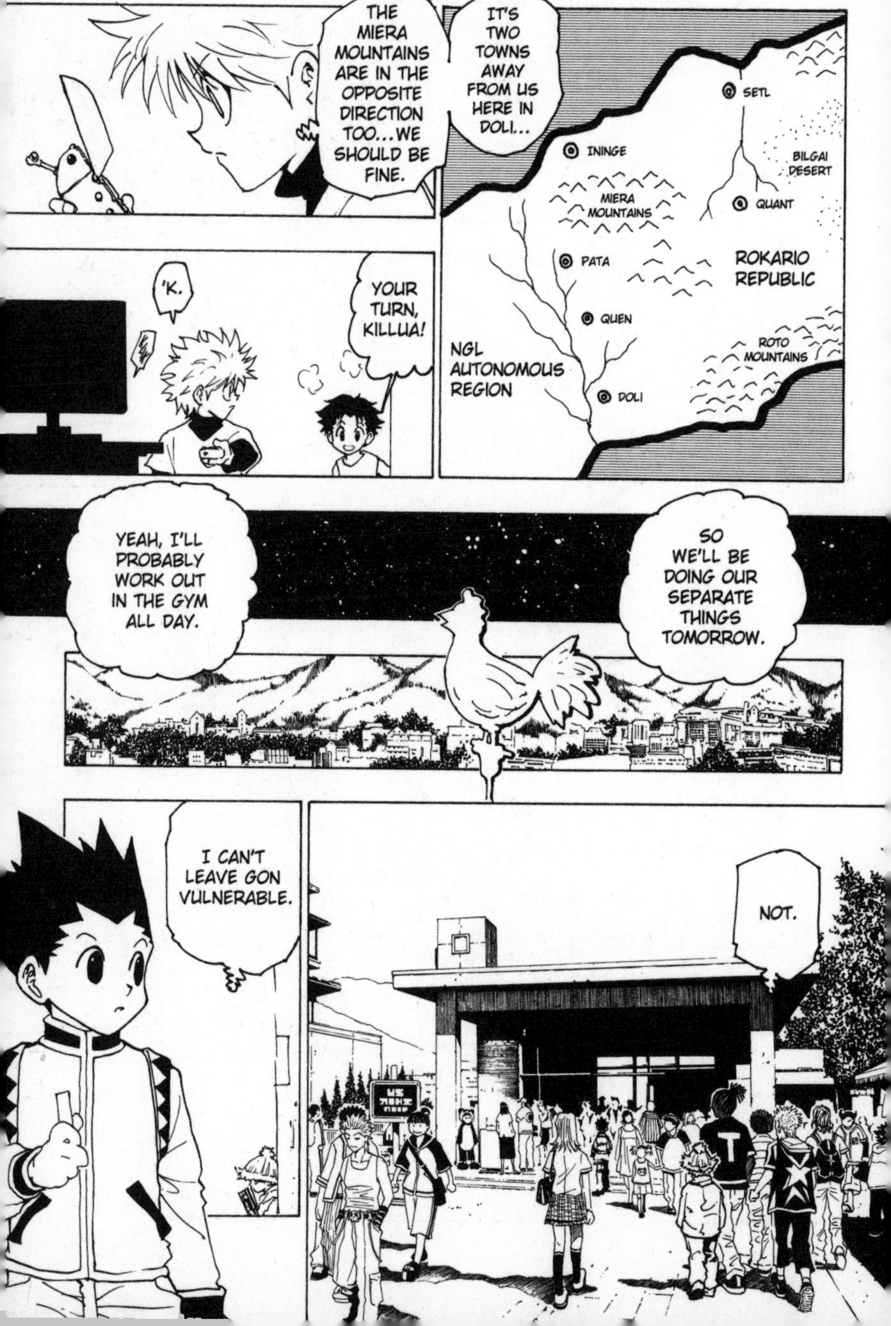
IT'S TWO TOWNS AWAY FROM US HERE IN DOLI...
SETL
ININGE
BILGAI DESERT
QUANT
MIERA MOUNTAINS
PATA
ROKARIO REPUBLIC
QUEN
ROTO MOUNTAINS
NGL AUTONOMOUS REGION
DOLI
THE MIERA MOUNTAINS ARE IN THE OPPOSITE DIRECTION TOO...WE SHOULD BE FINE.
YOUR TURN, KILLUA!
'K.
SO WE'LL BE DOING OUR SEPARATE THINGS TOMORROW.
YEAH, I'LL PROBABLY WORK OUT IN THE GYM ALL DAY.
NOT.
I CAN'T LEAVE GON VULNERABLE.

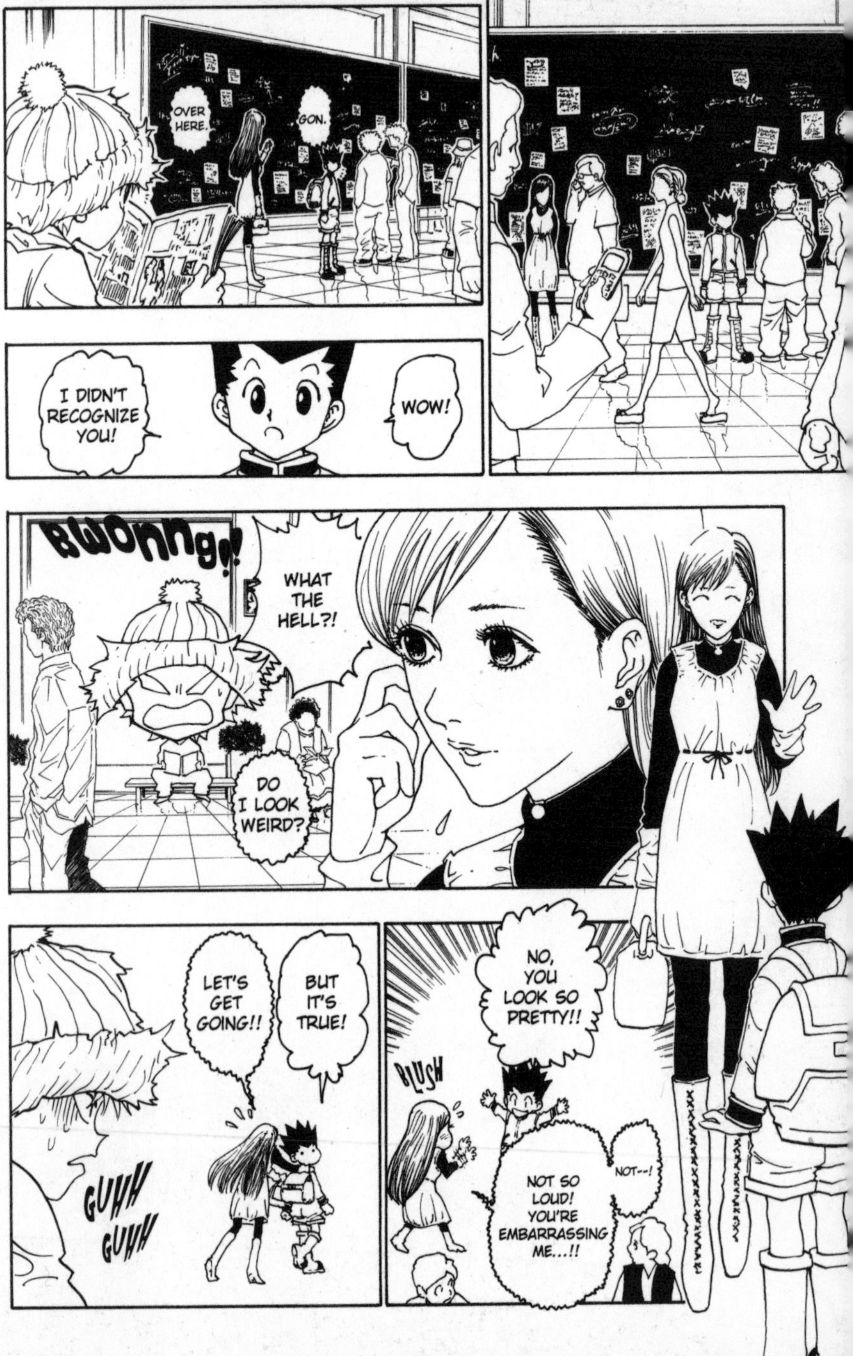
GON.
OVER HERE.
WOW!
I DIDN'T RECOGNIZE YOU!
WHAT THE HELL?!
BWONNG!!
DO I LOOK WEIRD?
NO, YOU LOOK SO PRETTY!!
BLUSH
NOT--!
NOT SO LOUD! YOU'RE EMBARRASSING ME...!!
BUT IT'S TRUE!
LET'S GET GOING!!
GUHH GUHH

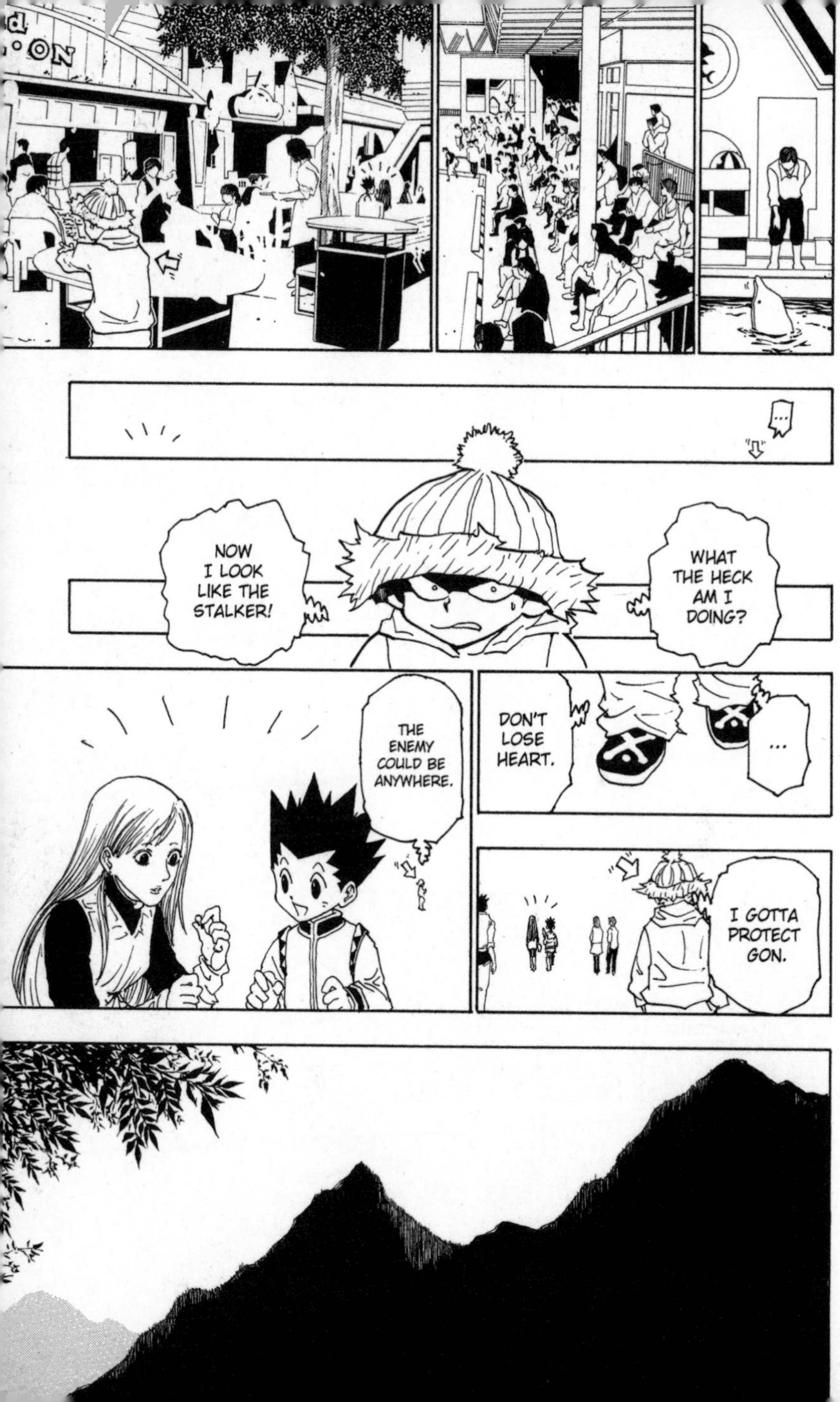
...
WHAT THE HECK AM I DOING?
NOW I LOOK LIKE THE STALKER!
...
DON'T LOSE HEART.
I GOTTA PROTECT GON.
THE ENEMY COULD BE ANYWHERE.

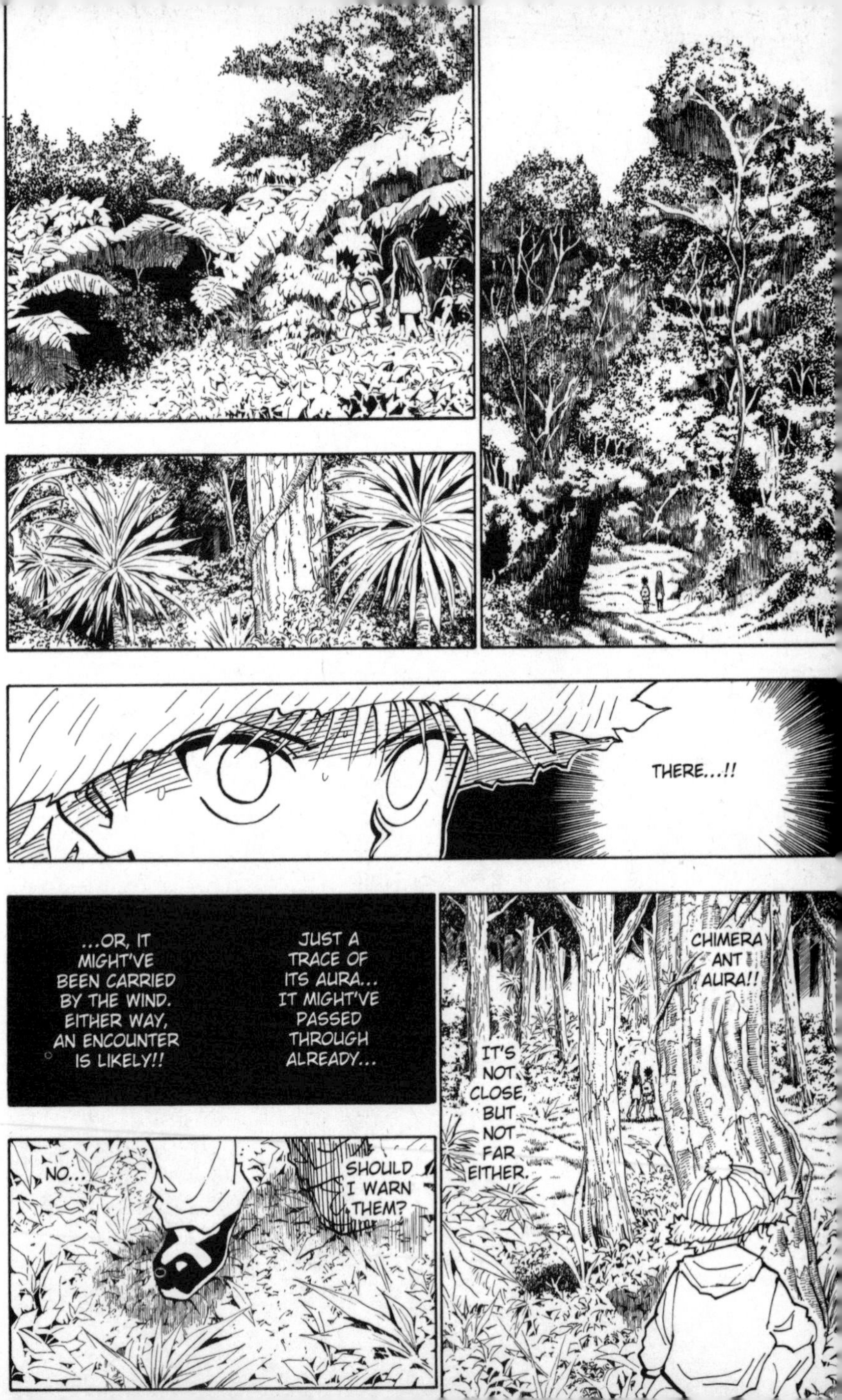
THERE...!!
CHIMERA ANT AURA!!
IT'S NOT CLOSE, BUT NOT FAR EITHER.
JUST A TRACE OF ITS AURA... IT MIGHT'VE PASSED THROUGH ALREADY...
...OR, IT MIGHT'VE BEEN CARRIED BY THE WIND. EITHER WAY, AN ENCOUNTER IS LIKELY!!
SHOULD I WARN THEM?
NO...

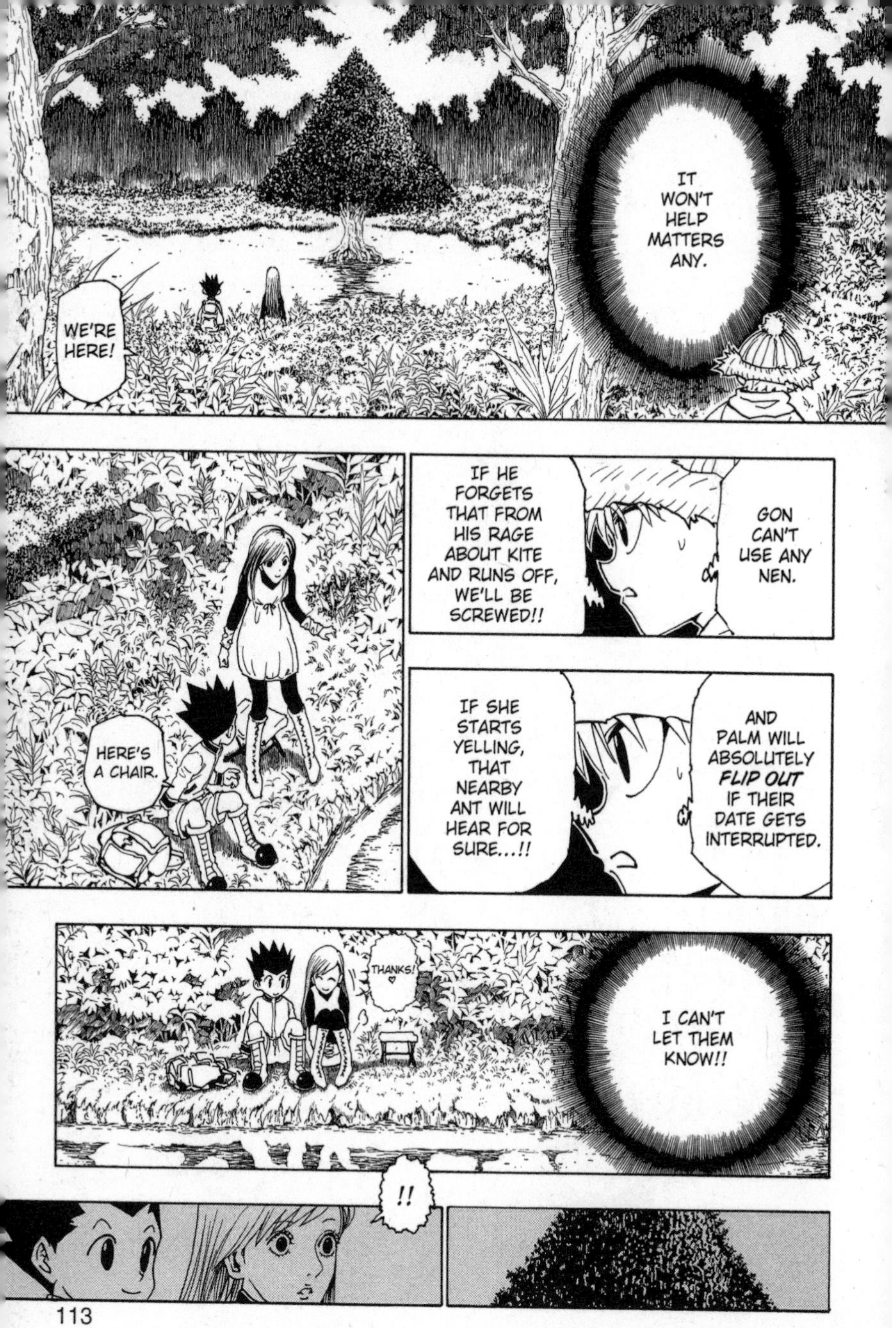
IT WON'T HELP MATTERS ANY.
WE'RE HERE!
GON CAN'T USE ANY NEN.
IF HE FORGETS THAT FROM HIS RAGE ABOUT KITE AND RUNS OFF, WE'LL BE SCREWED!!
AND PALM WILL ABSOLUTELY *FLIP OUT* IF THEIR DATE GETS INTERRUPTED.
IF SHE STARTS YELLING, THAT NEARBY ANT WILL HEAR FOR SURE...!!
HERE'S A CHAIR.
I CAN'T LET THEM KNOW!!
THANKS! ♥
!!

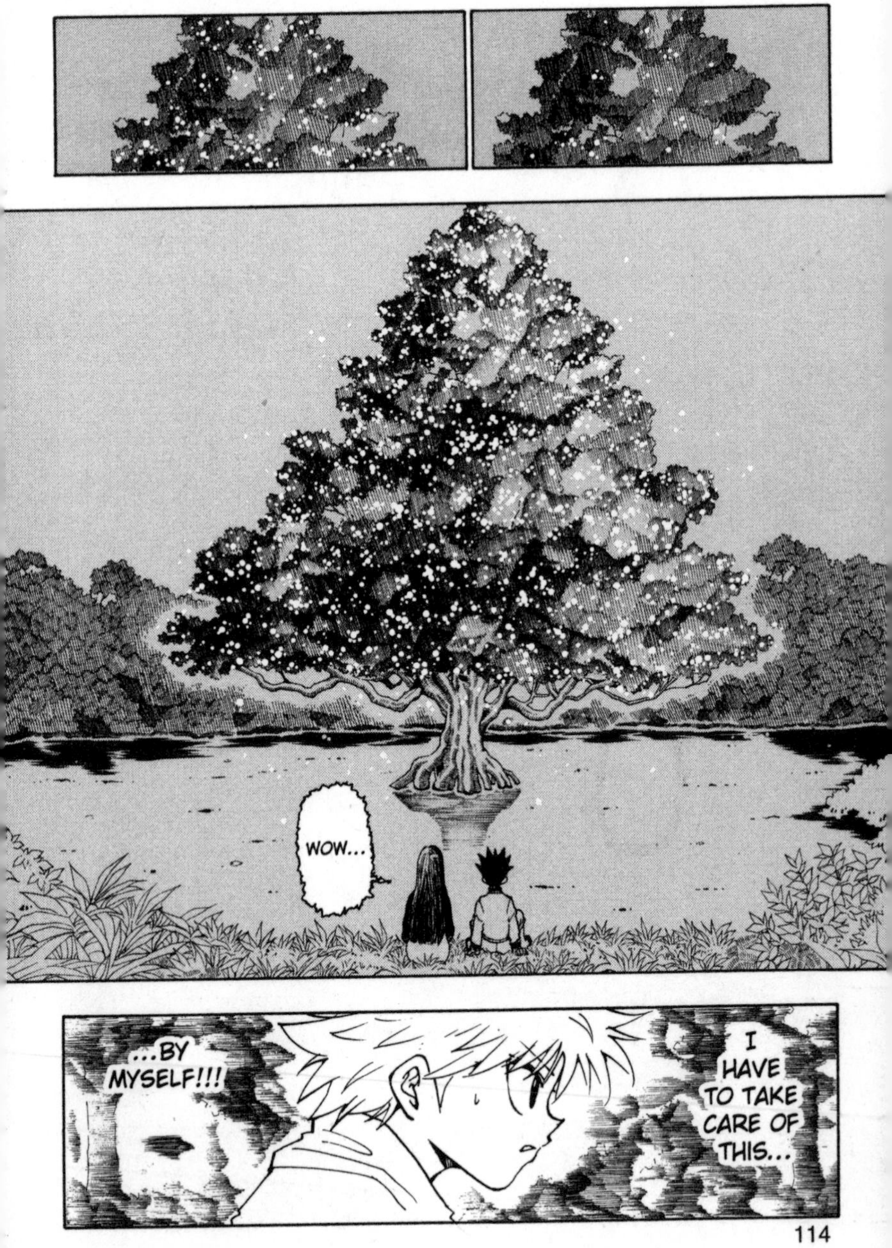
WOW...
I HAVE TO TAKE CARE OF THIS...
...BY MYSELF!!!

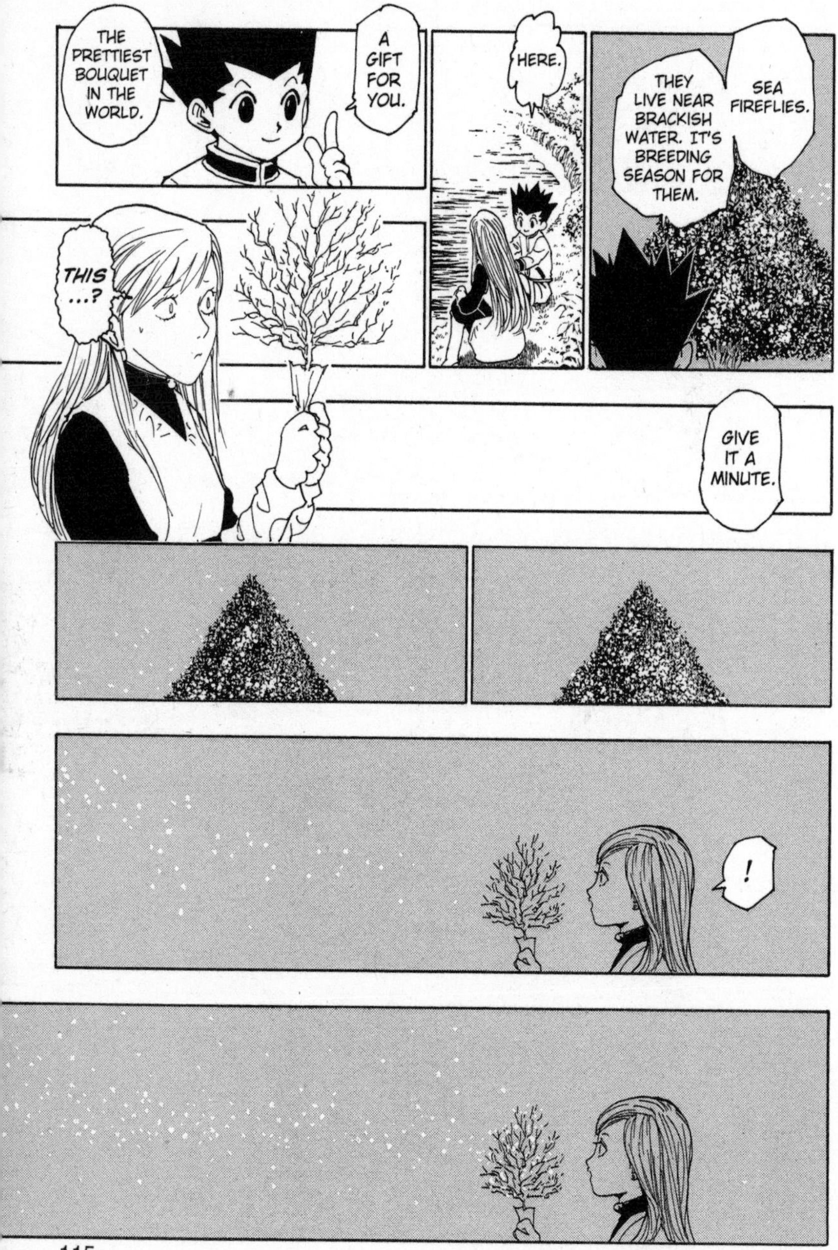
SEA FIREFLIES.
THEY LIVE NEAR BRACKISH WATER. IT'S BREEDING SEASON FOR THEM.
HERE.
A GIFT FOR YOU.
THE PRETTIEST BOUQUET IN THE WORLD.
THIS ...?
GIVE IT A MINUTE.
!

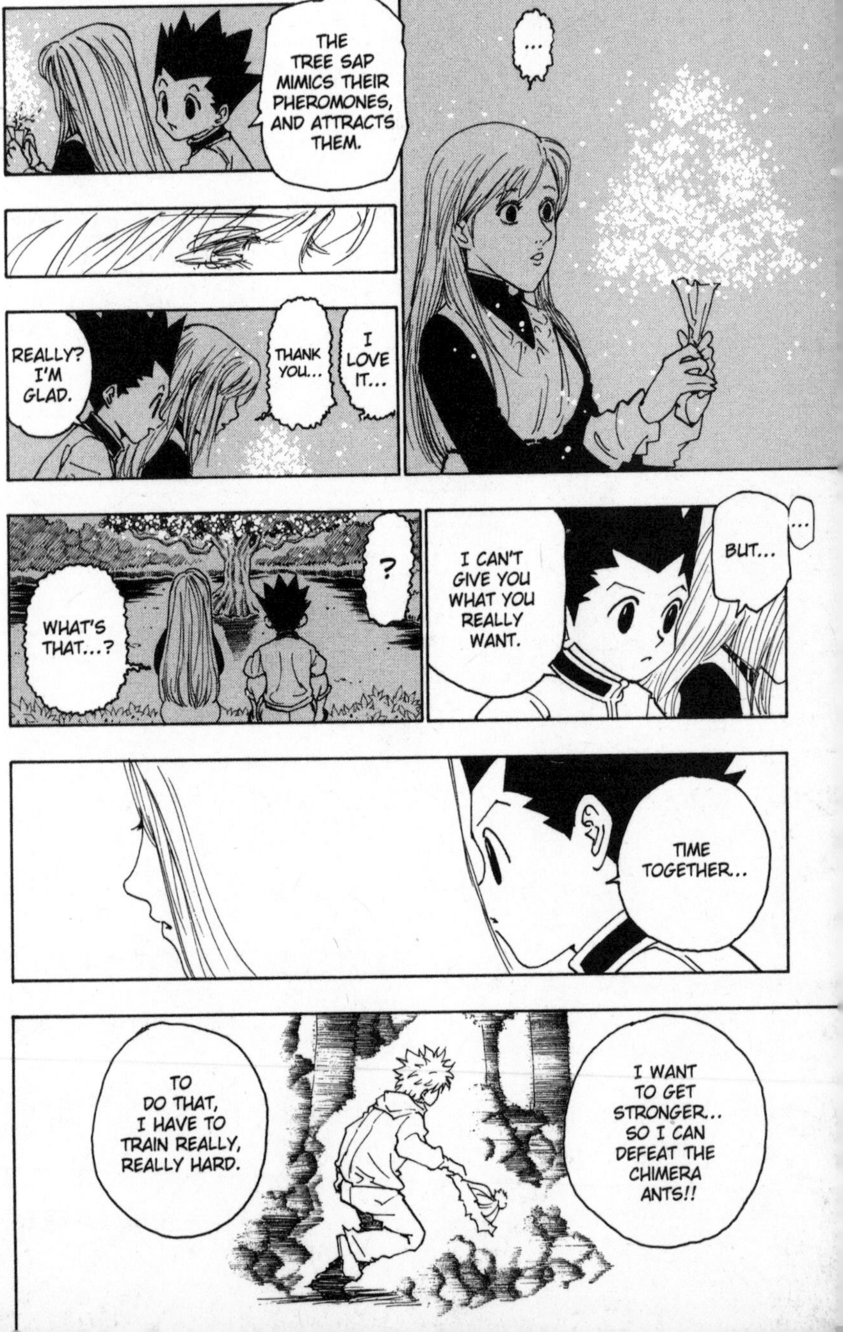
...
THE TREE SAP MIMICS THEIR PHEROMONES, AND ATTRACTS THEM.
I LOVE IT...
THANK YOU...
REALLY? I'M GLAD.
...
BUT...
I CAN'T GIVE YOU WHAT YOU REALLY WANT.
?
WHAT'S THAT...?
TIME TOGETHER...
I WANT TO GET STRONGER... SO I CAN DEFEAT THE CHIMERA ANTS!!
TO DO THAT, I HAVE TO TRAIN REALLY, REALLY HARD.

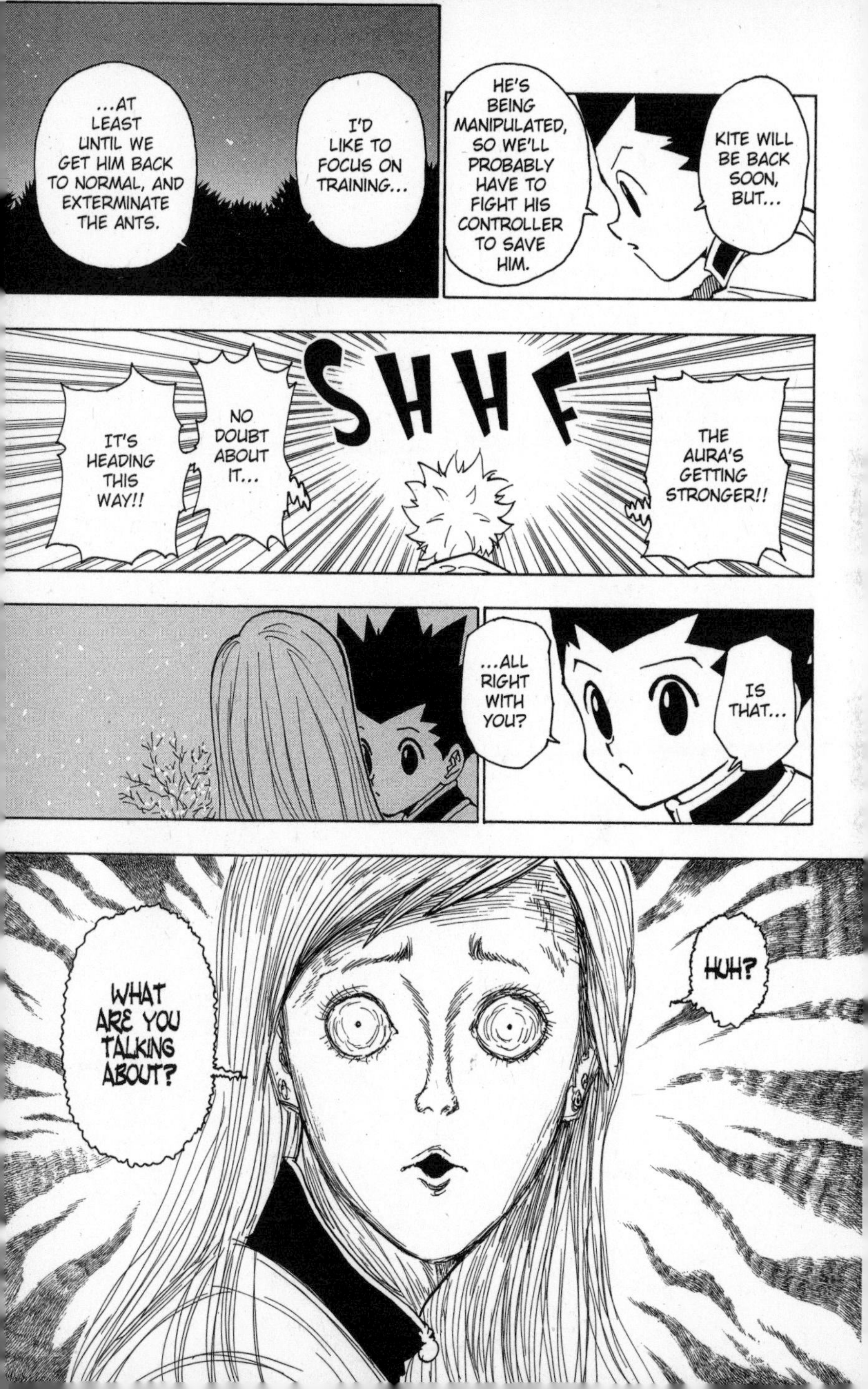
KITE WILL BE BACK SOON, BUT...
HE'S BEING MANIPULATED, SO WE'LL PROBABLY HAVE TO FIGHT HIS CONTROLLER TO SAVE HIM.
I'D LIKE TO FOCUS ON TRAINING...
...AT LEAST UNTIL WE GET HIM BACK TO NORMAL, AND EXTERMINATE THE ANTS.
THE AURA'S GETTING STRONGER!!
SHHF
NO DOUBT ABOUT IT...
IT'S HEADING THIS WAY!!
IS THAT...
...ALL RIGHT WITH YOU?
HUH?
WHAT ARE YOU TALKING ABOUT?

SKRITCH
SKRITCH

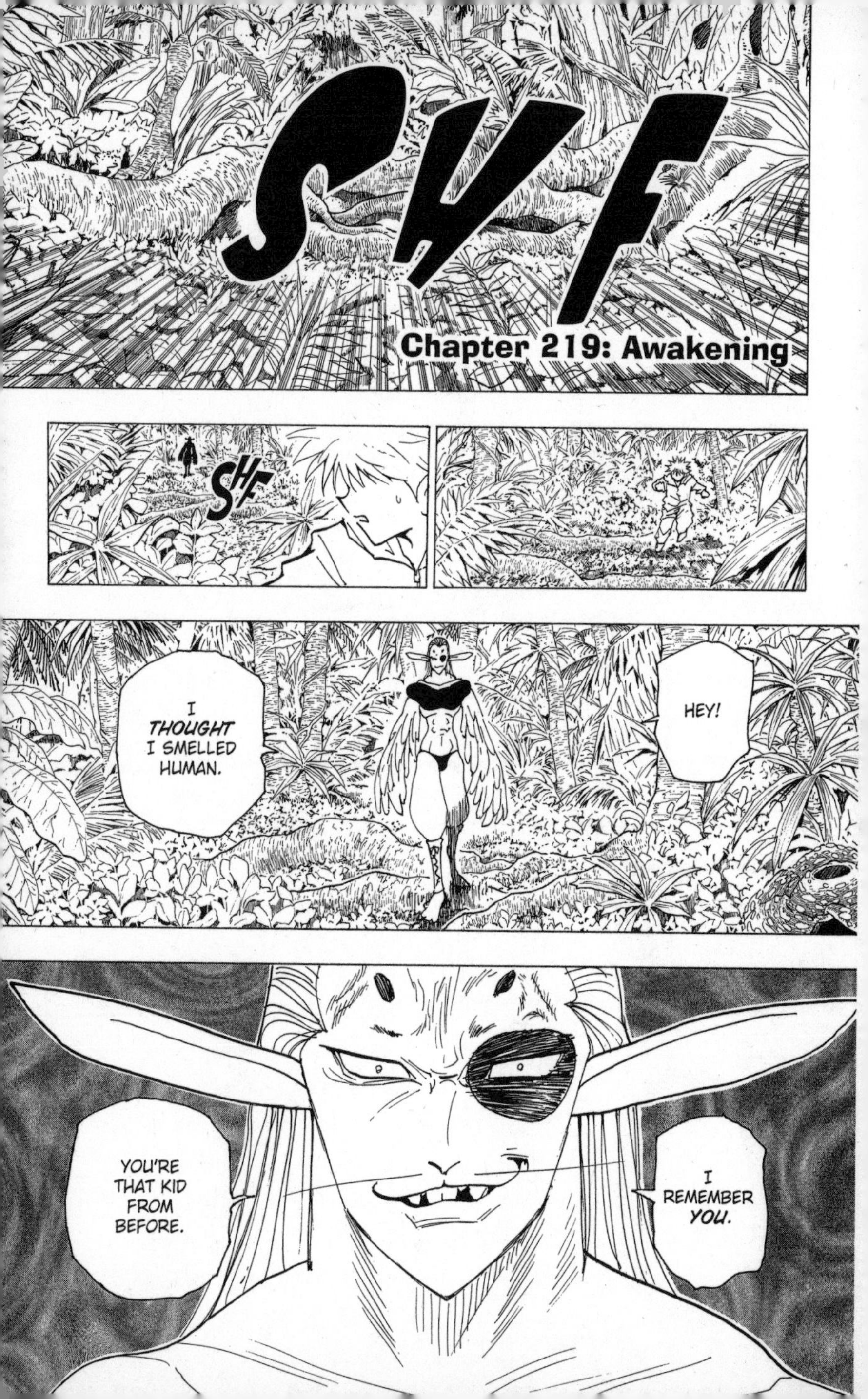
SVF
Chapter 219: Awakening
SHF
HEY!
I THOUGHT I SMELLED HUMAN.
I REMEMBER YOU.
YOU'RE THAT KID FROM BEFORE.

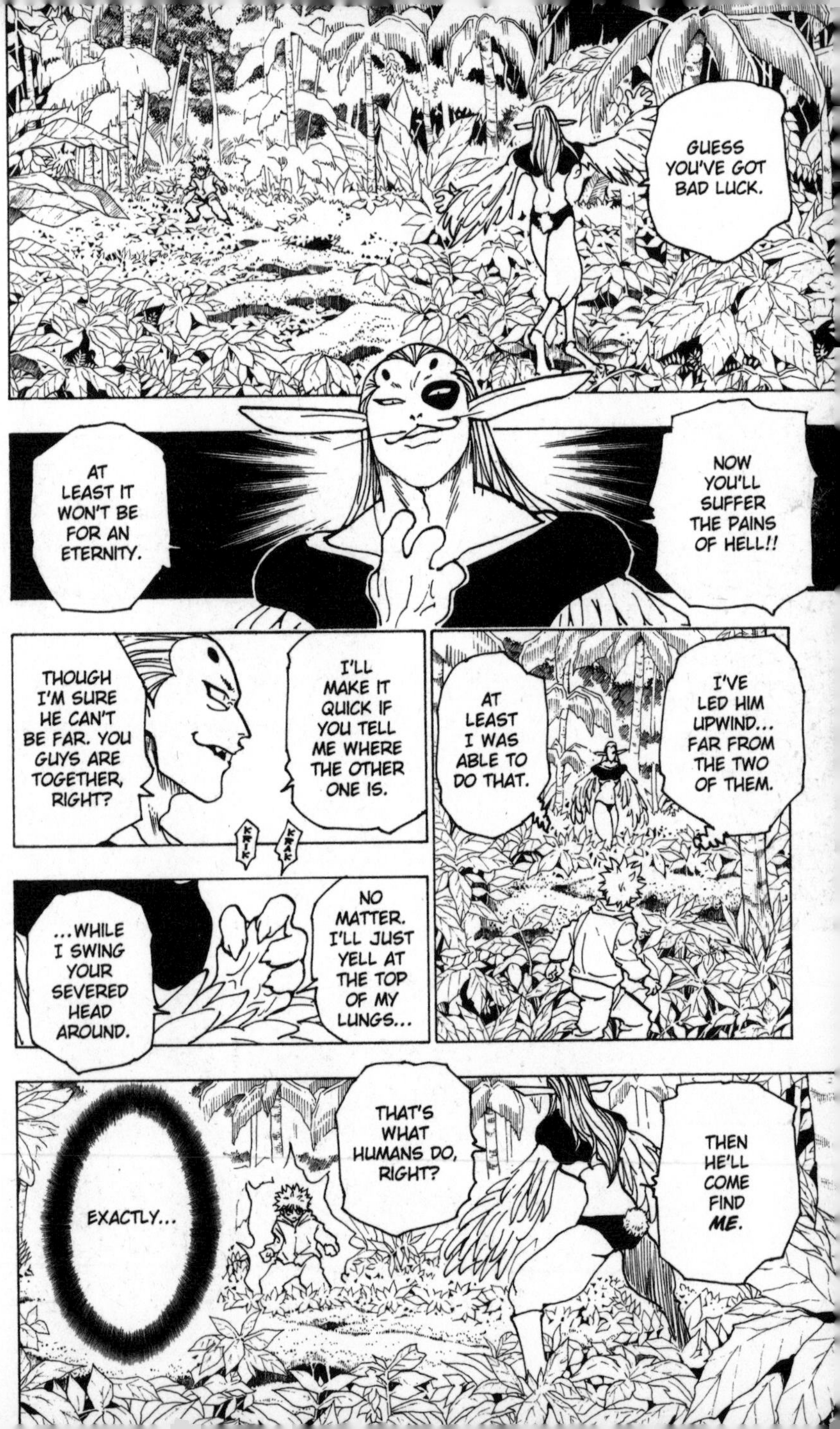
GUESS YOU'VE GOT BAD LUCK.
NOW YOU'LL SUFFER THE PAINS OF HELL!!
AT LEAST IT WON'T BE FOR AN ETERNITY.
I'VE LED HIM UPWIND... FAR FROM THE TWO OF THEM.
AT LEAST I WAS ABLE TO DO THAT.
I'LL MAKE IT QUICK IF YOU TELL ME WHERE THE OTHER ONE IS.
THOUGH I'M SURE HE CAN'T BE FAR. YOU GUYS ARE TOGETHER, RIGHT?
KRAK
KRIK
NO MATTER. I'LL JUST YELL AT THE TOP OF MY LUNGS...
...WHILE I SWING YOUR SEVERED HEAD AROUND.
THEN HE'LL COME FIND *ME*.
THAT'S WHAT HUMANS DO, RIGHT?
EXACTLY...

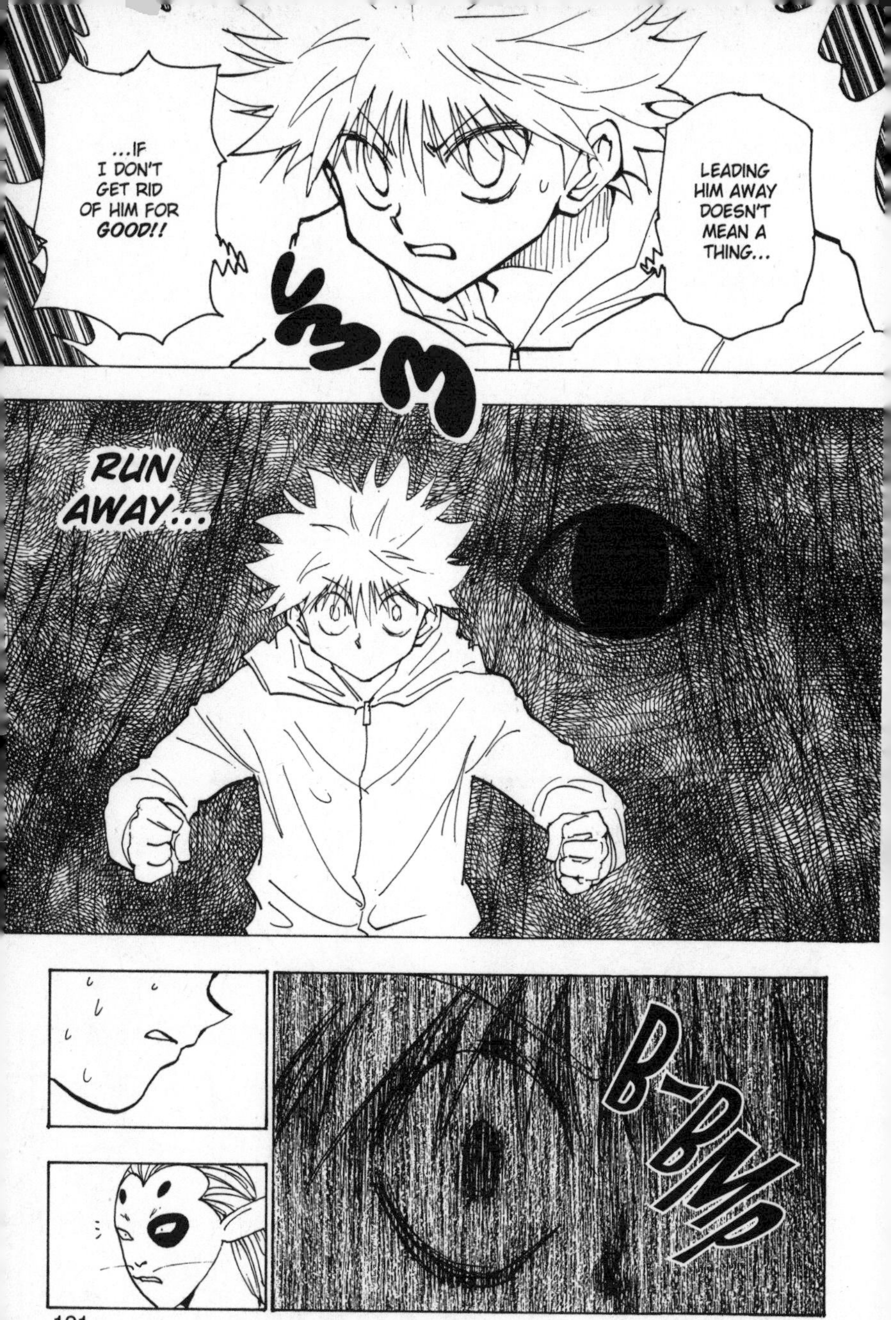

LEADING HIM AWAY DOESN'T MEAN A THING...
...IF I DON'T GET RID OF HIM FOR GOOD!!
UMM
RUN AWAY...
B-BMP

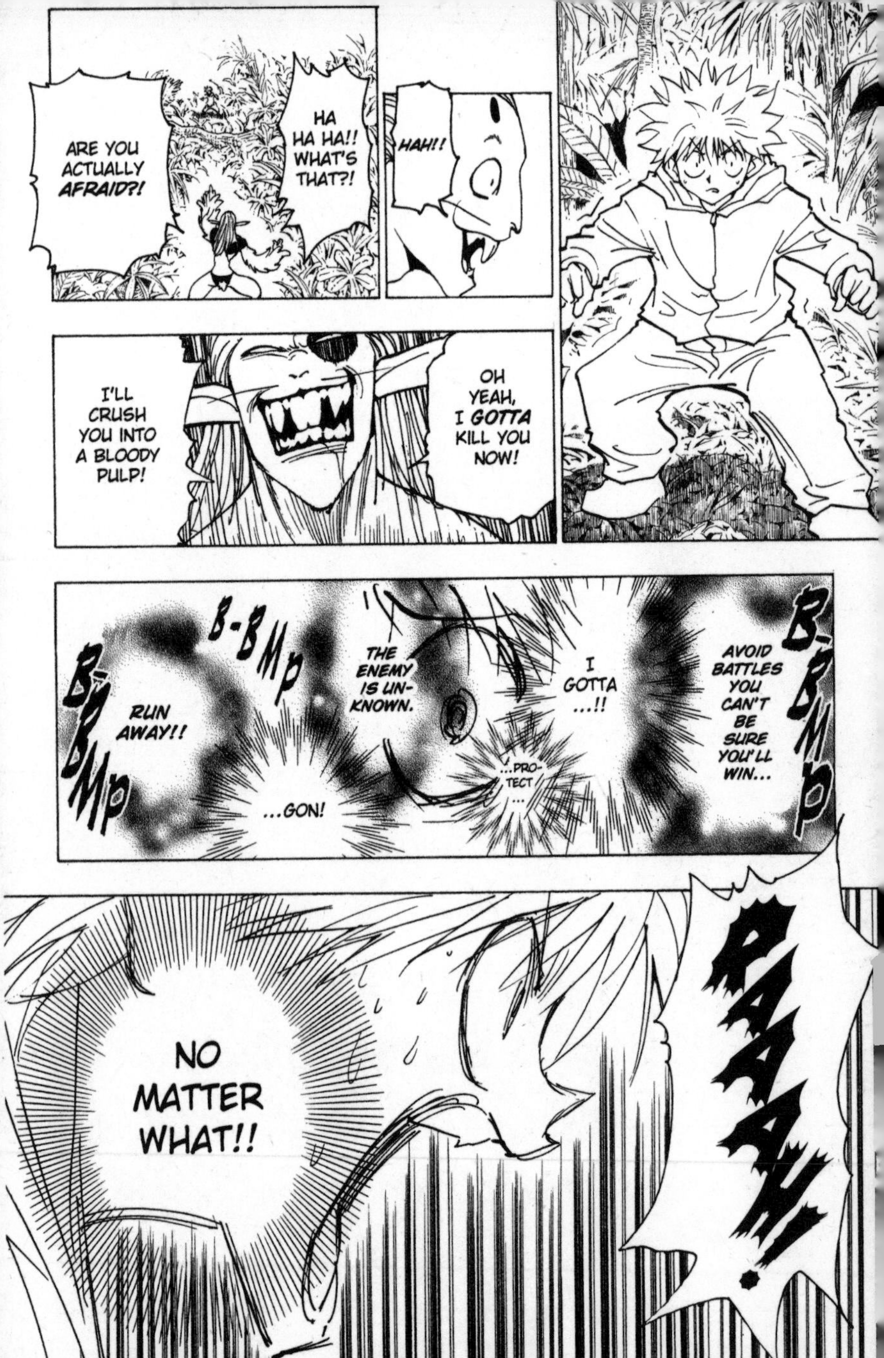
HAH!!
HA HA HA!! WHAT'S THAT?!
ARE YOU ACTUALLY AFRAID?!
OH YEAH, I GOTTA KILL YOU NOW!
I'LL CRUSH YOU INTO A BLOODY PULP!
B-BMP
AVOID BATTLES YOU CAN'T BE SURE YOU'LL WIN...
I GOTTA ...!!
...PRO-TECT...
THE ENEMY IS UN-KNOWN.
B-BMP
...GON!
RUN AWAY!!
B-BMP
RAAAH!!
NO MATTER WHAT!!

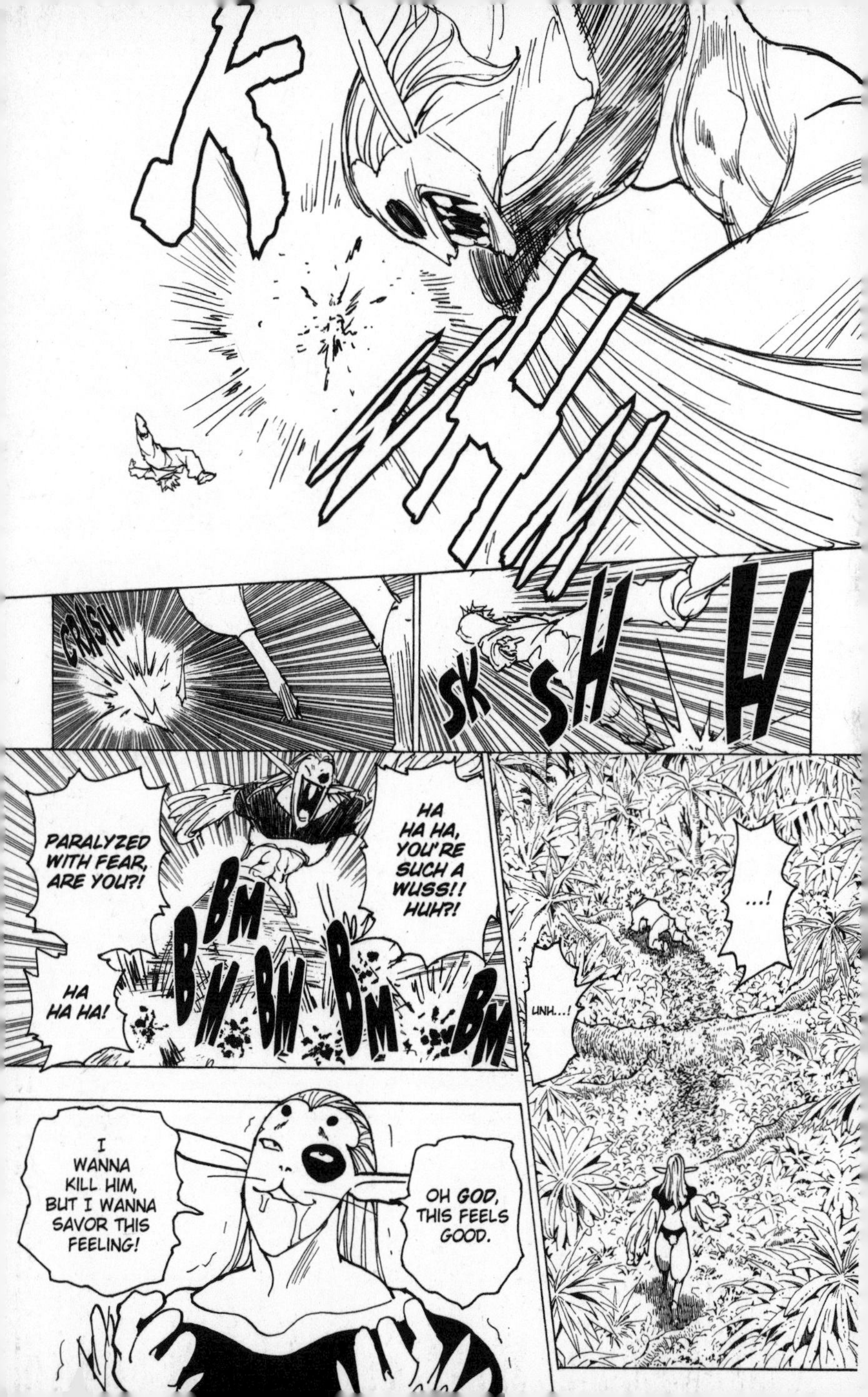
CRASH
...!
UNH...!
HA HA HA, YOU'RE SUCH A WUSS!! HUH?!
PARALYZED WITH FEAR, ARE YOU?!
HA HA HA!
BM BM BM BM BM BM
OH GOD, THIS FEELS GOOD.
I WANNA KILL HIM, BUT I WANNA SAVOR THIS FEELING!

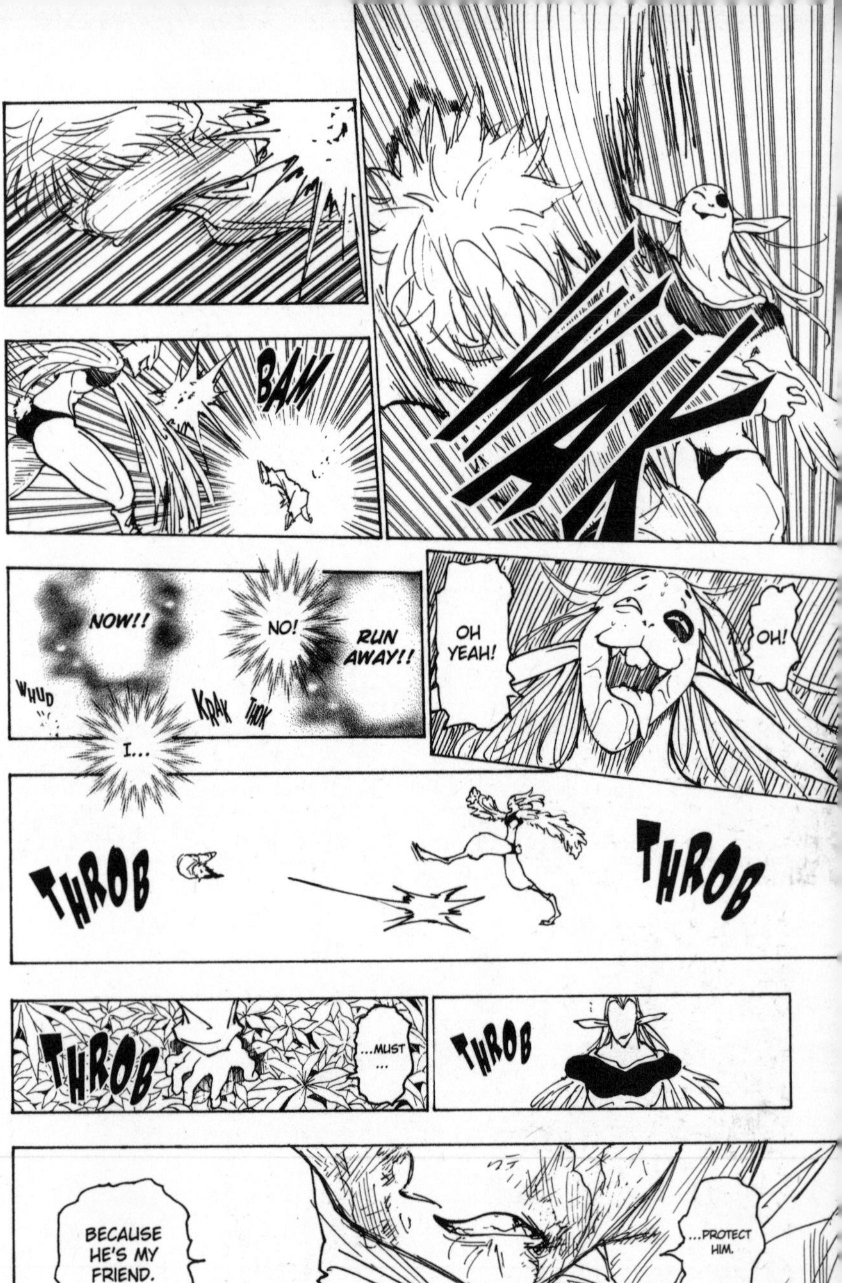
WAK
BAM
OH!
OH YEAH!
RUN AWAY!!
NO!
NOW!!
THOK
KRAK
WHUD
I...
THROB
THROB
THROB
...MUST ...
THROB
...PROTECT HIM.
BECAUSE HE'S MY FRIEND.

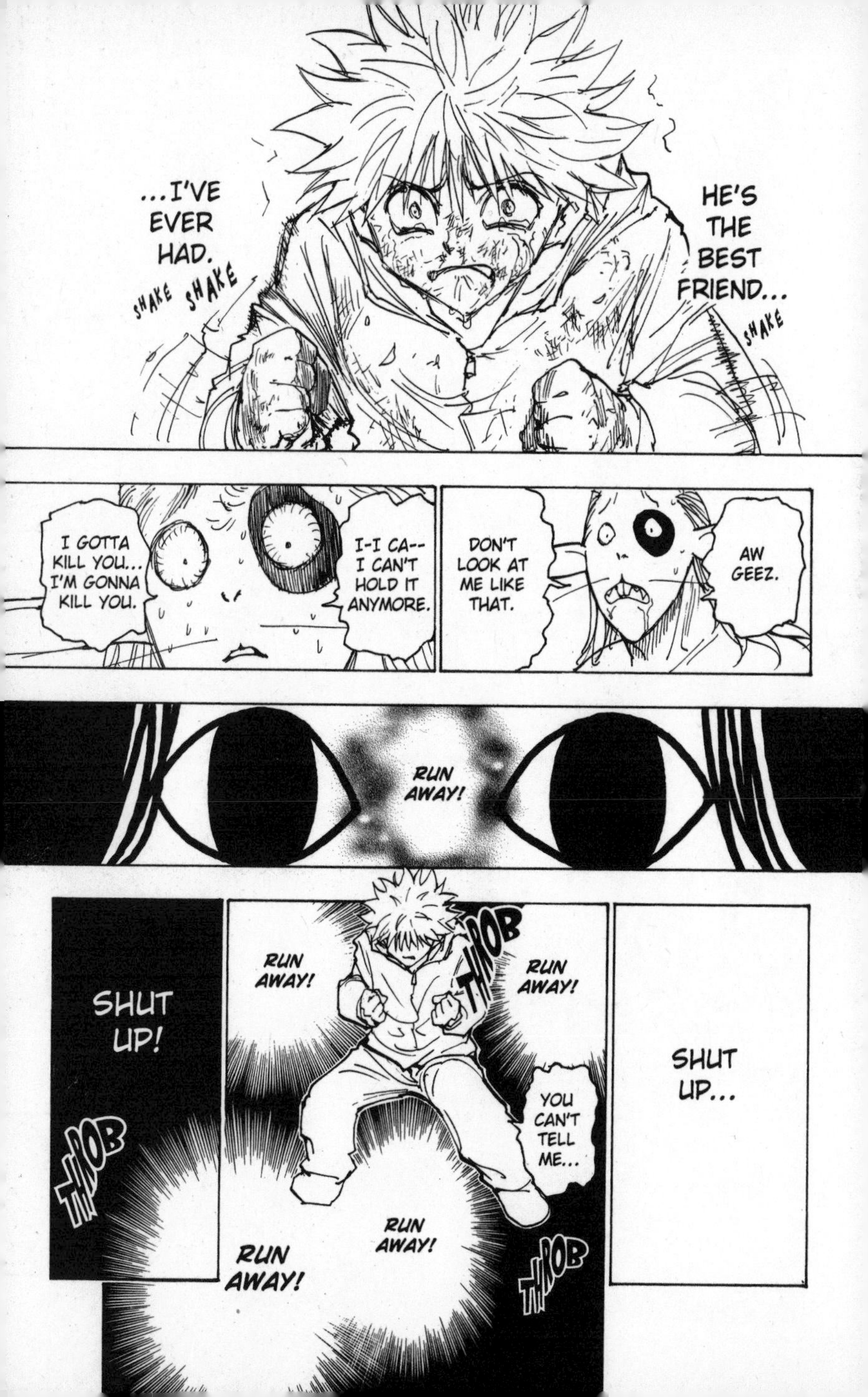
HE'S THE BEST FRIEND...
SHAKE
...I'VE EVER HAD.
SHAKE SHAKE
AW GEEZ.
DON'T LOOK AT ME LIKE THAT.
I-I CA-- I CAN'T HOLD IT ANYMORE.
I GOTTA KILL YOU... I'M GONNA KILL YOU.
RUN AWAY!
SHUT UP...
THROB
RUN AWAY!
RUN AWAY!
YOU CAN'T TELL ME...
RUN AWAY!
THROB
RUN AWAY!
SHUT UP!
THROB

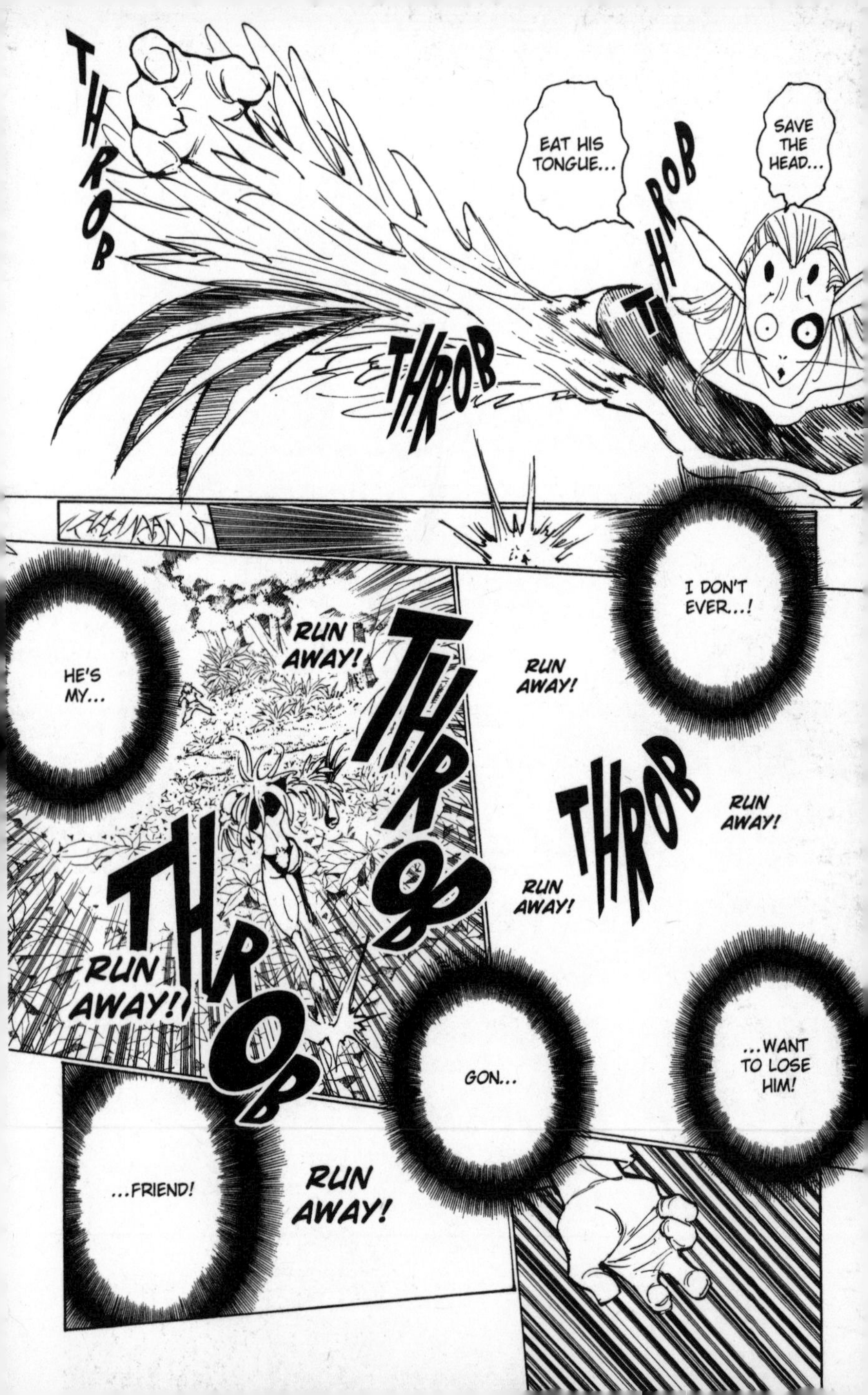
SAVE THE HEAD...
THROB
EAT HIS TONGUE...
THROB
THROB
I DON'T EVER...!
RUN AWAY!
RUN AWAY!
THROB
RUN AWAY!
RUN AWAY!
THROB
HE'S MY...
THROB
RUN AWAY!
...WANT TO LOSE HIM!
GON...
RUN AWAY!
...FRIEND!

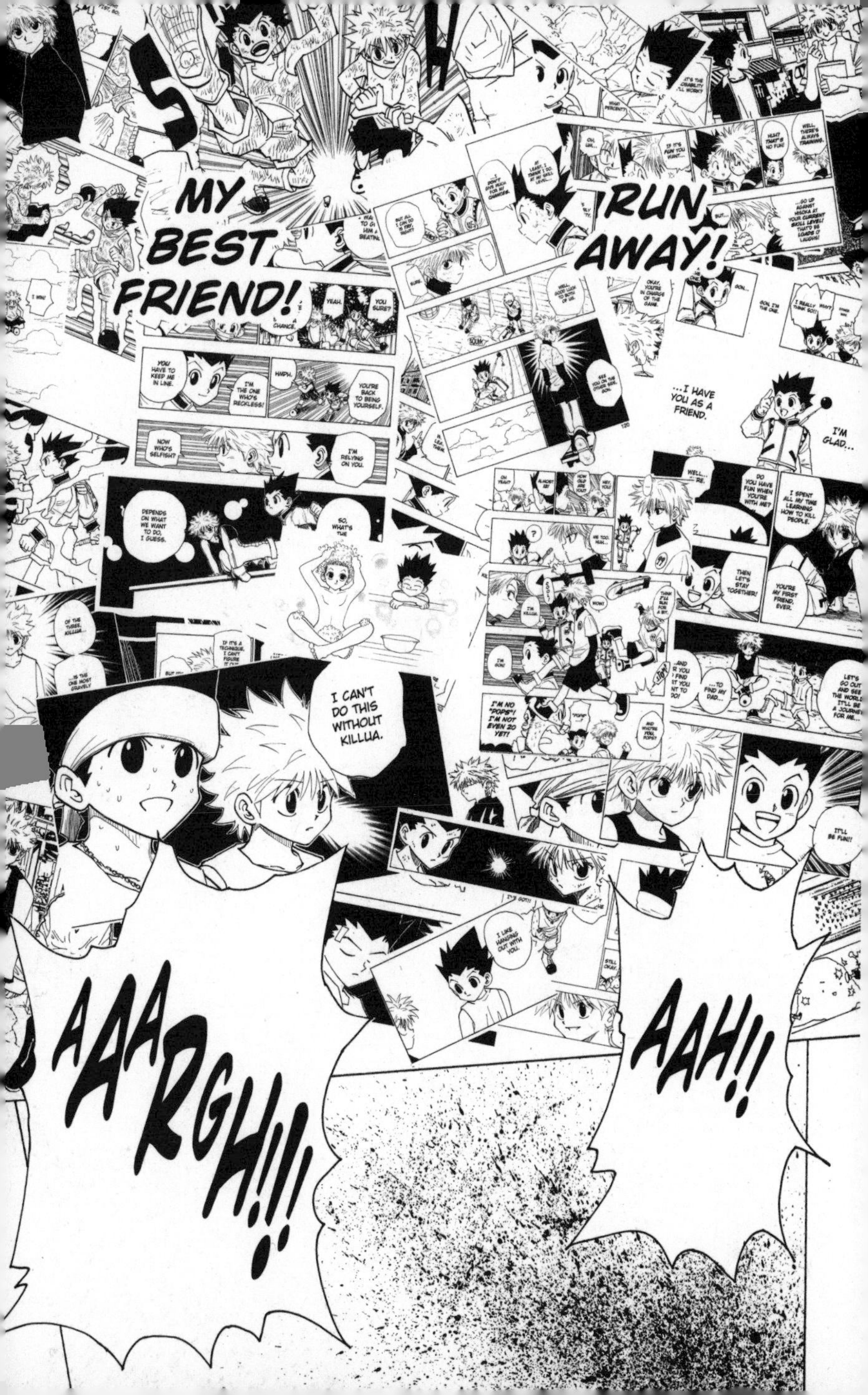
WELL, THERE'S ALWAYS TRAINING.
HUH? THAT'S NO FUN!
IF IT'S FUN YOU WANT...
...GO UP AGAINST HISOKA AT YOUR CURRENT SKILL LEVEL! THAT'D BE LOADS O' LAUGHS!
RUN AWAY!
MY BEST FRIEND!
OKAY. YOU'RE IN CHARGE OF THE GAME.
WELL, GOOD LUCK TO BOTH OF US.
YOU SURE?
YEAH.
YOU'RE BACK TO BEING YOURSELF.
HMPH.
I'M THE ONE WHO'S RECKLESS!
YOU! HAVE TO KEEP ME IN LINE.
I'M RELYING ON YOU.
NOW WHO'S SELFISH?
...I HAVE YOU AS A FRIEND.
I'M GLAD...
I SPENT ALL MY TIME LEARNING HOW TO KILL PEOPLE.
DO YOU HAVE FUN WHEN YOU'RE WITH ME?
YOU'RE MY FIRST FRIEND. EVER.
THEN LET'S STAY TOGETHER!
SO, WHAT'S THE
DEPENDS ON WHAT WE WANT TO DO, I GUESS.
OF THE THREE, KILLUA...
...IS THE ONE MOST GRAVELY
IF IT'S A TECHNIQUE, I CAN'T FIGURE
LET'S GO OUT AND SEE THE WORLD. IT'LL BE A JOURNEY FOR ME...
...TO FIND MY DAD...
AND WHO'RE YOU, POPS?
I'M NO "POPS"! I'M NOT EVEN 20 YET!
I CAN'T DO THIS WITHOUT KILLUA.
IT'LL BE FUN!!
I LIKE HANGING OUT WITH YOU.
AAH!!
AAARGH!!!

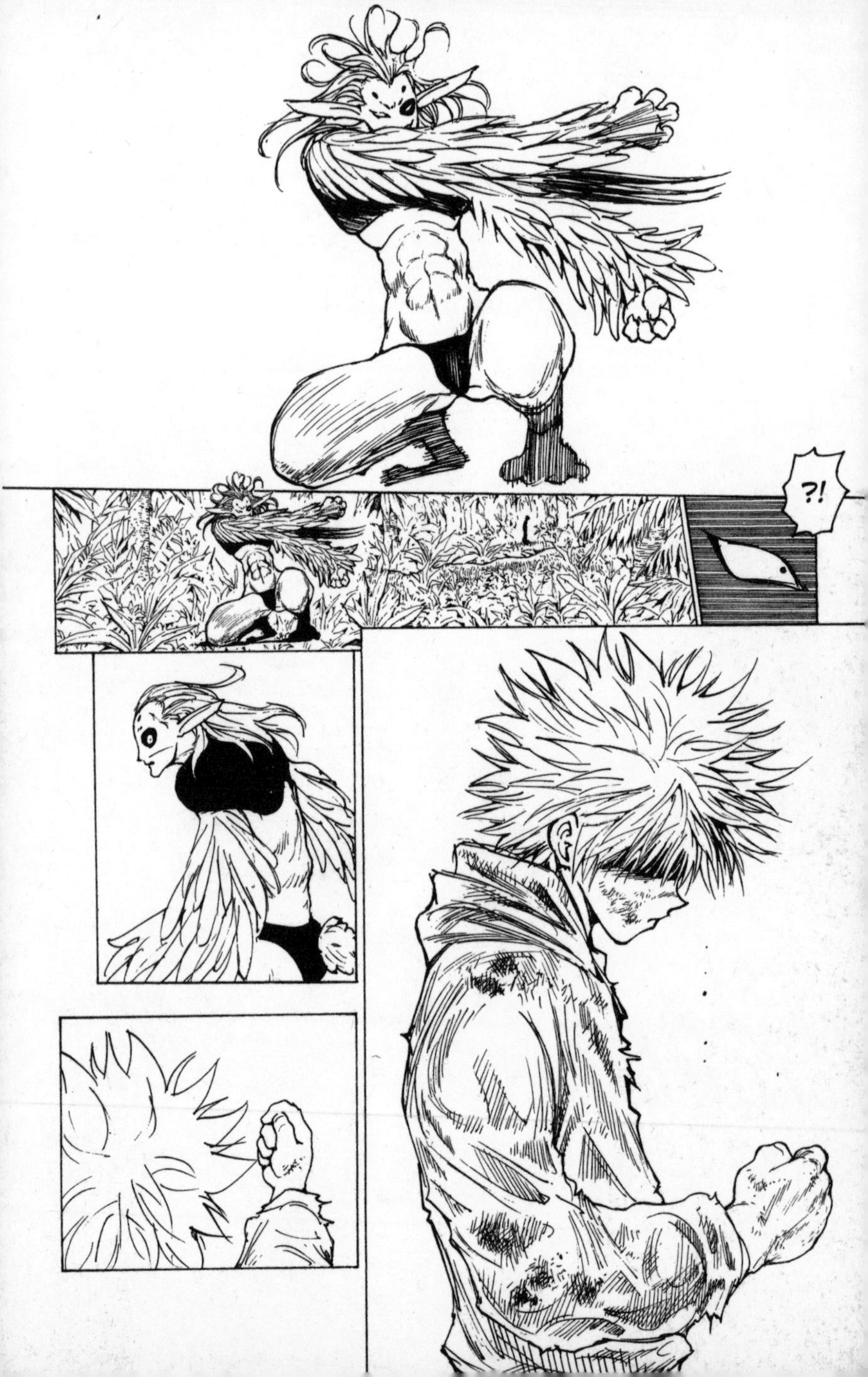
?!

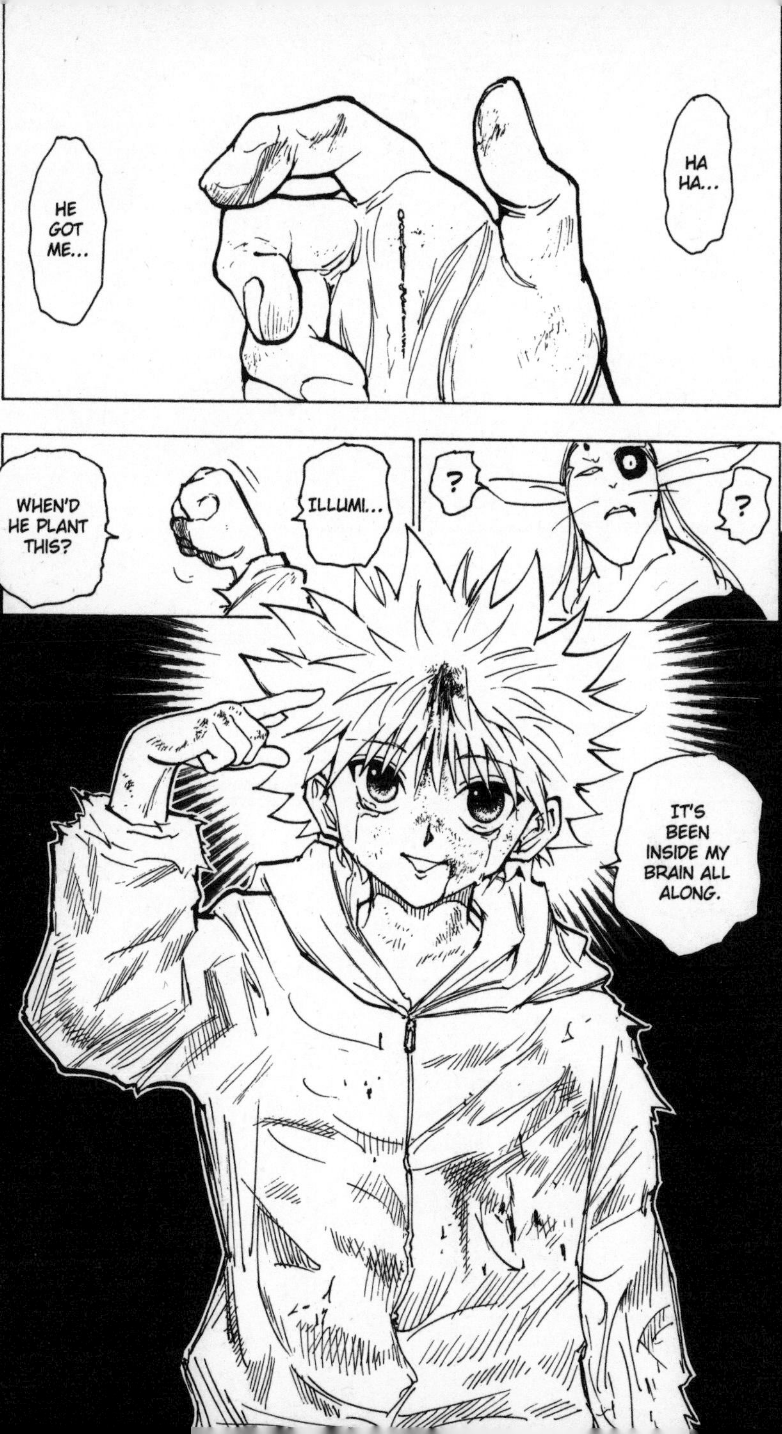
HA HA...
HE GOT ME...
?
?
ILLUMI...
WHEN'D HE PLANT THIS?
IT'S BEEN INSIDE MY BRAIN ALL ALONG.

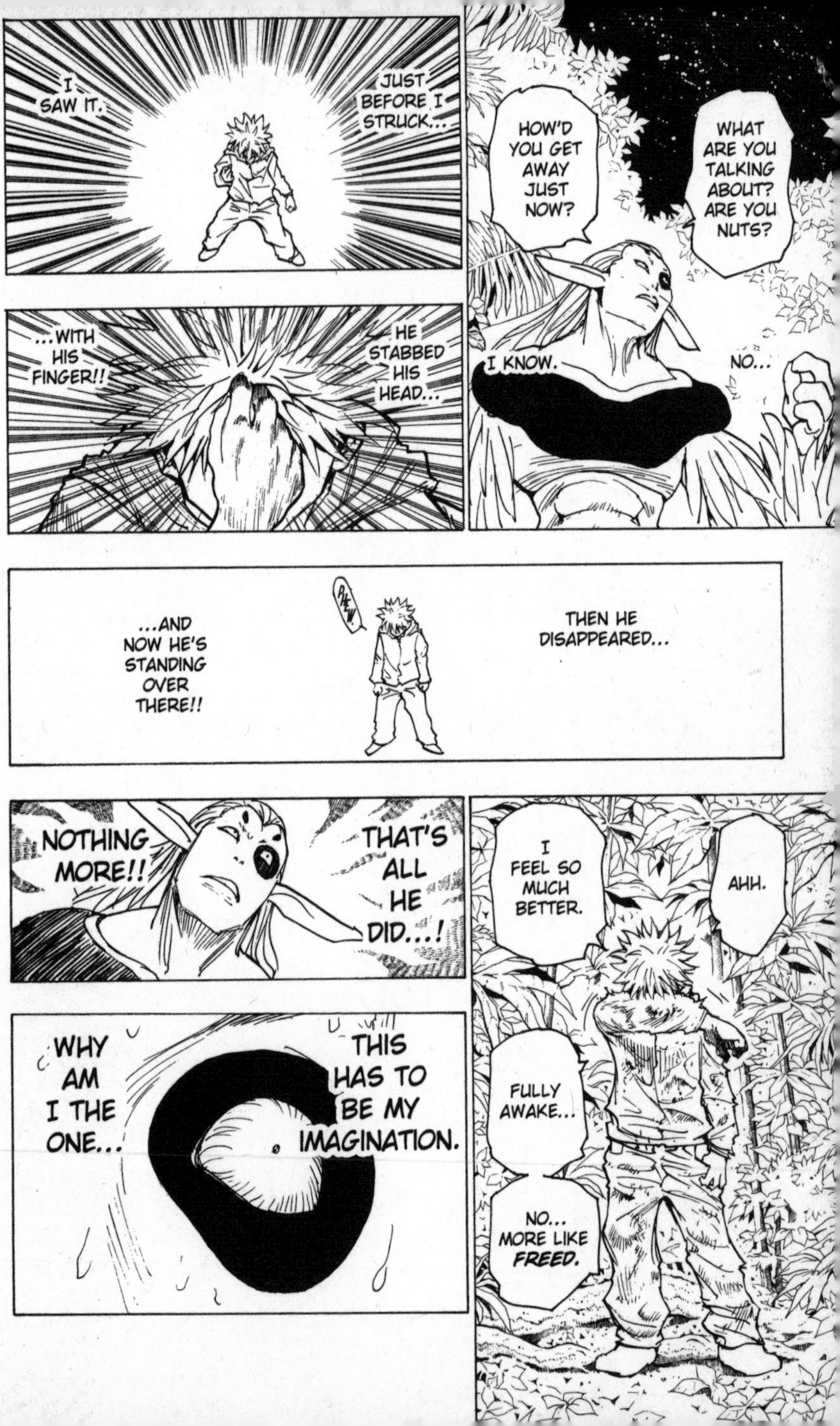
WHAT ARE YOU TALKING ABOUT? ARE YOU NUTS?
HOW'D YOU GET AWAY JUST NOW?
NO...
I KNOW.
JUST BEFORE I STRUCK...
I SAW IT.
HE STABBED HIS HEAD...
...WITH HIS FINGER!!
THEN HE DISAPPEARED...
PHEW
...AND NOW HE'S STANDING OVER THERE!!
AHH.
I FEEL SO MUCH BETTER.
FULLY AWAKE...
NO... MORE LIKE *FREED.*
THAT'S ALL HE DID...!
NOTHING MORE!!
THIS HAS TO BE MY IMAGINATION.
WHY AM I THE ONE...

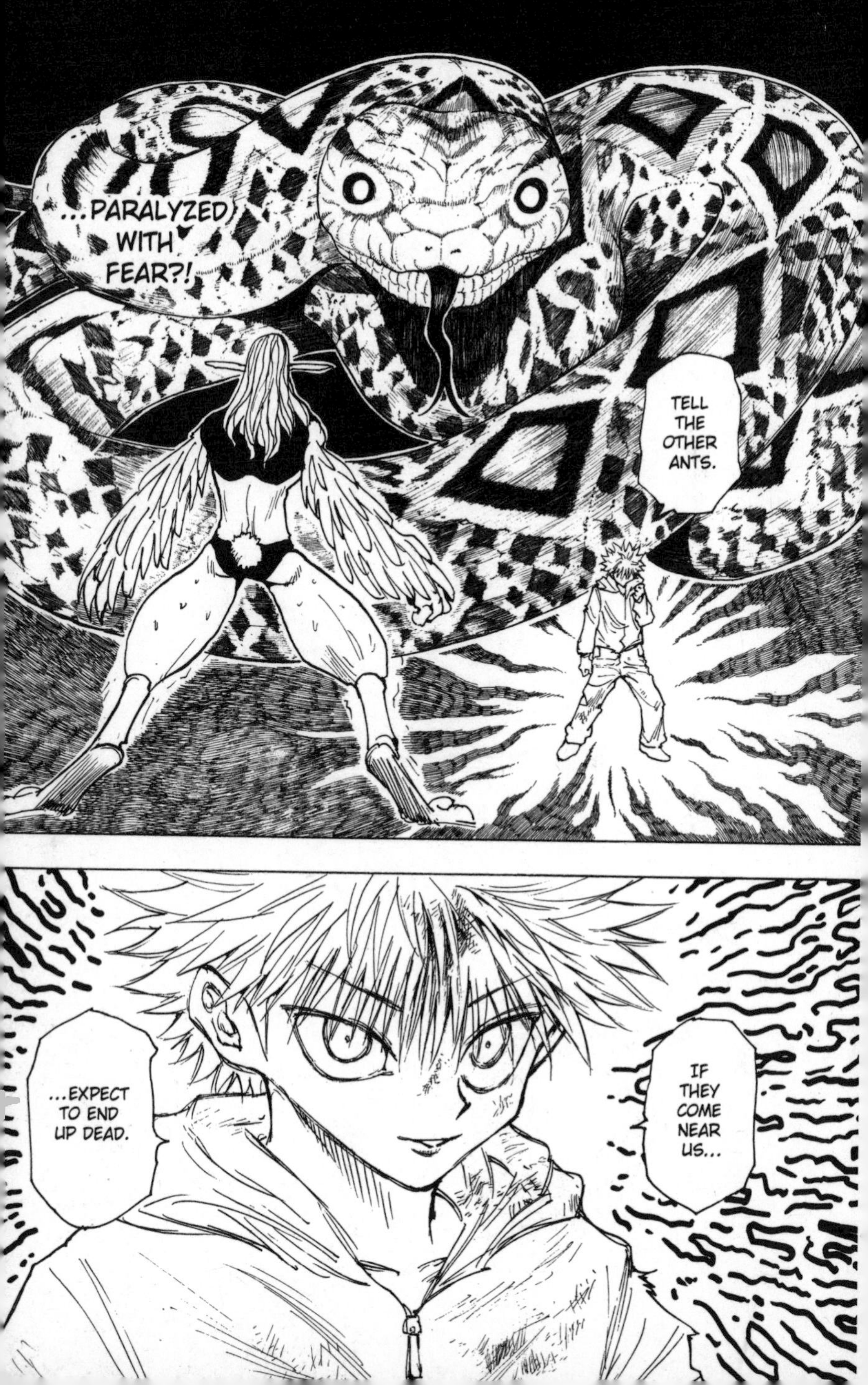
...PARALYZED WITH FEAR?!
TELL THE OTHER ANTS.
IF THEY COME NEAR US...
...EXPECT TO END UP DEAD.

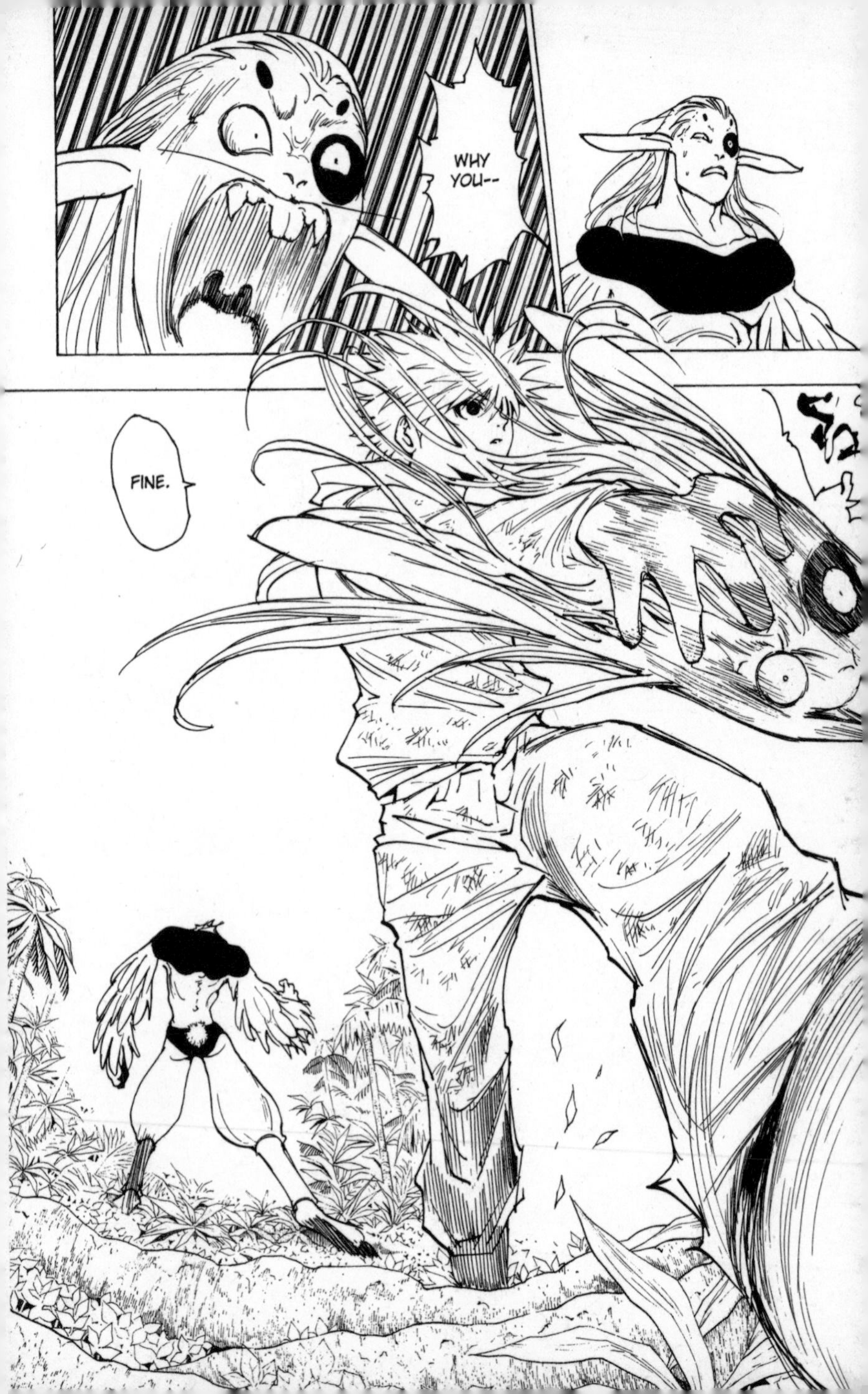
WHY YOU--
FINE.

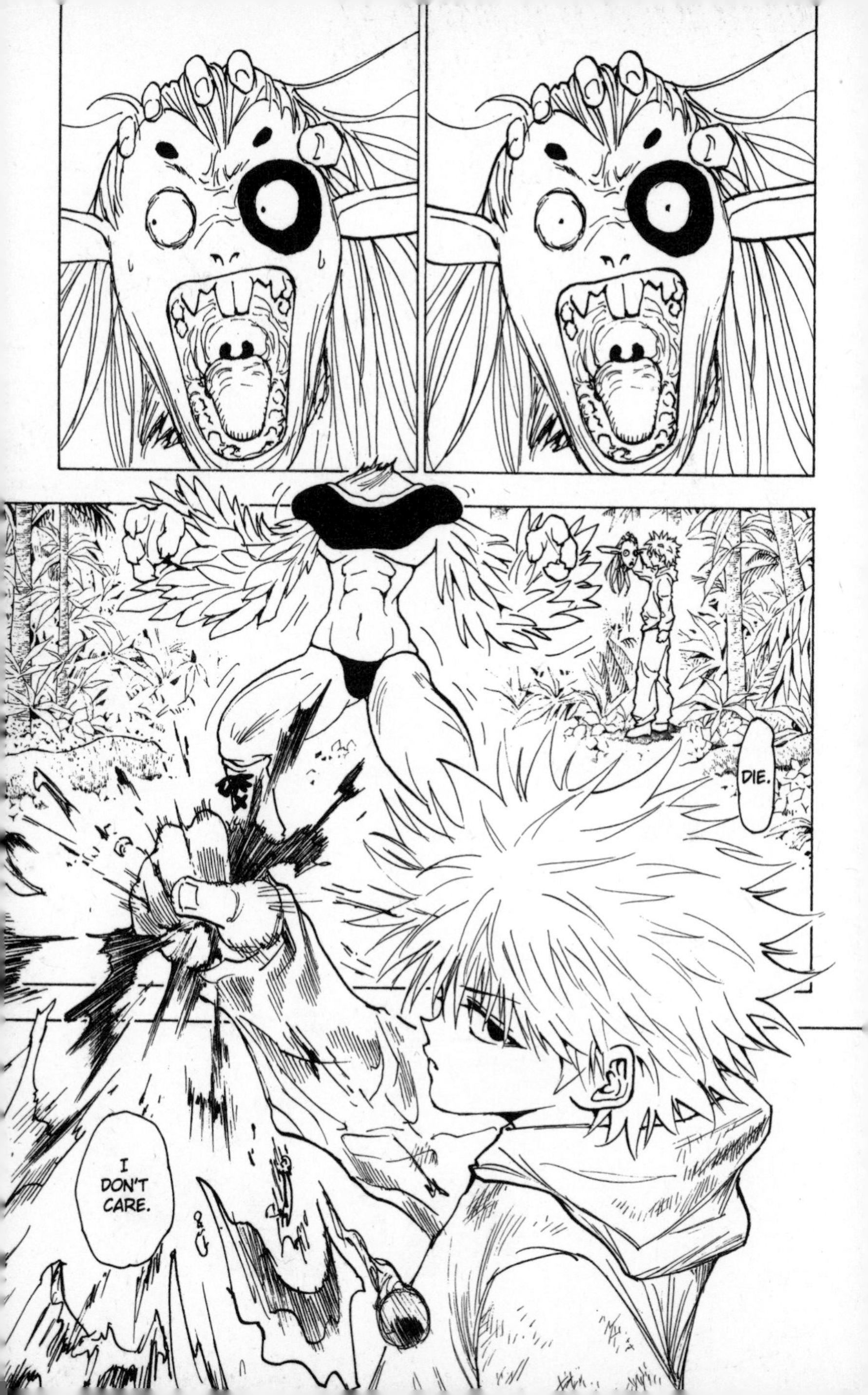
DIE.
I DON'T CARE.

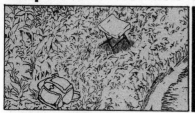

THEY'RE GONE...?! BUT THEIR STUFF IS STILL HERE!

DID ANOTHER ANT...?!

SSHHHF

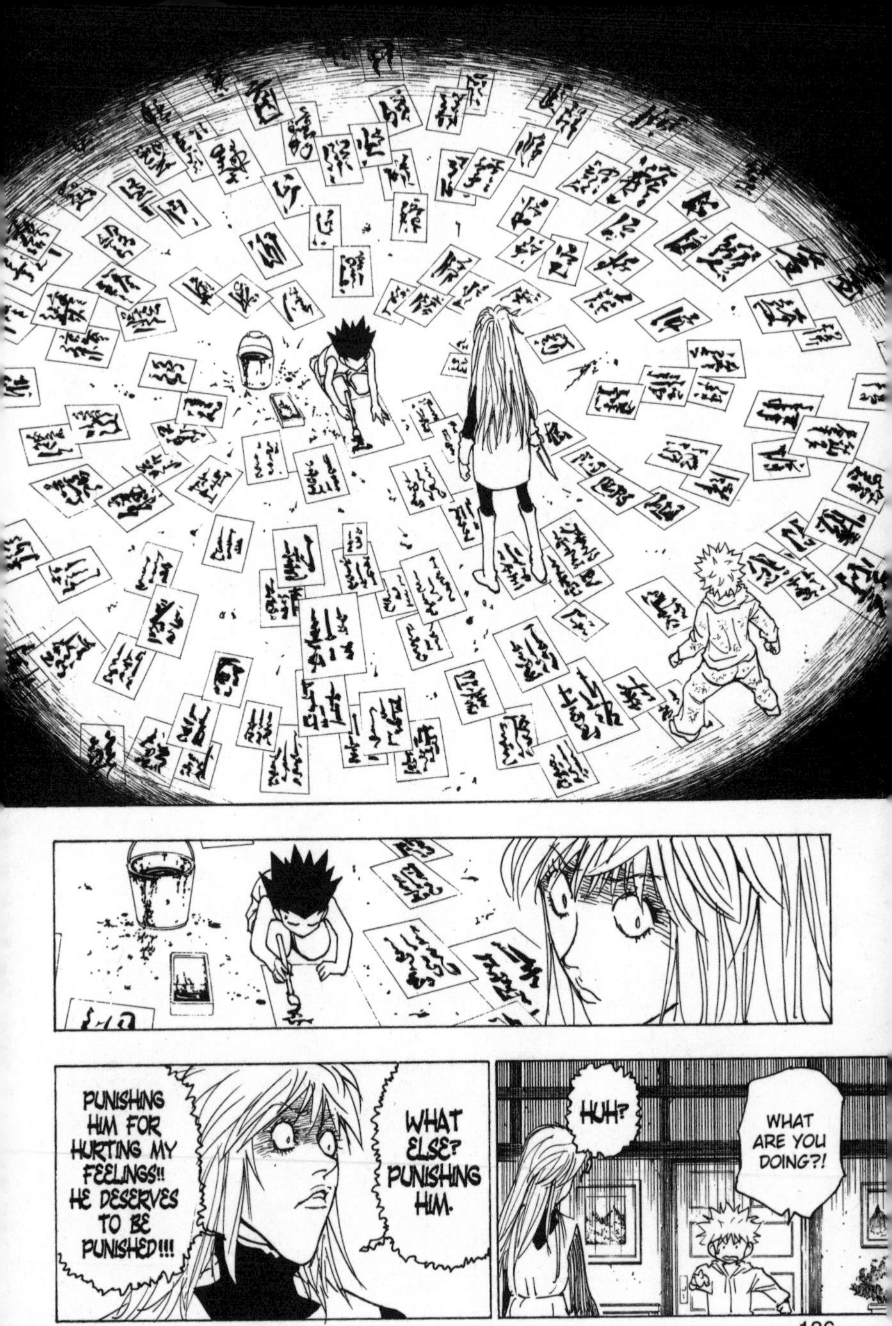
WHAT ARE YOU DOING?!
HUH?
WHAT ELSE? PUNISHING HIM.
PUNISHING HIM FOR HURTING MY FEELINGS!! HE DESERVES TO BE PUNISHED!!!

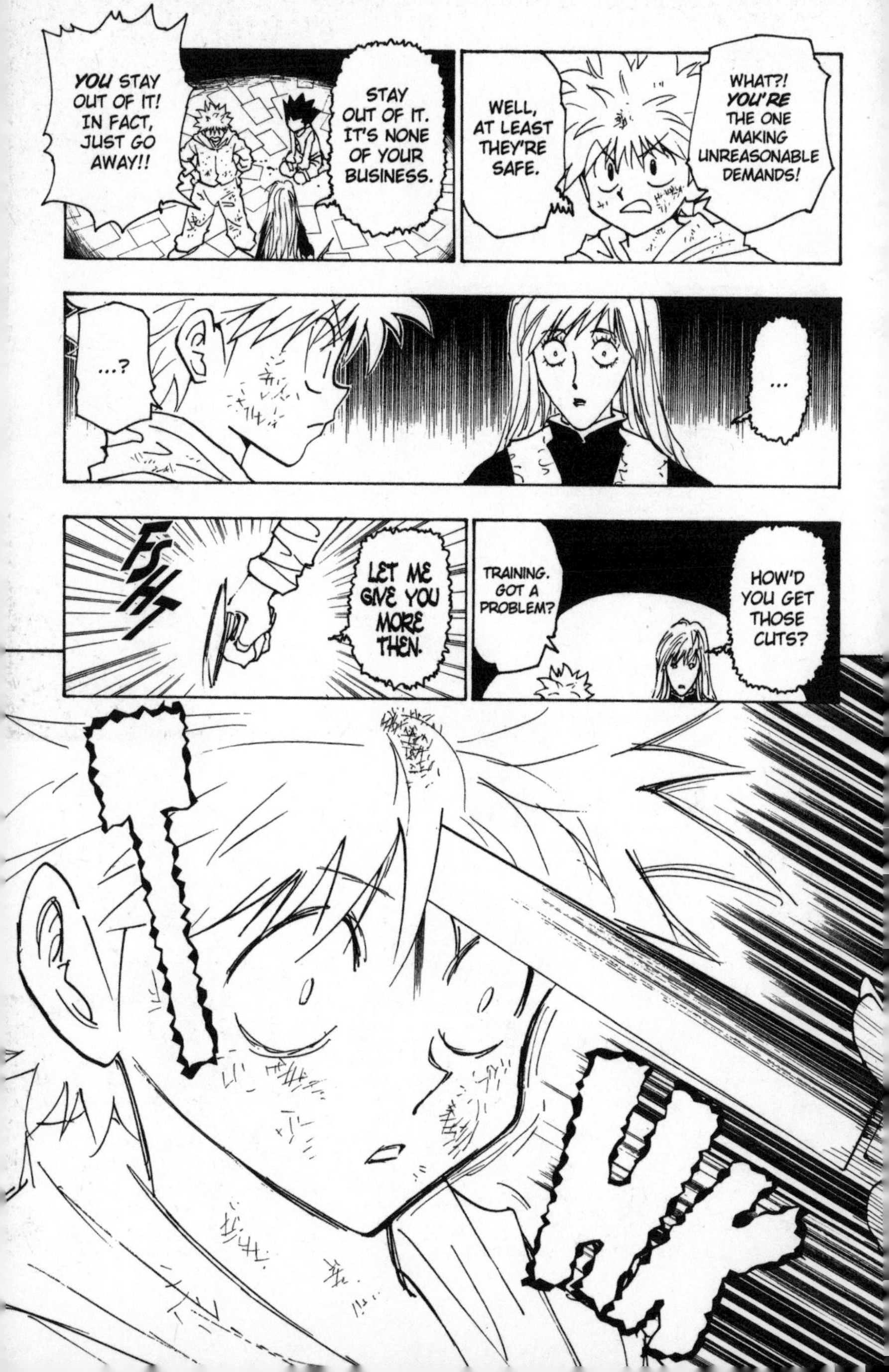
WHAT?! *YOU'RE* THE ONE MAKING UNREASONABLE DEMANDS!
WELL, AT LEAST THEY'RE SAFE.
STAY OUT OF IT. IT'S NONE OF YOUR BUSINESS.
YOU STAY OUT OF IT! IN FACT, JUST GO AWAY!!
...
...?
HOW'D YOU GET THOSE CUTS?
TRAINING. GOT A PROBLEM?
LET ME GIVE YOU MORE THEN.
FSHT

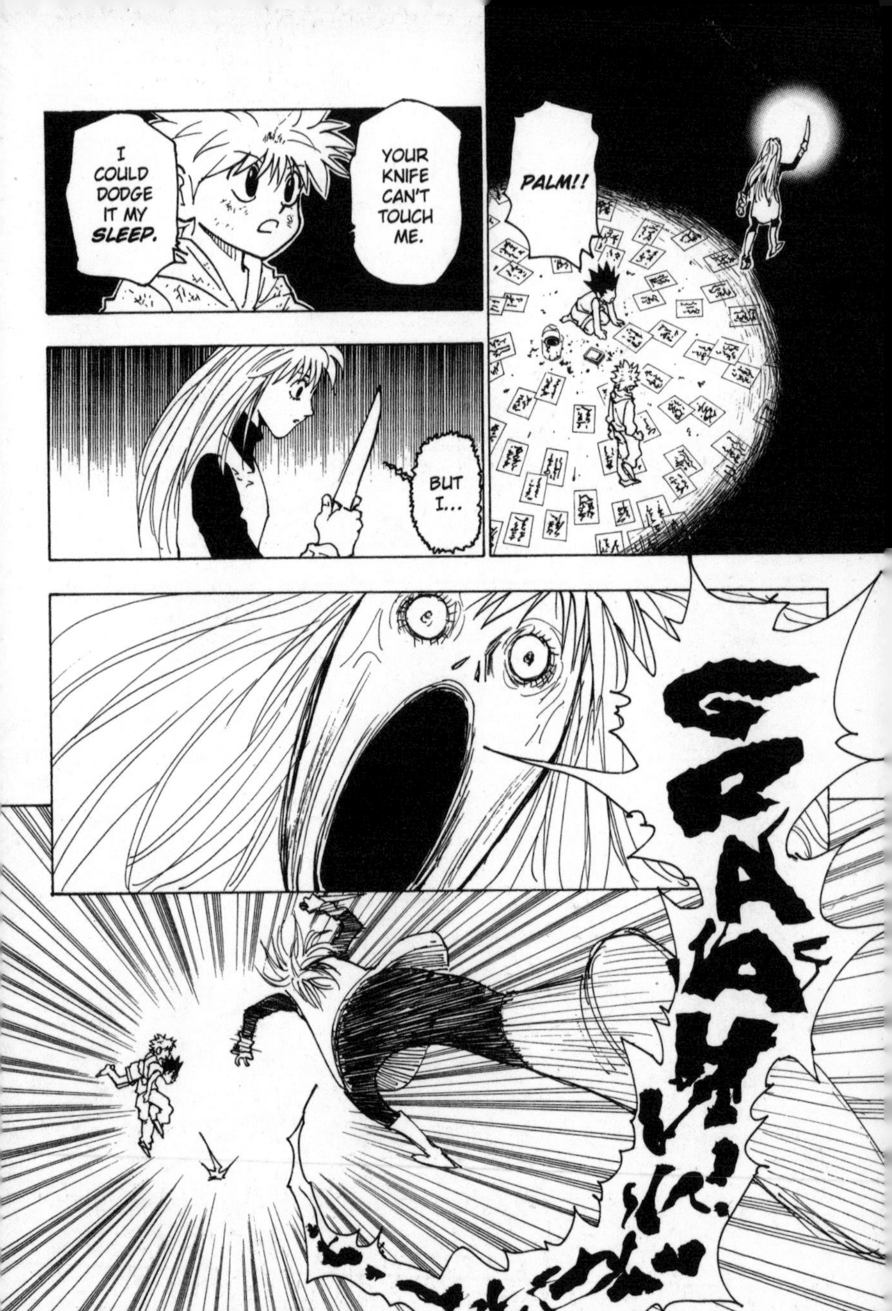
PALM!!
YOUR KNIFE CAN'T TOUCH ME.
I COULD DODGE IT MY SLEEP.
BUT I...
GRAAH!!

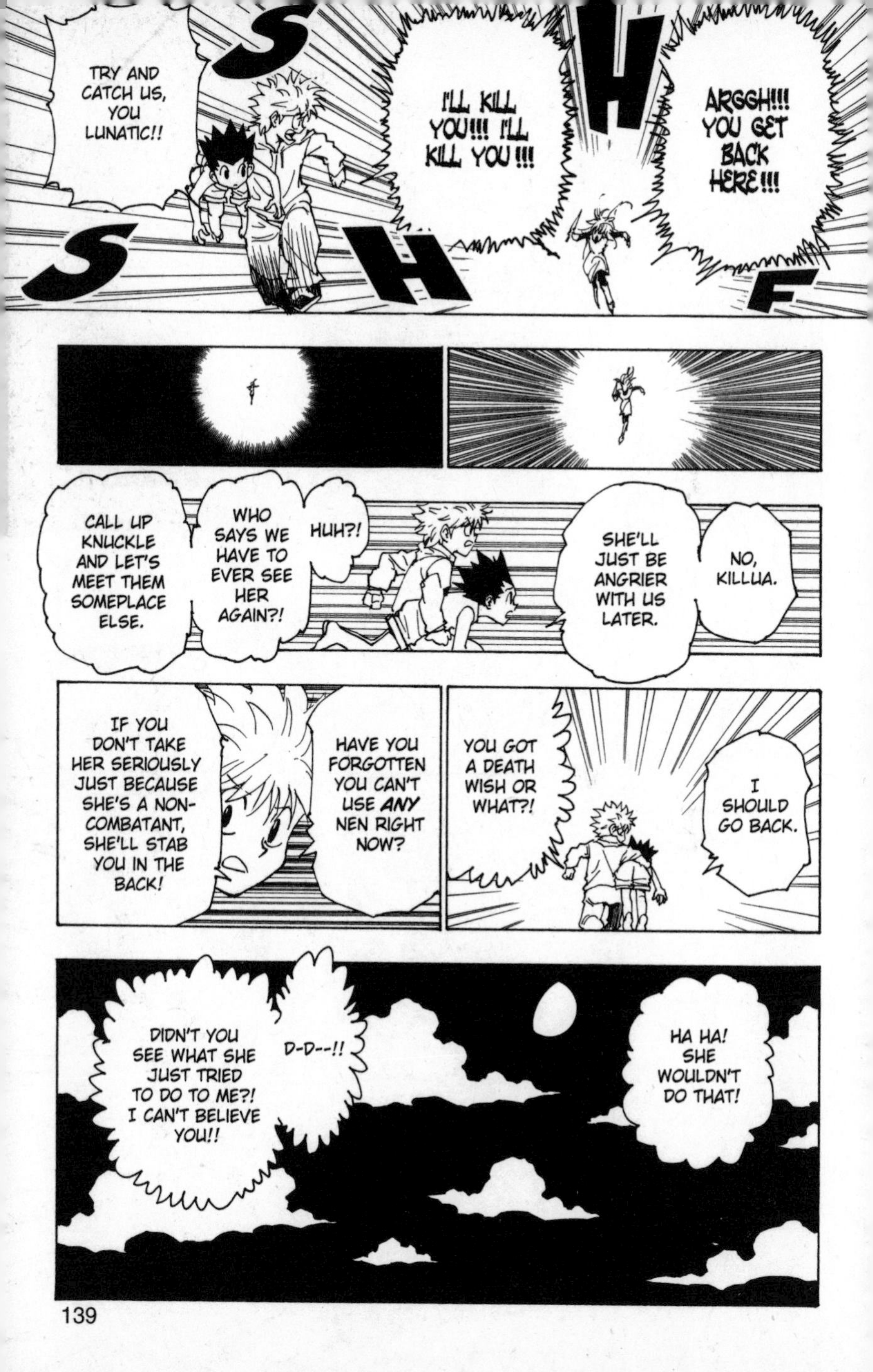
ARGGH!!! YOU GET BACK HERE!!!
I'LL KILL YOU!!! I'LL KILL YOU!!!
TRY AND CATCH US, YOU LUNATIC!!
NO, KILLUA.
SHE'LL JUST BE ANGRIER WITH US LATER.
HUH?!
WHO SAYS WE HAVE TO EVER SEE HER AGAIN?!
CALL UP KNUCKLE AND LET'S MEET THEM SOMEPLACE ELSE.
I SHOULD GO BACK.
YOU GOT A DEATH WISH OR WHAT?!
HAVE YOU FORGOTTEN YOU CAN'T USE ANY NEN RIGHT NOW?
IF YOU DON'T TAKE HER SERIOUSLY JUST BECAUSE SHE'S A NON-COMBATANT, SHE'LL STAB YOU IN THE BACK!
HA HA! SHE WOULDN'T DO THAT!
D-D--!!
DIDN'T YOU SEE WHAT SHE JUST TRIED TO DO TO ME?! I CAN'T BELIEVE YOU!!

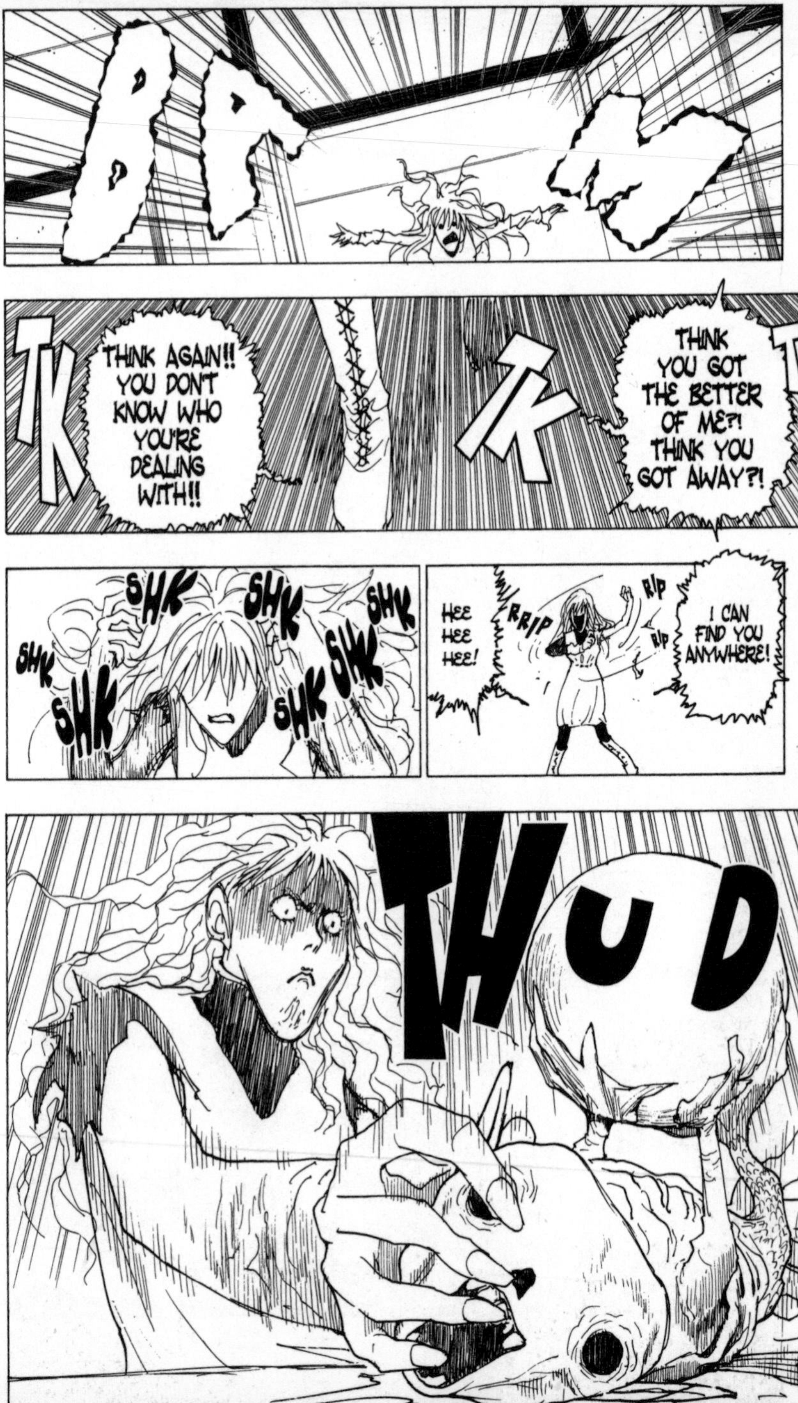
BAM
TK
THINK YOU GOT THE BETTER OF ME?! THINK YOU GOT AWAY?!
TK
THINK AGAIN!! YOU DON'T KNOW WHO YOU'RE DEALING WITH!!
TK
I CAN FIND YOU ANYWHERE!
RIP
RIP
RRIP
HEE HEE HEE!
SHK
SHK
SHK
SHK
SHK
SHK
SHK
THUD

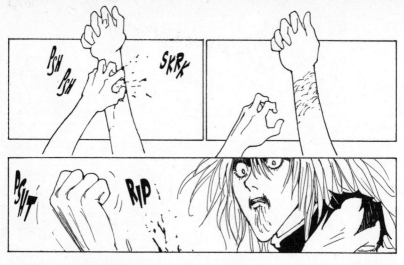

SKRK
PSH PSH
RIP
PSHT
PLP
PLP
PLP
MY DEAR LITTLE MERMAID.
TELL ME WHERE THAT INFERNAL BRAT, KILLUA, IS.
BRR
BRR
FWOO
THERE HE IS!
THE HOTEL BY THE TRAIN STATION...

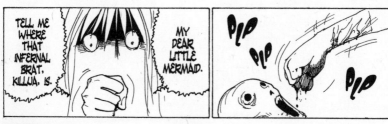

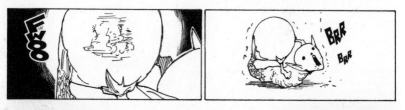

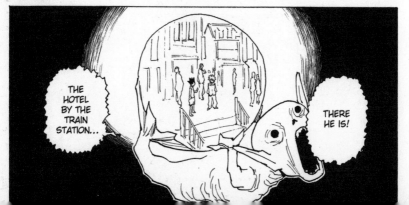

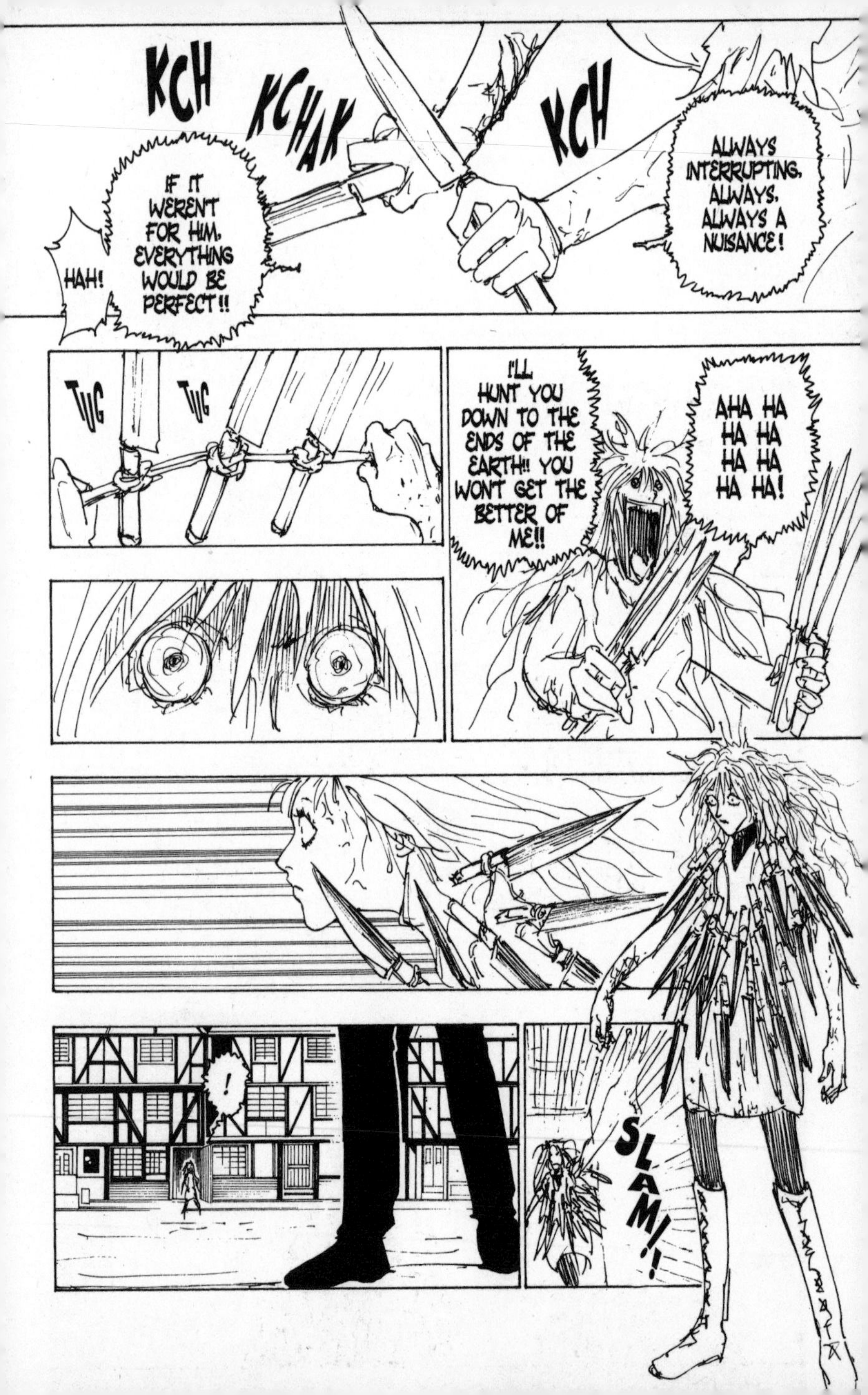
ALWAYS INTERRUPTING. ALWAYS. ALWAYS A NUISANCE!
KCH
KCHAK
KCH
IF IT WERENT FOR HIM, EVERYTHING WOULD BE PERFECT!!
HAH!
AHA HA HA HA HA HA HA HA!
I'LL HUNT YOU DOWN TO THE ENDS OF THE EARTH!! YOU WONT GET THE BETTER OF ME!!
TUG
TUG
SLAM!!
!

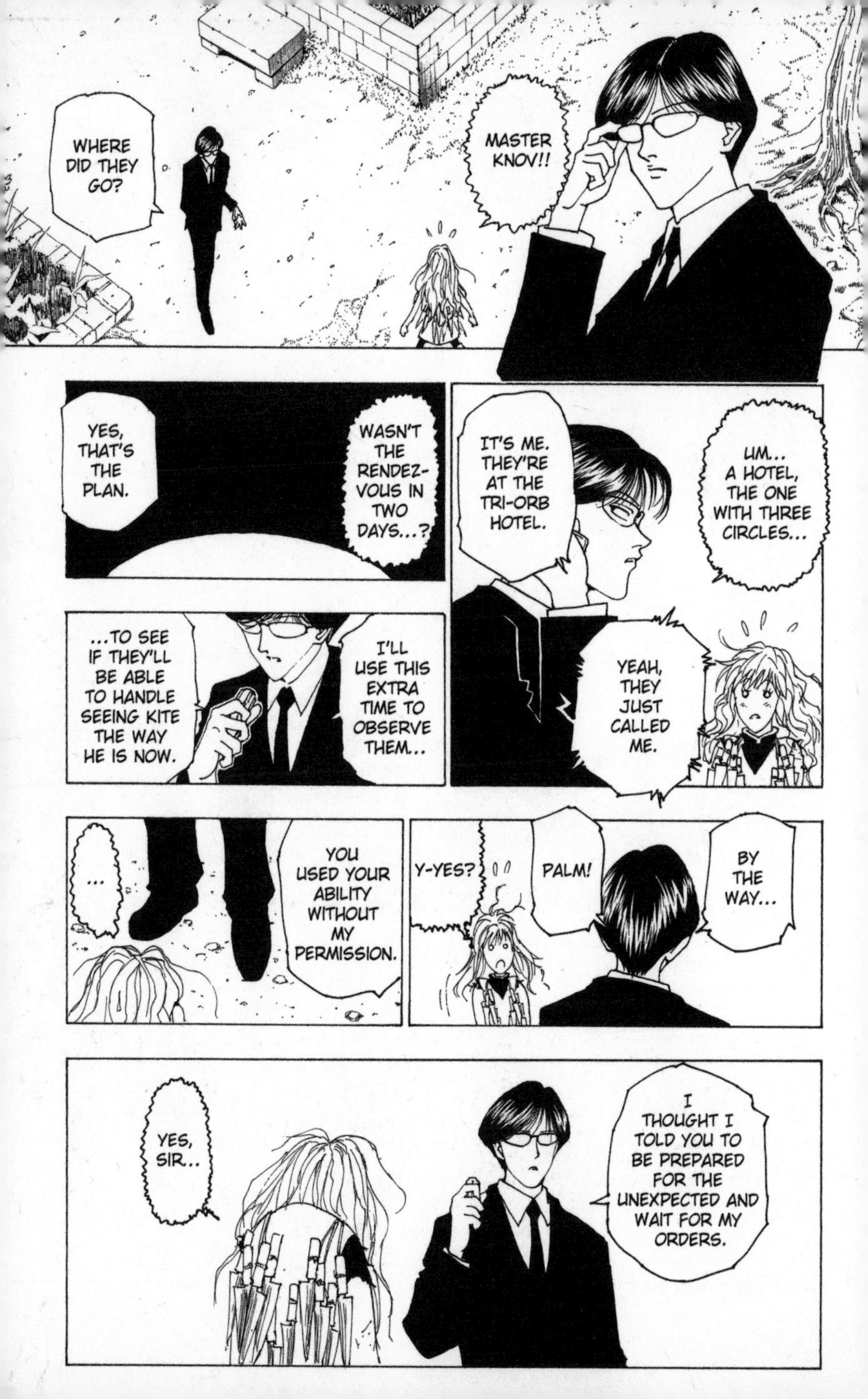
MASTER KNOV!!
WHERE DID THEY GO?
UM... A HOTEL, THE ONE WITH THREE CIRCLES...
IT'S ME. THEY'RE AT THE TRI-ORB HOTEL.
YEAH, THEY JUST CALLED ME.
WASN'T THE RENDEZ-VOUS IN TWO DAYS...?
YES, THAT'S THE PLAN.
I'LL USE THIS EXTRA TIME TO OBSERVE THEM...
...TO SEE IF THEY'LL BE ABLE TO HANDLE SEEING KITE THE WAY HE IS NOW.
BY THE WAY...
PALM!
Y-YES?
YOU USED YOUR ABILITY WITHOUT MY PERMISSION.
...
I THOUGHT I TOLD YOU TO BE PREPARED FOR THE UNEXPECTED AND WAIT FOR MY ORDERS.
YES, SIR...

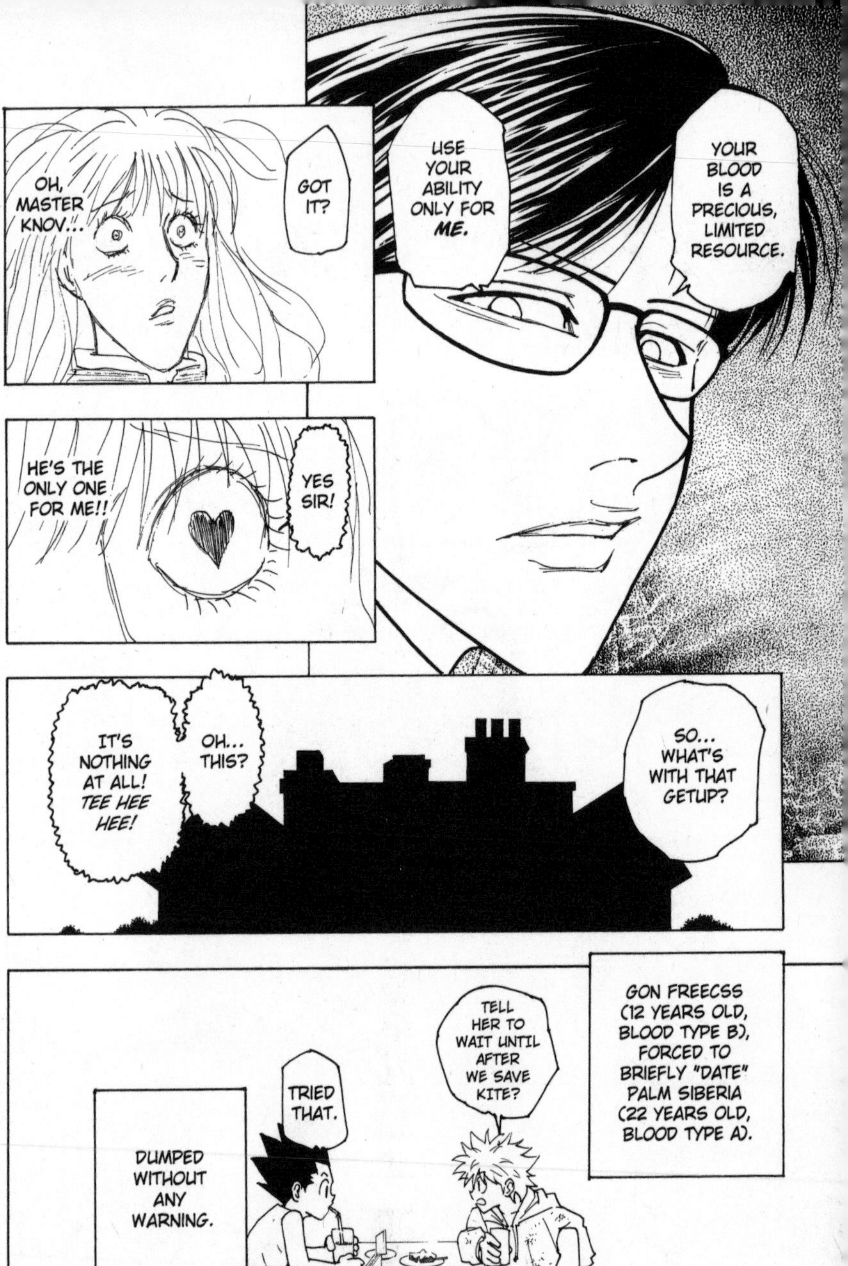
YOUR BLOOD IS A PRECIOUS, LIMITED RESOURCE.
USE YOUR ABILITY ONLY FOR *ME.*
GOT IT?
OH, MASTER KNOV...!
YES SIR!
HE'S THE ONLY ONE FOR ME!!
SO... WHAT'S WITH THAT GETUP?
OH... THIS?
IT'S NOTHING AT ALL! *TEE HEE HEE!*
GON FREECSS (12 YEARS OLD, BLOOD TYPE B), FORCED TO BRIEFLY "DATE" PALM SIBERIA (22 YEARS OLD, BLOOD TYPE A).
TELL HER TO WAIT UNTIL AFTER WE SAVE KITE?
TRIED THAT.
DUMPED WITHOUT ANY WARNING.

READ THIS WAY

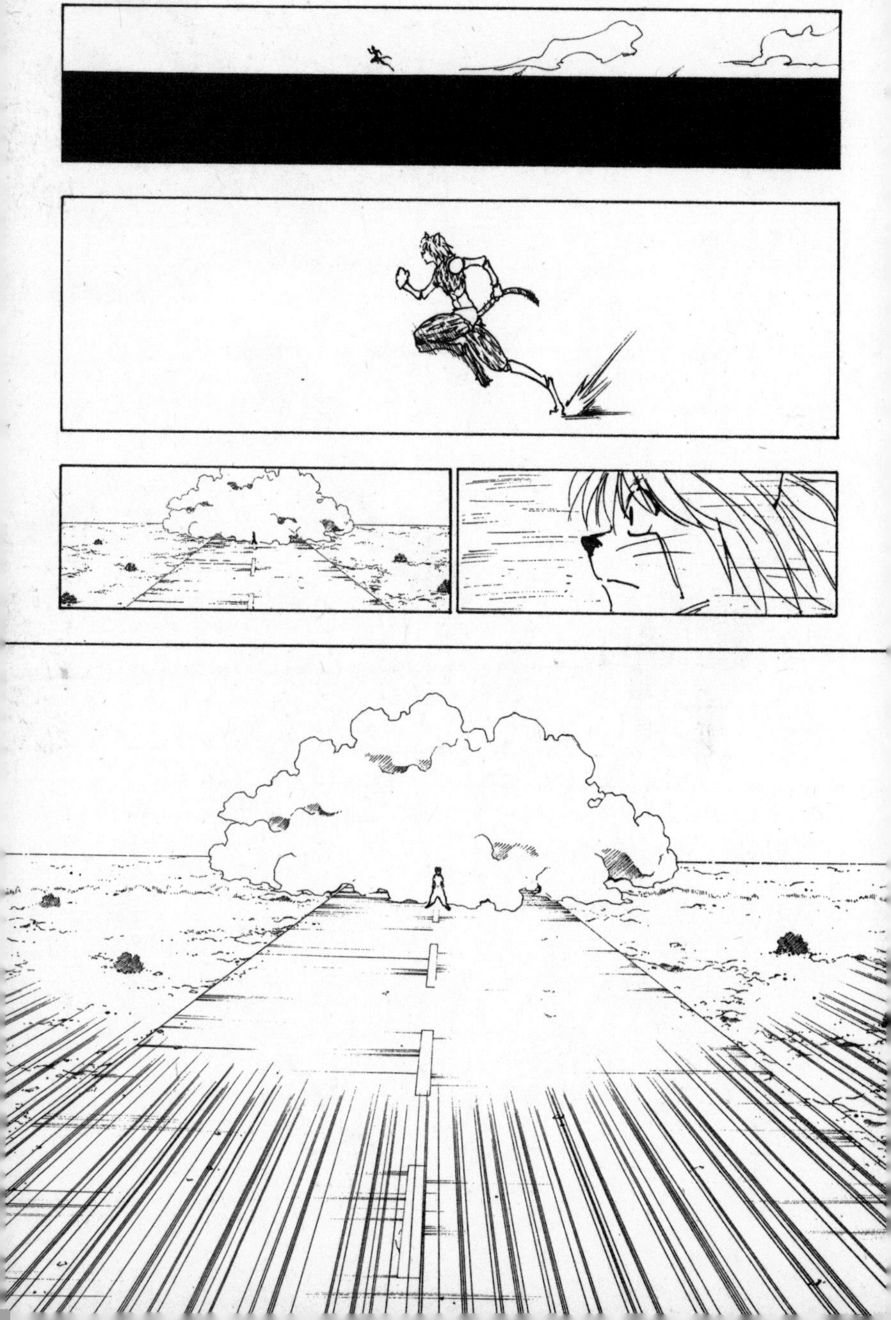

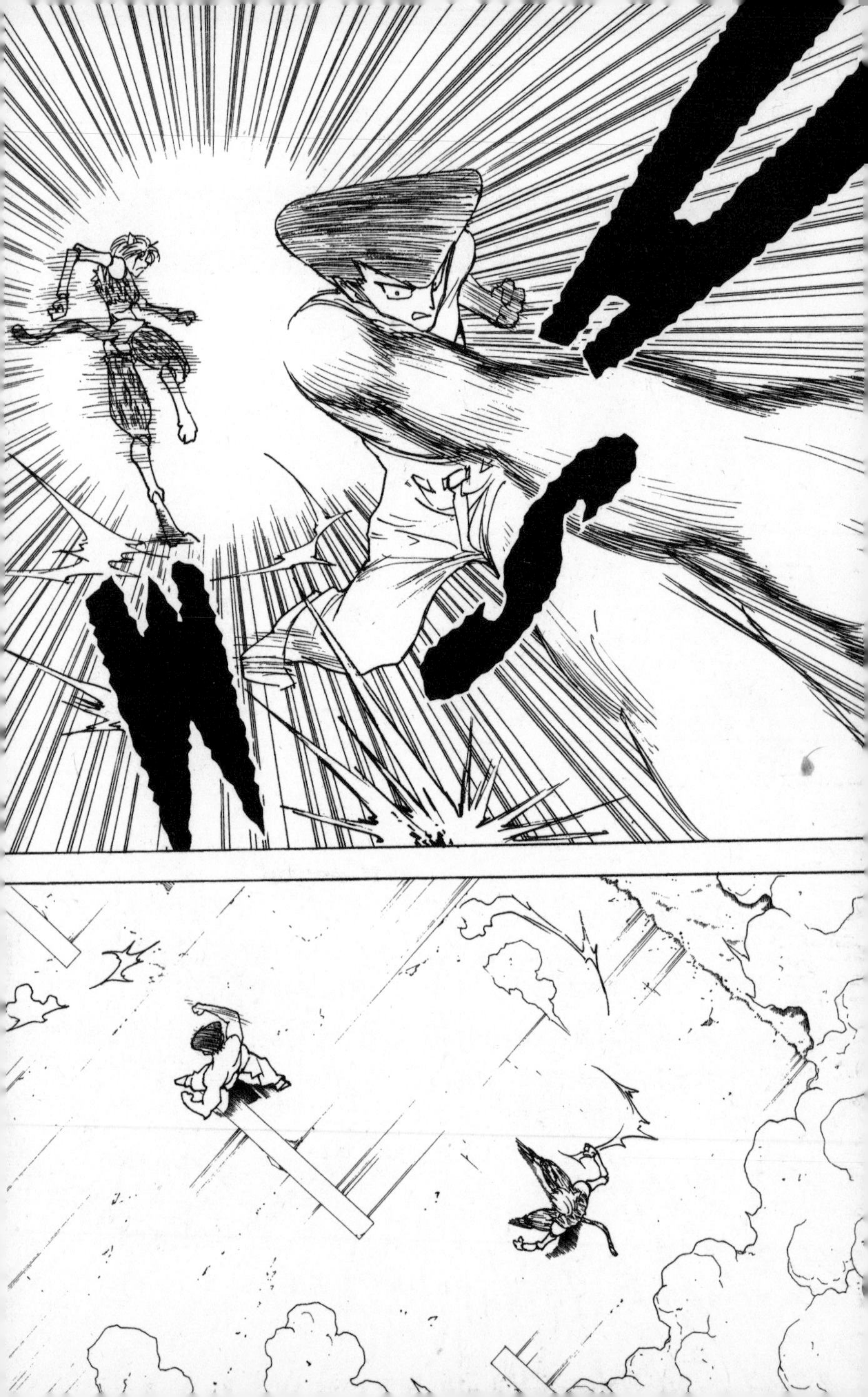

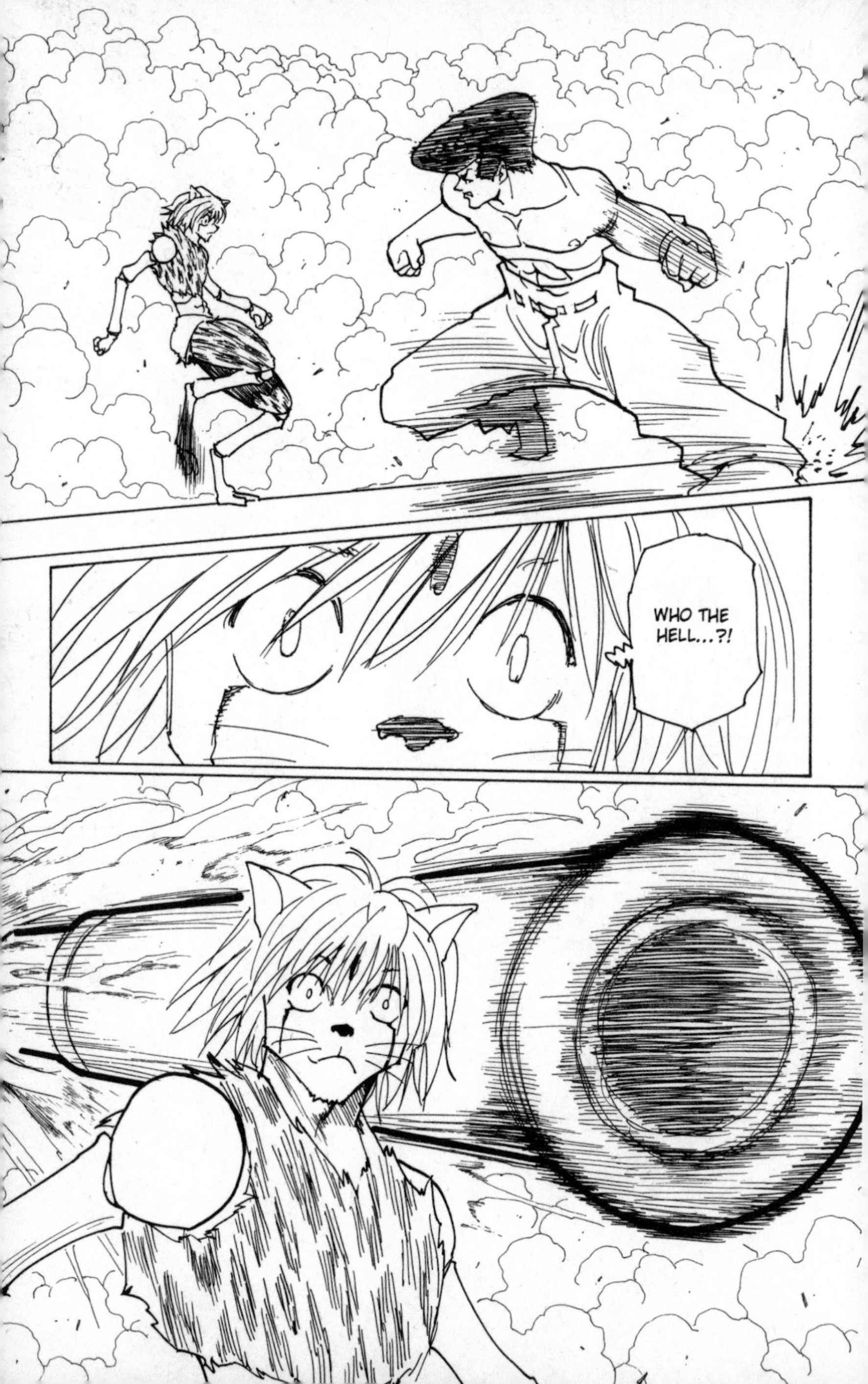
WHO THE HELL...?!

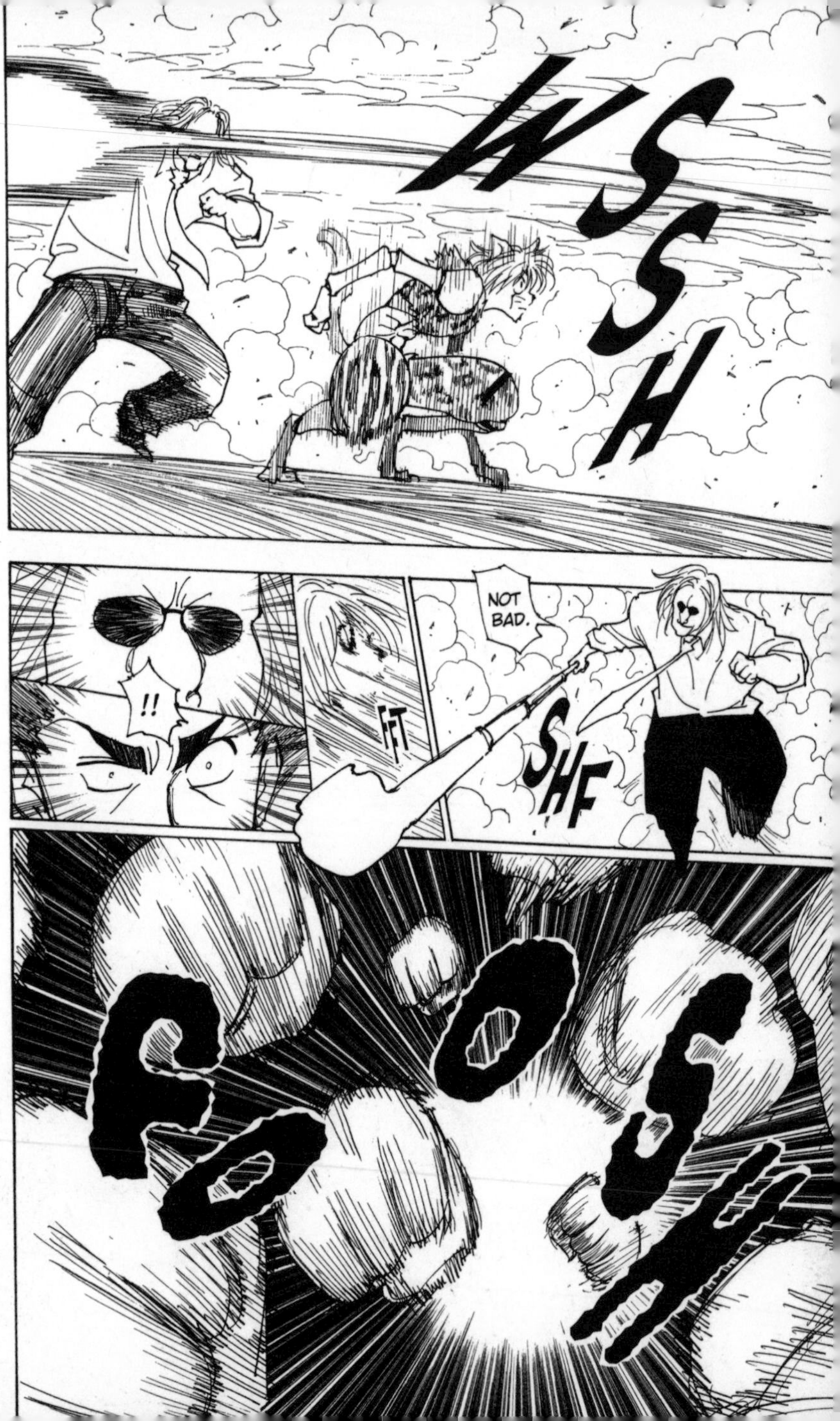
WSSH
NOT BAD.
SHF
FFT
!!
GOSH

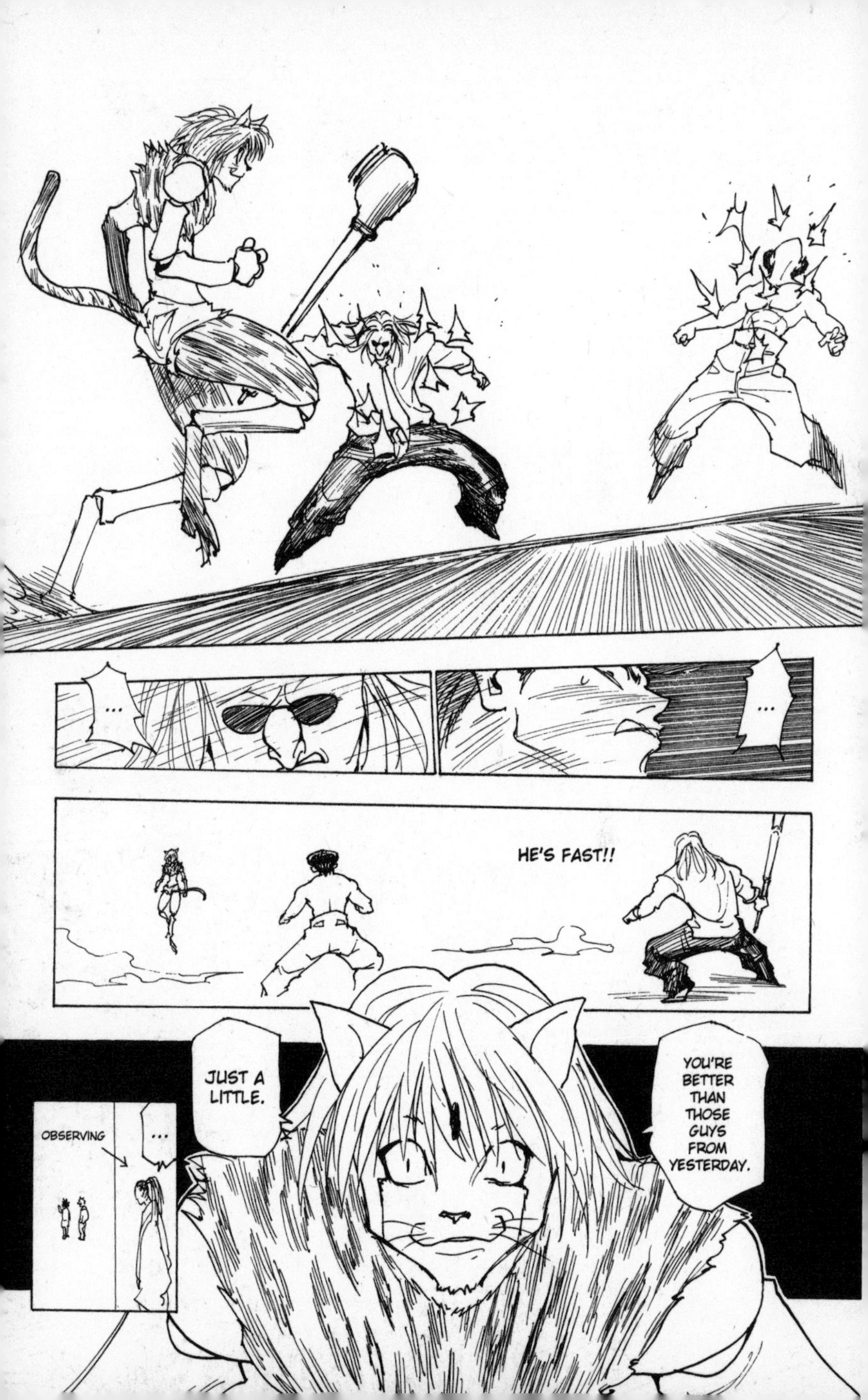
...
...
HE'S FAST!!
YOU'RE BETTER THAN THOSE GUYS FROM YESTERDAY.
JUST A LITTLE.
...
OBSERVING

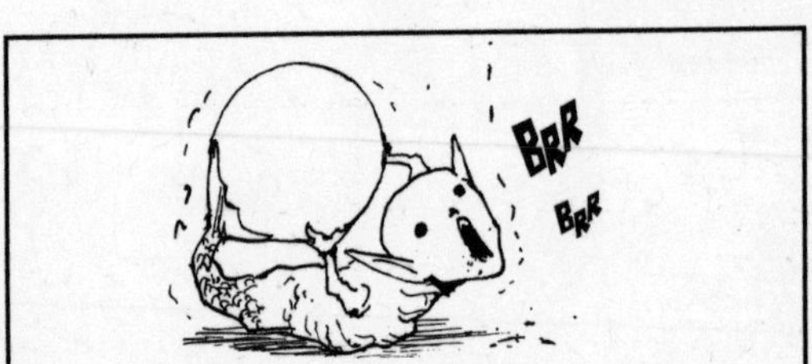
BRR
BRR

Chapter 221: Reunion: Part 2

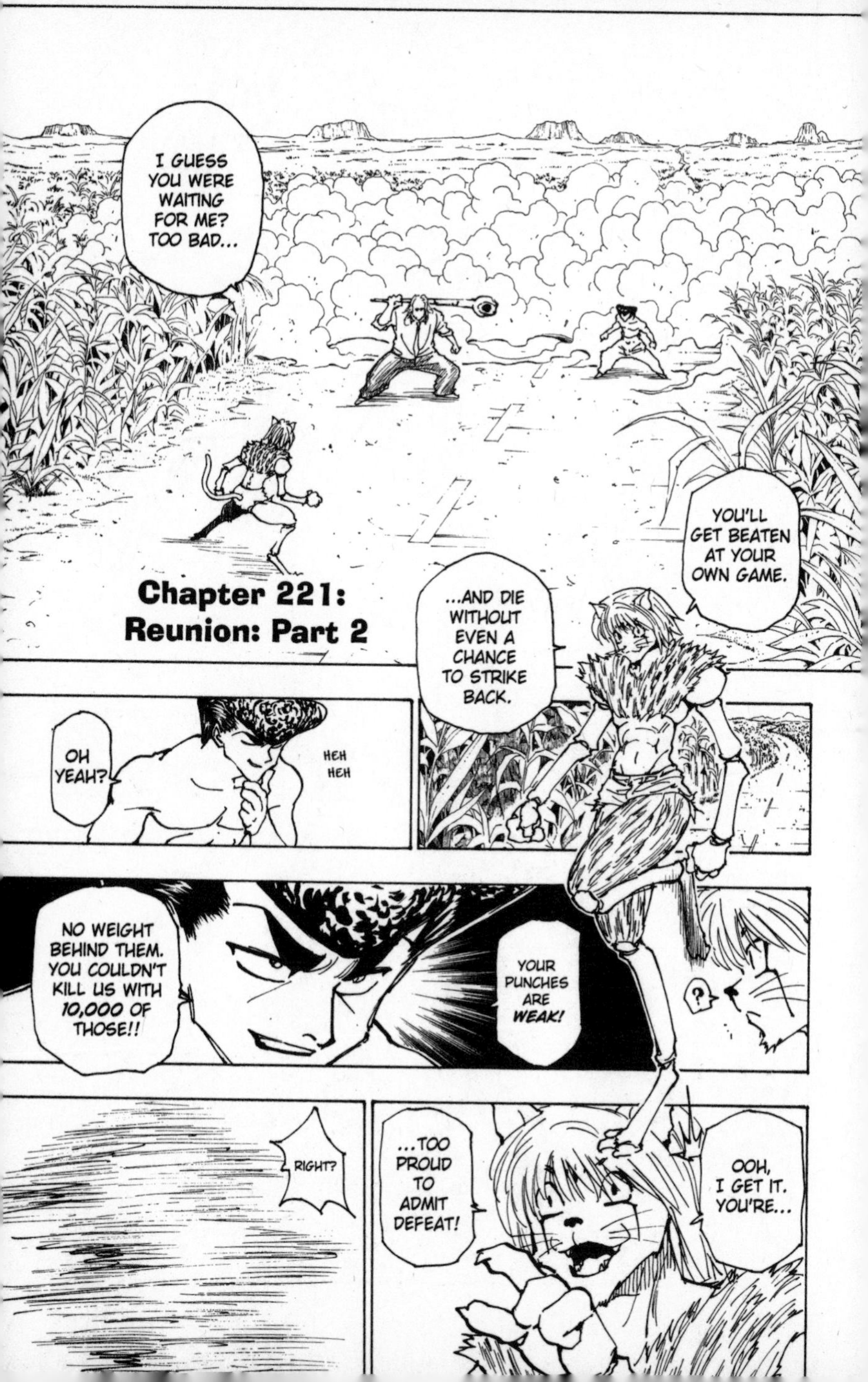
I GUESS YOU WERE WAITING FOR ME? TOO BAD...
YOU'LL GET BEATEN AT YOUR OWN GAME.
...AND DIE WITHOUT EVEN A CHANCE TO STRIKE BACK.
OH YEAH?
HEH HEH
YOUR PUNCHES ARE WEAK!
NO WEIGHT BEHIND THEM. YOU COULDN'T KILL US WITH 10,000 OF THOSE!!
?
OOH, I GET IT. YOU'RE...
...TOO PROUD TO ADMIT DEFEAT!
RIGHT?

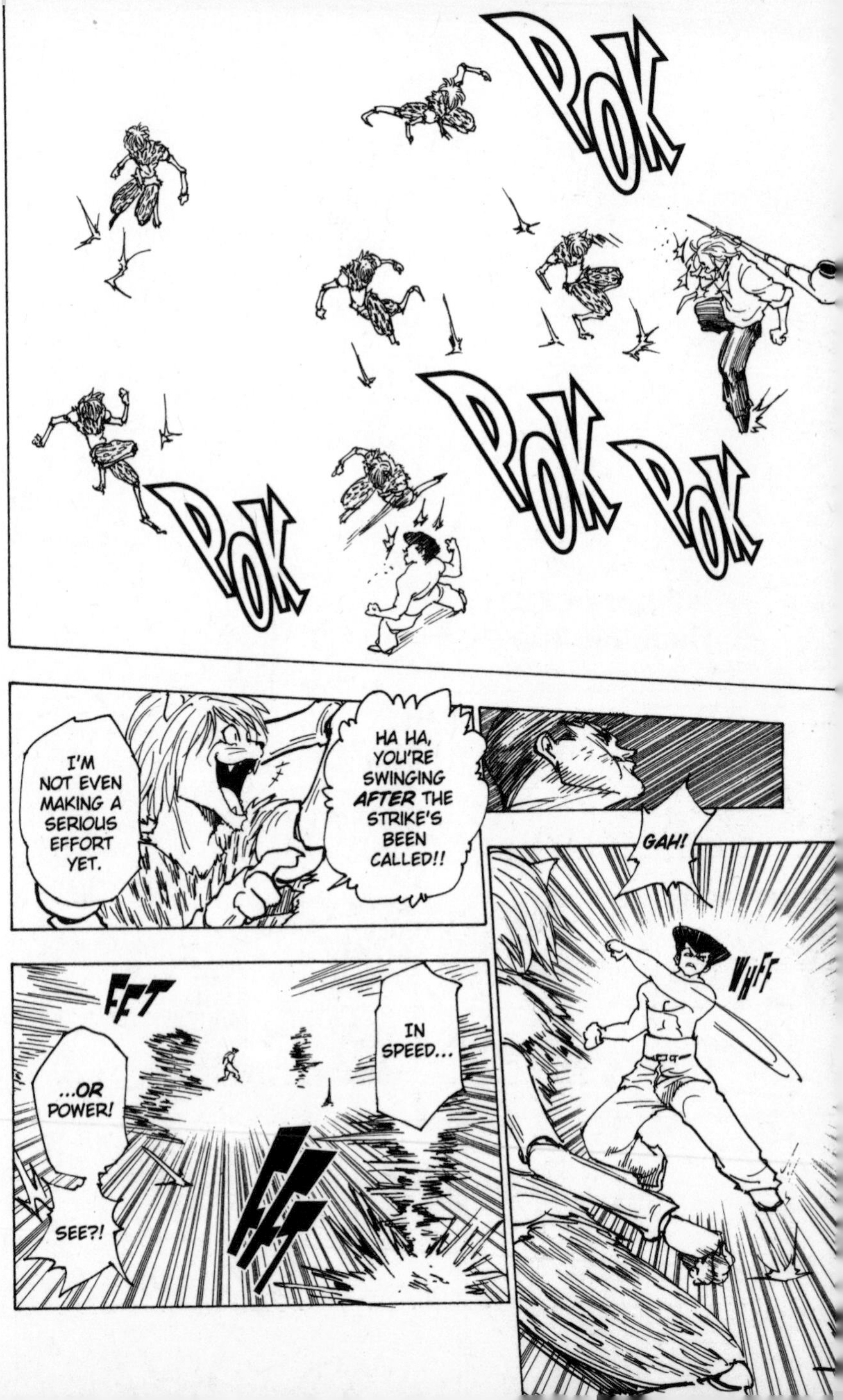
POK
POK
POK
POK
GAH!
HA HA, YOU'RE SWINGING *AFTER* THE STRIKE'S BEEN CALLED!!
I'M NOT EVEN MAKING A SERIOUS EFFORT YET.
WHFF
IN SPEED...
FFT
...OR POWER!
FFT
SEE?!

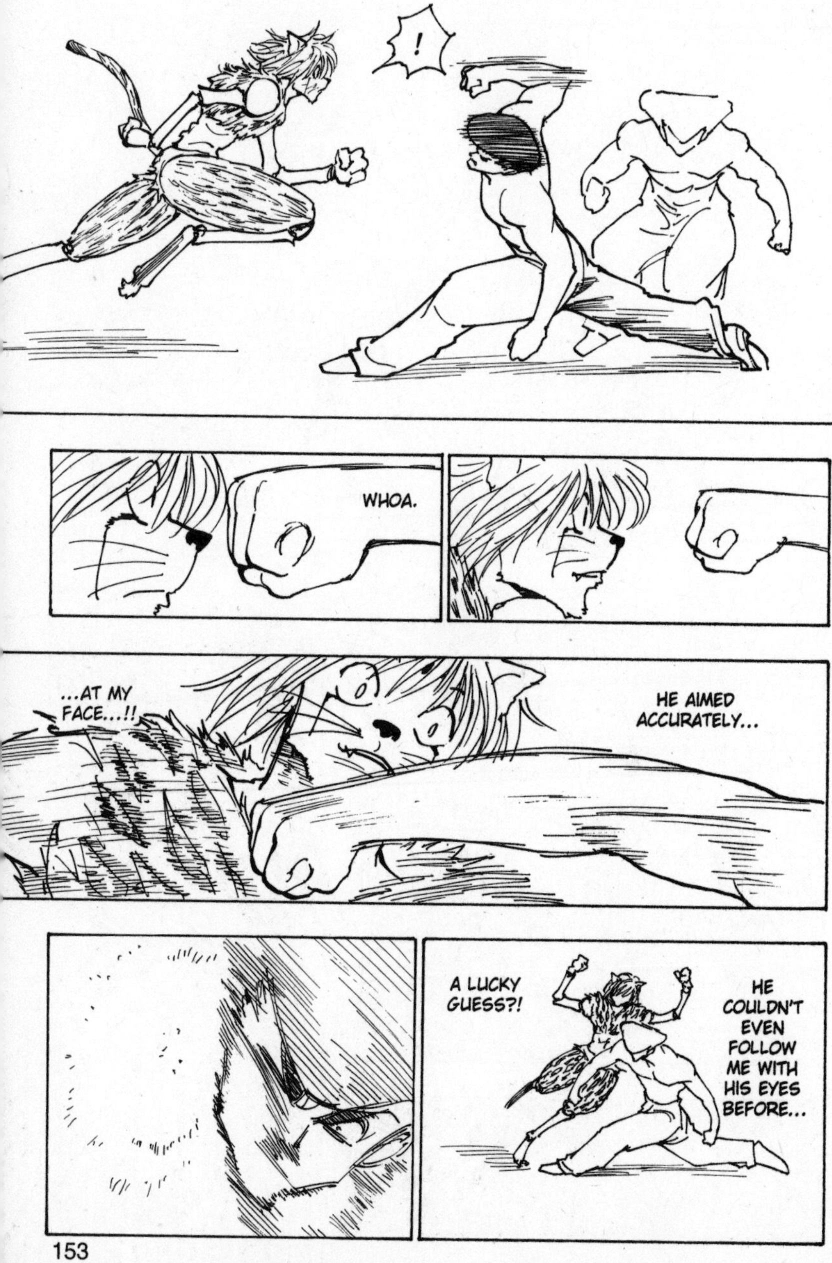
!
WHOA.
HE AIMED ACCURATELY...
...AT MY FACE...!!
HE COULDN'T EVEN FOLLOW ME WITH HIS EYES BEFORE...
A LUCKY GUESS?!

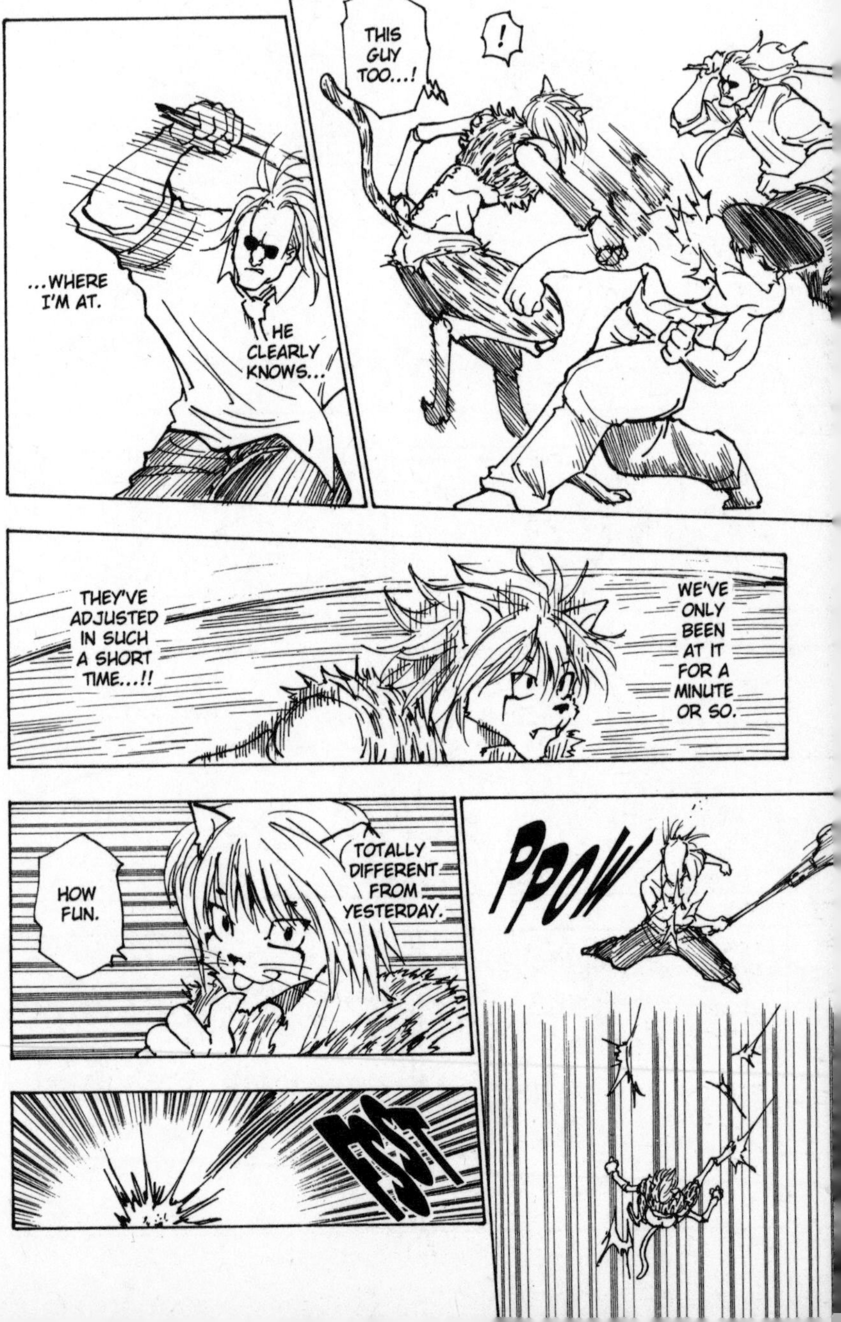

!
THIS GUY TOO...!
HE CLEARLY KNOWS...
...WHERE I'M AT.
WE'VE ONLY BEEN AT IT FOR A MINUTE OR SO.
THEY'VE ADJUSTED IN SUCH A SHORT TIME...!!
PPOW
TOTALLY DIFFERENT FROM YESTERDAY.
HOW FUN.
FSST

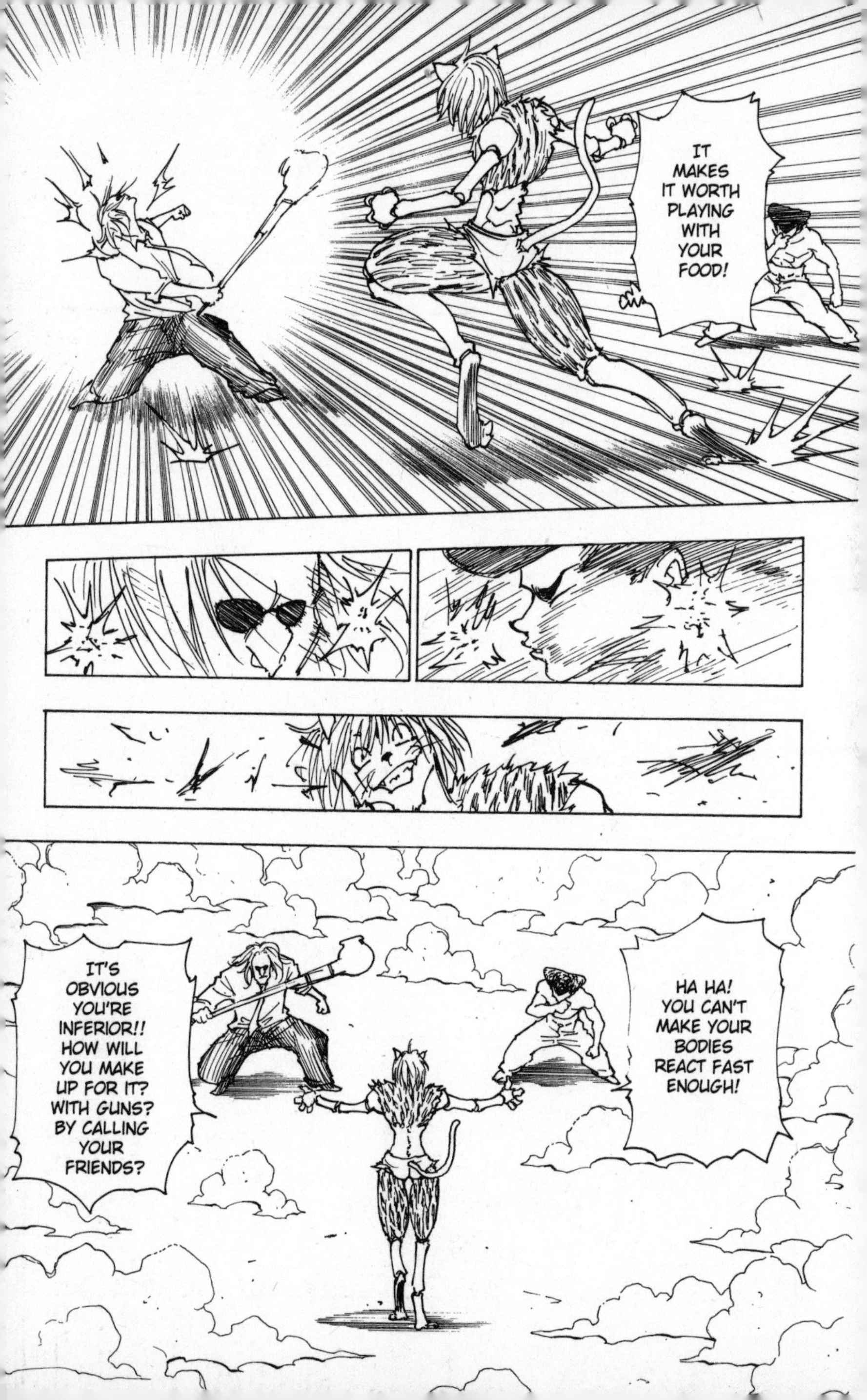
IT MAKES IT WORTH PLAYING WITH YOUR FOOD!
HA HA! YOU CAN'T MAKE YOUR BODIES REACT FAST ENOUGH!
IT'S OBVIOUS YOU'RE INFERIOR!! HOW WILL YOU MAKE UP FOR IT? WITH GUNS? BY CALLING YOUR FRIENDS?

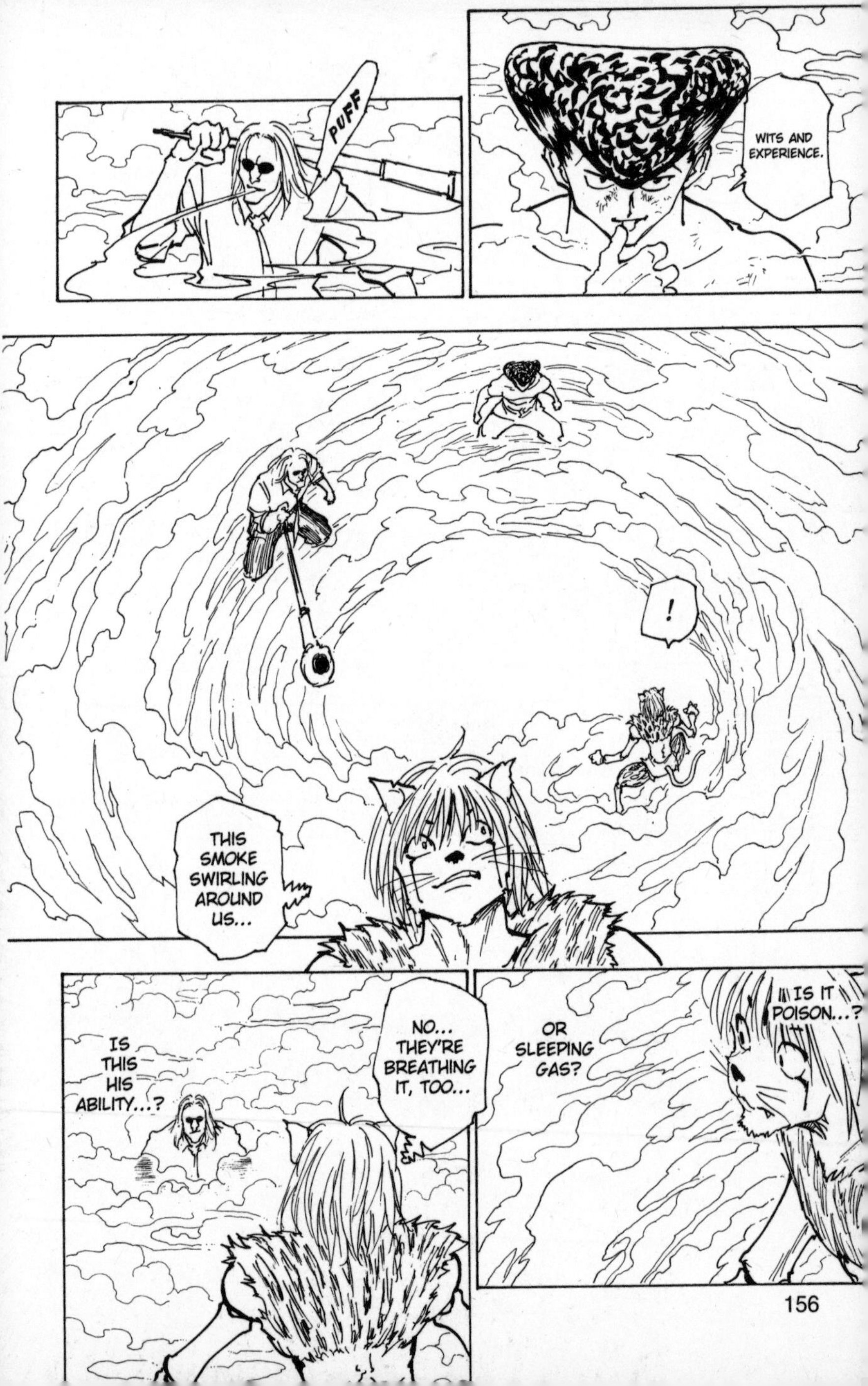

WITS AND EXPERIENCE.
PUFF
!
THIS SMOKE SWIRLING AROUND US...
IS IT POISON...?
OR SLEEPING GAS?
NO... THEY'RE BREATHING IT, TOO...
IS THIS HIS ABILITY...?

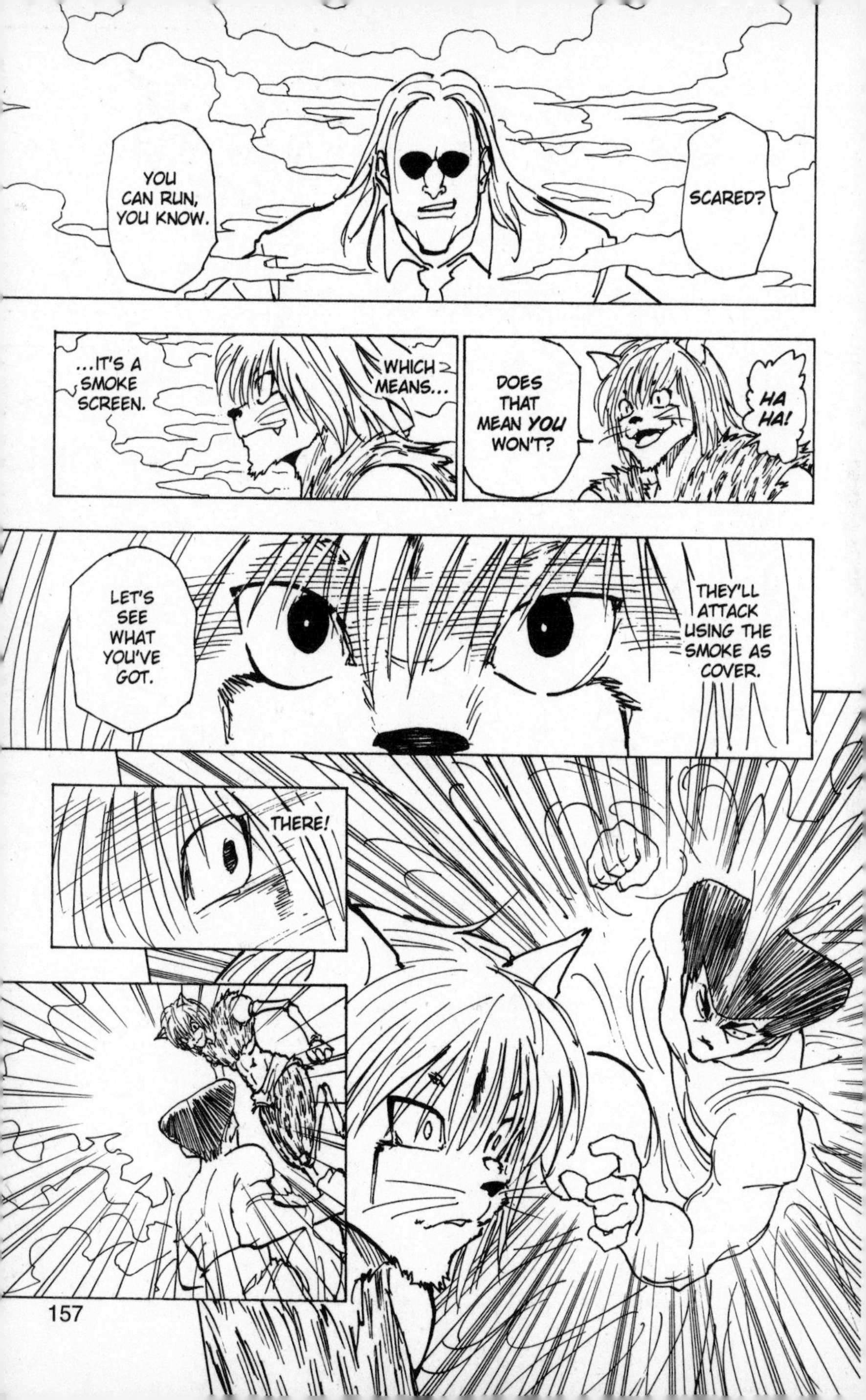
SCARED?
YOU CAN RUN, YOU KNOW.
HA HA!
DOES THAT MEAN *YOU* WON'T?
WHICH MEANS...
...IT'S A SMOKE SCREEN.
THEY'LL ATTACK USING THE SMOKE AS COVER.
LET'S SEE WHAT YOU'VE GOT.
THERE!

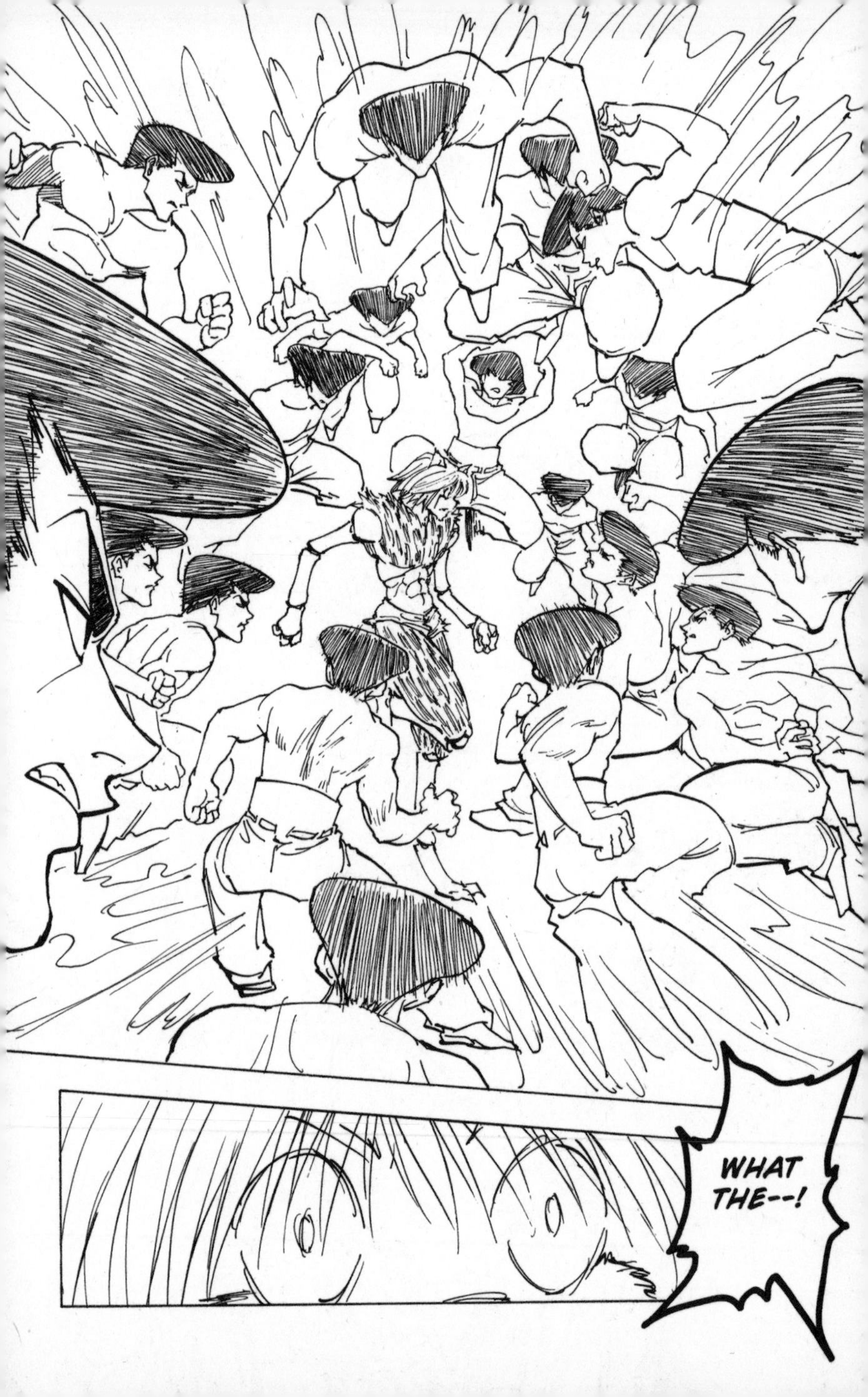
WHAT THE--!

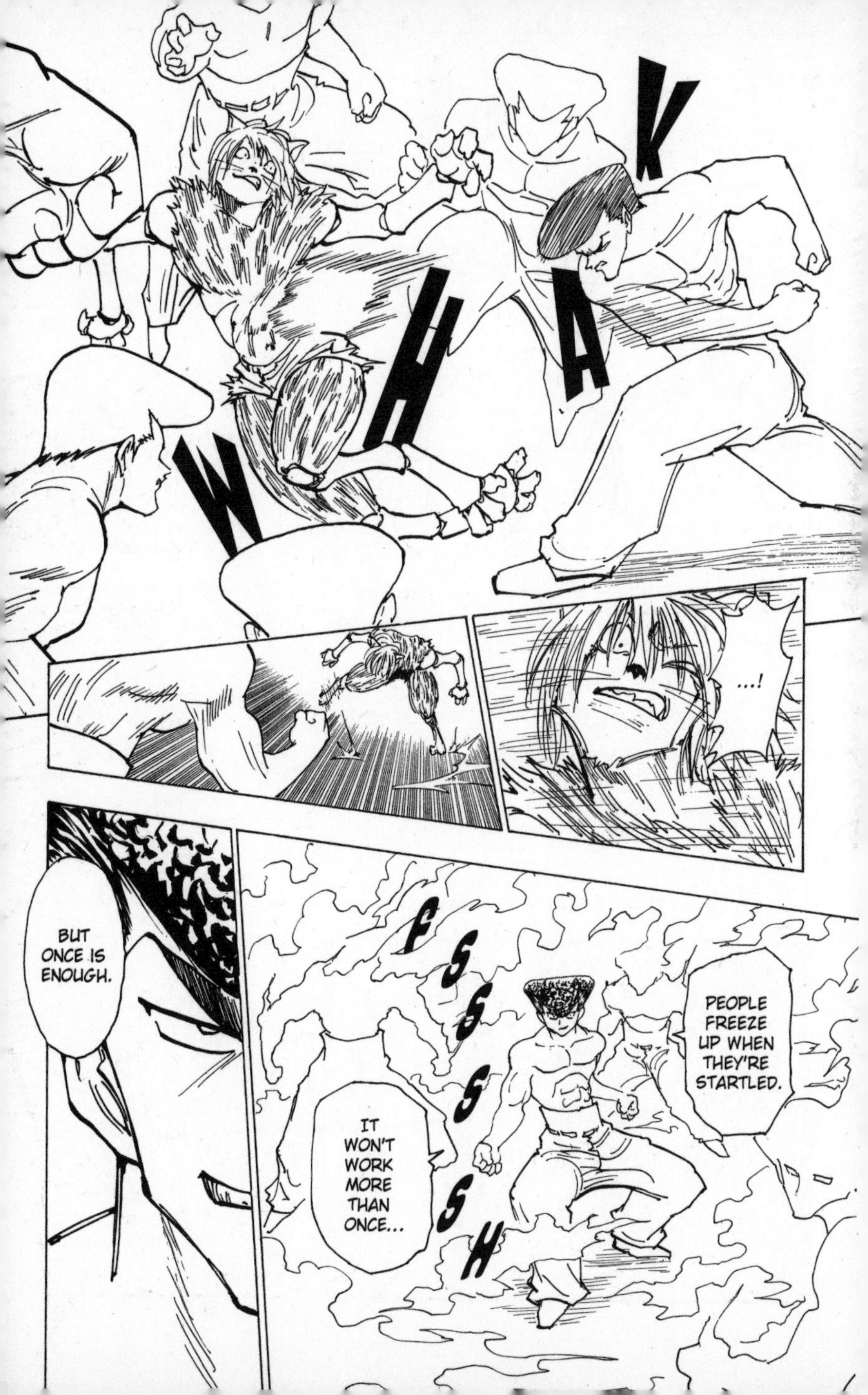
WHAK
...!
PEOPLE FREEZE UP WHEN THEY'RE STARTLED.
FSSSSH
IT WON'T WORK MORE THAN ONCE...
BUT ONCE IS ENOUGH.

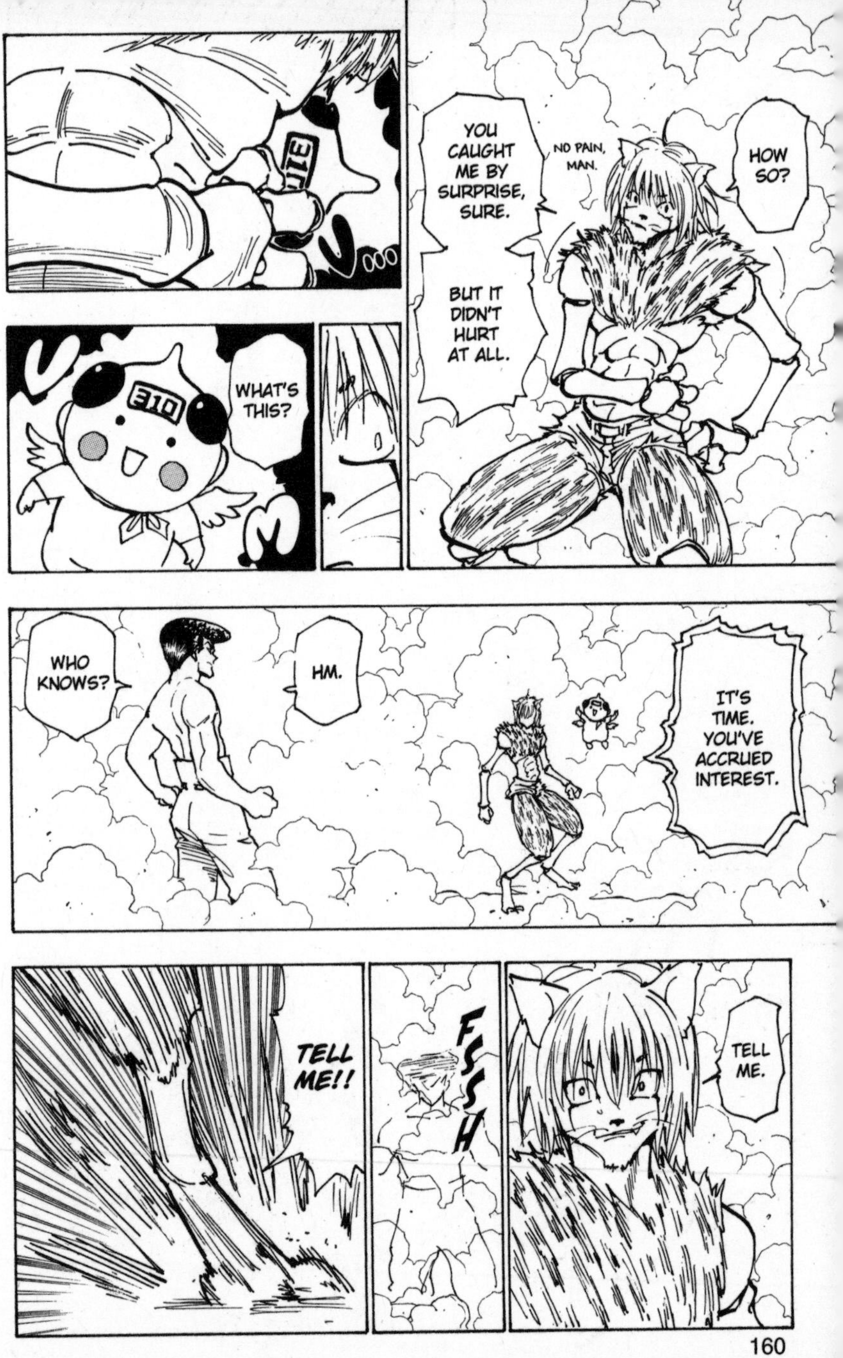
HOW SO?
NO PAIN, MAN.
YOU CAUGHT ME BY SURPRISE, SURE.
BUT IT DIDN'T HURT AT ALL.
310
WHAT'S THIS?
IT'S TIME. YOU'VE ACCRUED INTEREST.
HM.
WHO KNOWS?
TELL ME.
FSSH
TELL ME!!

READ THIS WAY

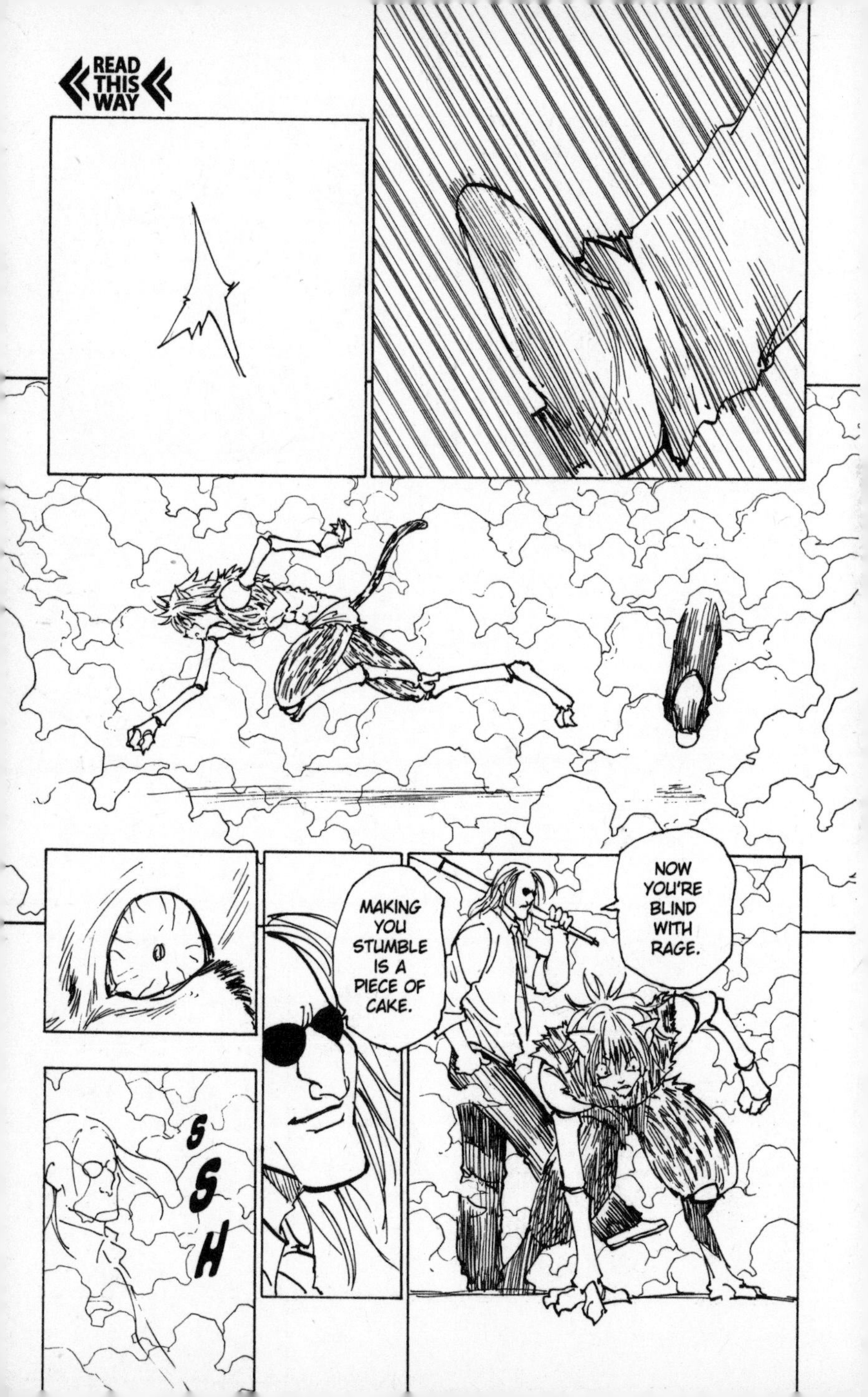

NOW YOU'RE BLIND WITH RAGE.
MAKING YOU STUMBLE IS A PIECE OF CAKE.
SSH

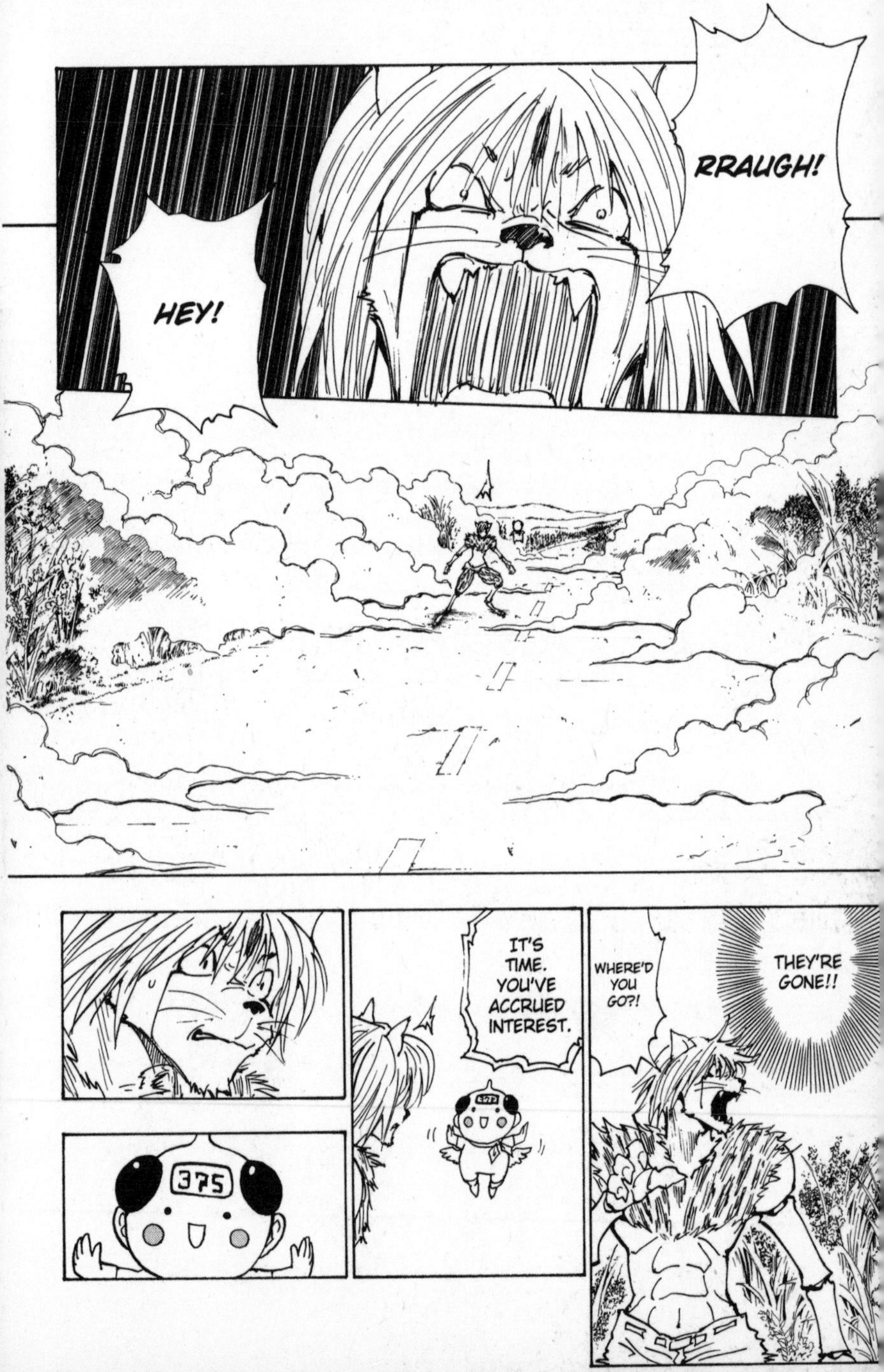
RRAUGH!
HEY!
THEY'RE GONE!!
WHERE'D YOU GO?!
IT'S TIME. YOU'VE ACCRUED INTEREST.
375

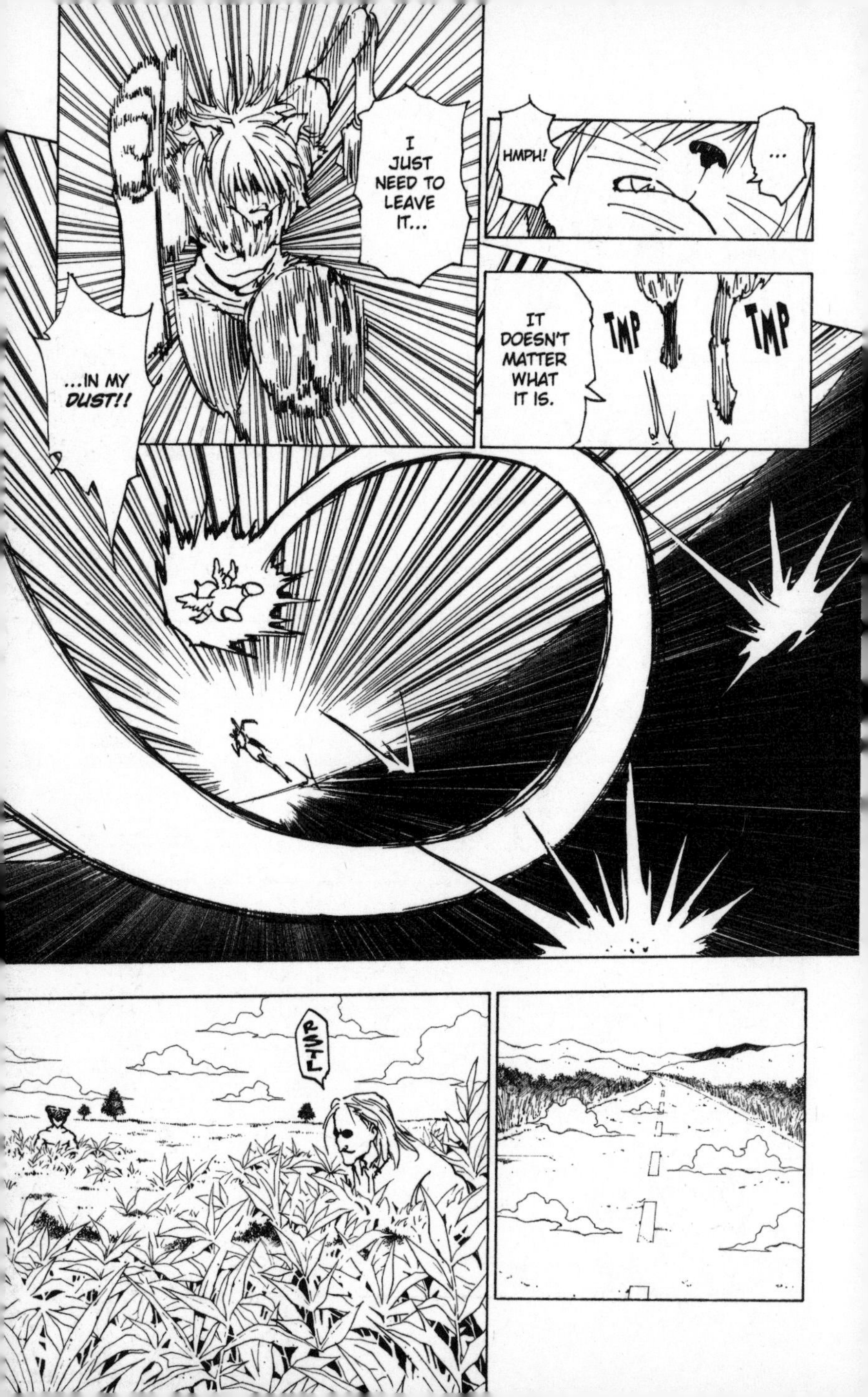
...
HMPH!
TMP
TMP
IT DOESN'T MATTER WHAT IT IS.
I JUST NEED TO LEAVE IT...
...IN MY DUST!!
RSTL

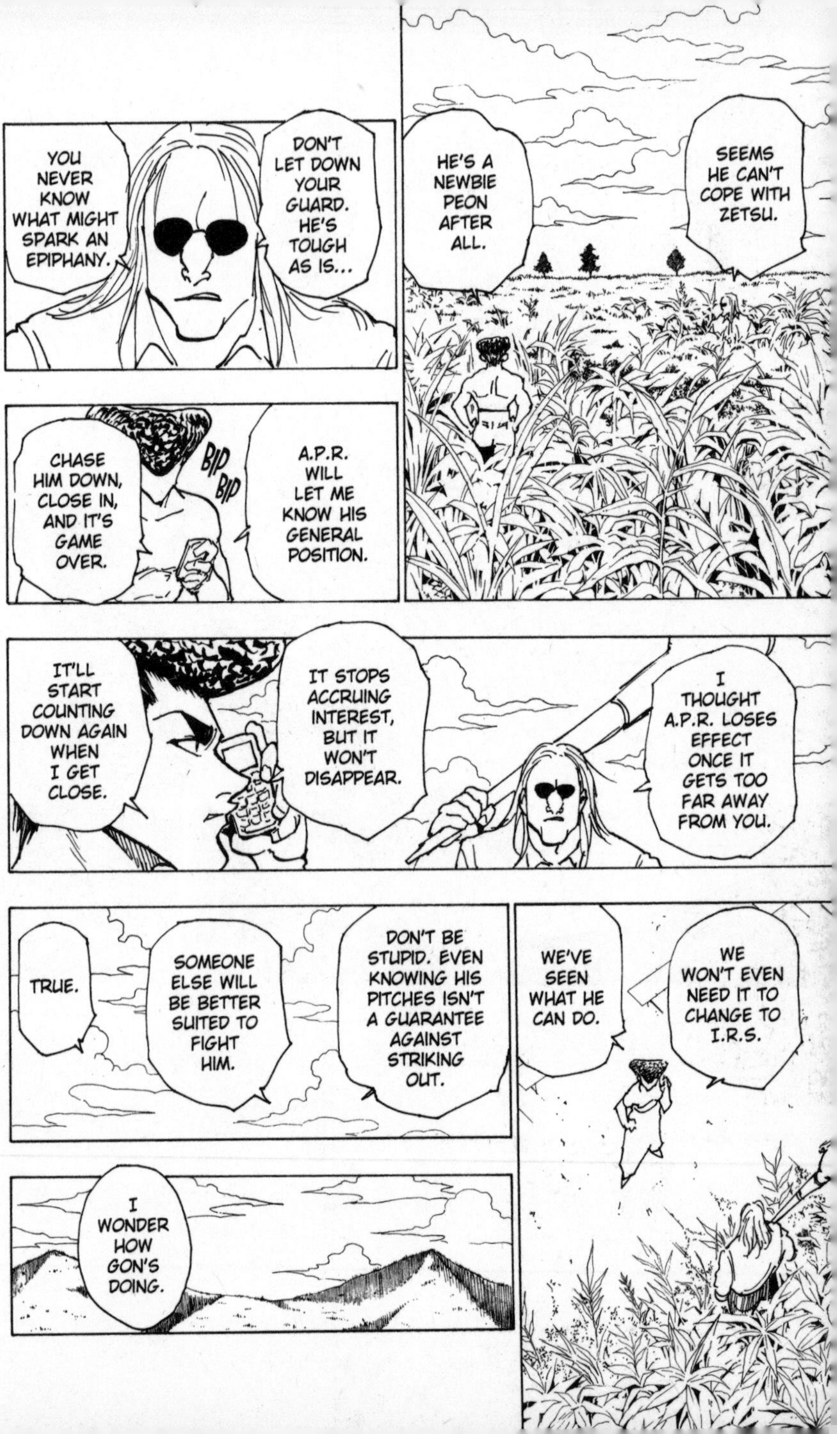
SEEMS HE CAN'T COPE WITH ZETSU.
HE'S A NEWBIE PEON AFTER ALL.
DON'T LET DOWN YOUR GUARD. HE'S TOUGH AS IS...
YOU NEVER KNOW WHAT MIGHT SPARK AN EPIPHANY.
A.P.R. WILL LET ME KNOW HIS GENERAL POSITION.
BIP BIP
CHASE HIM DOWN, CLOSE IN, AND IT'S GAME OVER.
I THOUGHT A.P.R. LOSES EFFECT ONCE IT GETS TOO FAR AWAY FROM YOU.
IT STOPS ACCRUING INTEREST, BUT IT WON'T DISAPPEAR.
IT'LL START COUNTING DOWN AGAIN WHEN I GET CLOSE.
WE WON'T EVEN NEED IT TO CHANGE TO I.R.S.
WE'VE SEEN WHAT HE CAN DO.
DON'T BE STUPID. EVEN KNOWING HIS PITCHES ISN'T A GUARANTEE AGAINST STRIKING OUT.
SOMEONE ELSE WILL BE BETTER SUITED TO FIGHT HIM.
TRUE.
I WONDER HOW GON'S DOING.

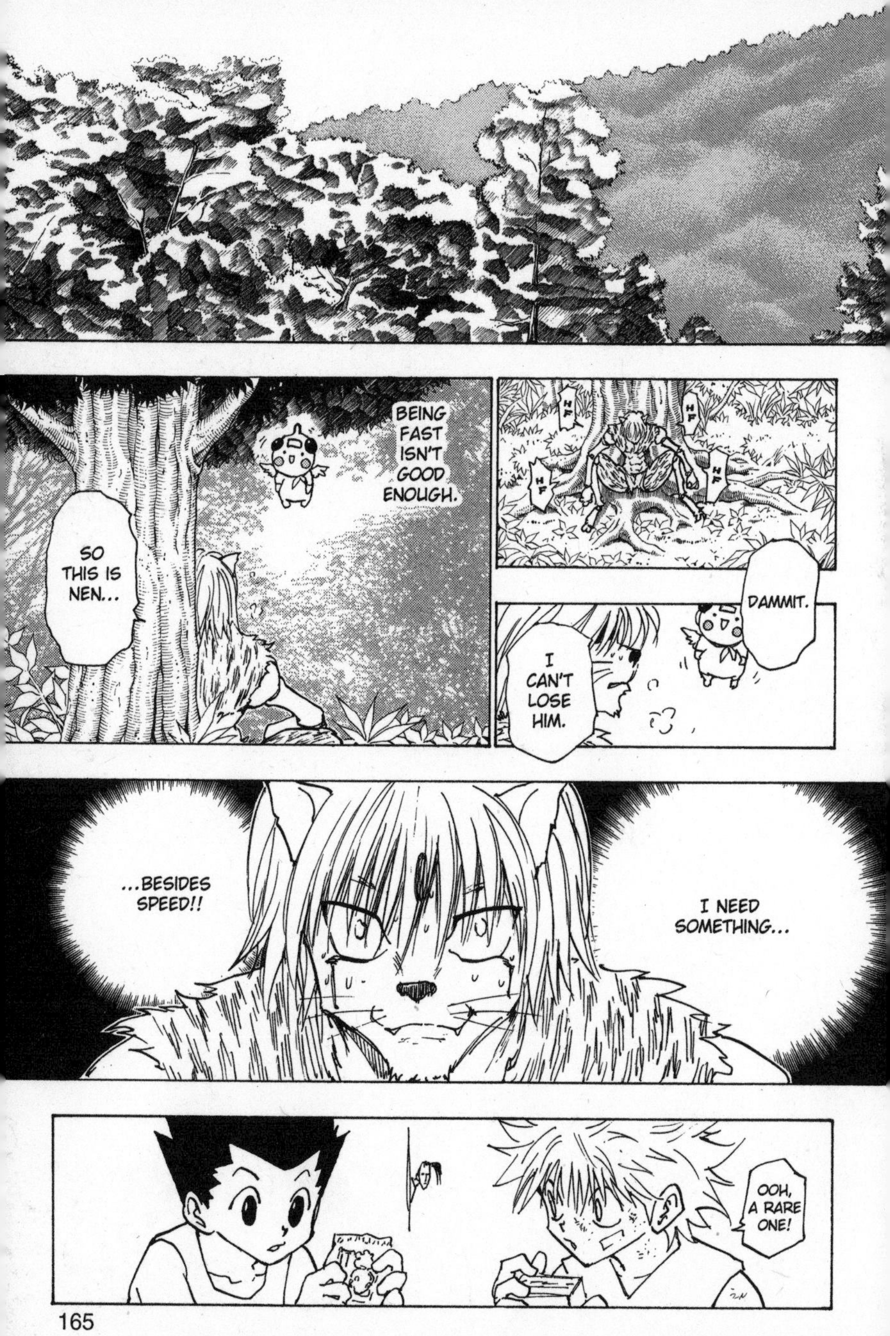
HF
HF
HF
HF
DAMMIT.
I CAN'T LOSE HIM.
BEING FAST ISN'T GOOD ENOUGH.
SO THIS IS NEN...
I NEED SOMETHING...
...BESIDES SPEED!!
OOH, A RARE ONE!

Chapter 222: Reunion: Part 3

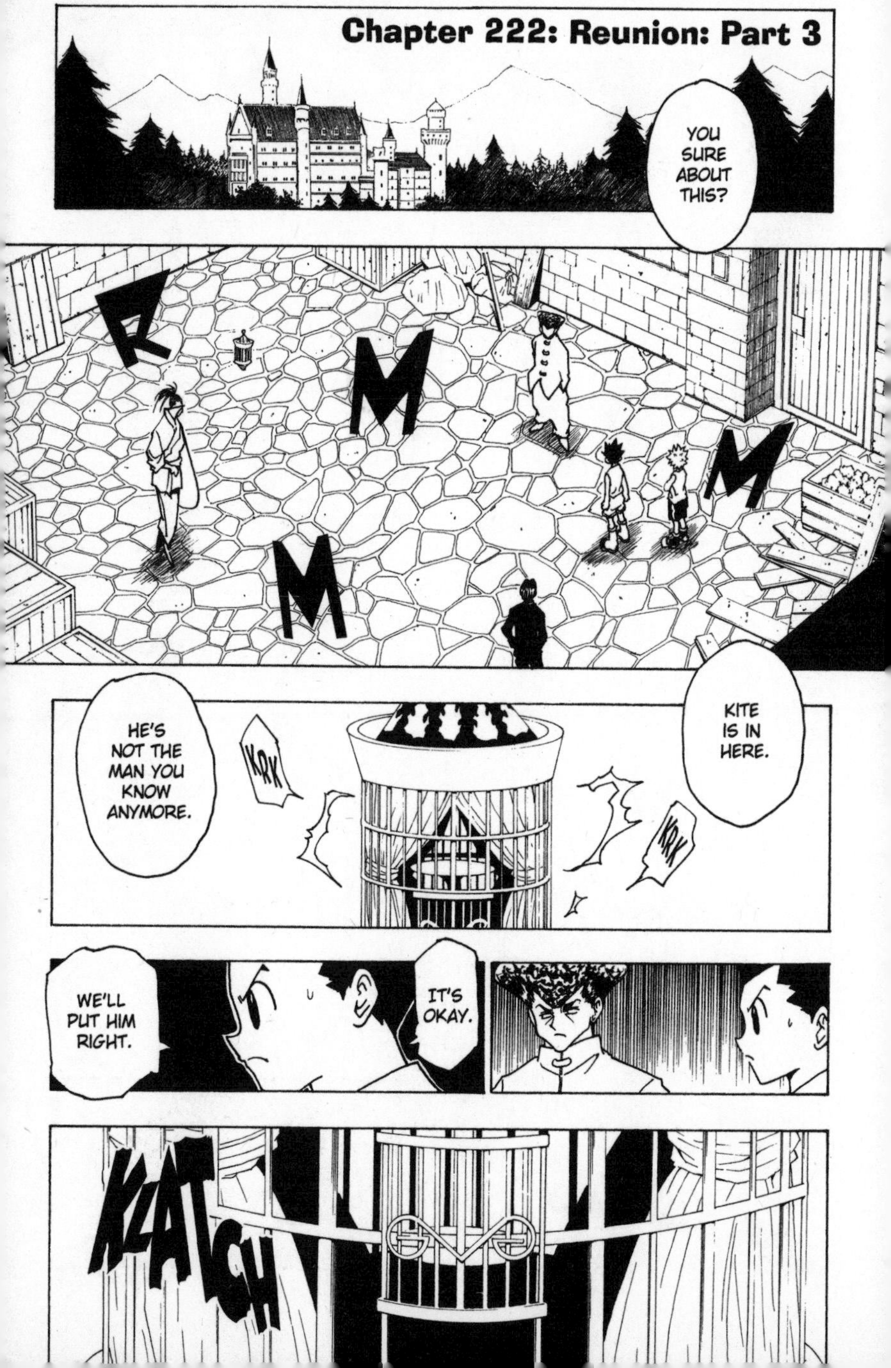
YOU SURE ABOUT THIS?
RMMM
KITE IS IN HERE.
KRK
KRK
HE'S NOT THE MAN YOU KNOW ANYMORE.
IT'S OKAY.
WE'LL PUT HIM RIGHT.
KLATCH

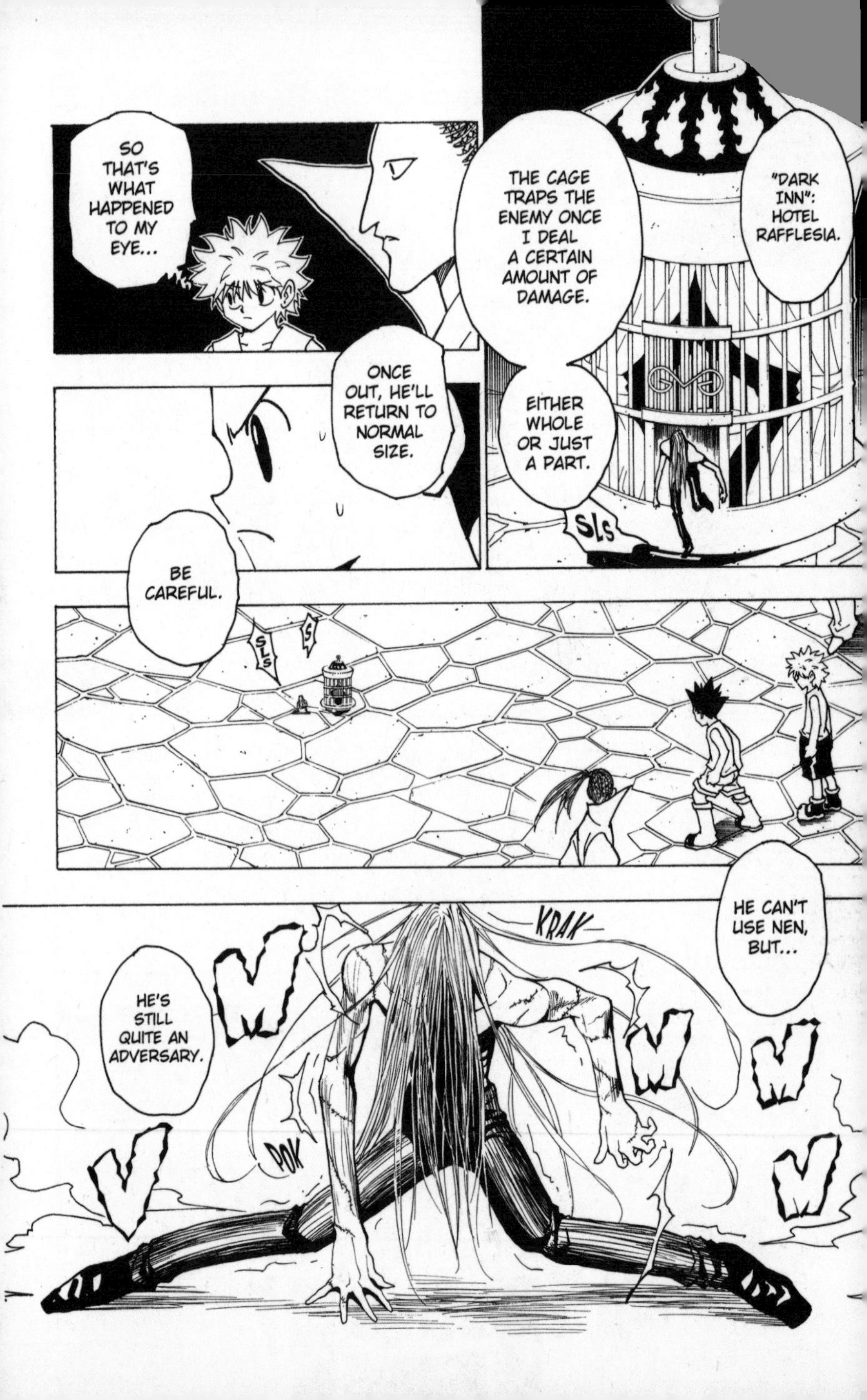
"DARK INN": HOTEL RAFFLESIA.
THE CAGE TRAPS THE ENEMY ONCE I DEAL A CERTAIN AMOUNT OF DAMAGE.
SO THAT'S WHAT HAPPENED TO MY EYE...
EITHER WHOLE OR JUST A PART.
SLS
ONCE OUT, HE'LL RETURN TO NORMAL SIZE.
BE CAREFUL.
S
SLS
HE CAN'T USE NEN, BUT...
KRAK
HE'S STILL QUITE AN ADVERSARY.
POK

READ THIS WAY

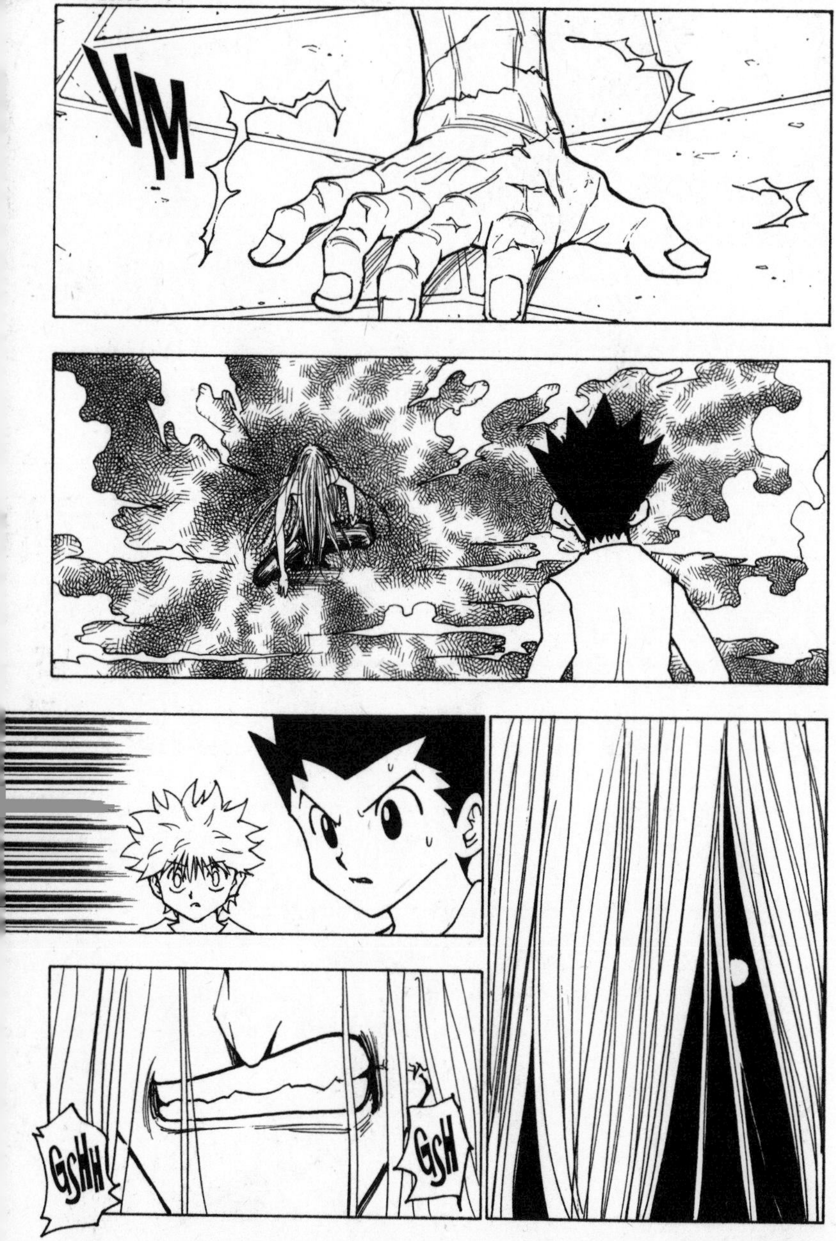
VM
GSH
GSHH

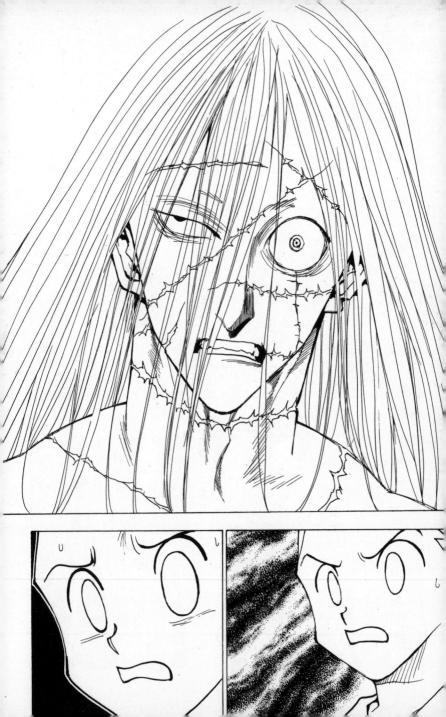

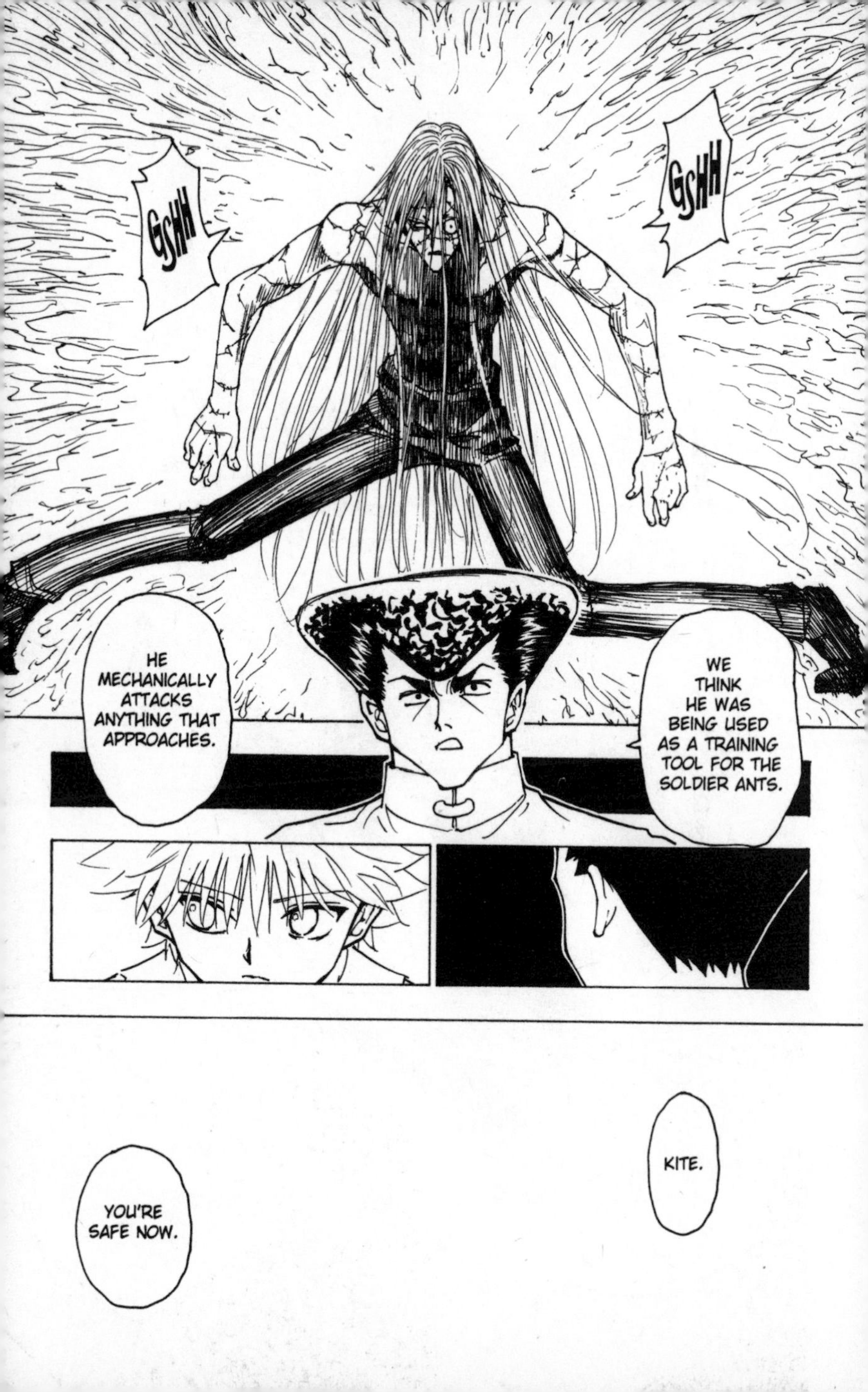
GSHH
GSHH
WE THINK HE WAS BEING USED AS A TRAINING TOOL FOR THE SOLDIER ANTS.
HE MECHANICALLY ATTACKS ANYTHING THAT APPROACHES.
KITE.
YOU'RE SAFE NOW.

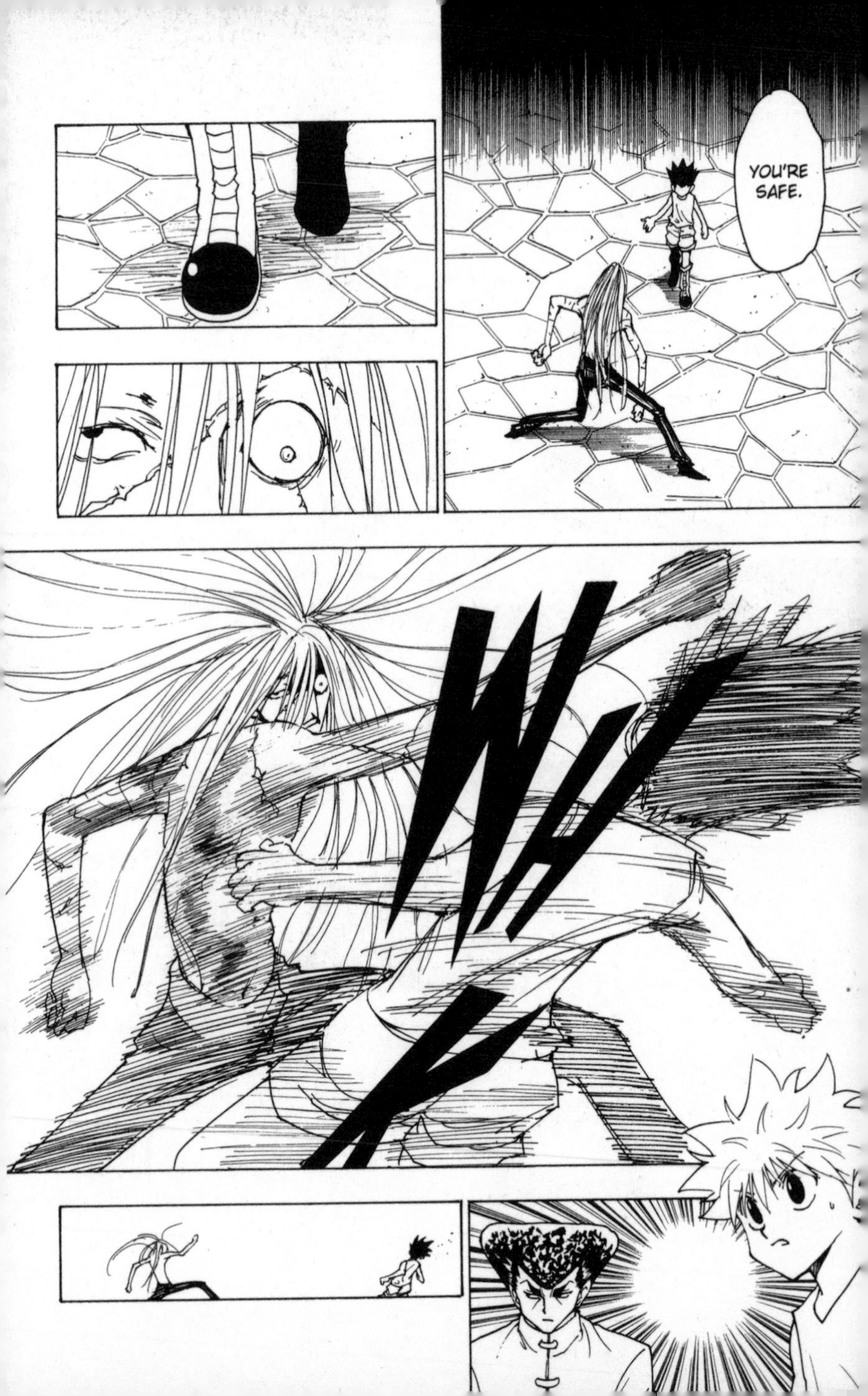
YOU'RE SAFE.

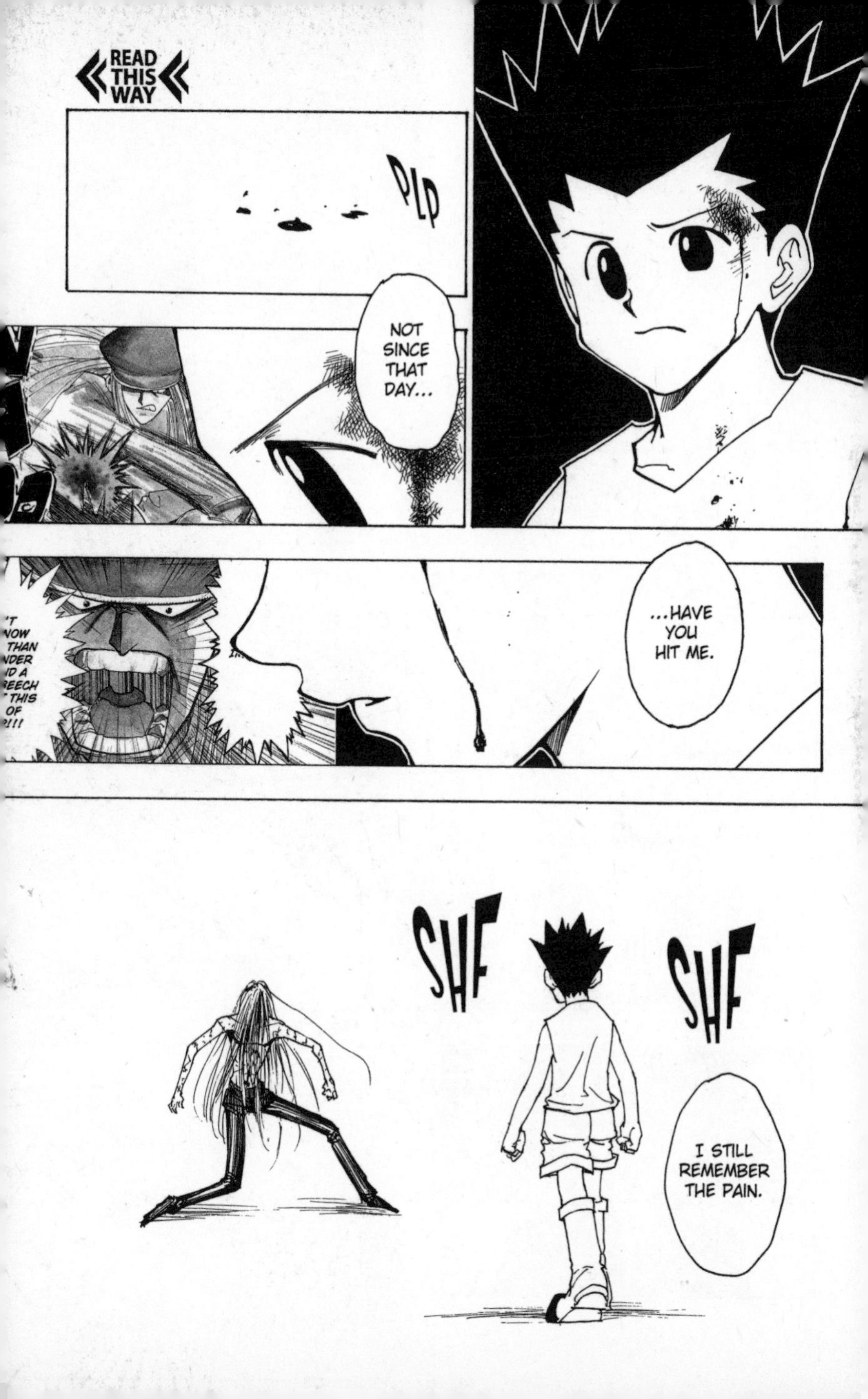
READ THIS WAY
PLP
NOT SINCE THAT DAY...
...HAVE YOU HIT ME.
SHF
SHF
I STILL REMEMBER THE PAIN.

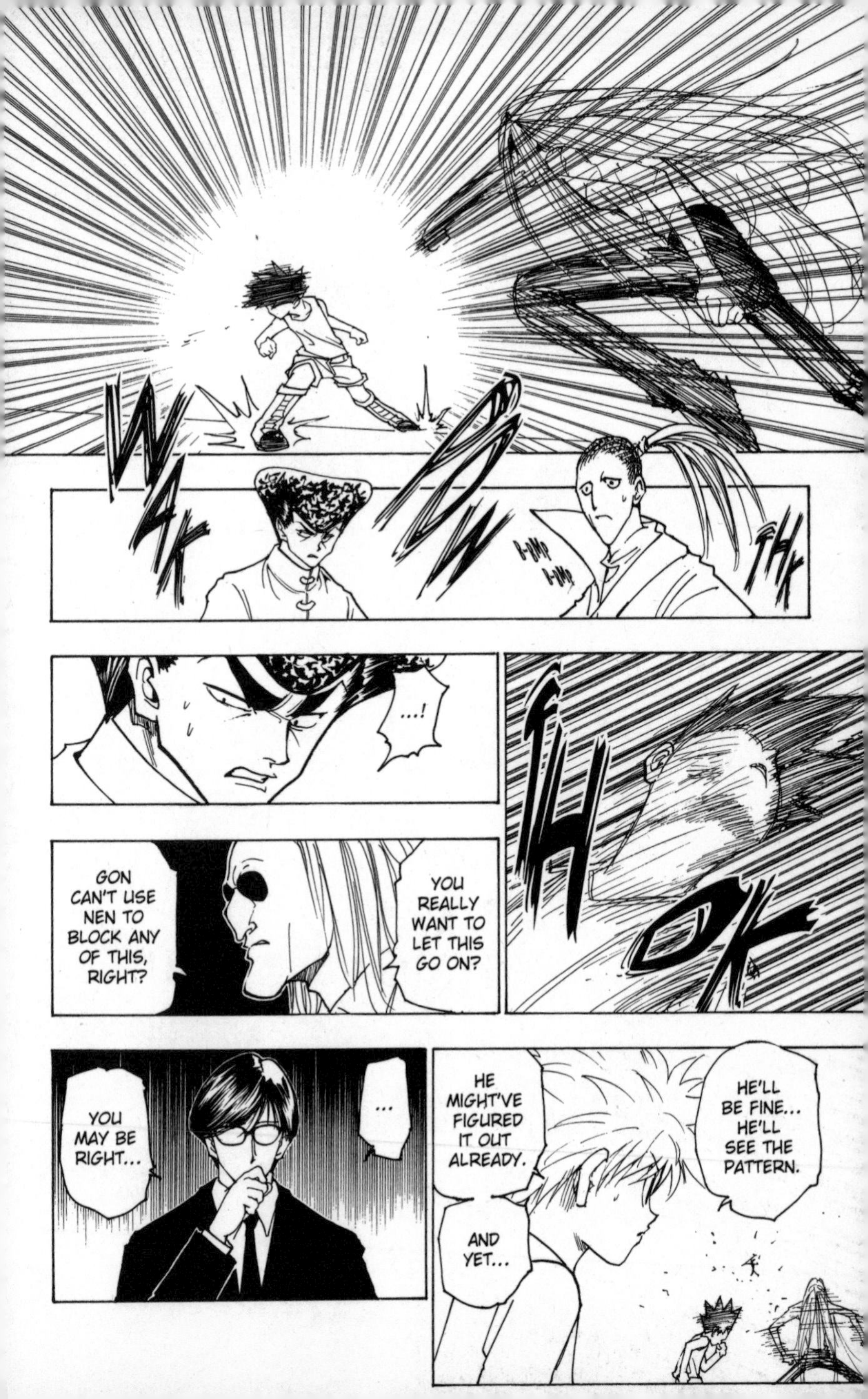
WAK
THK
B-BMP
B-BMP
...!
YOU REALLY WANT TO LET THIS GO ON?
GON CAN'T USE NEN TO BLOCK ANY OF THIS, RIGHT?
HE'LL BE FINE... HE'LL SEE THE PATTERN.
HE MIGHT'VE FIGURED IT OUT ALREADY.
AND YET...
...
YOU MAY BE RIGHT...

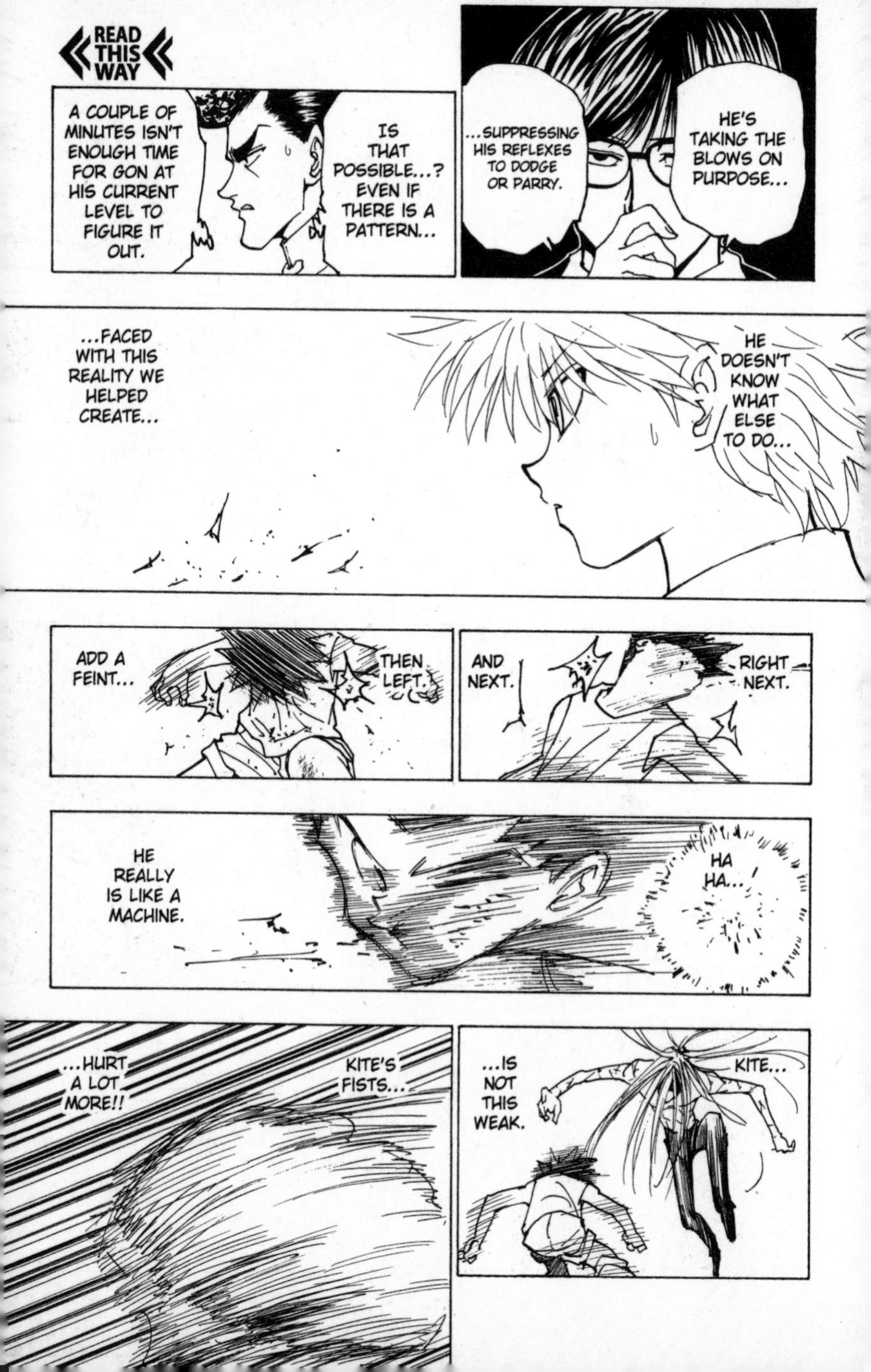
READ THIS WAY
HE'S TAKING THE BLOWS ON PURPOSE...
...SUPPRESSING HIS REFLEXES TO DODGE OR PARRY.
IS THAT POSSIBLE...? EVEN IF THERE IS A PATTERN...
A COUPLE OF MINUTES ISN'T ENOUGH TIME FOR GON AT HIS CURRENT LEVEL TO FIGURE IT OUT.
HE DOESN'T KNOW WHAT ELSE TO DO...
...FACED WITH THIS REALITY WE HELPED CREATE...
RIGHT NEXT.
AND NEXT.
THEN LEFT.
ADD A FEINT...
HA HA...!
HE REALLY IS LIKE A MACHINE.
KITE...
...IS NOT THIS WEAK.
KITE'S FISTS...
...HURT A LOT MORE!!

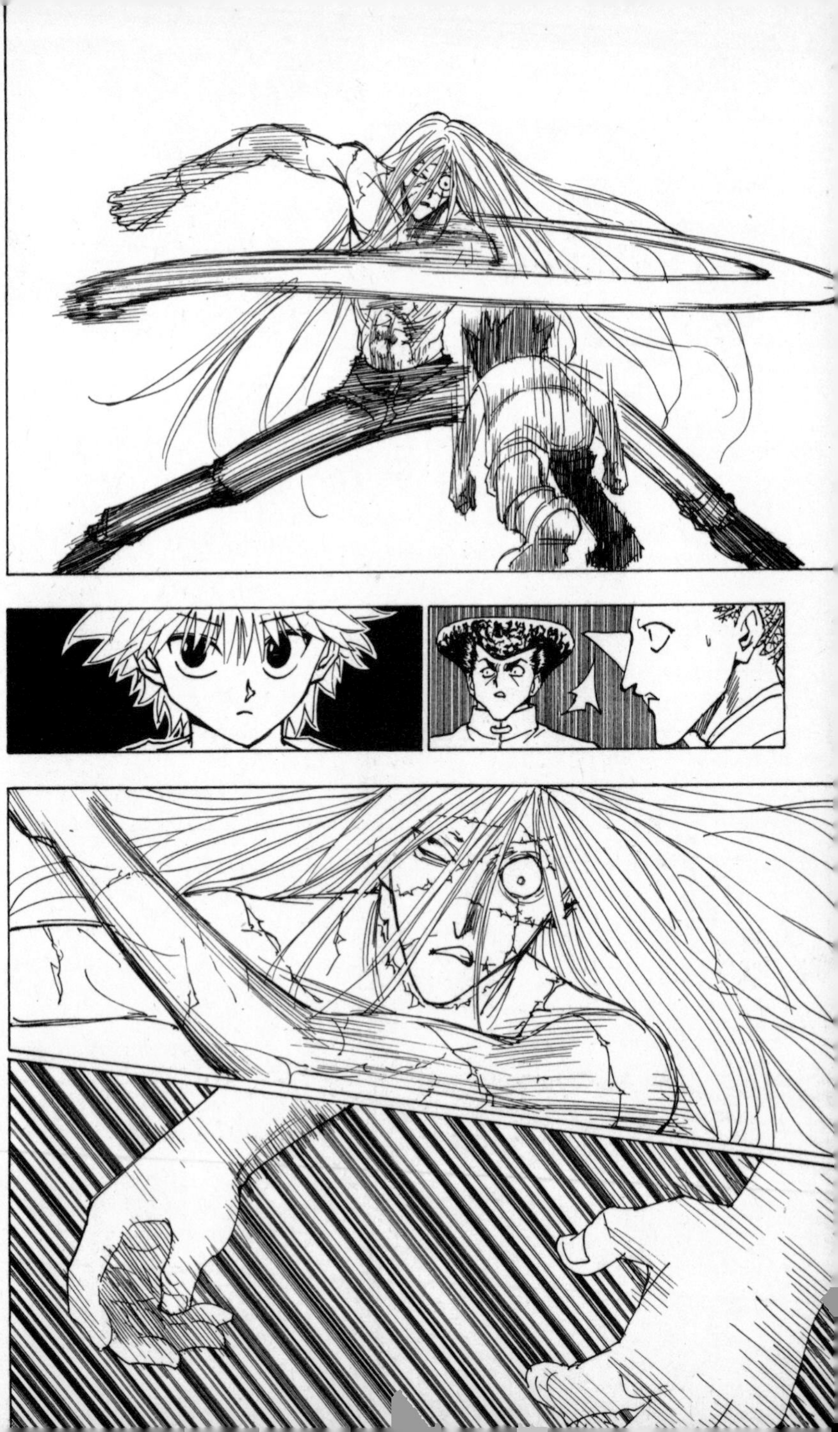

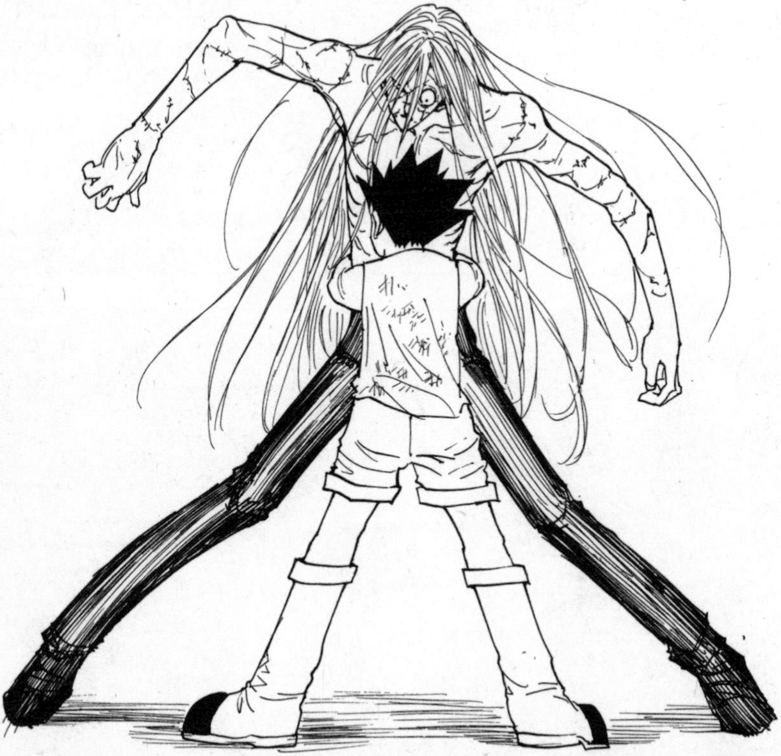

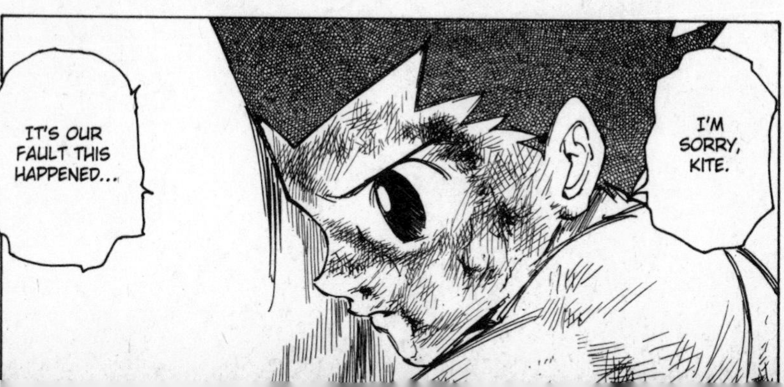
I'M SORRY, KITE.
IT'S OUR FAULT THIS HAPPENED...

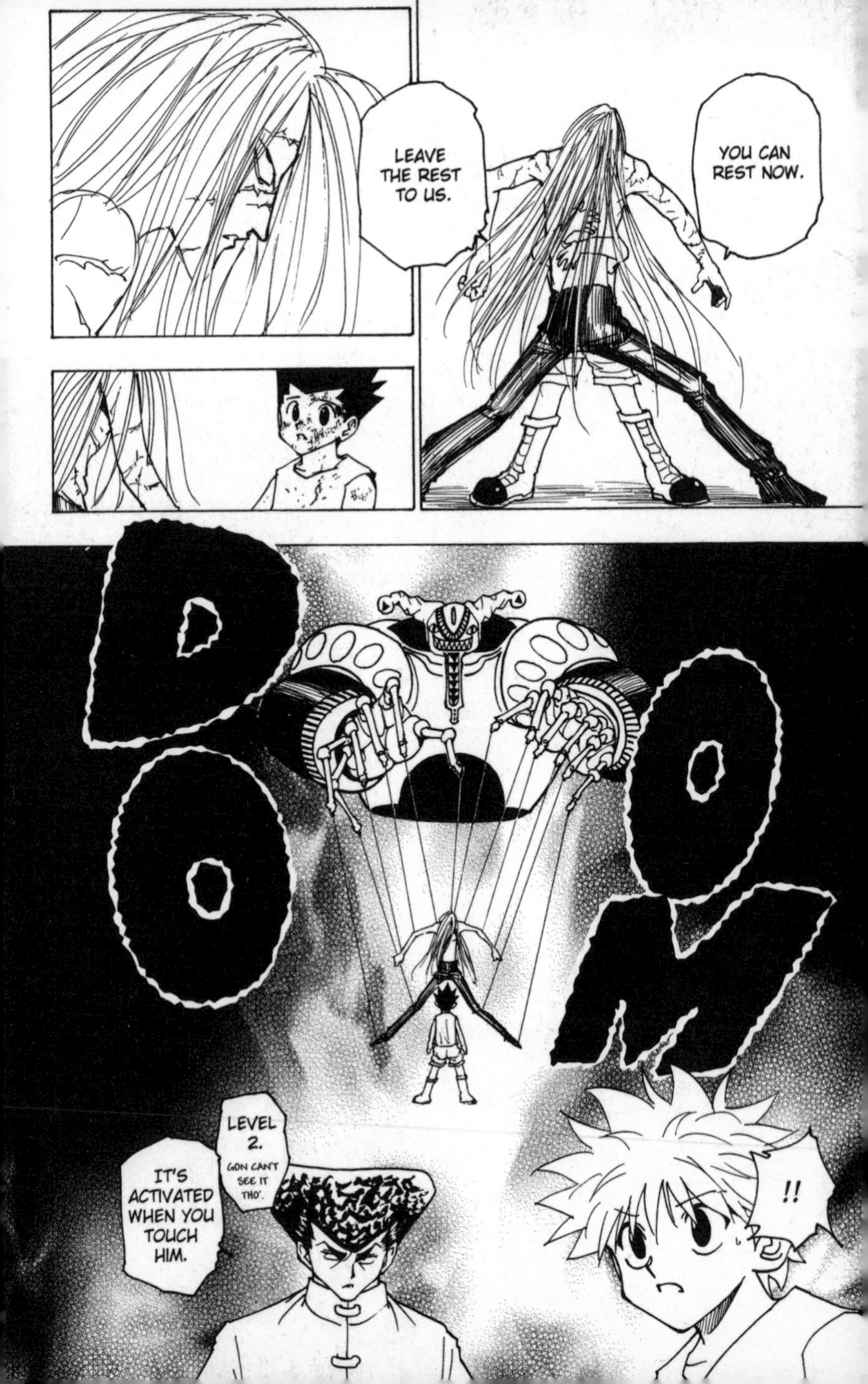
YOU CAN REST NOW.
LEAVE THE REST TO US.
BOOM
!!
LEVEL 2.
GON CAN'T SEE IT THO'.
IT'S ACTIVATED WHEN YOU TOUCH HIM.

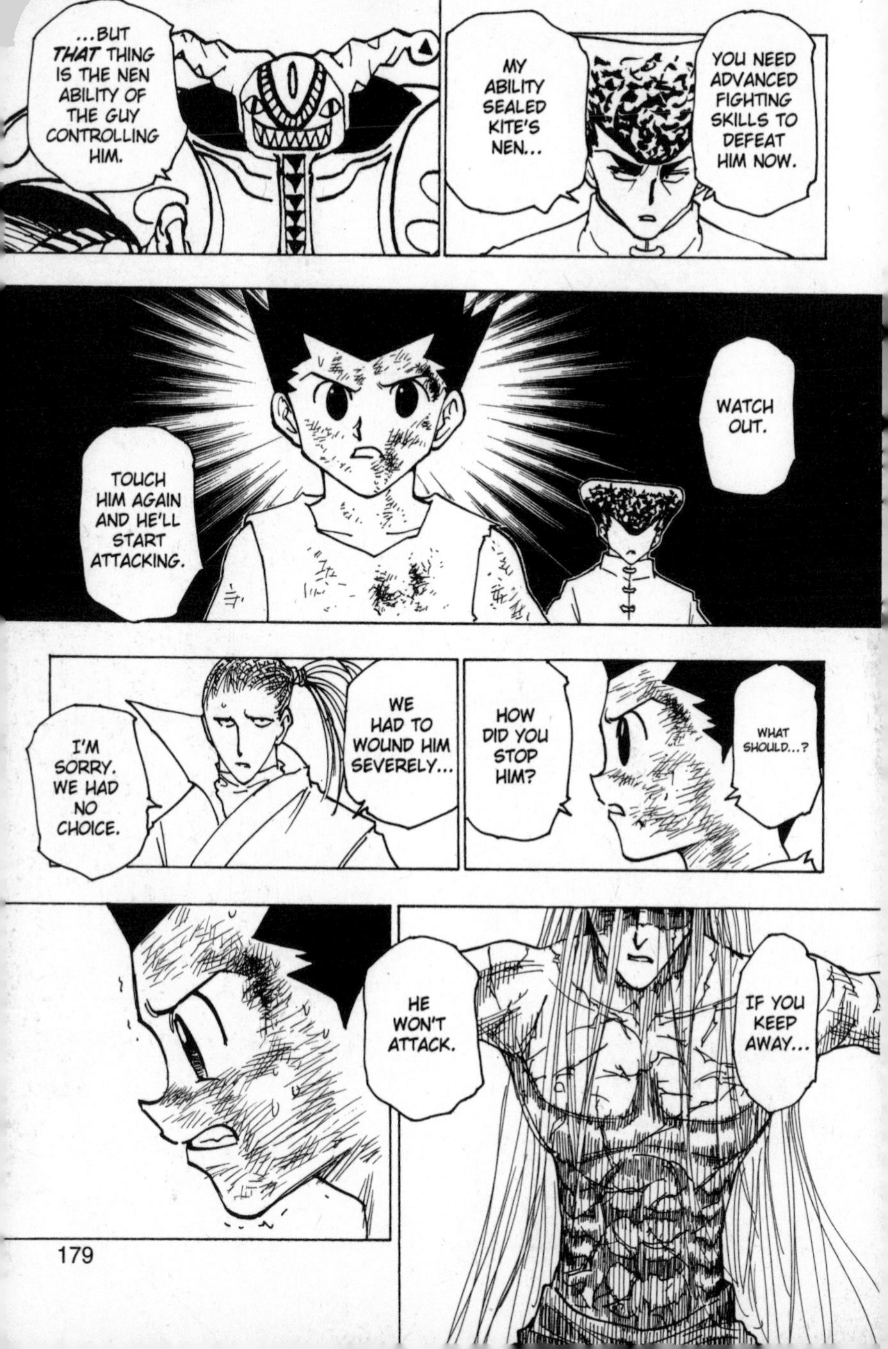
YOU NEED ADVANCED FIGHTING SKILLS TO DEFEAT HIM NOW.
MY ABILITY SEALED KITE'S NEN...
...BUT *THAT* THING IS THE NEN ABILITY OF THE GUY CONTROLLING HIM.
WATCH OUT.
TOUCH HIM AGAIN AND HE'LL START ATTACKING.
WHAT SHOULD...?
HOW DID YOU STOP HIM?
WE HAD TO WOUND HIM SEVERELY...
I'M SORRY. WE HAD NO CHOICE.
IF YOU KEEP AWAY...
HE WON'T ATTACK.

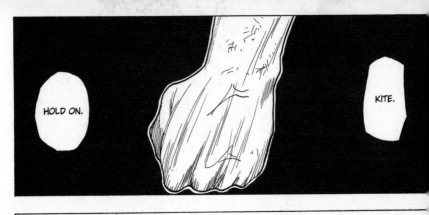

HOLD ON.

KITE.

WE'LL PUT YOU RIGHT.

KILLUA...

BRR

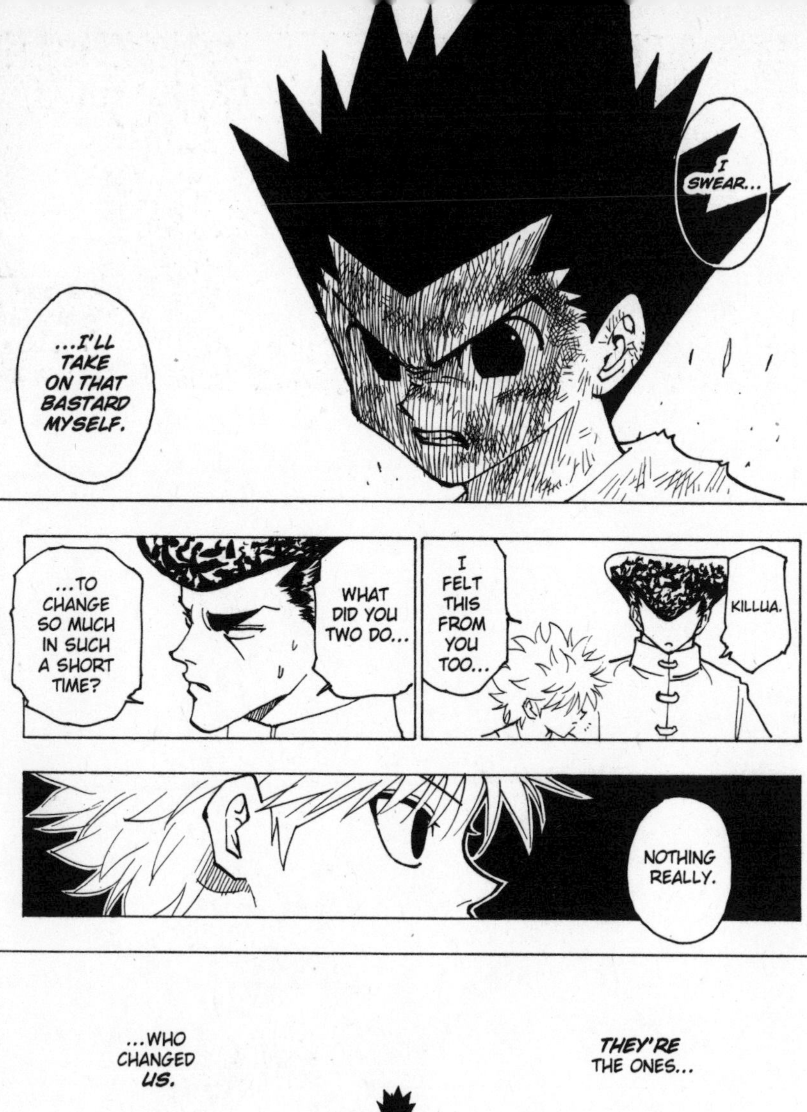
I SWEAR...
...I'LL TAKE ON THAT BASTARD MYSELF.
KILLUA.
I FELT THIS FROM YOU TOO...
WHAT DID YOU TWO DO...
...TO CHANGE SO MUCH IN SUCH A SHORT TIME?
NOTHING REALLY.
THEY'RE THE ONES...
...WHO CHANGED US.

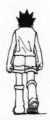

Chapter 223: 10: Part 1

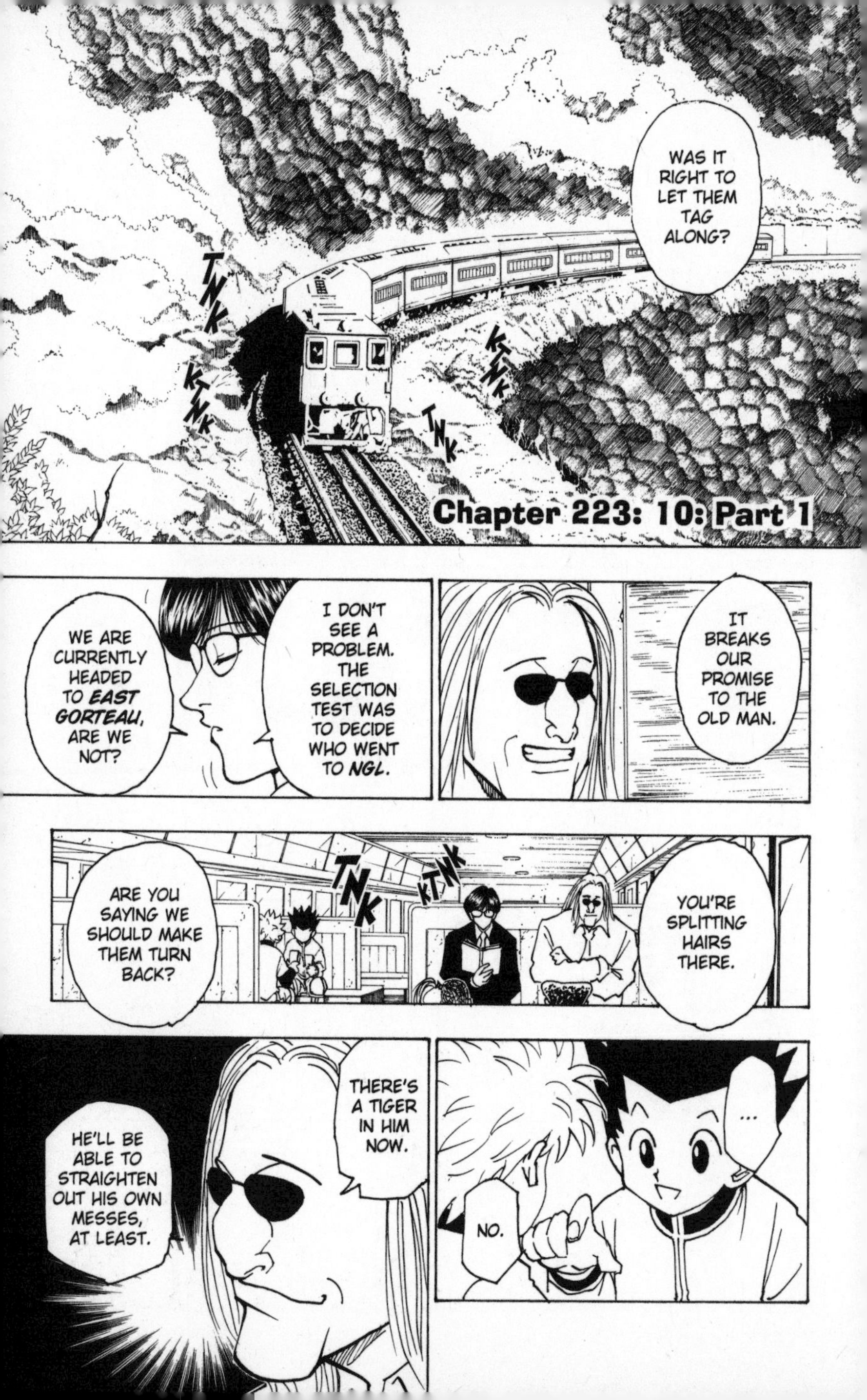
WAS IT RIGHT TO LET THEM TAG ALONG?
KTNK
TNK
TNK
KTNK
IT BREAKS OUR PROMISE TO THE OLD MAN.
I DON'T SEE A PROBLEM. THE SELECTION TEST WAS TO DECIDE WHO WENT TO *NGL*.
WE ARE CURRENTLY HEADED TO *EAST GORTEAU*, ARE WE NOT?
YOU'RE SPLITTING HAIRS THERE.
KTNK
TNK
ARE YOU SAYING WE SHOULD MAKE THEM TURN BACK?
...
NO.
THERE'S A TIGER IN HIM NOW.
HE'LL BE ABLE TO STRAIGHTEN OUT HIS OWN MESSES, AT LEAST.

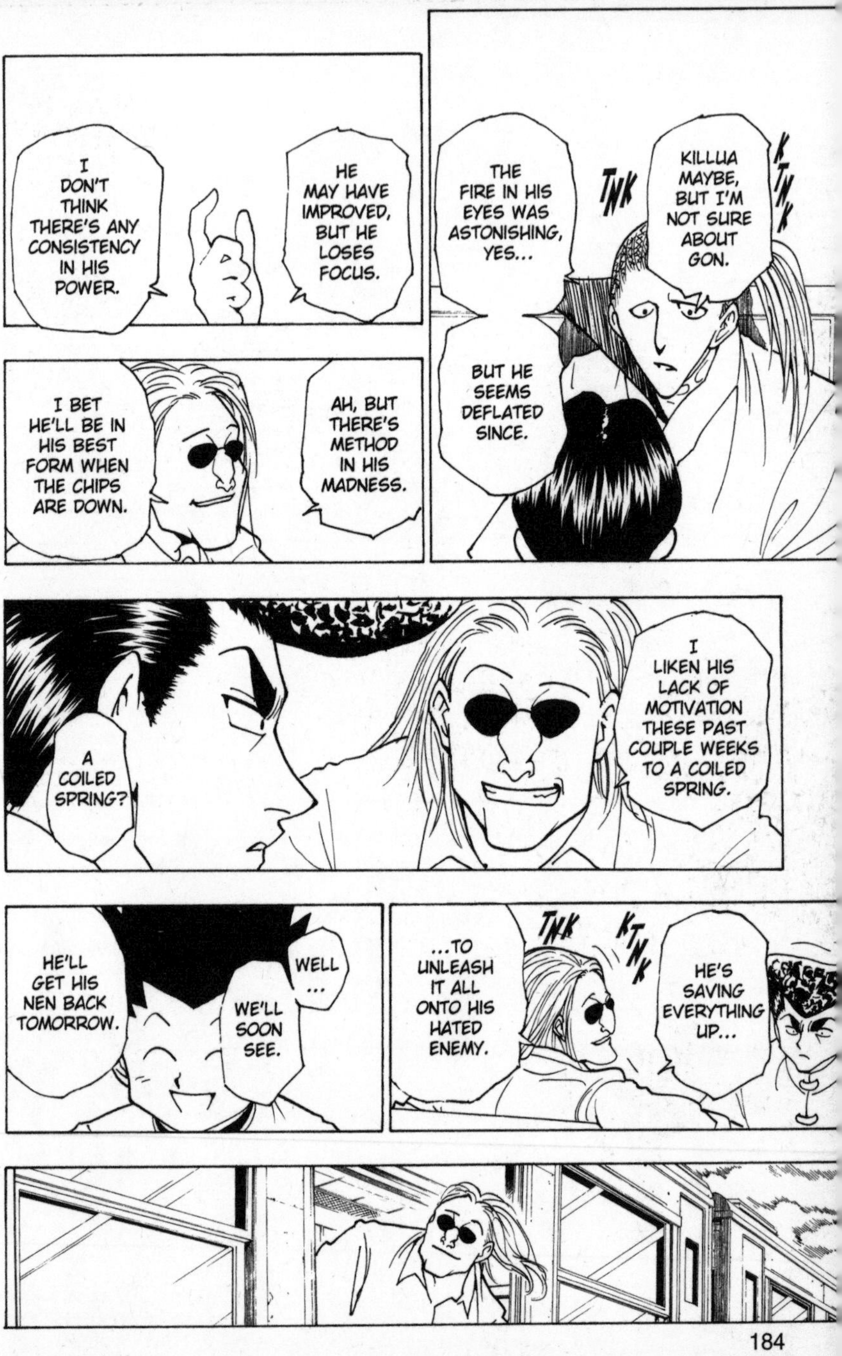
KTNK
TNK
KILLUA MAYBE, BUT I'M NOT SURE ABOUT GON.
THE FIRE IN HIS EYES WAS ASTONISHING, YES...
BUT HE SEEMS DEFLATED SINCE.
HE MAY HAVE IMPROVED, BUT HE LOSES FOCUS.
I DON'T THINK THERE'S ANY CONSISTENCY IN HIS POWER.
AH, BUT THERE'S METHOD IN HIS MADNESS.
I BET HE'LL BE IN HIS BEST FORM WHEN THE CHIPS ARE DOWN.
I LIKEN HIS LACK OF MOTIVATION THESE PAST COUPLE WEEKS TO A COILED SPRING.
A COILED SPRING?
KTNK
TNK
HE'S SAVING EVERYTHING UP...
...TO UNLEASH IT ALL ONTO HIS HATED ENEMY.
WELL...
WE'LL SOON SEE.
HE'LL GET HIS NEN BACK TOMORROW.

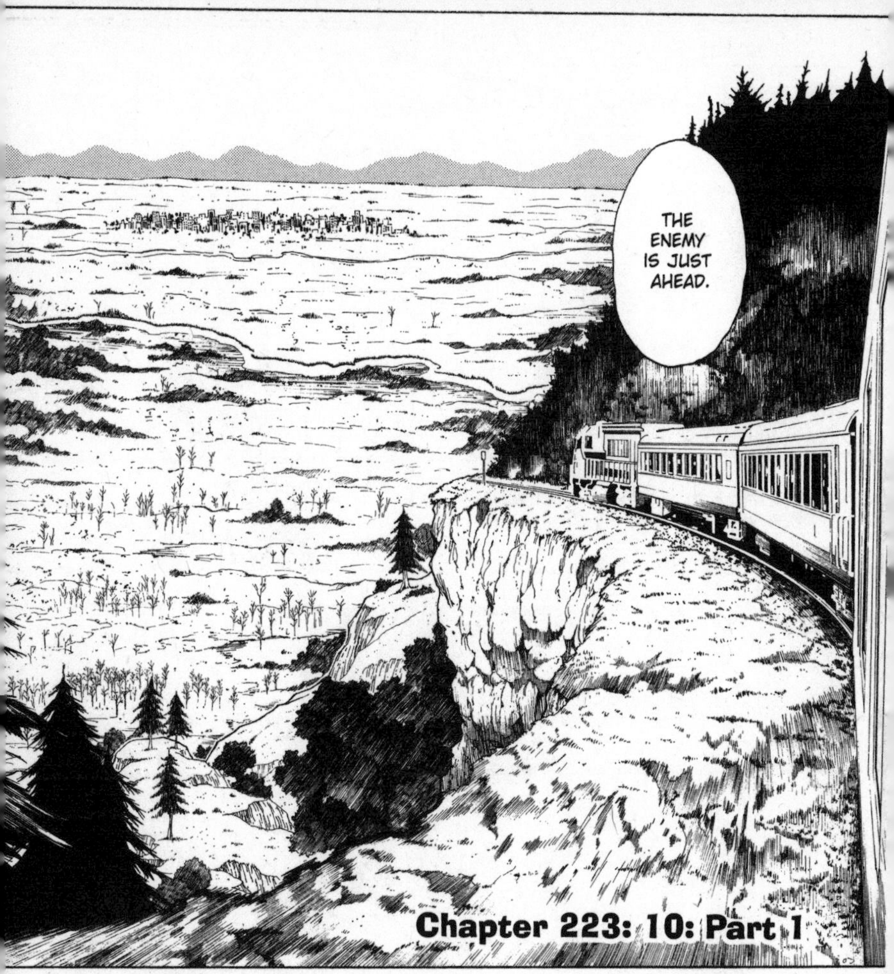
THE ENEMY IS JUST AHEAD.
Chapter 223: 10: Part 1
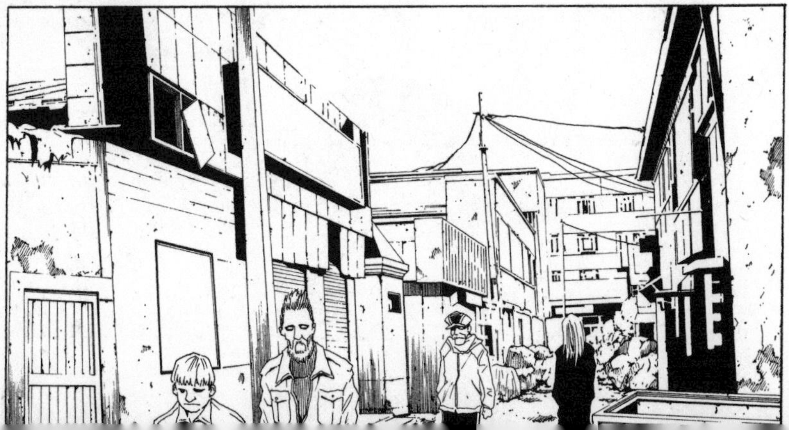

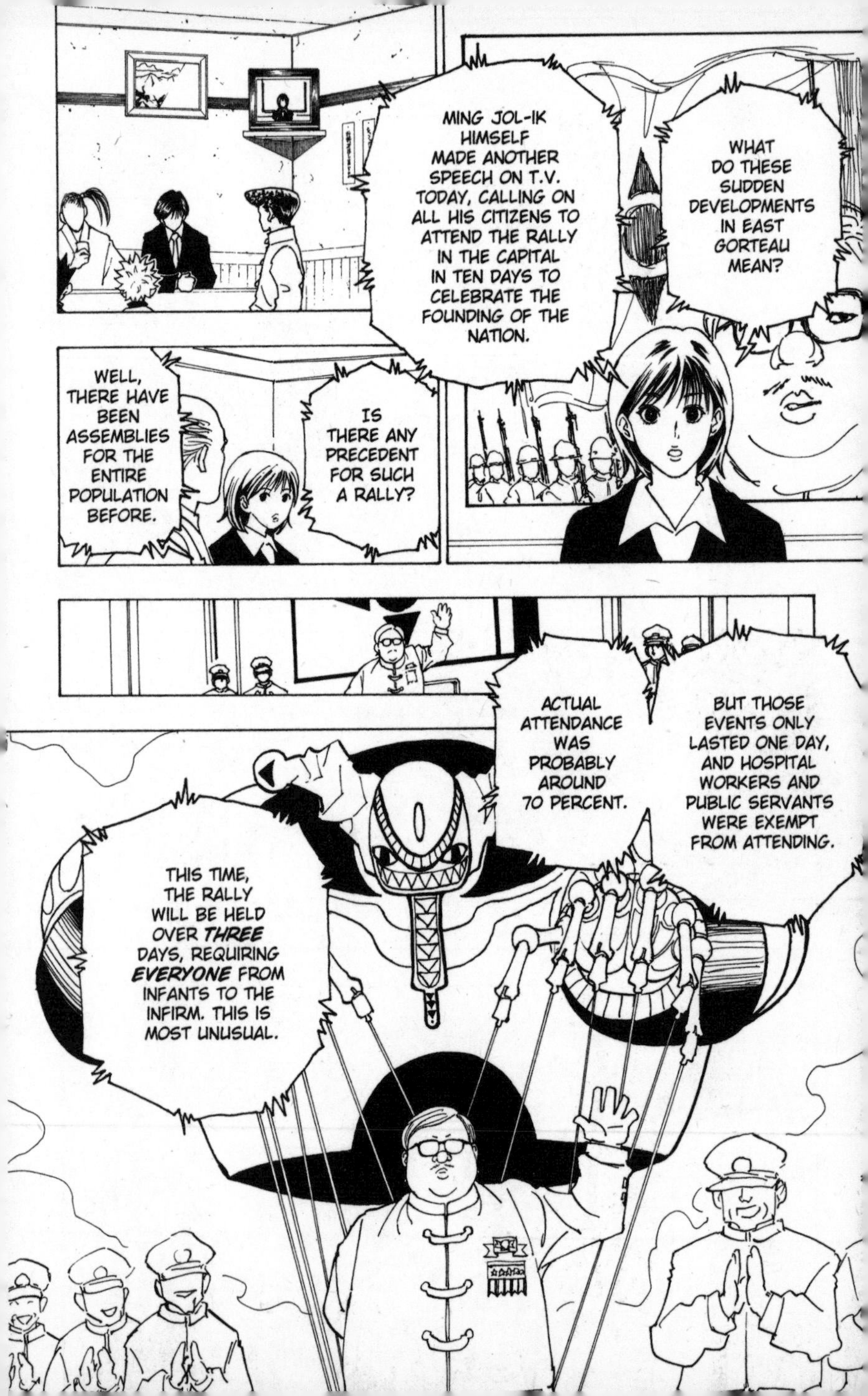
WHAT DO THESE SUDDEN DEVELOPMENTS IN EAST GORTEAU MEAN?
MING JOL-IK HIMSELF MADE ANOTHER SPEECH ON T.V. TODAY, CALLING ON ALL HIS CITIZENS TO ATTEND THE RALLY IN THE CAPITAL IN TEN DAYS TO CELEBRATE THE FOUNDING OF THE NATION.
IS THERE ANY PRECEDENT FOR SUCH A RALLY?
WELL, THERE HAVE BEEN ASSEMBLIES FOR THE ENTIRE POPULATION BEFORE.
BUT THOSE EVENTS ONLY LASTED ONE DAY, AND HOSPITAL WORKERS AND PUBLIC SERVANTS WERE EXEMPT FROM ATTENDING.
ACTUAL ATTENDANCE WAS PROBABLY AROUND 70 PERCENT.
THIS TIME, THE RALLY WILL BE HELD OVER ***THREE*** DAYS, REQUIRING ***EVERYONE*** FROM INFANTS TO THE INFIRM. THIS IS MOST UNUSUAL.

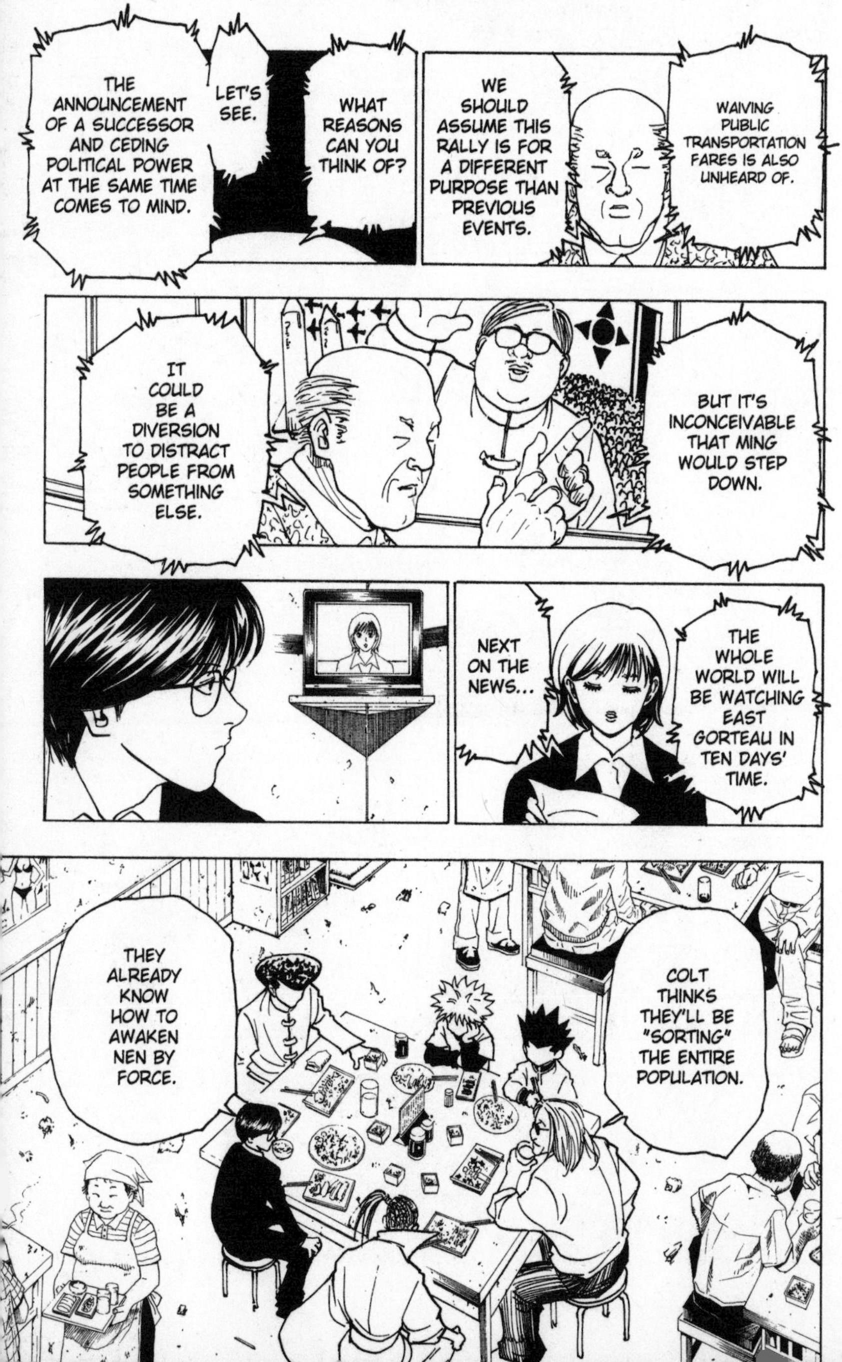
WAIVING PUBLIC TRANSPORTATION FARES IS ALSO UNHEARD OF.
WE SHOULD ASSUME THIS RALLY IS FOR A DIFFERENT PURPOSE THAN PREVIOUS EVENTS.
WHAT REASONS CAN YOU THINK OF?
LET'S SEE.
THE ANNOUNCEMENT OF A SUCCESSOR AND CEDING POLITICAL POWER AT THE SAME TIME COMES TO MIND.
BUT IT'S INCONCEIVABLE THAT MING WOULD STEP DOWN.
IT COULD BE A DIVERSION TO DISTRACT PEOPLE FROM SOMETHING ELSE.
THE WHOLE WORLD WILL BE WATCHING EAST GORTEAU IN TEN DAYS' TIME.
NEXT ON THE NEWS...
COLT THINKS THEY'LL BE "SORTING" THE ENTIRE POPULATION.
THEY ALREADY KNOW HOW TO AWAKEN NEN BY FORCE.

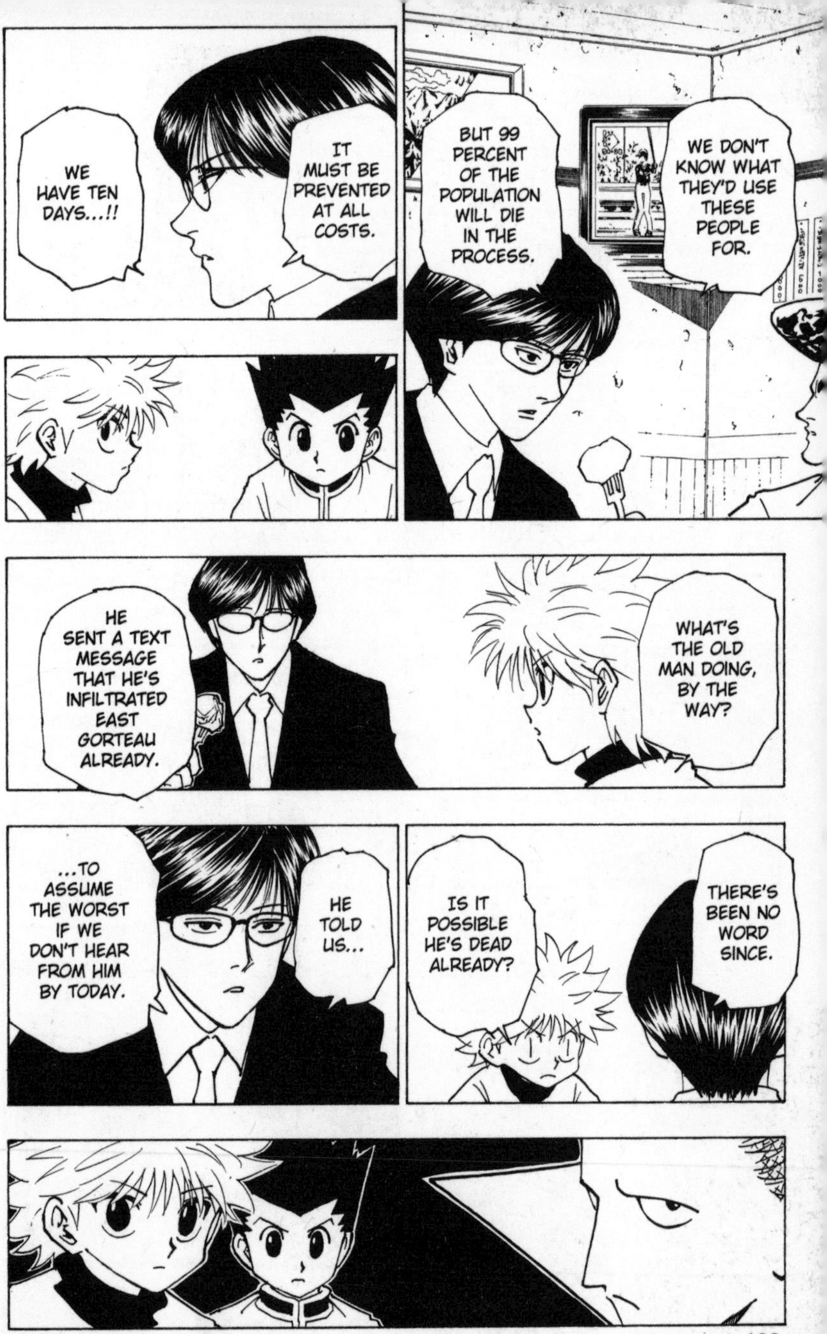
WE DON'T KNOW WHAT THEY'D USE THESE PEOPLE FOR.
BUT 99 PERCENT OF THE POPULATION WILL DIE IN THE PROCESS.
IT MUST BE PREVENTED AT ALL COSTS.
WE HAVE TEN DAYS...!!
WHAT'S THE OLD MAN DOING, BY THE WAY?
HE SENT A TEXT MESSAGE THAT HE'S INFILTRATED EAST GORTEAU ALREADY.
THERE'S BEEN NO WORD SINCE.
IS IT POSSIBLE HE'S DEAD ALREADY?
HE TOLD US...
...TO ASSUME THE WORST IF WE DON'T HEAR FROM HIM BY TODAY.

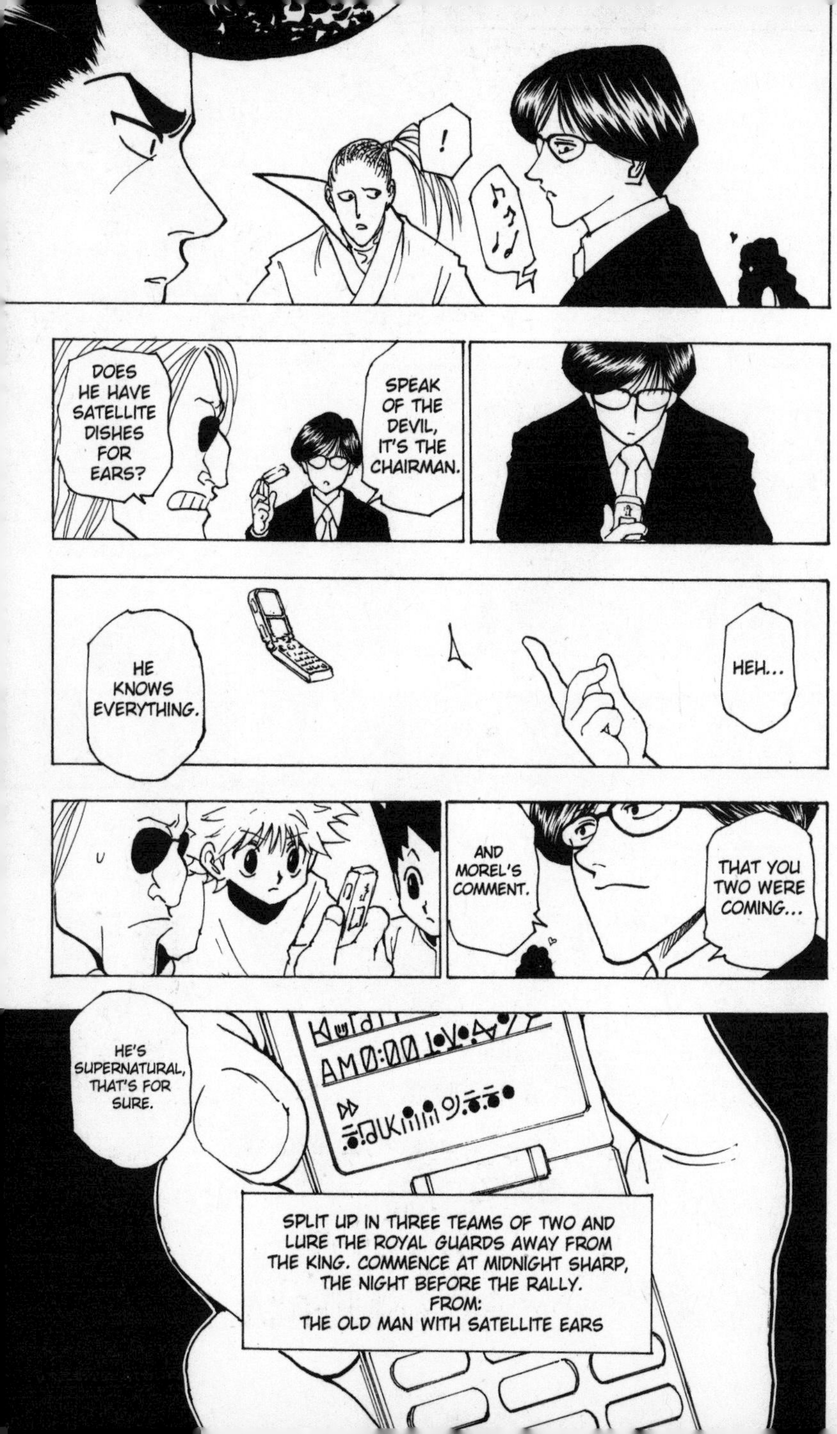
!
SPEAK OF THE DEVIL, IT'S THE CHAIRMAN.
DOES HE HAVE SATELLITE DISHES FOR EARS?
HEH...
HE KNOWS EVERYTHING.
THAT YOU TWO WERE COMING...
AND MOREL'S COMMENT.
HE'S SUPERNATURAL, THAT'S FOR SURE.
SPLIT UP IN THREE TEAMS OF TWO AND LURE THE ROYAL GUARDS AWAY FROM THE KING. COMMENCE AT MIDNIGHT SHARP, THE NIGHT BEFORE THE RALLY. FROM: THE OLD MAN WITH SATELLITE EARS

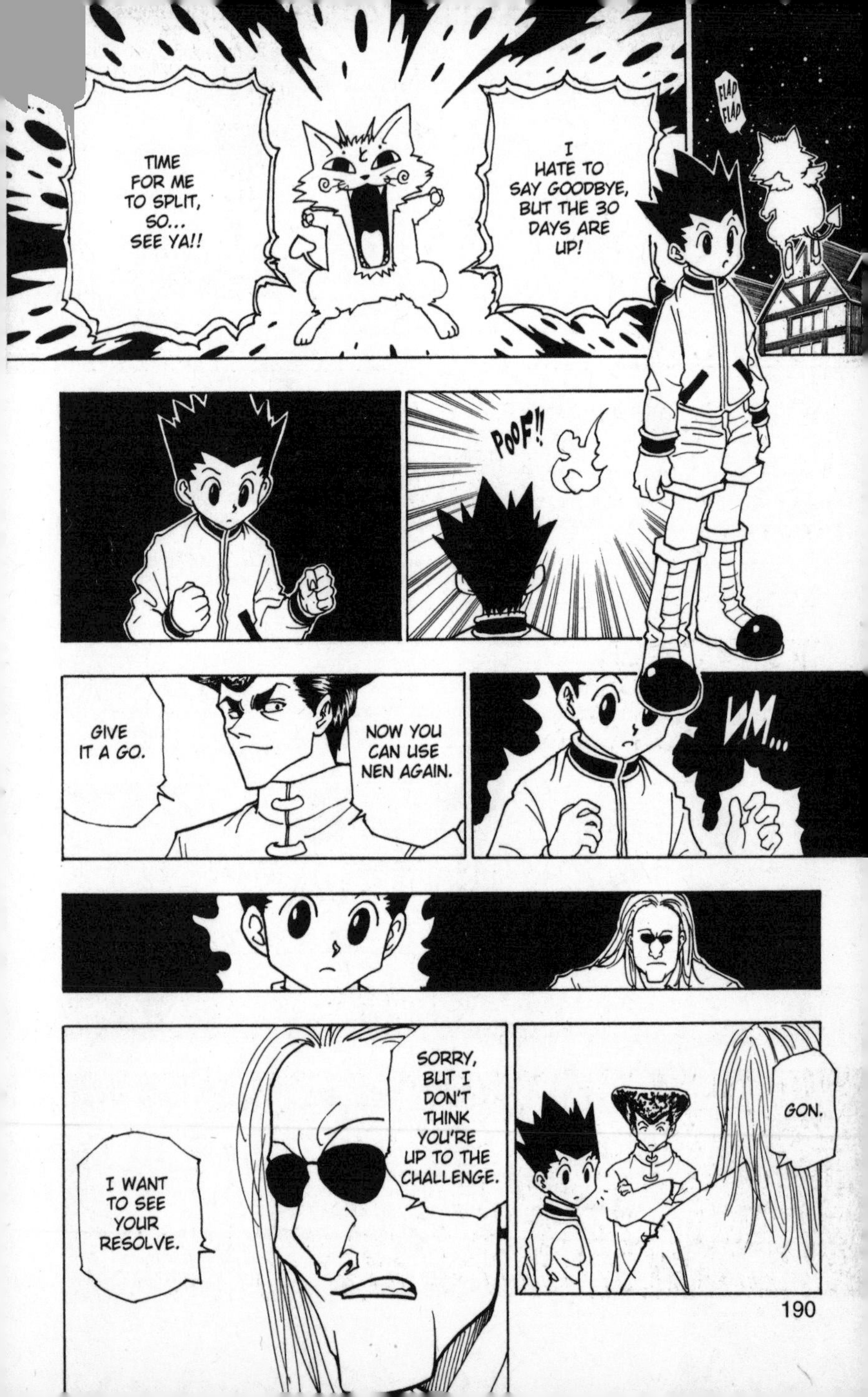
FLAP FLAP
I HATE TO SAY GOODBYE, BUT THE 30 DAYS ARE UP!
TIME FOR ME TO SPLIT, SO... SEE YA!!
POOF!!
VM...
NOW YOU CAN USE NEN AGAIN.
GIVE IT A GO.
GON.
SORRY, BUT I DON'T THINK YOU'RE UP TO THE CHALLENGE.
I WANT TO SEE YOUR RESOLVE.

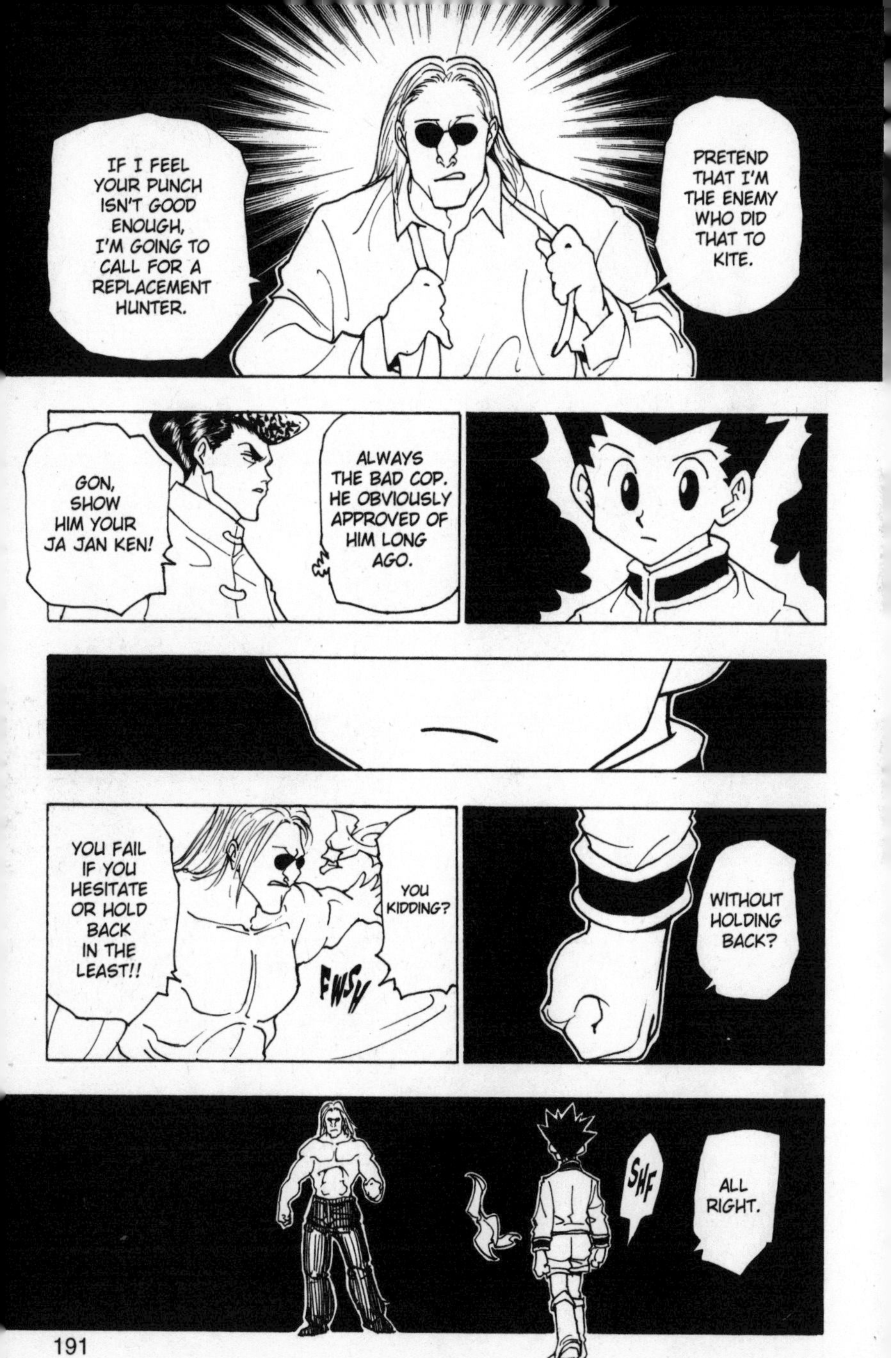
PRETEND THAT I'M THE ENEMY WHO DID THAT TO KITE.
IF I FEEL YOUR PUNCH ISN'T GOOD ENOUGH, I'M GOING TO CALL FOR A REPLACEMENT HUNTER.
ALWAYS THE BAD COP. HE OBVIOUSLY APPROVED OF HIM LONG AGO.
GON, SHOW HIM YOUR JA JAN KEN!
WITHOUT HOLDING BACK?
YOU KIDDING?
YOU FAIL IF YOU HESITATE OR HOLD BACK IN THE LEAST!!
FWSH
ALL RIGHT.
SHF

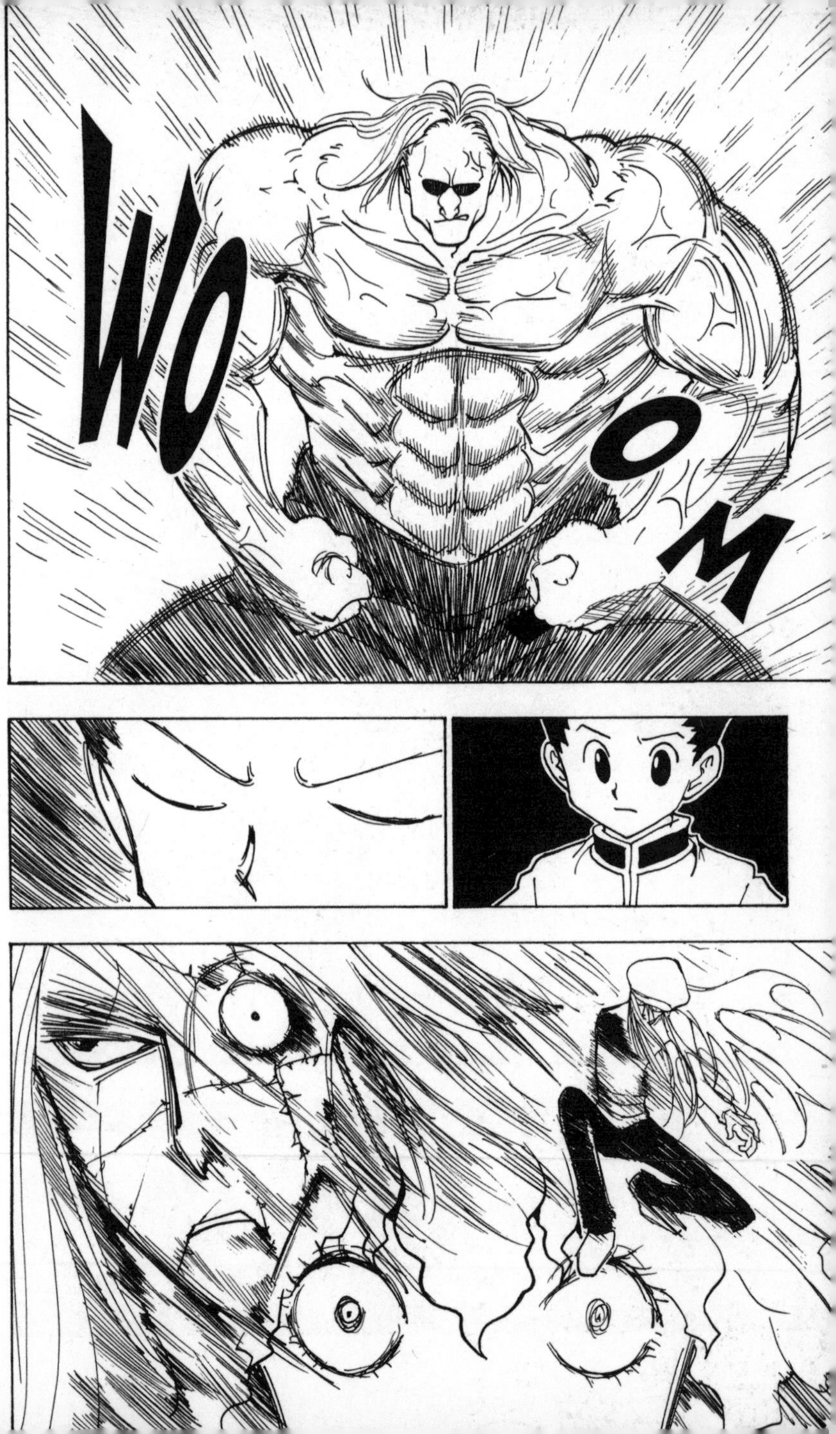
WOOM

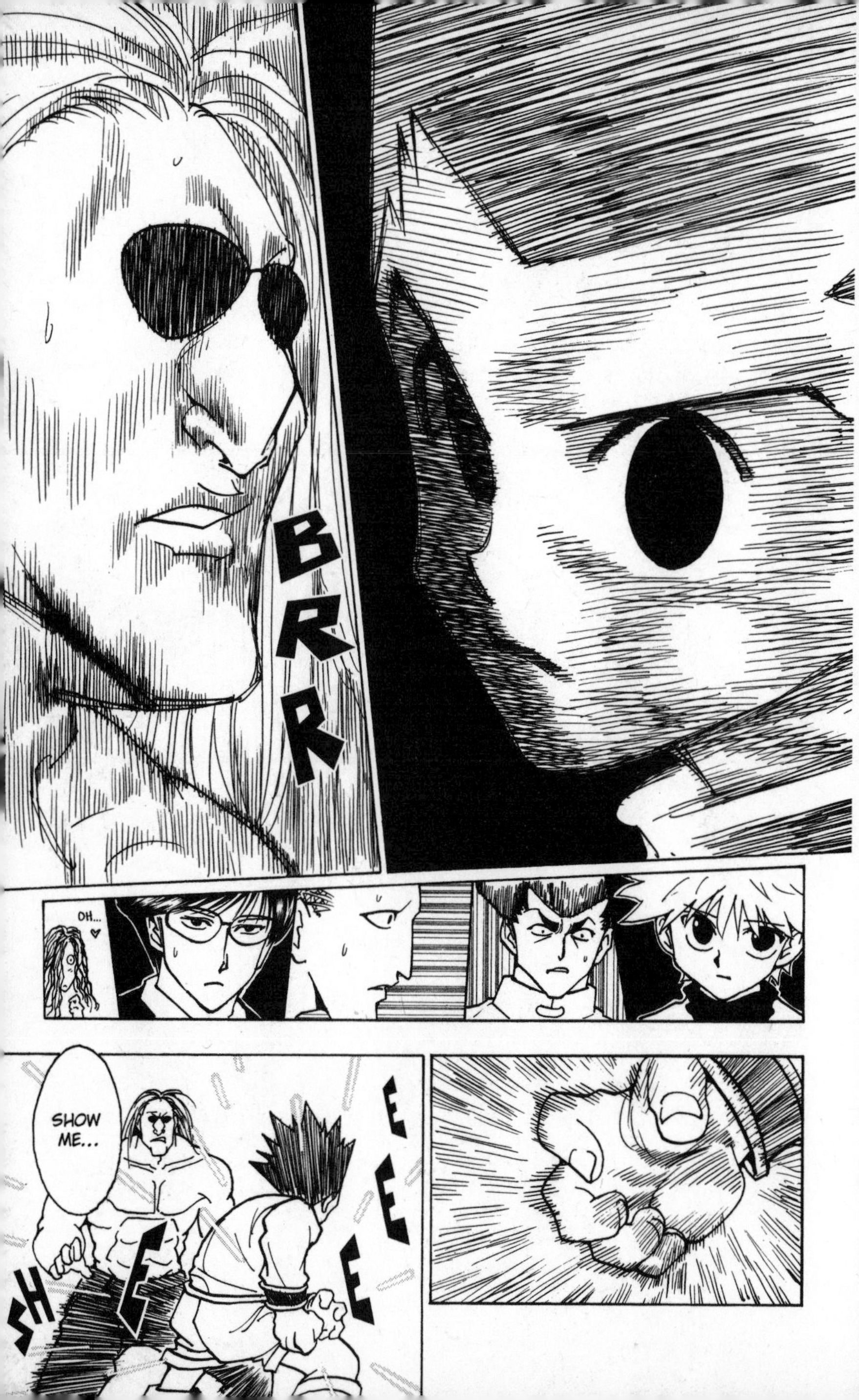
BRRR
OH... ♥
SHOW ME...
SHEEEE

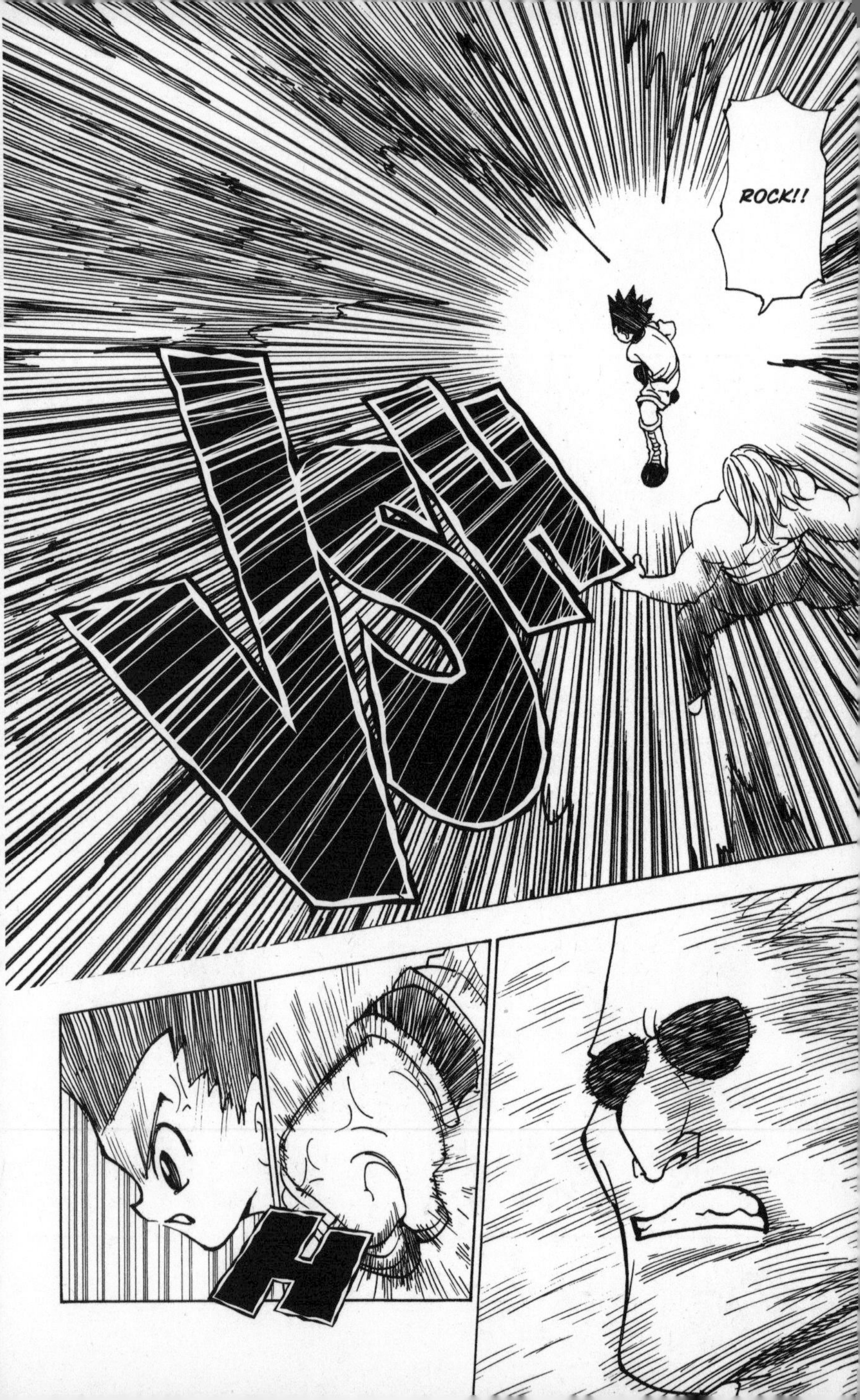
ROCK!!
WSH
H

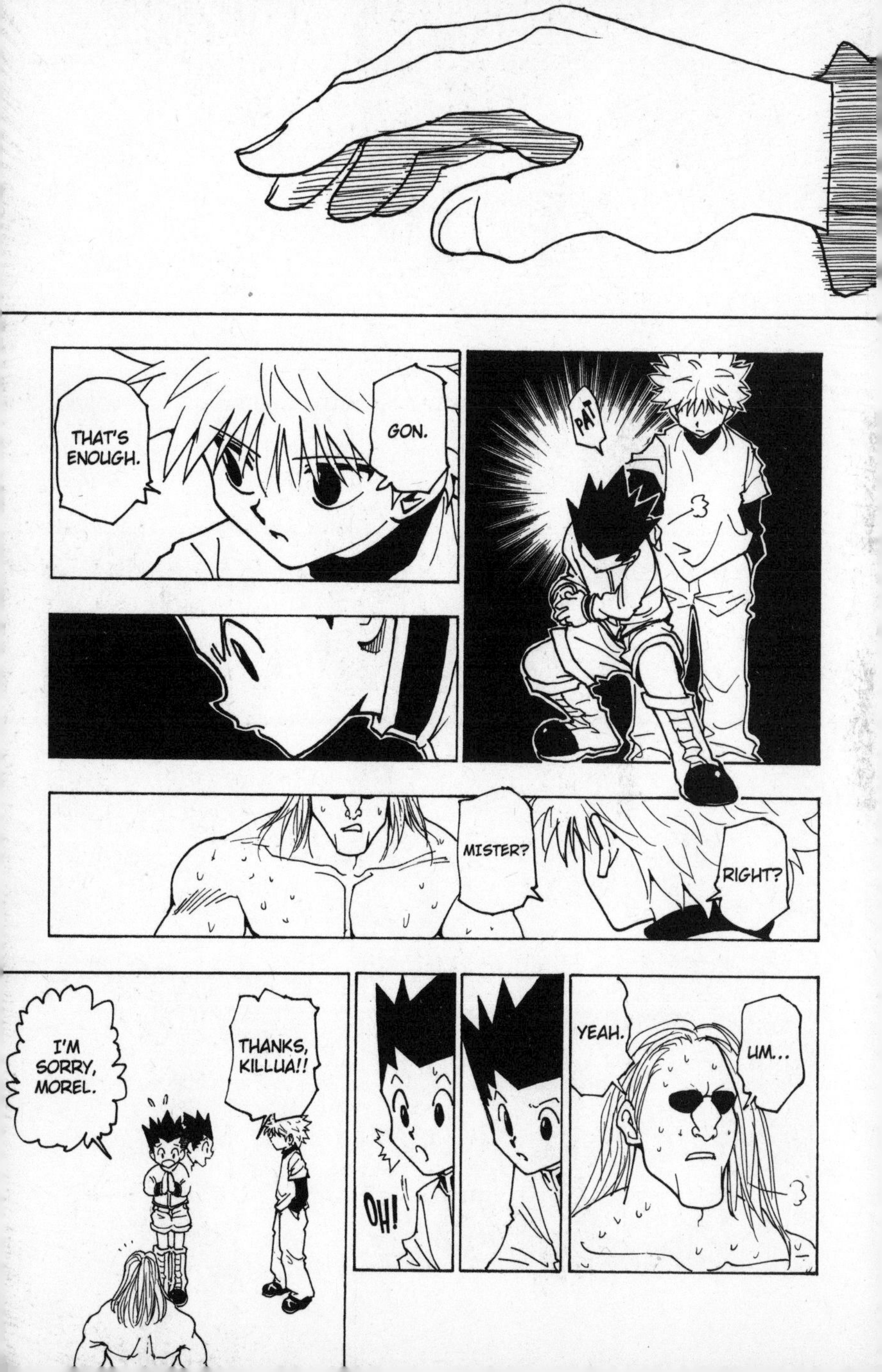
PAT
GON.
THAT'S ENOUGH.
RIGHT?
MISTER?
UM...
YEAH.
OH!
THANKS, KILLUA!!
I'M SORRY, MOREL.

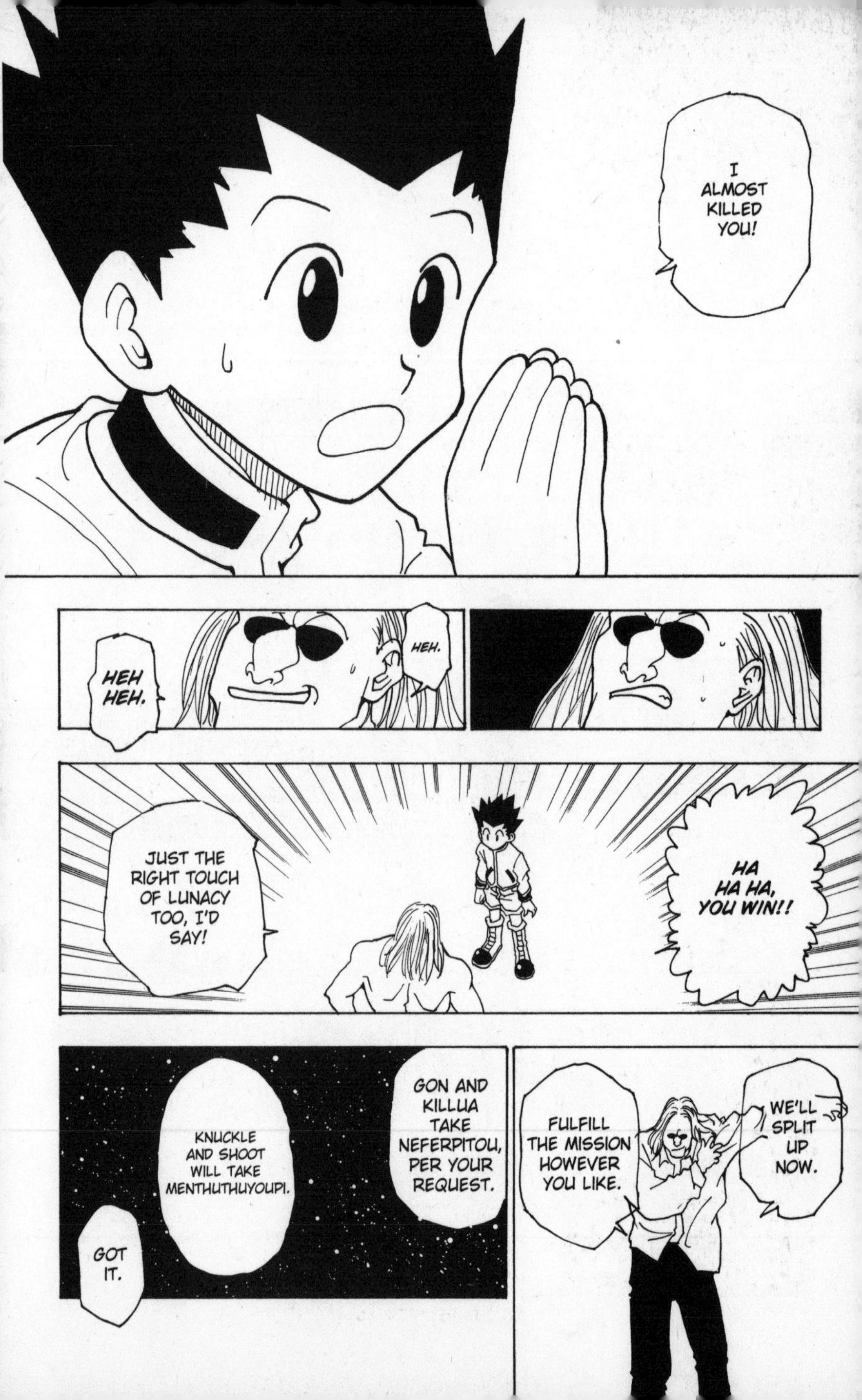
I ALMOST KILLED YOU!
HEH.
HEH HEH.
HA HA HA, YOU WIN!!
JUST THE RIGHT TOUCH OF LUNACY TOO, I'D SAY!
WE'LL SPLIT UP NOW.
FULFILL THE MISSION HOWEVER YOU LIKE.
GON AND KILLUA TAKE NEFERPITOU, PER YOUR REQUEST.
KNUCKLE AND SHOOT WILL TAKE MENTHUTHUYOUPI.
GOT IT.

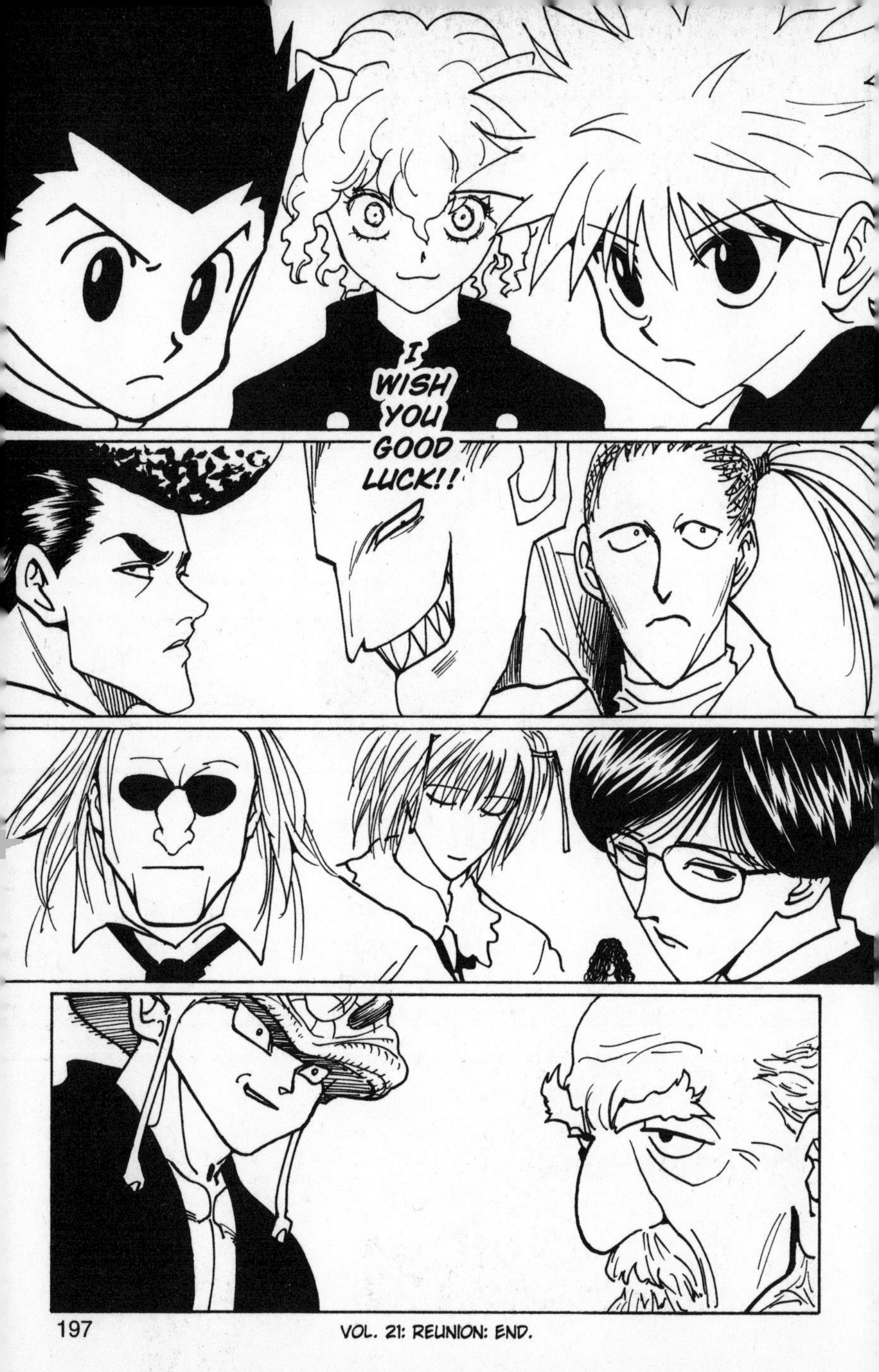
I WISH YOU GOOD LUCK!!

VOL. 21: REUNION: END.

Coming Next Volume...

With the termination of the Queen's reign, the Chimera Ants have left the nest! Spreading out to new territories, each is determined to become the next King. But they shoulda known better than to come a knockin' in Meteor City—the hometown of the Spiders! When the antsy Mistress Zazan sets up her fortress as the new Queen, she didn't expect *these* "insects" as her new citizens!

Available now!

IN A SAVAGE WORLD RULED BY THE PURSUIT OF THE MOST DELICIOUS FOODS, IT'S EITHER EAT OR BE EATEN!

"The most bizarrely entertaining manga out there on comic shelves. *Toriko* is a great series. If you're looking for a weirdly fun book or a fighting manga with a bizarre take, this is the story for you to read."

—ComicAttack.com

TORIKO

Story and Art by Mitsutoshi Shimabukuro

In an era where the world's gone crazy for increasingly bizarre gourmet foods, only Gourmet Hunter Toriko can hunt down the ferocious ingredients that supply the world's best restaurants. Join Toriko as he tracks and defeats the tastiest and most dangerous animals with his bare hands.

Change Your Perspective—Get BIG

Relive Kenshin's journey with the new VIZBIG Editions, featuring:

- Three volumes in one
- Exclusive cover designs
- Color manga pages
- Larger trim size
- Color artwork
- Bonus content

And more!

★ ★ ★ ★ ★ ★ ★ ★ ★ ★ ★ ★ ★ ★ ★ ★ ★

See why **Bigger is Better**—
start your VIZBIG collection today!

www.shonenjump.com

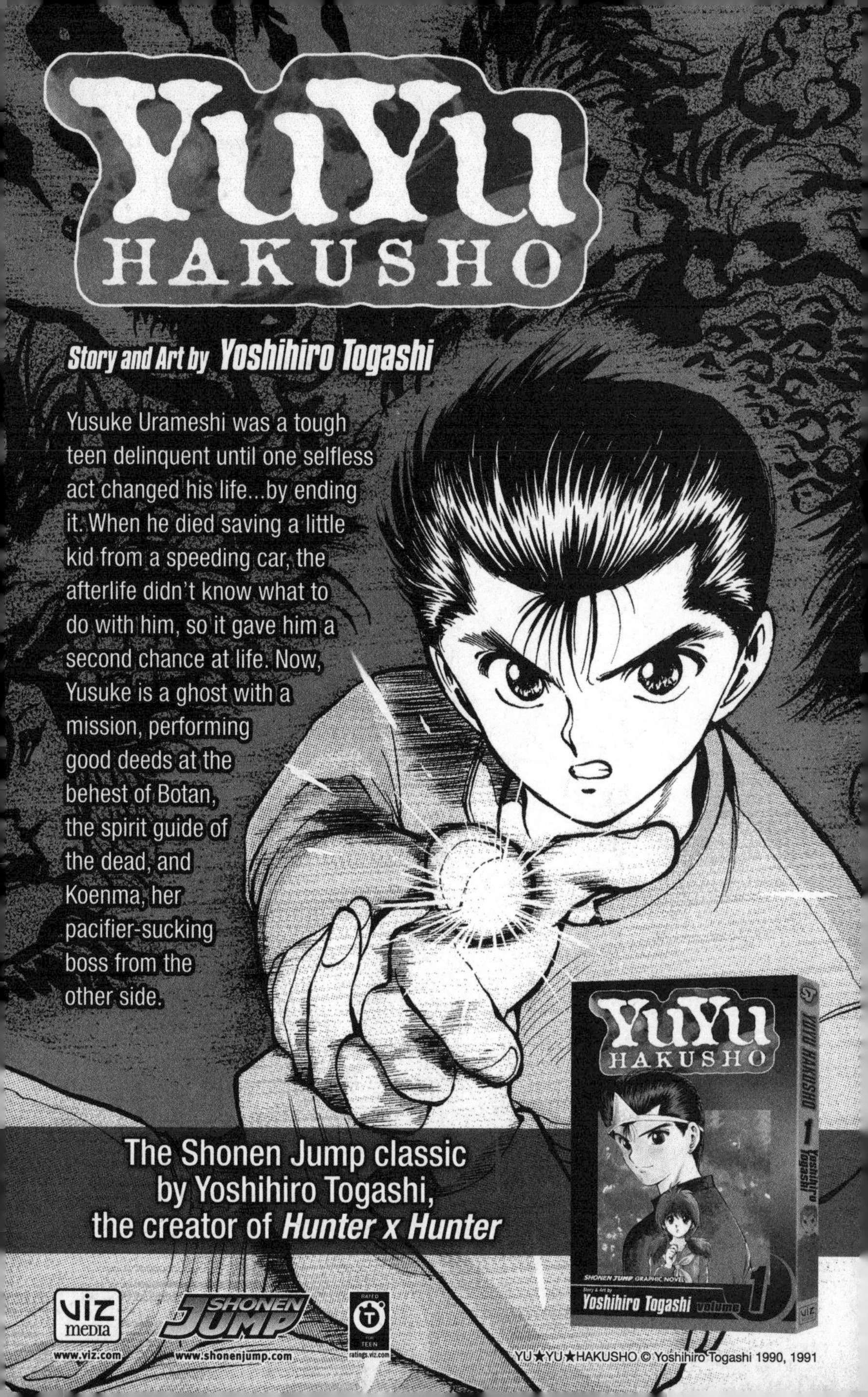
YuYu
HAKUSHO
Story and Art by Yoshihiro Togashi
Yusuke Urameshi was a tough teen delinquent until one selfless act changed his life...by ending it. When he died saving a little kid from a speeding car, the afterlife didn't know what to do with him, so it gave him a second chance at life. Now, Yusuke is a ghost with a mission, performing good deeds at the behest of Botan, the spirit guide of the dead, and Koenma, her pacifier-sucking boss from the other side.
YuYu HAKUSHO
SHONEN JUMP GRAPHIC NOVEL
Story & Art by
Yoshihiro Togashi volume 1
The Shonen Jump classic by Yoshihiro Togashi, the creator of Hunter x Hunter
viz media
www.viz.com
SHONEN JUMP
www.shonenjump.com
RATED T TEEN
ratings.viz.com
YU★YU★HAKUSHO © Yoshihiro Togashi 1990, 1991

EYESHIELD 21

STORY BY RIICHIRO INAGAKI
ART BY YUSUKE MURATA

From the artist of *One-Punch Man!*

Wimpy Sena Kobayakawa has been running away from bullies all his life. But when the football gear comes on, things change—Sena's speed and uncanny ability to elude big bullies just might give him what it takes to become a great high school football hero! Catch all the bone-crushing action and slapstick comedy of Japan's hottest football manga!

VIZ media

SHONEN JUMP ADVANCED

RATED **T** FOR OLDER TEEN ratings.viz.com

www.viz.com   www.shonenjump.com

EYESHIELD 21 © 2002 by Riichiro Inagaki, Yusuke Murata/SHUEISHA Inc.

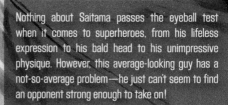

A PREMIUM BOX SET OF THE FIRST TWO STORY ARCS OF ONE PIECE!

A PIRATE'S TREASURE FOR ANY MANGA FAN!

STORY AND ART BY EIICHIRO ODA

Comes with **EXCLUSIVE POSTER** and the **ROMANCE DAWN** mini-comic!

As a child, Monkey D. Luffy dreamed of becoming King of the Pirates. But his life changed when he accidentally gained the power to stretch like rubber...at the cost of never being able to swim again! Years later, Luffy sets off in search of the "One Piece," said to be the greatest treasure in the world...

This box set includes VOLUMES 1-23, which comprise the EAST BLUE and BAROQUE WORKS story arcs.

EXCLUSIVE PREMIUMS and GREAT SAVINGS over buying the individual volumes!

You're Reading in the Wrong Direction!!

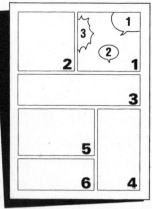

Whoops! Guess what? You're starting at the wrong end of the comic!

...It's true! In keeping with the original Japanese format, **Hunter x Hunter** is meant to be read from right to left, starting in the upper-right corner.

Unlike English, which is read from left to right, Japanese is read from right to left, meaning that action, sound effects and word-balloon order are completely reversed... something which can make readers unfamiliar with Japanese feel pretty backwards themselves. For this reason, manga or Japanese comics published in the U.S. in English have sometimes been published "flopped"— that is, printed in exact reverse order, as though seen from the other side of a mirror.

By flopping pages, U.S. publishers can avoid confusing readers, but the compromise is not without its downside. For one thing, a character in a flopped manga series who once wore in the original Japanese version a T-shirt emblazoned with "M A Y" (as in "the merry month of") now wears one which reads "Y A M"! Additionally, many manga creators in Japan are themselves unhappy with the process, as some feel the mirror-imaging of their art skews their original intentions.

We are proud to bring you Yoshihiro Togashi's **Hunter x Hunter** in the original unflopped format. For now, though, turn to the other side of the book and let the adventure begin...!

—Editor